Thinking as Communicating

This book is an attempt to change our thinking about thinking. Anna Sfard undertakes this task convinced that many long-standing, seemingly irresolvable quandaries regarding human development originate in ambiguities of the existing discourses on thinking. Standing on the shoulders of Vygotsky and Wittgenstein, the author defines thinking as a form of communication. The disappearance of the time-honored thinking-communicating dichotomy is epitomized by Sfard's term, *commognition*, which combines communication with cognition. The commognitive tenet implies that verbal communication with its distinctive property of recursive self-reference may be the primary source of humans' unique ability to accumulate the complexity of their action from one generation to another. The explanatory power of the commognitive framework and the manner in which it contributes to our understanding of human development is illustrated through commognitive analysis of mathematical discourse accompanied by vignettes from mathematics classrooms.

Anna Sfard is based at the University of Haifa in Israel and holds a joint appointment as Lappan-Phillips-Fitzgerald Professor of Mathematics Education at Michigan State University and as Professor of Mathematics at the University of London. In a series of studies in Israel, Canada, and the United States, she has been investigating the development of mathematical thinking in both history and individual learning. Results of these studies, both theoretical and empirical, have been published in more than 100 articles and edited volumes, many of which have been widely cited.

LEARNING IN DOING: SOCIAL, COGNITIVE, AND
COMPUTATIONAL PERSPECTIVES

SERIES EDITOR *EMERITUS*
John Seely Brown, *Xerox Palo Alto Research Center*

GENERAL EDITORS
Roy Pea, *Professor of Education and the Learning Sciences and Director, Stanford Center for Innovations in Learning, Stanford University*

Christian Heath, *The Management Centre, King's College, London*

Lucy A. Suchman, *Centre for Science Studies and Department of Sociology, Lancaster University, UK*

Continued after the Index

To my parents, Janina and Zygmunt Bauman

Thinking as Communicating

Human Development, the Growth of Discourses, and Mathematizing

ANNA SFARD

The University of Haifa, Israel
Michigan State University

CAMBRIDGE
UNIVERSITY PRESS

CAMBRIDGE UNIVERSITY PRESS
Cambridge, New York, Melbourne, Madrid, Cape Town, Singapore,
São Paulo, Delhi, Dubai, Tokyo

Cambridge University Press
32 Avenue of the Americas, New York, NY 10013-2473, USA

www.cambridge.org
Information on this title: www.cambridge.org/9780521161541

First published 2008
Reprinted 2009 (twice)
First paperback edition 2010

Printed in the United States of America

A catalog record for this publication is available from the British Library.

Library of Congress Cataloging in Publication Data

Sfard, Anna.
Thinking as communicating: Human development, the growth of discourses, and
mathematizing / Anna Sfard.
   p. cm. – (Learning in doing)
Includes bibliographical references and index.
ISBN 978-0-521-86737-5 (hardback)
1. Mathematics – Language. 2. Thought and thinking. I. Title. II. Series.
QA42.S43 2008
153–dc22   2007018212

ISBN 978-0-521-86737-5 Hardback
ISBN 978-0-521-16154-1 Paperback

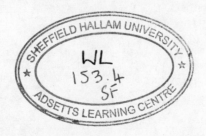

Contents

Series Foreword

This series for Cambridge University Press is widely known as an international forum for studies of situated learning and cognition. Innovative contributions are being made by anthropology; by cognitive, developmental, and cultural psychology; by computer science; by education; and by social theory. These contributions are providing the basis for new ways of understanding the social, historical, and contextual nature of learning, thinking, and practice that emerges from human activity. The empirical settings of these research inquiries range from the classroom to the workplace, to the high-technology office, and to learning in the streets and in other communities of practice. The situated nature of learning and remembering through activity is a central fact. It may appear obvious that human minds develop in social situations and extend their sphere of activity and communicative competencies. But cognitive theories of knowledge representation and learning alone have not provided sufficient insight into these relationships. This series was born of the conviction that new exciting interdisciplinary syntheses are underway as scholars and practitioners from diverse fields seek to develop theory and empirical investigations adequate for characterizing the complex relations of social and mental life, and for understanding successful learning wherever it occurs. The series invites contributions that advance our understanding of these seminal issues.

Roy Pea
Christian Heath
Lucy Suchman

Introduction

> If we see knowing not as having an essence, to be described by scientists or philosophers, but rather as a right, by current standards, to believe, then we are well on the way to seeing *conversation* as the ultimate context within which knowledge is to be understood. Our focus shifts from the relation between human beings and the objects of their inquiry to the relation between alternative standards of justification, and from there to the actual changes in those standards which make up intellectual history.
>
> Richard Rorty[1]

This book is a result of years-long attempts to change my own thinking about thinking, a task seemingly as improbable as breaking a hammer by hitting it with itself. In this unlikely undertaking, I have been inspired by Lev Vygotsky, the Byelorussian psychologist who devoted his life to "characterizing the uniquely human aspects of behavior,"[2] and by Ludwig Wittgenstein, the Austrian-British philosopher who insisted that no substantial progress can be made in this kind of endeavor unless the ways we talk, and thus think, about uniquely human "forms of life" undergo extensive revisions.

My admittedly ambitious undertaking had modest beginnings. I was initially interested in learning and teaching mathematics. Like many others before me, I was mystified by what could best be described as vagaries of the human mind: Whereas some people juggled numbers, polygons, and functions effortlessly, some others were petrified at the very mention of numbers or geometric figures. Many of those who erred in their use of mathematical terms and techniques seemed to err in systematic, surprisingly

---

[1] Rorty (1979, pp. 389–390).
[2] Vygotsky (1978, p. 1).

similar ways. And then there was the wonder of little children doing strange things with numbers before gradually becoming able to handle them the standard way. Above all, however, one could not but puzzle over why the persistent attempts to improve mathematics learning over many decades, if not centuries, did not seem to have any sustainable effect. After years of grappling with these and similar phenomena, I realized that one cannot crack the puzzles of mathematical thinking without taking a good look at human thinking at large. I ended up wondering with Vygotsky about how the unique human abilities "have been formed in the course of human history" and about "the way they develop over an individual's lifetime."[3]

I soon discovered that whoever forays into this exciting territory dooms herself to an uneasy life. The first predicament of the student of human development is her being torn between two conflicting wishes: the wish to be scientific, whatever this word means to her, and the desire to capture the gist of those phenomena that are unique to humans. Whenever one of these needs is taken care of, the other one appears to be inherently unsatisfiable. Indeed, across history, the tug-of-war between the two goals, that of scientific reproducibility, rigor, and cumulativeness, on the one hand, and that of doing justice to the complexity of the "uniquely human," on the other, resulted in the pendulum-like movement between the reductionist and the "gestaltist" poles. Reductionist theories, of which behaviorism is arguably the most extreme example, can boast the scientific operationality of their vocabulary, but they eventually kill their object by throwing away some of its vital parts. Socioculturally minded followers of Vygotsky, on the other hand, aware of the futility of the search conducted "under the lamp" rather than in those dark places where answers to their questions may really be hiding, fail to communicate their rich ideas clearly enough to give rise to well-defined programs of study.

Today, our sense of helplessness may well be at its most acute. New technologies afford unprecedented insights into human phenomena and produce high-resolution evidence of the utmost complexity of human forms of life. With audio and video recorders as standard ingredients of the researcher's toolkit, the fleeting human action acquires permanence and becomes researchable in ways unknown to our predecessors. When carefully documented and transcribed, even the most common of everyday conversations prove to be a complex, multifaceted phenomenon, and an inexhaustible source of wonderings. This makes us as aware as ever of the fact that our ability to analyze and explain lags behind our ability to observe

---

[3] Ibid.

and to see. In this respect, our current situation is comparable to that of the 17th-century scientists faced with the newly invented microscope: Powerful, high-resolution lenses that reveal what was never noticed before are yet to be matched by an equally powerful analytic apparatus.

Inadequacies of conceptual tools are what Wittgenstein had in mind when he complained, more than half a century ago, about the state of research on human thinking. "Psychological concepts are just everyday concepts," he said, whereas what we need are "concepts newly fashioned by science for its own purpose."[4] These words seem to have as much force today as they had when they were written. Lacking a designated, operationally defined vocabulary, the study of humans remains plagued by resilient dilemmas. Just look at time-honored controversies about human development that recur time and again, alas in different disguises, throughout history. Take, for example, the famous "nature versus nurture" dilemma, the "mind and body" problem, or the controversy about the "transfer of learning." All these quandaries have an appearance of disagreements about empirical facts but may, in reality, be a matter of lexical ambiguities. The blurriness of the vocabulary is the most obvious explanation for our inability to overcome the differences and build on each other's work: Unknown to ourselves, we are likely to be using the same words – *nature, nurture, mind, transfer* – in different ways. Similarly, our inability to capture the complexity of human phenomena may well be a matter of an inadequacy of our analytic methods, the weakness that, in the absence of explicit, operational definitions, seems incurable.

At a closer look, the lack of operationality is only the beginning of the researcher's problem. Without clear definitions, one is left at the mercy of metaphors, that is, of concepts created by transferring familiar words into unfamiliar territories. Indeed, if we are able to use words such as *nurture* or *transfer* in the context of human learning and development, it is because both these terms are known to us from everyday discourse. The services rendered by metaphors, however, are not without a price: Together with the unwritten guidelines for how to incorporate the old term into new contexts are hordes of unforeseen metaphorical entailments, some of which may interfere with the task of gaining useful insights into the observed phenomena. Whereas the use of metaphor cannot be barred – after all, this is one of the principal mechanisms of discourse building – the risks of metaphorical projections may be considerably reduced by providing the metaphorically engendered notions with operational definitions.

[4] Wittgenstein (1980, § 62).

Being explicit and operational about one's own use of words, however, is not an easy matter. Some people circumvent the challenge by turning to numbers. Precise measurement seems such an obvious antidote to the uncertainties of descriptive narratives! Rather than merely describing what the child does when grappling with mathematical problems, those who speak "numberese" would look at students' solutions, divide them into categories, and check distributions. Rather than scrutinizing the utterances of a girl executing an arithmetic operation, they would measure her IQ, consider her grades, and decide whether the numbers justify labeling her as "learning disabled." Never mind the fact that in the quantitative discourse the numbers may be originating in categorizations as underdefined as those that belong to its "qualitative" counterpart (after all, there is no reason to assume that the words signifying things to be counted, when not defined in operational terms, are more operational than any other). Forget the fact that in their zeal to produce simplicity, order, and unification, the quantitatively minded interlocutors are likely to gloss over potentially significant individual differences. It is only too tempting to believe that numbers can say it all and that when they speak, there is no need to worry about words.

I do worry about words, though, and this book is the result of this concern. In spite of my liking for numbers – after all, I am the native of mathematics – I am acutely aware of the perils of the purely numerical talk. The uneasy option of operationalizing the discourse about uniquely human forms of life seems the only alternative. On the following pages, I take a close look at basic terms such as *thinking, learning,* and *communication* and try to define them with the help of clear, publicly accessible criteria. If this operationalizing effort raises some brows – if some readers protest, saying that thinking and communication are natural phenomena and thus not anything that people should bother to define – let me remind them that defining relates to the ways we talk about the world, not the world as such, and it is up to us, not to nature, to decide how to match our words with phenomena. And to readers who feel that I am trying to tell them how to talk, let me explain that this, too, is not the case. All I want is to be understood the way I intend, on my own terms. For me, being explicit about my use of words is simply a matter of "conceptual accountability," of being committed to, and responsible for, the effectiveness of my communication with others.

The conceptualization I am about to propose may be regarded as an almost self-imposing entailment of what was explicitly said by Vygotsky and what was implied by Wittgenstein. The point of departure is Vygotsky's claim that historically established, collectively implemented activities are developmentally prior to all our uniquely human skills. Being one of these skills, human thinking must also have a collective predecessor. Obviously, interpersonal communication is the only candidate. In this book, therefore, thinking is defined as the *individualized version of interpersonal communication* – as a communicative interaction in which one person plays the roles of all interlocutors. The term *commognition*, a combination of *communication* and *cognition*, stresses that interpersonal communication and individual thinking are two facets of the same phenomenon.

In the nine chapters of this book, the introduction to the commognitive perspective is accompanied by a careful examination of its theoretical consequences and its implications for research and for educational practice. The task is implemented in two steps. Part I (chapters 1 through 4) is devoted to the double project of telling a story of human thinking and creating a language in which this story may usefully be told. After presenting a number of time-honored controversies regarding human learning and problem solving (chapter 1), and after tracing the roots of these quandaries to certain linguistic ambiguities (chapter 2), the commognitive vision is introduced as a possible cure for at least some of the persistent dilemmas and uncertainties (chapter 3). Although it is repeatedly stressed that language is not the only medium in which communication, and thus thinking, can take place, it is now claimed that verbal communication may well be the primary source of the distinctively human forms of life (chapter 4). Indeed, if one were to name a single feature that would set humankind apart from all the others in the eyes of a hypothetical extraterrestrial observer, the most likely choice would be our ability to accumulate complexity of action, that is, the fact that our forms of life, unlike those of other species, evolve and grow in intricacy and sophistication from one generation to another, constantly redefining the nature and range of individual development. It may now be argued that this gradual growth is made possible by the fact that our activities are verbally mediated. More specifically, thanks to the special property of human language known as recursivity, the activity-mediating discourses and the resulting texts become the primary repository of the gradually increasing complexity. Consistent with this vision, research on human development becomes the study of the growth of discourses.

In part II I return to the questions that started me on this project: I use the commognitive lens to make sense of one special type of discourse called *mathematical*. By choosing mathematics I hope to be able to illustrate the power of the commognitive framework with a particular clarity. Mathematical thinking has been psychologists' favorite object of study since the advent of the disciplined inquiry into human cognition. Widely regarded as perhaps the most striking instantiation of the human capacity for abstraction and complexity, mathematics is also a paragon of rigor and clarity: It is decomposable into relatively neatly delineated, hierarchically organized layers that allow for many different levels of engagement and performance. The tradition of using mathematics as a medium within which to address general questions about human thinking goes back to Jean Piaget[5] and continues with the wide variety of developmental psychologists and misconception seekers, ending up, at least for now, with the sociocultural thinkers who vowed to reclaim the place of the social within the time-honored trinity world–society–individual.[6] Throughout history, students of the human mind were often divided on questions of epistemology, methodology, and the meaning of observed phenomena, but they always agreed that mathematical thinking is a perfect setting for uncovering general truths about human development.[7]

In the four chapters devoted to mathematical thinking, I develop the commognitive vision of mathematics as a type of discourse – as a well-defined form of communication, made distinct by its vocabulary, visual mediators, routines, and the narratives it produces (chapter 5). The questions of the nature and origins of the objects of mathematical discourse are then addressed, and the claim is made that mathematics is an autopoietic system – one that spurs its own development and produces its own objects (chapter 6). I follow with a close glimpse at uniquely mathematical ways of communicating (chapter 7) and at the gains of communicating in these special ways (chapter 8). All along, particular attention is given to the question of how mathematical discourse comes into being and how and why it subsequently evolves. The vision of mathematics as a discourse, and thus as a form of human activity, makes it possible to identify mechanisms that are common to the historical development of mathematics and to its individual learning. Having stated all this, I return to the initial quandaries and ask myself whether the commognitive vision has yielded the wished-for resolution. At the same time, I wonder about a series of new puzzles, some of them already being taken care of and some others still waiting to be transformed into researchable questions (chapter 9).

Throughout the book, theoretical musings are interspersed with numerous empirical instantiations. Although the examples are mostly mathematical, they are rather elementary and easily accessible to anybody who knows

---

[5] E.g., Piaget (1952).

[6] E.g., Lave (1988) and Walkerdine (1988).

[7] H. J. Reed and J. Lave (1979) make a compelling case for using mathematics as a "laboratory" for studying human thinking in their article with the telltale title "Arithmetic as a tool for investigating the relation between culture and cognition."

a thing or two about basic arithmetic. The mathematical slant, therefore, should not deter nonmathematical readers, not even those who suffer from mathematical anxiety. It is also worth mentioning that the book may be read in different ways, depending on one's needs and foci. Those interested mainly in theorizing about human thinking may satisfy themselves with part I, where references to mathematics are scarce. Those who reach for this book because of their interest in mathematical thinking can head directly to part II. The glossary at the end of the volume will help them, if necessary, with concise explanations of basic terms and tenets.

Acknowledgments

An argument...in which the parties express disagreement is nonetheless co-constructed.

Jacoby and Ochs, 1995[1]

Once we agree that thinking is an individualized form of interpersonal communication, we must also concede that whatever one creates is a product of collective doing. Even when sitting alone at her desk and deeply immersed in thoughts, a person is engaged in a conversation with others. As is any human artifact, therefore, this book is full of "echoes and reverberations" of conversations that occurred at many different times and places, involving numerous people whom I never met, and probably many others of whom I haven't even heard. Being "filled with others' words,"[2] this text has therefore more contributors than I am aware of. When echoing other authors' words or when taking exception with what they said, I have dragged them into this conversation, sometimes intentionally and sometimes unconsciously. If their roles were revealed, not all of these involuntary contributors would probably agree to take any credit for the final product. Nevertheless, I would dearly like to acknowledge them all. Unfortunately, I can express my gratitude only to those few people of whose contribution I am aware, hoping to be forgiven by all the others.

Let me begin with Lev Semionovitch Vygotsky and Ludwig Wittgenstein, two giants whose shoulders proved wide enough to accommodate legions of followers and a wide variety of interpreters. Although libraries have already been filled with exegetic treatises, the Byelorussian psychologist and the Austrian-born philosopher continue to inspire new ideas even

[1] Jacoby and Ochs (1995, p. 171).
[2] Bakhtin (1999, p. 130).

as I am writing these lines. This, it seems, is due to one important feature their writings have in common: rather than provide information, they address the reader as a partner in thinking; rather than presenting a completed edifice with all the scaffolding removed, they extend an invitation for a guided tour of the construction site; rather than present firm convictions, they share the "doubt that comes *after* belief."[3] These two writers had a major impact on my thinking; I can only hope they had a similar effect on my ability to share it.

I am indebted to a number of people who stirred my fascination with the phenomenon called mathematics and thereby with human thinking. The list begins with the elementary school teacher, Mr. Żendara, who said, "Open, sesame" and led our group of 11- and 12-year-olds into the cave full of mathematical wonders; it continues with the high school mathematics teacher, Aniela Ehrenfeught, whose enthusiasm for mathematics was truly contagious; and it culminates with the long list of university professors, whose live shows of awe-inspiring acrobatics on the highest levels of mathematical abstraction ignited their students' interest in the miracle of human cognition.

Ellice Forman kicked the writing project off by declaring me "the person who needs a book" and alerting me to the option of Cambridge University Press (this was Ellice's gentle way of telling me that my texts were too long and too theoretical to be published as journal articles). Another friendly kick, this time by Joan Ferrini-Mundy, jettisoned me out of the box straight into transcontinental commuting. It took me to Michigan State University, where I found all I needed to complete this project: a peaceful environment and a consolidated group of colleagues and students who challenged me with difficult questions. Glenda Lappan, Betty Phillips, and George Leroi joined Joan in making my stay possible, while Nathalie Sinclair, Nick Jackiw, Helen Featherstone, and Jeanne Wald, with their sustained interest, constant encouragement, and stimulating conversation over countless coffees, lunches, and dinners, made this stay no less enjoyable than fruitful. I consider myself lucky to have the friendship of all these special individuals.

Most of the empirical studies featured in these pages were collective endeavors in which I was but one of several researchers. I am grateful to Carolyn Kieran, Liora Linchevsky, Miriam Ben-Yehuda, Anna Prusak, Irit Lavie, and Sharon Avgil for their collaboration and their multifarious contributions. A less direct, but no less important, input was that of graduate students who, on both sides of the Atlantic Ocean, mulled over intricacies of human learning and often had the courage to announce that as far as they

---

[3] Wittgenstein (1969, p. 23e).

were concerned, the queens and kings of educational research had been suffering from a scarcity of attire. Sincere thanks go also to those who delved into successive versions of different parts of this book to reemerge with tons of high-quality grist for my mill. Among them, let me count Jihad Al-Shwaikh, Shai Caspi, Paul Cobb, Helen Featherstone, Einat Heyd-Metzuyanim, Talli Nachlieli, Jill Newton, Andreas Ryve, Nathalie Sinclair, Michal Tabach, Eran Tavor, and Hava Tuval. The incisive, often quite critical comments of these first readers pushed the project forward, albeit not always in the directions the critics themselves considered desirable.

I was fortunate to benefit from the erudition and connoisseurship of Roy Pea, the editor of the Learning in Doing series and an expert on learning sciences (according to Roy's own definition, an expert is a person who "notice[s] features of situations and problems that escape the attention of novices").[4] Four anonymous reviewers have to be thanked for flagging pitfalls and inspiring additional searches. Eric Schwartz, Helen Wheeler, and Susan Thornton of Cambridge University Press walked me gently through the mazes of publishing processes, and for this joint trip they will always be remembered with fondness. To Jean Beland and Georgia Old from Michigan State University I am grateful for helping me through the labyrinths of manuscript preparation.

I am grateful to the publishers of the *Journal for Research in Mathematics Education* (copyright 2005 by the National Council of Teachers of Mathematics. All Rights Reserved); *For the Learning of Mathematics*; *Mind, Culture, and Activity*; and *Cognition and Instruction* for letting me use fragments of my former writings that they published.

My family is present between the covers of this volume no less than Wittgenstein and Vygotsky, even if not so explicitly. Michael Sfard and Emi Sfard made a paramount contribution by giving me the opportunity to watch two exemplary cases of human development in real time and in a close-up. Their early experience as mathematics learners inspired some of the stories told on these pages. Emi, who grew up to favor images over numbers, made yet another contribution to this volume by preparing its cover illustration. Leon Sfard, my constant interlocutor and my most helpful critic, should probably be regarded as a cocreator of this text. Indeed, even if eavesdroppers can hear only one voice, this book is a record of our ongoing dialogue. I am unspeakably grateful to this dear little crowd of mine for coaxing me into the mood for writing and for giving me the strength and emotional resilience to persevere until the completion of this project – and well beyond.

---

[4] Bransford et al. (2006, p. 25).

Part I

Discourse on Thinking

1   Puzzling about (Mathematical) Thinking

One . . . fact must astonish us, or rather would astonish us if we were not too much accustomed to it: How does it happen that there are people who do not understand mathematics? If the science invokes only the rules of logic, those accepted by all well-formed minds, how does it happen that there are so many people who are entirely impervious to it?

Henri Poincaré[1]

Full of puzzles, mathematics is a puzzle in itself. Anybody who knows anything about it is likely to have questions to ask. Most of us marvel about how abstract mathematics is and wonder how one can come to grips with anything as complex and as detached from anything tangible as this. The concern of those who do manage the complexity, as did the French mathematician and philosopher of science Henri Poincaré, is just the opposite: The fortunate few who "speak mathematics" as effortlessly as they converse in their mother tongue have a hard time understanding other people's difficulty. From a certain point in our lives, it seems, mathematical understanding becomes an "all or nothing" phenomenon – either you have it, or you don't – and being in any of these two camps appears so natural that you are unable to imagine what it means to be in the other.

But the bafflement with regard to mathematics goes further than that. Literature about human thinking is teeming with resilient mathematics-related puzzles. Some of these puzzles are well known and have been fueling vocal debates for a long time now; some others are still waiting for broader attention. Let me instantiate both types of quandaries with a number of examples. Each of the five stories that follow begins with a brief description of a well-documented controversy and continues with additional teasing

[1] Poincaré (1952, p. 47).

questions that must occur to us the moment we manage to see a familiar situation in unfamiliar light. No solutions will be proposed at this time, and when the chapter ends, some readers may feel left midair, and rather annoyingly so. May I thus ask for your patience: Grappling with the conundrums that follow is going to take this whole book. In this chapter, my aims are to present the maladies of the present research on thinking and prepare the ground for diagnosing their sources. The attempt to follow with a cure will be made in the remaining chapters. I do hope that the long journey toward a better understanding of thinking will be not any less rewarding than the prizes that wait at its end.

1. The Quandary of *Number*

Puzzling phenomena related to mathematics can be observed already in the earliest stages in a child's development. Some of the best known and most discussed of such phenomena were first noticed and documented by the Swiss psychologist Jean Piaget.[2] To put it in Piaget's own language, young children do not *conserve number*; that is, they are not aware of the fact that mere spatial rearrangements do not change cardinality of sets of objects (or, to put it more simply, as long as nothing was added or taken away, the counting process, if repeated, always ends with the same number-word).

A child's awareness of the conservation of number is tested with the help of specially designed tasks. In one of such tasks the child is shown two numerically equivalent sets of counters arranged in parallel rows of equal length and density. The one-to-one correspondence of the counters is thus readily visible when the child is asked, "Which of the rows has more marbles?" In this situation, even young interviewees are reported to give the expected answer. One of the rows is then stretched so as to become longer without becoming more numerous and the child is asked the comparison question again. On the basis of their performance, most 4- and 5-year-olds are believed to be at the "preconservation" stage: When requested to compare the rows of the unequal length, even those of them who previously answered that "no row has more" now point to the one that has been stretched. This phenomenon appears particularly surprising in the view of the fact that by the age of 4 the majority of children have already mastered the art of counting up to 10 or 20.[3] Why is it that children who can count

---

[2] Piaget (1952).

[3] This mastery has been described by Rochelle Gelman and her colleagues (e.g., Gelman & Gallistel, 1978) as the ability to observe three principles of counting: the principle of *one-to-one correspondence*, that is, of assigning exactly one number-word to each element

properly do not turn to counting when presented with the question "Which of the two rows has more marbles?" "They do not yet conserve number" is a traditional Piagetian answer. Piaget's perplexing finding, as well as his diagnoses, led to a long series of additional studies in which 4- and 5-year-old children were presented with tasks best solved with the help of counting, such as set comparison or construction of numerically equivalent sets. All these studies confirmed at least one of Piaget's observations: Although skillful in counting, children tend to perform certain tasks with nonnumerical methods, which more often than not lead them to "nonstandard" results.

Over the last several decades these phenomena and their Piagetian interpretation generated much discussion.[4] For example, Margret Donaldson and James McGarrigle[5] speculated that children may have at least two good reasons to modify their answers after the change in the arrangement of sets, with none of these reasons translating into the young learners' "inability to conserve number." First, it seemed plausible that rather than relating the words *has more* to the cardinality of sets, the children attend to the immediately visible properties of the rows, such as length. Second, according to the rules of the learning–teaching game widely practiced both in schools and in children's homes, the very reiteration of the question may be interpreted by the young interviewees as a prompt for a change in the answer.[6]

In the attempt to have a closer look at this phenomenon, my colleague Irit Lavie and I have launched an *Incipient Numerical Thinking Study*.[7] Our "subjects" were Irit's 4-year-old daughter, Roni, and Roni's 7-months-older friend Eynat (see Figure 1.1), and our intention was to conduct an experiment similar to those described earlier: We would ask the girls to compare sets of counters. Although in the end our study led to findings not unlike those obtained by Piaget and his followers, it also became a source of new, previously unreported quandaries. One vignette from this study suffices to exemplify certain striking, previously unreported aspects of the children's performances. Episode 1.1, presented in the following, is the beginning of the first 20-minute-long conversation between the two

---

of the set that is being counted; the principle of *constant order*, that is, of always saying the number-words in the same linear arrangement; and the principle of *cardinality*, that is, the awareness of the fact that correct counting of the given set, if repeated, must end with the same number-word.

[4] See, e.g., Mehler and Bever (1967) and McGarrigle and Donaldson (1974).

[5] McGarrigle and Donaldson (1974).

[6] Mehan (1979).

[7] This is a longitudinal study ongoing since 2002. Eynat, whom Roni has known since birth, is a daughter of Roni's parents' friends. Both couples are well-educated professionals. The event took place in Roni's house. For a detailed report on the first part of this study see Sfard and Lavie (2005).

Figure 1.1. Roni and Eynat.

girls and Roni's mother. The event took place in Roni's house. Two sets of marbles were presented to the girls in identical closed boxes, with the marbles themselves invisible through the opaque walls.[8]

Episode 1.1. Comparing sets of marbles

Speaker	What is said	What is done
1. Mother	I brought you two boxes. Do you know what is there in the boxes?	Puts two identical closed opaque boxes, A and B, on the carpet, next to the girls.
2. Roni	Yes, marbles.	
3a. Mother	Right, there are marbles in the boxes.	
3b. Mother	I want you to tell me in which box there are more marbles.	While saying this, points to box A close to Eynat, then to box B.
3c. Eynat		Points to box A, which is closer to her.
3d. Roni		Points to box A.
4. Mother	In this one? How do you know?	Points to box A.

[8] The conversation was held in Hebrew. While translating to English, I made an effort to preserve the idiosyncrasies of the children's word use (thus expressions such as "this is the biggest than this one" and "it is more huge than that.")

5.	Roni	Because this is the biggest than this one. It is the most.	While saying "than this one" points to box B, which is closer to her.
6.	Mother	Eynat, how do you know?	
7.	Eynat	Because . . . cause it is more huge than that.	Repeats Roni's pointing movement to box B when saying "than that."
8.	Mother	Yes? This is more huge than that? Roni, what do you say?	Repeats Roni's pointing movement to box B when saying "than that."
9.	Roni	That this is also more huge than this.	Repeats Roni's pointing movement to box B when saying "than that."
. . . . . .		. . . . . .	. . . . . .
10a.	Mother	Do you want to open and discover? Let's open and see what there is inside. Take a look now.	
10b.	Roni		Abruptly grabs box A, which is closer to Eynat and which was previously chosen as the one with more marbles.
11.	Roni	1 . . . 1 . . . 1 . . . 2, 3, 4, 5, 6, 7, 8.	Opens box A and counts correctly.
12.	Eynat	1, 2, 3, 4, 5, 6.	Opens box B and counts correctly.
13.	Mother	So, what do you say?	
14.	Roni	6.	
15.	Mother	Six what? You say 6 what? What does it mean "six"? Explain.	
16.	Roni	That this is too many.	
17.	Mother	That this is too much? Eynat, what do you say?	
18.	Eynat	That this too is a little.	
19.	Mother	That it seems to you a little? Where do you think there are more marbles?	

Episode 1.1 *(continued)*

20. Roni	I think here.	Points to box A, which is now close to her (and in which she found eight marbles).
21. Mother	You think here? And what do you think, Eynat?	
22. Eynat	Also here.	

As predicted by the mother, the girls have shown full mastery of counting. In spite of this, they did not bother to count the marbles or even to open the boxes when asked to compare the invisible contents. Their immediate response was the choice of one of the closed boxes ([3c], [3d]). Not only did they make this instant move and agree in their decision, but they were also perfectly able to "justify" their action in a way that could have appeared adequate if not for the fact that the girls had no grounds for the comparative claims, such as "this is the biggest than this one" ([5]), "It is the most" ([7]), and "it is more huge than that" ([9]). If the startled mother had hoped that her interrogation about the reasons for the choices ([4], [6], [8]) would stimulate opening the boxes and counting the marbles, she was quickly disillusioned: Nothing less than the explicit request to open the boxes ([10a]) seemed to help.

By now, we are so familiar with the fact that "children who know how to count may not use counting to compare sets with respect to number"[9] that the episode may fail to surprise us, at least at the first reading. And yet, knowing what children usually *do not* do is not enough to account for what they *actually do*. Our young interviewees' insistence on deciding which box "has more marbles" without performing any explorations is a puzzle, one that has not been noted or accounted for in the previous studies. Unlike in conservation tasks, Roni and Eynat made their claims about the inequality without actually seeing the sets, so we cannot ascribe their choices to any visible differences between the objects of comparison. Neither can the children's surprising decision be seen as motivated by the rule "Repeated question means 'Change your answer!'": The girls chose one of the indistinguishable boxes already the first time round, before the parents had a chance to reiterate their request. Well, they were playing a guessing game, somebody may say. This would mean that the children knew they would have to verify their guess by counting the contents of the two boxes. However,

[9] Nunes and Bryant (1996, p. 35).

neither of them seemed inclined actually to perform such a verifying procedure, and when they eventually did, there was no sign they were concerned with the question whether the present answer matches the former direct choice. Moreover, the hypothesis of a guessing game, even if confirmed, still leaves many questions unanswered: Why were the girls in such perfect accord about their choices even though these choices seemed arbitrary? What was it that evidently made the chosen box so highly desirable? (Note that each of the girls wanted this box for herself; see for example, [10b].) Why after making the seemingly inexplicable decisions were the children able to answer the request for justification? On what grounds did they claim that what they chose is "the biggest" or "more huge"? Many different conjectures may be formulated in an attempt to respond to all these queries, but it seems that a real breakthrough in our understanding of children's number-related actions is unlikely to occur unless there is some fundamental change in our thinking about numerical thinking.

It seems that in order to come to grips with these and similar phenomena, one needs to go beyond the Piagetian frame of mind. Indeed, if there is little in the past research to help us account for what we saw in this study, it is probably because theory-guided researchers attend to nothing except for those actions of their interviewees that they have classified in advance as relevant to their study, and for the Piagetian investigator, the conversation that preceded opening of the boxes would be dismissable as mere "noise." The analysis of the remaining half of the event might even lead her to the claim that Roni and Eynat had a satisfactory command of numerical comparisons, although this is not the vision that emerges when the second part of the episode is analyzed in the context of the first.

2. The Quandary of *Abstraction* (and *Transfer*)

The most common explanation of the widespread failure in more advanced school-type mathematics is its highly *abstract* character. Abstracting, the specialty of scientists at large and of mathematicians in particular, has always been a highly valued activity, appreciated for its power to produce useful generalizations. It has been believed that if people engage in abstract thinking in spite of its difficulty, they do so because of the natural tendency of the human mind for organizing one's experience with the help of unifying patterns and structures. It may thus be surprising that the notion of abstraction has been getting bad press lately. True, the troubles did not really start today. The idea of abstraction boggled the minds of philosophers and of psychologists from the birth of their disciplines, and critical voices, pointing to abstraction-engendered conceptual dilemmas, could be heard for centuries. And yet, never before was it suggested, as it is now, that the term *abstraction* be simply removed from the discourse on learning.[10]

To get a flavor of the phenomena that shook researchers' confidence in the human propensity for abstracting, let us look at the brief episode that originates in the study of Brazilian street vendors conducted by Teresinha Nunes, Annalucia Schliemann, and David Carraher.[11] The 12-year-old child, M, selling coconuts at the price of 35 cruzeiros per unit, is approached by a customer.

Customer: I'm going to take four coconuts. How much is that?

M, the child: There will be one hundred five, plus thirty, that's one thirty-five . . . one coconut is thirty-five . . . that is . . . one forty!

Some time later, the child is asked to perform the numerical calculation $4 \cdot 35$ without any direct reference to coconuts or money.

Child: Four times five is twenty, carry the two; two plus three is five, times four is twenty. [Answer written: 200]

The new result, so dramatically different from the former, may seem puzzling to anybody who knows a thing or two about mathematics. To put it in the researchers' own words, "How is it possible that children capable of solving a computational problem in the natural situation will fail to solve the same problem when it is taken out of its context?"[12] Solving "the same problem" in different situations means being able to view the two situations as, in a sense, the same, or at least as sufficiently similar to allow for application of the same algorithm. Being able to notice the sameness (or just the similarity) is the gist of abstracting, and the capacity for abstracting is said to be part and parcel of the human ability to "transfer knowledge" – to recycle old problem-solving procedures in new situations. What puzzled the implementers of the Brazilian study was the fact that this latter ability seemed to be absent in M, as well as in practically all the other young street vendors whom they interviewed.

One may try to account for these findings simply by saying that the main reason for the disparity between the Brazilian childrens' performances in the street and in school-like situations was their insufficient schooling. M's inability to cope with the abstract task is understandable in the view of

[10] Lave and Wenger (1991).
[11] Nunes, Schliemann, and Carraher (1993, p. 24).
[12] Ibid., p. 23.

his almost complete lack of school learning. And yet, the question remains why it did not occur to the child to use in the school-like situation the very same algorithm that made him so successful in the street. This query becomes even more nagging in the view of the results of other cross-cultural and cross-situational studies, most of which indicated that people who are extremely skillful in solving everyday mathematical problems may have considerable difficulty with learning abstract equivalents of the real-life procedures. Consider, for example, the findings of the study conducted by Michael Cole and his colleagues in the 1960s in Liberia. Although the Kpelle people, whom the researchers observed, have shown great agility in operations involving quantities of rice and in money transactions, they seemed almost impervious to school mathematics. "Teachers complained that when they presented a problem like $2 + 6 = ?$ as an example in the classroom and then asked $3 + 5 = ?$ on a test, students were likely to protest that the test was unfair because it contained material not covered in the lesson."[13] Even in retrospect, Cole cannot overcome his bafflement:

> The question aroused by these observations remains with me to this day. Judged by the way they do puzzles or study for mathematics in school, the Kpelle appeared dumb; judged by their behavior in markets, taxis, and many other settings, they appeared smart (at least, smarter than one American visitor). How could people be so dumb and so smart at the same time?[14]

These findings are not unlike the results of many other cross-cultural and cross-situational studies, notably those on dairy warehouse workers,[15] on American shoppers and weight-watchers,[16] and on Nepalese shopkeepers.[17] In our own study, we have seen that a child may have difficulty putting together everyday and abstract mathematical procedures even if she has a reasonable knowledge of school mathematics. Consider, for example, two excerpts from an interview with a 12-year-old seventh grader,[18] whom I shall call Ron. In the first part of the conversation, the child was playing the role of a shop attendant and the interviewer presented herself as a client. The products were represented by cards featuring their names along with their authentic prices. The "vendor" and the "buyer" had a certain amount

---

[13] Cole (1996, p. 73). Compare Cole et al. (1971); Hoyles et al. (2001); Lave (1988); Scribner (1997); Scribner and Cole (1981).

[14] Cole (1996, p. 74).

[15] Scribner (1997).

[16] Lave (1988).

[17] Beach (1995).

[18] The interview was conducted in Hebrew by Liron Dekel (2003) as a part of her master's thesis.

of real coins and banknotes at their disposal. In the episode that follows, the shop attendant is calculating the sum to be paid by the buyer, who is asking for three cans of tuna fish for 4.99 shekel each and for two bottles of mineral water for 1.10 shekel each.[19]

Episode 1.2. Utilizing rounding procedure and distributivity

67. Interviewer:	Three cans of tuna and two bottles of water.	The necessary operation: $3 \cdot 4.99\text{is} + 2 \cdot 1.10\text{is}$	
68. Ron:	[. . . .][20] Two twenty [2.20] [. . . . .] Can I round the sums up?		
69. Interviewer:	Just tell me how much I am supposed to pay.		
70. Ron:	[. . . . .] I think it is 17 [IS] and 17 agoras. [17.17] [. . . . .] Perhaps not. Let me see. I calculated this as 5. . . . It makes 15, because I multiplied by 3. Minus 3 agoras from the 99, and it makes 14 and 97 agoras. I added 97 agoras and the 20 agoras of the water and this means I have to add shekel and 17 agoras. It is already 15 and 17 agoras. I added the 2 shekels of the water and this made 17 shekels and 17 agoras.	Performs: $3 \cdot 5\text{is} = 15\text{is}$ $15\text{is} - 3 \text{ ag} = 14.97\text{is}$ $97\text{ag} + 20 \text{ ag} = 1.17\text{is}$ $14\text{is} + 1.17\text{is} = 15.17\text{is}$ $15.17\text{is} + 2\text{is} = 17.17\text{is}$	

The shopping tasks were followed by purely numerical assignments, one of which was the multiplication $24 \cdot 9$. Ron performed the operation on the basis of the distributive property and without using the rounding procedure, which might have given the result more quickly.

192. Ron:	[reads] 24 times 9 [. . . . . .] 20 times 9 is 180. 9 times 4 is 36. 80 plus 36 is [. . . . .] 116. 180 plus 36 is 226.	$24 \cdot 9$

[19] The Israeli shekel (IS) is the Israeli monetary unit; 1 shekel is equivalent to 100 agoras.
[20] The dots in square brackets represent pauses; two dots are equivalent to a break of one second in speech.

In spite of his skillfulness in applying the rounding procedure and in taking advantage of distributivity, which he displayed both here and in the previous task with money, Ron did not have recourse to these methods while trying to perform a more complex calculation, $49 \cdot 16$:

196.	Ron:	40 times 16. 40 times 10 is 400. 9 times 6 is 54. It's 454.	$40 \cdot 10 = 400$ $9 \cdot 6 = 54$ $400 + 54 = 454$
197.	Interviewer:	Is this reasonable?	
198.	Ron:	Why not?	

The interviewer waited for a few moments and then decided to prompt the boy toward the use of the rounding procedure.

199.	Interviewer:	Look again at the expression. Are there other similar numbers you could...	$49 \cdot 16$
200.	Ron:	What do you mean?	
201.	Interviewer:	49 is like...	
202.	Ron:	[.....] 64?	64 was a number obtained in one of the former purely numerical tasks
203.	Interviewer:	Do you remember what we did while shopping?	
204.	Ron:	[........] When we had 99 agoras?	looks at the prices written on the product cards
205.	Interviewer:	Yes. What did we do then?	
206.	Ron:	We took 1 agora away... It is 50 times 10 minus [....] I turned 49 into 50 [....] 50 times 10 is 500 [....] and 50 times six is 300. It is 800 [....]; and then... 166? No, 346.	$50 \cdot 10 - \cdots$ $50 \cdot 10 = 500$ $50 \cdot 6 = 300$ $500 + 300 = 800$ $800 - 166?$ $800 - 346?$
207.	Interviewer:	You subtract 346?	
208.	Ron:	Yes, 346.	

Ron's present difficulty with utilizing the rounding procedure and the distributive property, which clearly contrasts with the facility he demonstrated while applying both of them in the "real life" situation, may be due to the difference in the numbers involved. However, it may also be a result of the fact that this time, the calculations were performed on the "bare" numbers and not on the familiar notes and coins that evidently mediated – either in their actual or only imagined form – the earlier real life calculation, not to mention the possibility that Ron might simply have no reason to associate the paper-and-pencil numerical tasks with the money transactions. After all, numerical tasks are performed in schools to show one's mastery of formal computational procedures, not merely to produce an answer. Whichever is the reason, the question is what can be done to overcome this compartmentalization of techniques.

According to many researchers, the bulky findings that indicate the strong dependence of human actions on the situations in which the actions take place seem to undermine the assumption that motivates school curricula, according to which abstract concepts and procedures, once learned, will readily "transfer" to new situations whenever a possibility offers itself:

> Recent investigations of learning...challenge...separating of what is learned from how it is learned and used. The activity in which knowledge is developed and deployed, it is now argued, is not separable from or ancillary to learning or cognition. Nor is it neutral. Rather, it is an integral part of what is learned. Situations might be said to coproduce knowledge through activity. Learning and cognition, it is now possible to argue, are fundamentally situated.[21]

The resulting criticism of the ideas of abstraction and transfer goes from moderate to radical – from one that focuses on common faults in our understanding of the concept to one that posits its outright untenability. In the radical version, the notion of abstraction, seen as practically inseparable from the issue of the generality of knowledge and from the concept of learning transfer, is being accused of taking into cognitive research tacit assumptions that are bound to lead this research astray. Thus, for example, the first theorists who proposed to conceptualize learning in terms of participation in certain well-defined practices rather than in terms of "acquiring knowledge" declared that they "challenge...the very meaning of abstraction and/or generalization" and "reject conventional readings of the generalizability and/or abstraction of 'knowledge.'"[22] In the moderate version, the proposal is not so much to abandon the idea of abstraction as

[21] Brown, Collins, and Duguid (1989, p. 32).
[22] Lave and Wenger (1991, p. 37).

to be more aware of the hazards of its careless conceptualization and of its perfunctory applications. Referring to the heated controversies between those who wish to retain the traditionally conceived idea of abstraction and those who reject it, says James Greeno:[23] "On the issue of abstraction . . . the disagreement . . . is about theoretical formulations, rather than being about empirical claim." And further, while

> [although] abstract representations can facilitate learning when students share the interpretive conventions that are intended in their use . . . abstract instruction can also be ineffective regarding some important purposes if what is taught in the classroom does not communicate important meanings and significance of symbolic expressions and procedures.

Whether phenomena such as those described earlier should be taken as showing the inherent, insurmountable situatedness of learning remains a moot point. The discussion on the nature and place of abstraction in human thinking is going on and on and does not show any signs of approaching definite conclusions.[24] Whatever the interpretation and conclusions drawn from the cross-cultural and cross-situational studies, however, one thing is certain: These studies' findings present us with a dilemma. On the one hand, we seem to have good reasons to doubt the effectiveness of what Greeno calls "abstract learning," well exemplified by the type of learning that takes place in mathematics classrooms; on the other hand, even if often disappointing in its immediate results, this type of learning still seems to be the quickest path to useful reorganization of practices that constitute our lives.[25] Indeed, neither the human civilization nor our everyday activities would have developed the way they did if not for our capacity for abstracting and generalizing.[26]

---

[23] Greeno (1997, p. 13).

[24] See, e.g., Brown et al. (1989); Lave (1988); Lave and Wenger (1991); also see the recent debate in *Educational Researcher*: Anderson et al. (1996); Cobb and Bowers (1999); Donmoyer (1996); Greeno (1997); Sfard (1998).

[25] At this point, two disclaimers are in order. First, when speaking about school-type learning (rather than just school learning) I stress that what really counts, in the present context, is the nature of this learning and not the setting where it takes place. Second, lest I be misunderstood as claiming that everyday usefulness is the only possible reason for school learning, let me clarify that if I restrict the present debate to the question of practical impact of school mathematics, it is only because this is the topic around which the recent controversy revolves.

[26] To those who tend to dismiss this last statement because of their objections to the direction taken by our civilization, let me say that my stance is inquisitive, not normative. Whether one is pleased or displeased with the current state of affairs, nobody can deny that human culture is what sets us apart from other species, and that this uniqueness merits researchers'

3. The Quandary of *Misconceptions*

Some difficulties with mathematics are widespread and well known to every teacher. In spite of their commonness, many of them are a constant source of bewilderment. Among the most intriguing phenomena commonplace in a mathematical classroom are those that have become known as *misconceptions*. We are said to be witnessing a misconception whenever a student is using a certain concept, say function, in a way that, although systematic and invariant across contexts, differs from the way this concept is used by experts. Researchers interpret this phenomenon as showing that children, in the process of learning mathematics, tend to *"create their own meanings – meanings that are not appropriate at all."*[27] The words *not appropriate* refer not so much to the inner coherence of students' thinking as to possible disparities between students' conceptions and the generally accepted versions of the same ideas. Thus, for example, studies have repeatedly shown that the overwhelming majority of high school students tend to believe in the algorithmic nature of functions. This conviction persists in spite of the fact that the definition, which most of the learners can repeat without difficulty, does not require any kind of behavioral "regularity."[28] Similarly, young children are known to believe that the operation of multiplication must increase the multiplied number, whereas division must make it smaller.[29] A child's idiosyncratic notions tend to be consistent one with another and are sometimes very difficult to change. All this has been widely documented.[30]

Although today our knowledge on the ways in which children think about numbers, functions, proofs, and other mathematical ideas is impressively rich, there are many questions that the theory of misconceptions leaves open. For example, one cannot stop puzzling in the face of the fact that the same misconceptions are held by children speaking different languages, learning with different teachers and according to different curricula,

---

attention. It seems that one issue that is still in need of more investigation is the mechanism through which school-type learning leads to lasting reorganization of human activities and to the incessant, consequential growth in their complexity.

[27] Davis (1988, p. 9).

[28] Malik (1980); Markovits, Eylon, and Bruckheimer (1986); Sfard (1992); Vinner and Dreyfus (1989).

[29] Fishbein (1987, 1989); Fischbein, Deri, Nello, and Marino (1985); Harel, Behr, Post, and Lesh (1989).

[30] Smith, diSessa, and Rochelle (1993); Confrey (1990); see also studies on related ideas, e.g., *concept images* as in Tall and Vinner (1981); Vinner (1983) or *tacit models* as in Fischbein (1989); see also the tightly related, burgeoning research on conceptual change, e.g., Schnotz, Vosniadou, and Carretero (1999); Vosniadou (1994).

and using different textbooks. How is it that the "misconceiving" children agree among themselves about how to disagree with the definition? Such a well-coordinated rebellion against generally accepted rules of word use cannot be dismissed as just accidental "erring."

The phenomenon of misconceptions is known in other domains of knowledge as well, notably in science, but in mathematics, the striking regularity of the "mistaken" ways of thinking is particularly perplexing. Indeed, the fact that many children hold misconceptions about Earth can be accounted for by saying that the classroom is not the only, perhaps even not the most influential, source of one's knowledge about Earth. A child's own experiences in the world are the primary type of "material" of which her ideas about Earth are forged. Because these experiences are similar in different individuals, no wonder that people's "private" misconceptions are similar one to another as well. And yet, this explanation does not seem to hold for mathematical concepts, many of which are unknown to children at the time they begin learning about them in school. Thus, how can one account for the well-coordinated "distortion" of such a notion as, say, function, which, when first encountered in school, does not have any obvious "real world" counterpart? One becomes even more bewildered when one notices the strange similarity between children's misconceptions and the early historical versions of the concepts. Thus, for example, the first definitions presented function simply as formulas.[31] In this case, it was justified to claim that functions express certain algorithmic regularities – a claim that today counts as a misconception. How do abstract mathematical concepts created by mathematicians get life of their own and start dictating to their creators what to think? Why do today's children think the same way as mathematicians of the past?[32]

The trouble with the idea of misconception does not stop here. In addition to its being insufficiently understood, the notion turns out to be of only limited value as an explanatory tool, supposed to help in accounting for what is actually happening when children grapple with mathematical problems. The classroom episode that follows, taken from the *Montreal Algebra Study*,[33] presents one unsuccessful problem-solving attempt that,

---

[31] One of the earliest definitions was formulated in 1718 by Johann Bernoulli. It presented a *function* as "a variable quantity composed in any manner whatever of this variable and of constants." It was followed by that given in 1737 by Euler, which defined *function* as an "analytic expression" (Kline, 1980).

[32] See Piaget and Garcia (1989) and Sfard (1992, 1995) for reflections on parallels between historical and ontogenic development of mathematical thinking. The idea that there must be such parallels was one of the basic assumptions of Piaget's genetic epistemology.

[33] This study, directed by Carolyn Kieran and me, was implemented in 1992–1994 in a Montreal middle school situated in an affluent area. The aim of the 30-session-long teaching

A function *g(x)* is partly represented by Figure 1.2. Answer the questions in the box.

x	g(x)
0	-5
1	0
2	5
3	10
4	15
5	20

(1) What is $g(6)$? _____
(2) What is $g(10)$? _____
(3) The students in grade 7 were
      asked to write an expression
      for the function *g(x)*.
Evan wrote *g(x)* = 5(*x* – 1)
Amy wrote *g(x)* = 3(*x* – 3) + 2(*x* – 2)
Stuart wrote *g(x)* = 5*x* – 5
Who is right? Why?

Figure 1.2. Slope episode – the worksheet.

although it seems to be involving misconceptions, cannot be explained by this fact alone. In the episode, two 12-year-old boys, Ari and Gur, are grappling together with one of a long series of problems supposed to usher them into algebraic thinking and to help them in learning about function. The boys are dealing with the first of the three questions in Figure 1.2. On the worksheet, function $g(x)$ has been introduced with the help of the partial table of values and the question requires finding the value of $g(6)$, which does not appear in the table. Before proceeding, the reader is advised to take a good look at Ari and Gur's exchange and try to answer some obvious questions: Do the boys know how to cope with the problem? Do they display satisfactory understanding of the situation? Does the collaboration contribute in any visible way to their learning? If either of the students experiences difficulty, what is the nature of the problem? How could he be helped? What would be an effective way of overcoming – or preventing altogether – the difficulty he is facing?

Episode 1.3. Finding a value of a function

1. Ari: Wait, how do we find out the slope again?
          No, no, no, no. Slope, no, wait, intercept
          is negative 5. Slope

sequence designed for the sake of the study was to introduce the students to algebra while investigating their ways of constructing algebraic concepts and testing certain hypotheses about possible ways of spurring these constructions. The present episode is taken from the 21st meeting. More information on the study, as well as another outlook on the present episode, may be found in Kieran and Sfard (1999) and Sfard and Kieran (2001a, 2001b).

2.	Gur:	What are you talking about?	
3.	Ari:	I'm talking about this....	points to the -5 in the right column
		It's 5.	is moving his eyes to the next row
4.	Gur:	It doesn't matter if it's on (mumble)	
5.	Ari:	5x. Right?	Writes the formula $g(x) = 5x - 5$ on his worksheet
6.	Gur:	What's that?	pointing to the expression
7.	Ari:	It's the formula, so you can figure it out.	
8.	Gur:	Oh. How'd you get that formula?	
9.	Ari:	and you replace the x by 6.	
10.	Gur:	Oh. Ok, I...	
11.	Ari:	Look. Cause the, um the slope, is the zero.	
		Ah, no, the intercept is the zero.	points to the 0 in the left column
12.	Gur:	Oh, yeah, yeah, yeah. So you got your	
13.	Ari:	And then you see how many is in between each, like from zero to what	while saying "each," Ari points to both columns; while saying "from zero to what," he points to the x column
14.	Gur:	And the slope is, so the slope is 1.	the left counterpart of the right column 0 is 1
15.	Ari:	Hum? No, the slope, see you look at zero,	circles the zero in the x column on Gur's sheet
16.	Gur:	Oh that zero, ok. So the slope is minus 5	
17.	Ari:	Yeah. And	
18.	Gur:	How are you supposed to get the other ones?	
19.	Ari:	You look how many times it's going down, like we did before. So it's going down by ones. So then it's easy.	first points to x column ("going down by ones"), then the g(x) column ("by

Example 1.3 *(continued)*

		This is ah … by fives. See, it's going down by ones, so you just look here	fives"), and again to g(x) column ("look here")
20.	Gur:	Oh. So it's 5	
21.	Ari:	Yeah. 5x plus	
22.	Gur:	Negative 5.	
23.	Ari:	Do you understand?	
24.	Gur:	Negative 5. Yeah, yeah, ok. So what is g 6?	
25.	Ari:	5 times 6 is 30, plus negative 5 is 25. So we did get it right.	
26.	Gur:	No, but it's – in this column there?	points to x column
27.	Ari:	Yeah	
28.	Gur:	Oh, then that makes sense. It's 30 What is g 10? … 40	writes "30" moves to the next question on the worksheet
29.	Ari:	20, ah 40. No, 45.	
30.	Gur:	No,	
31.	Ari:	45	
32.	Gur:	because 20	
33.	Ari:	10 times 5 is 50, minus	
34.	Gur:	Well, 5 is 20, so 10 must have 40	points to the two entries in the last row
35.	Ari:	times 5	circles the 10 in g(10) on Gur's sheet
36.	Gur:	Oh, we do that thing. Ok, just trying to find it.	
37.	Ari:	Yeah	
38.	Gur:	Cause I was thinking cause 5 is 20,	points again to the last row of the table
39.	Ari:	It's 45. Yeah	
40.	Gur:	(mumble) So it's 45.	

A cursory glance at the transcript suffices to see that Ari proceeds smoothly and effectively, whereas Gur is unable to cope with the task. Moreover, in spite of Ari's apparently adequate algebraic skills, the conversation that accompanies the process of solving does not seem to help Gur.

So far so good: The basic question about the overall effectiveness of the students' problem-solving efforts does not pose any special difficulty. A difficulty arises when we attempt a move beyond this crude evaluation and venture a quest for a deeper insight into the boys' thinking. Let us try, for example, to diagnose the nature of Gur's problem. The first thing to say would be that "Gur does not understand the concept of function" or, more precisely, "He does not understand what the formula and the table are all about, what is their relation, and how they should be used in the present context." Although certainly true, this statement has little explanatory power. What Tolstoy said about unhappiness seems to be true also about the lack of understanding: Whoever lacks understanding fails to understand in his or her own way. We do not know much if we cannot say anything specific about the unique nature of Gur's incomprehension.

Rather than asking *whether* students understand, we now ask *how* they understand. It is here that the notion of misconception comes in handy. We could say, for example, that Gur's conception of function, unlike his partner's, is still quite faulty. One look at the transcript now, and we identify the familiar nature of the inadequacy: The sequence [28]–[34] shows that Gur holds the ill-conceived idea of proportionality, according to which values of a function should be proportional to the values of the argument.[34] "Misconception of proportionality" is so common that it even made its way to a popular TV sitcom, *Friends*. In one episode, a person tries to prevent an 18-year-old youth from marrying a 44-year-old woman. He says: "She is so much older than you are. And think about the future: When you are 36, she will be 88." "Yeah, I know," says the boy.

The fact that Gur holds the well-known misconception about function, as significant as it surely is, does not seem to satisfy our need for explanation. The misconception-based account leaves us in the dark about many aspects of the preceding conversation and, more specifically, about the reasons for Gur's choices and responses. The misconception that certainly plays a role in the last part of the exchange does not account for Gur's earlier responses to the notion of formula. These responses seem as unexpected as they are unhelpful. Moreover, although it is obvious that Gur does struggle for understanding, and although the ideas he wishes to

[34] The proportionality belief is a variant of the well-known misconception according to which any function should be linear; see, e.g., Markovitz et al. (1986); Van Dooren, De Bock, Janssens, and Verschaffel (2005); Vinner and Dreyfus (1989).

understand do not appear to be very complex (indeed, what could be more straightforward than the principle of plugging a number into the formula in order to calculate the value of the function for this number?), all his efforts prove strangely ineffective – they do not seem to make him one step closer to the understanding of the solution that Ari repeatedly tries to explain. It is not easy to decide which kind of action by the more knowledgeable peer could be of some genuine help.

This example seems to reinforce the conclusion drawn from our two former dilemmas: In order to make sense of what people are doing while engaging in mathematical thinking (or in any thinking at all, for that matter), we need not just additional data, but also, and above all, more developed ways of looking, organized into more penetrating theories of thinking and learning.

4. The Quandary of *Learning Disability*

Within the current tradition, failure in learning is believed to stem from certain inadequacies in one's cognitive processes. Some of these inadequacies, such as those that produce the common misconceptions just described, are regarded as "normal," that is, as natural, almost inevitable, relatively mild perturbations in the otherwise linear growth of knowledge. Some other difficulties are seen as indicating a more serious condition known as learning disability or LD, for short. Historically, this distinction has its roots in the old nature/nurture dichotomy that assumes the possibility of setting apart phenomena originating in biological factors from those that have their roots in environmental influences. Indeed, the decision to distinguish certain cases of unsuccessful learning from all the others stems from the belief that some difficulties indicate a neurologically grounded "cognitive defect."[35] Over time, this approach has proved problematic in several respects, and the resulting research has stumbled upon difficulties.

First, as a result of the proposed distinction, learning difficulties in mathematics have been studied by two different professional communities who do not really communicate with one another. Specialists in LD speak about deficient *cognitive* and *metacognitive skills* and insufficient *neurological functioning* as the main characteristics of students who have persistent difficulties in mathematics.[36] In contrast, specialists in mathematics education frame

---

[35] Kosc (1974).

[36] Chinn (1996); Garnett (1992); Goldman, Pellegrino, and Mertz (1988); Steeves and Tomey (1998).

mathematics learning difficulties in the neo-Piagetian language of *misconceptions*,[37] faulty *mental schemes* or *tacit models*,[38] flawed *concept images*,[39] and *buggy algorithms*.[40] The lack of a common language between these two communities reduces their chances of engaging in useful exchanges of ideas or building upon each other's research.

Second, the notion of LD, which some researchers consider indispensable in accounting for more extreme cases of mathematical failure, seems inherently problematic. "Many of the difficulties experienced by the LD field emanate from a failure to answer the seeming straightforward question, 'What is a learning disability?'" admit the authors of an article.[41] The reasons for confusion are many. As long as there are no easily accessible high-resolution methods for studying cerebral mechanisms, descriptions that speak about the existence of neurological faults cannot be truly operative. Aware of this difficulty, LD researchers have been trying to bypass any explicit mention of neurological factors. At present, the most widely accepted definition of LD, proposed by developmental psychologists, refers to children "who possess 'normal' intellectual ability – they are not mentally retarded – but do not seem to profit from sound instruction despite the fact that they are motivated to learn."[42] However, even those who adopt this definition are well aware of its numerous pitfalls. Many of them acknowledge that the distinction between difficulty experienced *despite* instruction and difficulty that develops *because of* instruction is not as straightforward as the definition seems to imply. No wonder, then, that the results attained with diagnostic methods based on this distinction are regarded by many as debatable.[43] Some authors argue that psychologists who "located [a] child's problem beneath his skin and between his ears"[44] engage in practices that, through their very dynamics, construct rather than merely identify LD. This latter criticism is in tune with more general attacks on the epistemological premises underlying both LD research and the study of misconceptions.[45] I expand on these epistemological issues in the next chapter.

To shed some additional light on the dilemma of learning disability and to present the problem in more concrete terms, let me introduce two

---

[37] Smith et al. (1993).
[38] Dreyfus (1991); Fischbein (1989); Hershkowitz (1989).
[39] Tall and Vinner (1981); Vinner (1991).
[40] Brown and Burton (1978).
[41] Kavale and Forness (1997, p. 3).
[42] Ginsburg (1997, p. 27); cf. Shaywitz, Escobar, Shaywitz, Fletcher, and Makuch (1992).
[43] Geary, Hoard, and Hamson (1999); Ginsburg (1997) .
[44] Mehan (1996, p. 268).
[45] McDermott (1993); Mehan (1996); Varenne and McDermott (1998).

18-year-old high school students, Mira and Talli, who participated in the Learning Difficulty Study[46] (LD study) conducted by Miriam Ben-Yehuda, Ilana Lavie, Liora Linchevski, and me. At the time we met them, Mira and Talli were 11th-grade students in a special vocational school for adolescents who had long histories of maladjustment, low achievement, and distinct learning difficulties. Because of their discontinuous educational histories, both were older than the norm for their class. Mira had prepared herself for a secretarial job and Talli expected to become a hairdresser. Both were described by their mathematics teacher as "extremely weak" in arithmetic. While interviewing them, we had ample opportunity to see that, indeed, the state of their arithmetic fell well below what one would expect from an 18-year-old. Even simple multiplication of whole numbers seemed to exceed their computational capacities.

Mira, when asked to tell us the history of her mathematics learning, asserted that as a young child she did not experience any difficulty with calculations. She claimed that her difficulties began some time later:

> In the fourth grade, when we started to multiply...I lost the way....I thought it was not for me....I did want to know how to do it....Sometimes I can do things and succeed...But when I have to think hard, I give up....The multiplication table...no use in trying to remember. It is so confusing.

The interviewer followed with the question "How much is $7 \cdot 16$?" When Mira experienced difficulty multiplying 6 by 7, the following exchange took place:

Episode 1.4a. Mira calculates $7 \cdot 16$

1. Interviewer:	Do you know how much 6 times 7 is?	
2. Mira:	No.	
3. Interviewer:	And if I asked you to figure it out, what would you do?	
4. Mira:	I would use my fingers. Would count seven times.	
5. Interviewer:	Show us.	
6. Mira:	No.	
7. Interviewer:	Please do.	
8. Mira:	No. I do it silently, so that people won't see.	

---

[46] The full report on the study can be found in Ben-Yehuda, Lavie, Linchevski, and Sfard (2005).

Later, when Talli tackled the same question "How much is 7 · 16?" her computational skills did not appear to be much more advanced:

Episode 1.4b. Talli calculates 7 · 16

53. Talli:	I'm not good at multiplication table.	
56. Interviewer:	100? 3000? 500? 5? It does not need to be exact.	
57. Talli:	Approximately 50…	
…..	…..	…..
67. Talli:	I take down the 7, multiply the 6 by the 7 and the 7 by the 1, and get the answer.	
68. Interviewer:	Do it, please.	
……	……	…..
71. Talli:	6 multiplied by 7 is 36. Okay? I am asking you. [laughs].	$6 \cdot 7 = 36?$
……	………	……
75. Interviewer:	6 multiplied by 7 is 42. Ok? What do you do next?	
76. Talli:	I take it down. [mumbling] 1 multiplied by 7, it gives 7. So it gives 742.	Writes: ^{4} 16 ·7 122

Their common difficulty with multiplication notwithstanding, Mira and Talli differed in more than one way. The teacher told us that Talli, in spite of her problems, was a student "with a genuine potential." In contrast, she described Mira as the "weakest student" in her class, who clearly did not have "much chance." The teacher also warned us that any effort we made to perform arithmetic with Mira would be "a waste of time." The teacher's assessment seemed to be in tune with the girls' appearance and demeanor. Mira wore provocative clothes and heavy makeup, and she behaved and spoke like a helpless child. In contrast, Talli's stern look and plain dark clothes gave the impression of a no-nonsense, mature person who knew exactly what she wanted. And yet later, while listening to the girls at length, we became skeptical about the teacher's remarks about their "mathematical potential."

To understand the nature of the conundrum with which we were faced, let us take a look at what was known about Mira and Talli before our investigation began. Our two interviewees' stories, as told by the rich records we found in their school files, may have differed in details but resembled one another in several important respects.

According to these records, in the course of the first 18 years of their lives, both girls experienced more misfortune and suffering than can be found in other people's entire life spans. Mira, who was the sixth and last child in her family, and whose father stopped working when she was still very young, was subject to sexual assault at the age of 7. The case had no legal follow-up, but the girl received professional assistance and some time later moved to her married brother's house. Talli, the oldest of three siblings, was 8 years old when her mother began a struggle with a terminal illness. After her mother's death 5 years later, she was sent by her deeply religious father to a boarding school, never to return home. She never agreed to see her father again.

Our interviewees' educational histories were rather discontinuous. Both were frequently moved from one school to another, never spending more than a couple of years in one place and sometimes having to join children several years younger. Under the occasional care of social workers and psychologists, each of them underwent certain diagnostic examinations at one time or another. In their school files, we found the results of IQ tests, in which they both scored around average, with their IQ performance scores slightly surpassing their verbal scores. In addition, each file contained a number of general evaluations written at different times by psychologists, social workers, and teachers. In these documents, Mira was described as "having normal intellectual ability, with certain emotional impediments and slight learning disabilities." The LD diagnosis was supported with statements about limitations in Mira's "short term and long term memory" and her "difficulties in areas requiring automation." Although Talli was found to have similar difficulties and limitations, in her case the findings did not lead to an explicit claim about LD. Both girls were said to have a "deficiency in acquired knowledge" and to possess "much unrealized potential." In addition, Mira was described as suffering from occasional "attacks of anxiety" and from a "fear of failure" that manifested itself at times of crisis in withdrawal and in "extreme avoidance." She was also said to be "mentally strong and prepared to invest in those areas in which she had genuine interest." Talli was described as "strongly motivated" to learn, but also as occasionally turning to "suppression mechanisms" while trying to overcome anxieties or to cope with her sense of loneliness.

Finally, the two files contained numerous records about the girls' mathematics histories. Various tests and teachers' assessments invariably pointed to a serious deficiency in both Mira's and Talli's arithmetical skills. This general agreement notwithstanding, the two interviewees did differ in the quality of their mathematical performance, at least according to their teachers. In vocational tests that she underwent at the age of 16, Mira received the lowest possible score. No mention of this kind of test appeared in Talli's file, but a current teacher's assessment described Talli as "strong in comparison to the school average" and as having a "good command over the four basic arithmetical operations." In both 10th and 11th grade, her final grades in arithmetic were 95%. In contrast, Mira scored only 75% in both cases.

The stories of Mira and Talli left us with many disquieting questions. First, how can one explain the teachers' positive evaluation of Talli's arithmetic skills? This assessment contrasted strongly with what we saw ourselves in the course of the interview. Second, and more importantly, why is it that the young women did not manage to learn the most basic arithmetic even though they were clearly given many opportunities over the years? They were preoccupied with other, more important problems, somebody might say. This is certainly true, and yet, this obvious answer did not seem to delve deeply enough. Indeed, what is the exact nature of the interplay between life hardships and the ability to learn? In this context, what is the status of Mira's LD diagnosis? Was the LD offered as an independent reason for her failure in learning, preexisting her misfortunes, or was it considered as, in a sense, a result of her life adversities? The list of questions remains long. Most of them may probably be summarized as follows: "What is it that made arithmetic so difficult a target for the two girls, and how was this difficulty related to other spheres of their lives?" Dilemmas such as these continue to perplex teachers, remedial specialists, and researchers, whereas the notion of learning disability, rather than help in solving these quandaries, seems to complicate the matters even further.

5. The Quandary of *Understanding*

One theme common to all the four dilemmas presented earlier is that of *understanding*. Each of the quandaries could have been formulated as a question about whether, how, or why people do or do not understand mathematics, sometimes even under the most favorable of circumstances. The interest in the issue of understanding has been pervasive in psychological, anthropological, and educational literature ever since the landmark call for *meaningful learning*, or *learning-with-understanding*, which, more than seven decades ago, signaled the end of the behaviorist era and the beginning of the new direction in the study of human cognition. When W. A. Brownell issued the plea for the "full recognition of the value of children's experiences" and for making "arithmetic less a challenge to pupil's memory and more a challenge to his intelligence,"[47] his words sounded innovative, and even defiant. Eventually, these words helped to lift the behaviorist ban on the inquiry into the "black box" of mind. Once the permission to look "inside the human head" was given, the issue of understanding turned into one of the central topics of research. Cognitive psychology equated understanding with perfecting mental representations and defined learning-with-understanding as one that effectively relates new knowledge to knowledge already possessed. With its roots in Piaget's theory of mental schemes and with its many branches in the quickly developing new science of cognition, this approach flourished for a few decades, spawning a massive flow of research.[48]

In spite of the impressive advances, researchers agree today that pinpointing the exact meaning of the word *understanding* and finding ways to make the principle of learning-with-understanding operative are extremely difficult tasks. The difficulty begins with the elusiveness of the experience that makes us say, "I understand": This experience is difficult to achieve and to sustain, and it is even more difficult to capture and to explain. Let me give a personal example. I can clearly remember the event that, for the first time, made me aware of the degree of my ignorance in this respect. I was a beginning teacher and I discovered to my surprise that students who had a good command of systems of linear equations might still be unable to deal with such questions as "For what value of parameter q does the given system of linear equations have no solution?" I approached the difficulty nonchalantly, confident that the students would be able to overcome the obstacle in an hour or two. Contrary to my expectations, several days passed before I felt that the class could cope with parameters. But even then the situation was not as good as I hoped for: At the final test only one student managed to produce fully satisfactory solutions to all the problems. In a private conversation with him I remarked, "It seems that you are the only one in this class who really understood the subject." To my distress, the praise was greeted with an angry response: "I didn't understand anything! I did what I did but I don't know why it worked." I tried to prove him wrong. I presented him with several other problems, one quite unlike the other, and he solved all of them without visible difficulty. I claimed that

[47] Brownell (1935, p. 31).
[48] See, e.g., Hiebert and Carpenter (1992).

this kind of question just cannot be answered by mechanical application of an algorithm. He kept insisting that he "did not understand anything." We ended up frustrated and puzzled. He felt he did not understand parameters, and I sensed that I did not understand understanding.

Reflections on my own history helped, but only to some extent. I could remember myself as a graduate mathematics student passing exams, often quite well, but not always having the sense of true understanding. Some time later I was happy to find out that even people who grew up to become well-known mathematicians were not altogether unfamiliar with this kind of experience. For example, Paul Halmos recalls in his "automatography":

> I was a student, sometimes pretty good and sometimes less good. Symbols didn't bother me. I could juggle them quite well ... [but] I was stumped by the infinitesimal subtlety of epsilonic analysis. I could read analytic proofs, remember them if I made an effort, and reproduce them, sort of, but I didn't really know what was going on.[49]

Halmos was fortunate enough eventually to find out what the "real knowing" was all about:

> One afternoon something happened. I remember standing at the blackboard in Room 213 of the mathematics building talking with Warren Ambrose and suddenly I understood epsilons. I understood what limits were, and all of the stuff that people had been drilling into me became clear. I sat down that afternoon with the calculus textbook by Granville, Smith, and Longley. All of that stuff that previously had not made any sense became obvious.[50]

As implied in this story, what people call "true" understanding must involve something that goes beyond the operative ability of solving problems and of proving theorems. But although a person may have no difficulty with diagnosing the degree of his or her understanding, he or she does not find it equally easy to name the criteria according to which such assessment is made. Many articles and books have already been written in which an attempt was made to understand what understanding is all about, but we still seem to be groping in the dark while trying to capture the gist of this fugitive something that makes us feel we had grasped an essence of a concept, a relation, or a proof.

Yet another illustration for the elusiveness of the notion of understanding, at large, and of the term *learning-with-understanding*, in particular,

---

[49] Halmos (1985, p. 47).
[50] Albers and Alexanderson (1985, p. 123).

comes from the following conversation between a preservice teacher and Noa, a 7-year-old girl:

Episode 1.5. What is the biggest number?

1. Teacher:	Can you count to 10?
2. Noa:	Yes. 1, 2, 3, 4, 5, 6, 7, 8, 9, 10.
3. Teacher:	Do you know more than ten?
4. Noa:	Yes. 1, 2, 3, 4, 5, 6, 7, 8, 9, 10,11, 12, 13, 14, 15, 16, 17, 18, 19, 20.
5. Teacher:	What is the biggest number you can think of?
6. Noa:	Million.
7. Teacher:	What happens when we add one to million?
8. Noa:	Million and one.
9. Teacher:	Is it bigger than million?
10. Noa:	Yes.
11. Teacher:	So what is the biggest number?
12. Noa:	Two million.
13. Teacher:	And if we add one to two million?
14. Noa:	It's more than two million.
15. Teacher:	So can one arrive at the biggest number?
16. Noa:	Yes.
17. Teacher:	Let's assume that *googol* is the biggest number. Can we add one to googol?
18. Noa:	Yes. There are numbers bigger than googol.
19. Teacher:	So what is the biggest number?
20. Noa:	There is no such number!
21. Teacher:	Why is there no biggest number?
22. Noa:	Because there is always a number which is bigger than that?

Clearly, this very brief exchange becomes for Noa an opportunity for learning. The girl begins the dialogue convinced that there is a number that can be called "the biggest" and she ends emphatically stating the opposite: "There is no such number!" The question is whether this learning may be regarded as learning-with-understanding, and whether it is therefore the desirable kind of learning. To answer this question, one has to look at the way in which the learning occurs. The seemingly most natural thing to say if one approaches the task from the traditional perspective is that the teacher leads the girl to realize the contradiction in her conception of number: Noa views the number set as finite, but she also seems aware of the fact that adding 1 to any number leads to an even bigger number. These two facts, put together, lead to what is called in literature "a cognitive conflict"[51] – a situation supposed to push a person toward revision of her number schema. This is what Noa eventually does. On the face of it, the change occurs as a result of rational considerations and may thus count as an instance of learning with understanding.

And yet, something seems missing in this explanation. Why is it that Noa stays quite unimpressed by the contradiction the first time she is asked about the number obtained by adding 1? Why doesn't she modify her answer when exposed to the discrepancy for the second time? Why is it that when she eventually puts together the two contradicting claims – the claim that adding 1 is always possible and always leads to a bigger number, on the one hand, and the claim that there is such a thing as *the* biggest number, on the other hand – her conclusion ends with a question mark rather than with a firm assertion (see [22])? Isn't the girl aware of the logical necessity of this conclusion?

In light of the previous observations, it is hardly surprising that methods of "meaningful" teaching "are still not well known, and most mathematics teachers probably must rely on a set of intuitions about quantitative thinking that involves both the importance of meaning – however defined – and computation."[52] James Hiebert and Thomas Carpenter echo this concern when saying that promoting learning with understanding "has been like searching for the Holy Grail," and they add, "There is a persistent belief in the merits of the goal, but designing school learning environments that successfully promote understanding has been difficult."[53] The mild complaint by researchers who belong to the traditional cognitivist school of thought turns into an essential doubt in the mouth of adherents of alternative conceptual frameworks. The difficulty seems so pervasive, they say, one begins wondering whether finding answers to the nagging questions is only a matter of time. Some representatives of new schools of thought go so far as to consider the possibility that the very idea of understanding

---

[51] See, e.g., Tall and Schwartzenberger (1978).
[52] Mayer (1983, p. 72).
[53] Hiebert and Carpenter (1992, p. 65).

may be, in fact, theoretically intractable and thus essentially inapplicable either in research or in everyday schooling practice.[54] As in the previous four cases, one may conclude that nothing less than reconceptualization may be necessary to make the quandary disappear.

6. Puzzling about Thinking – in a Nutshell

Five persistent, vexing quandaries were presented in this chapter to show that in spite of the long history of thinking about human thinking at large, and of mathematical thinking in particular, those who try to understand this complex phenomenon may well have yet a long way to go. Indeed, the stories just told left us with a long list of unanswered questions. Just to quote a few representative examples:

- Why is it that children who can count without a glitch do not use counting when asked to compare sets of objects? How can we account for what they actually do? More generally, where does numerical thinking begin, how is its incipient version different from our own, and how does it become, eventually, just like that of any other adult person?
- Why is it that even well-educated people do not apply abstract mathematical procedures in situations in which such use could help them with problems they are trying to solve? More generally, why does people's thinking appear so much dependent on particularities of the situations in which it takes place? Are there any teaching strategies that could be used to counteract this situatedness?
- How can one explain the fact that a child who learned a mathematical concept from a teacher or a textbook "errs" about this concept in a systematic way? How can we account for the fact that some of these mistakes are shared by a great many children all around the world? Even more puzzlingly, how is it that students' "misconceptions" are often very much like those of the scientists or mathematicians who were the first to think about the concepts in question? Most importantly, because the theory of misconceptions, even if perfected, does not seem likely to suffice as a framework for studying learning of mathematics or science, what is it that this theory is missing?
- If the condition known as "learning disability" is supposed to originate in "natural" rather than environmental factors, why does it seem

---

[54] Edwards (1993); Lerman (1999).

so tightly related to life stories of those who are diagnosed as learn-ing disabled? Which of the two occurs first: learning disability or life hardships? Besides, without direct access to physiological factors, how are we supposed to distinguish between learning disabilities and "normal" learning difficulties?

- Although we do not seem to hesitate in deciding whether we under-stand something or not, and although we are only too quick to diag-nose other people's understanding, we have considerable difficulty trying to articulate our criteria for this kind of judgment. What is it that we do not yet understand about understanding?

These five quandaries, when taken together, lead to the inevitable conclusion: If in spite of the long history of research so many questions about thinking remain unanswered, it may well be that the reason lies in our ways of thinking about thinking. Examining this conjecture is the theme of the next chapter.

2 Objectification

The greatest magician...would be the one who would cast over himself a spell so complete that he would take his own phantasmagorias as autonomous appearances....We (the undivided divinity operating within us) have dreamt the world. We have dreamt it as firm, mysterious, visible, ubiquitous in space and durable in time.

Jorge Luis Borges[1]

They recalled that all nouns...have only a metaphorical value.

Jorge Luis Borges[2]

Our investigation is therefore a grammatical one. Such an investigation sheds light on our problem by clearing misunderstandings away. Misunderstandings concerning the use of words, caused, among other things, by certain analogies between the forms of expression in different regions of language.

Ludwig Wittgenstein[3]

The claim, made in the last chapter, that some foundational work may be needed before the resilient, long-standing quandaries can be resolved will now be reinforced by showing that these quandaries may, in fact, be the product of the way we speak. More specifically, it is posited that the source of the problem is in the way we think about human activities in general and, in particular, in the way we communicate with others and with ourselves about the activity of thinking, mathematical or otherwise. I am arguing that the different keywords around which the five quandaries

---

[1] Borges (1962/1964, p. 202).
[2] Ibid., p. 11.
[3] Wittgenstein (1953/2003, p. 43e).

revolve are not operational enough to ensure effective communication. I also show that most of them are metaphorical in nature, and metaphors are often like Trojan horses that enter discourses with hidden armies of unhelpful entailments. But let me begin with an attempt to answer the basic question of what research is and why it is so much dependent on our use of words.

1. What Is Research and What Makes It Ineffective?

The claim about the importance of words and their uses becomes clear once we realize that research is a form of communication. More specifically, research, whether psychological, sociological, or in natural science, can be defined as a particular, well-defined kind of discourse producing cogent narratives[4] with which other human practices can be mediated, modified, and gradually improved in their effectiveness and productivity (in a more traditional language, such research-engendered narratives are known as "scientific facts" that constitute the "body of knowledge"). This definition is consonant with the assumption that discourse plays a constitutive role in all human practices and with the claim made by the Soviet psychologist Lev Vygotsky almost eight decades ago that the "the dialectic unity [between speech and practical action] in the human adult is the very essence of human complex behavior."[5] In the case of natural sciences, the research-produced and practice-mediating narratives are likely to take the form of concise symbolic formulas, such as $E = mc^2$ or $N_2 + 3H_2 \rightarrow 2NH_3$, which are said to present "laws of nature." Such narratives mediate practices of tool building and thus help in making technological advances. In the case of social sciences, the aim is to mediate practices such as educating, treating psychological or social inadequacies of individuals and groups, and engineering organizational and institutional structures and mechanisms. The discursive mediation is supposed to make these practices optimally effective in achieving their respective goals. Narratives typical of sociology, psychology, education, or anthropology and the rules of their endorsement are quite different from those of natural sciences and of mathematics.

Let me now use the research-as-discourse conceptualization to reflect on the possible sources of the resilient quandaries reported in chapter 1.

---

[4] The words *discourse* and *narrative* are central to the conceptualization of thinking proposed in this book and, as such, should be explicitly defined. This will be done later. In the present context, we may satisfy ourselves with informal use.

[5] Vygotsky (1978, p. 24).

These controversies and dilemmas are representative of the pervasive uncertainties with which the research on human thinking at large, and the study of mathematical thinking in particular, have been riddled since their inception. Over decades, as the conceptual underpinnings of cognitive research evolved, the quandaries evolved as well, with some of them disappearing and other ones replacing them. At no point in history, however, could our thinking about our own thinking be described as having entered the stage of "normal science"[6] – the stage of a relatively steady, linear accumulation of knowledge, made possible by a wide conceptual consensus among researchers. Because of its apparent inability to give clear-cut answers to what seem to be basic theoretical and practical questions, the research on human thinking has always been researchers' own favorite target of scrutiny and criticism.[7] Since international comparative studies on school mathematics[8] confirmed that in many countries, the level of students' mathematical achievement was less than satisfactory, the ostensible weaknesses of the research have begun to attract public attention as well. The quandaries-plagued field of study has been described as fragmented, unable to accumulate knowledge, and incapable of living up to its major commitment of improving teaching and learning.[9]

In the view of the discursive definition of research, we may say that fragmentation and inability to accumulate knowledge mean that a given type of research fails to attain its communicational purpose. In this case, the keywords of the discourse become immediately suspect. Indeed, when a discourse does not work as expected, it is natural to ask whether all its participants are using words in the same manner. The plea for a responsible use of research keywords is as old as the research itself. Thus, for example, four decades ago Hubert Blumer listed three basic properties of "satisfactory concepts in empirical science": To count as such, a concept has to

1. point clearly to the individual instances of the class of empirical objects to which it refers;

---

[6] The term was coined by Thomas Kuhn (1962).

[7] In addition to the recent sources cited in the last chapter, e.g., Anderson et al. (1996); Brown et al. (1989); Cobb and Bowers (1999); Donmoyer (1996); Greeno (1997); Lave (1988); Lave and Wenger (1991); Sfard (1998), let me mention the criticism by Vygotsky (1987) that goes back to the first decades of the 20th century.

[8] See http://nces.ed.gov/timss/ for the results of TIMSS 2003 (Trends in International Science and Mathematics Education) and tp://www.pisa.oecd.org/ for the results of PISA 2006 (Programme for International Student Assessment).

[9] Burkhard and Schoenfeld (2003); Sfard (2003, 2005).

2. distinguish clearly this class of objects from other related classes of objects; and

3. enable the development of cumulative knowledge of the class of objects to which it refers.[10]

A close look at the keywords featured in the five quandaries presented in the preceding chapter would reveal that most of them fail all three conditions. Take, for example, the word *understanding* that lies at the core of the last dilemma and plays a significant role also in the other four. Although we are only too eager to inquire about our own and other people's understanding of mathematics and, subsequently, to make judgments about it, we are not necessarily as likely to come up with a ready-made answer to the question of what we actually mean when saying that somebody does or does not understand. Our difficulty with deciding what one should look at while diagnosing another person's understanding may be the primary source of our fifth quandary. Similarly, it is the researchers' inability to provide an operational definition of *learning disability* that generates our fourth dilemma. The other terms that play pivotal roles in the other quandaries – *abstraction, conception,* and *misconception,* and even the word *thinking,* around which all of the present discussion evolves – may or may not count as satisfactory in Blumer's sense, depending on whether we can provide them with operational definition – a definition that specifies what we should look at and what to ignore when trying to decide whether the word is applicable in a given situation.

A cursory look at randomly chosen professional publications would suffice to show that such definitions are few and far between. More often than not, authors seem to be assuming that the keywords of their specialized discourse are well known and that there is no reason to worry about disparities in their use. Such an assumption is as risky as it is ungrounded. Only too often, a close scrutiny would reveal that different writers are making different uses of the same words, and such different uses are likely to be grounded in differing premises about the nature and sources of the phenomena that the words denote. Leaving these functional disparities unacknowledged is a reliable prescription for disagreements that have every appearance of controversies over the accuracy of one's vision of reality although, in fact, resulting from differences in the way interlocutors match words with aspects of reality.

[10] Blumer (1969, p. 91).

Let me illustrate this latter claim with the example of the current debate on the origins of numerical thinking. As remarked, Piaget postulated that this kind of thinking does not begin until the child is already aware of "conservation of number," that is, until the child is at least 5 years old. Over the last several decades this claim generated much discussion, and not just about what should count as a proper interpretation of the conservation tasks, but also on the issue of the order and timing of events in the developmental sequence. On the basis of his comprehensive survey of the most recent research,[11] Stanislas Dehaene[12] speaks about "babies who count" – children as young as 2 months of age who appear to display sensitivity to changes in the cardinality of small sets. As a result, he sustains that a basic number sense is "wired in" in humans, and that it is clearly present from the very first days of the child's life.

As can be learned from a closer inspection of different texts produced in this debate, not many discussants care to explain operationally what they mean by the term *numerical thinking* (or by the word *thinking*, for that matter). Divided on the question of *when* this thinking begins, they rarely address such a preliminary query as *What kind of child's action should count as an indication of numerical thinking?* Once we become aware of the fact that the central notion remains unspecified, we realize that answering the question *When does numerical thinking begin?* is a matter of semantic decision rather than of empirical discovery. The declaration that numerical thinking begins with the child's awareness of number conservation may well be Piaget's definition of numerical thinking, rather than his conclusion from research findings. The same may be said about Dehaene's statement that numerical thinking is evidenced already by a change in the baby's reaction to a variation in the number of elements in small sets. Thus, the disagreement presented as regarding scientifically established "truths about the world" is, in fact, the issue of an unacknowledged difference in the discussants' keyword use. This kind of controversy can only be resolved by explicit defining, whereas the motives for preferring one possible definition to another would be related to what the participants consider as more useful.

Research on human activities in which many substantially different phenomena hide behind one unifying label may be not just ineffective – it may sometimes be harmful. Before I try to propose a cure, I need to search for deeper, hidden origins of the affliction.

---

[11] Simon, Hespos, and Rochat (1995); Starkey and Cooper (1980); Wynn (1992, 1995); Xu and Carrey (1996).
[12] Dehaene (1997).

2. Metaphors as Generators of New Discourses

The first question to ask in view of what has been said so far is *Why are we able to use specialized keywords without ever being exposed to their explicit definitions?* One look at some examples, say at the words *conservation*, *abstract*, *disability*, or *understanding*, and this initial query becomes easy to answer: These specialized words are usually borrowed from other, better known discourses, and as such, they appear familiar and ready for use even as they make their very first appearance in the unusual discursive context. At the time they turn into part of a scholarly discourse on thinking, these words seem not just meaningful but also fully determined. In this situation, when it is no longer up to the interlocutors to decide about the words' interpretation, using these words in ways dictated by one's former habits is the natural – indeed, the only possible – thing to do, whatever the context.

What was described in the last few lines, the action of "transplanting" words from one discourse to another, is known in professional literature as the mechanism of *metaphor*. Because of its centrality, this mechanism is worth some additional attention. Let me thus pause for a moment and try to answer such questions as what metaphors are, how they work, why we cannot live without them, and why using them may be somewhat risky.

It was Michael Reddy who, in the article entitled "The conduit metaphor," alerted us to the ubiquity of metaphors and to their constitutive role.[13] Using as an illustration the notion of *communication*, he has shown how words characteristic of one discourse may take us in a systematic way to another, seemingly unrelated one. In his example, he spoke about the figurative projection from the discourse on *transport* to that on *communication*. In the case of research on thinking and learning, the discourse of transport is easily recognizable as a metaphorical source of the talk about *learning transfer*. Note also the recursive nature of the definition of metaphor as "discursive transplant." As stated by Paul Ricoeur, "The paradox is that we can't talk about metaphor except by using a conceptual framework which itself is engendered out of metaphor."[14] This recursivity of metaphors, and thus their presence in practically every discursive action, is yet another indication of how essential they are to our ability of sense making. If the omnipresence of metaphors is not immediately obvious, it is because this very ubiquity renders most metaphors practically transparent. Besides, as noted by Israel Scheffler, "the line, even in science, between

[13] Reddy (1979).
[14] Ricoeur (1977, p. 66).

serious theory and metaphor is a thin one – if it can be drawn at all. . . . There is no obvious point at which we must say, 'Here the metaphors stop and the theories begin.'"[15]

Since Reddy's seminal publication, what came to be known as *conceptual mappings* turned into an object of vigorous inquiry.[16] Philosophers of science have acknowledged the fact that metaphors play a constitutive role and that no kind of research would be possible without them.[17] What had been traditionally regarded by researchers as not more than a tool for better understanding and for more effective memorizing of their theories, was now recognized as these theories' primary source. The word *metaphor*, which previously had been conceived as referring to a mere literary gimmick, became a pointer to a mechanism through which we become able to organize new experiences in terms of those with which we are already familiar.

Let me dwell on this last point a bit longer. Although the idea that new knowledge is germinated in old knowledge has been promoted by all theoreticians of human development, from Piaget to Vygotsky to contemporary cognitive scientists, the question of how the old is transformed into the new has remained a vexing puzzle. The quandary was first signaled by Plato in his dialogue *Meno*[18] and came to be known later as *the learning paradox*.[19] Although seen in many different guises throughout history, the question has always been the same: How can we want to acquire a knowledge of something that is not yet known to us? If we can only become cognizant of something by recognizing it on the basis of the knowledge we already possess, then nothing that does not yet belong to the assortment of the things we know can ever become one of them. Among those who accept the claim that production of knowledge is a discursive activity, the paradox may be recast in discursive terms: On the one hand, the only way to bring new discourses into being is by practicing them; after all, discourses exist only in action. On the other hand, how can one practice, or even just want to practice, a discourse whose rules have not yet been established? After all, if not grounded in rules known and observed by all the participants, communication cannot possibly succeed. Conclusion: Creating new discourses – or creating new knowledge – is inherently impossible. The recent work on metaphors as the agents of discursive change offers a way out of this entanglement. Metaphors owe their effectiveness as the harbingers and catalysts

[15] Scheffler (1991, p. 45).
[16] Johnson (1987); Lakoff (1987, 1993); Lakoff and Johnson (1980); Sacks (1978).
[17] Hesse (1966); Ortony (1993).
[18] Plato (1949).
[19] Fodor (1983); Bereiter (1985); Cobb, Yackel, and Wood (1992).

of discursive change to the fact that familiar words, even if transplanted into a new discursive context, can still be used according to those of the old rules that seem consonant with the new context. Think, for example, about your own ability to get an initial sense of what is being talked about when you come across a familiar colloquial term, such as *strain* or *messenger*, in a hitherto unfamiliar scientific context, where they appear in such expressions as *cognitive strain* or *messenger DNA*. Once the metaphorical term is introduced, the rules of its use are gradually modified, resulting in a whole new set of language games.[20]

When a new word is metaphorically introduced, our feeling of understanding is deceptive in that there is no guarantee others are using this word in the same way. This potential ambiguity is a threat to the effectiveness of communication, and it exposes interlocutors to all the usual risks of nonoperationalized word use. Whereas it is precisely the ambiguity of metaphors that makes the figurative projection dear to the poet, the scientist views the vagueness as the metaphors' major weakness. Having as their goal production of narratives that can help in practical activities, and thus being interested in optimal interpersonal coordination, scientists would not use a metaphorically introduced term unless it had been operationalized. Jerome Bruner describes the transition from a metaphor to its operationalized, "scientific" version in a beautifully metaphorical way. After stating that metaphors are "crutches to help us get up the abstract mountain," the author notes:

> Once up, we throw them away (even hide them) in favor of a formal, logically consistent theory that (with luck) can be stated in mathematical or near-mathematical terms. The formal models that emerge are shared, carefully guarded against attack, and prescribe ways of life for their users. The metaphors that are added in this achievement are usually forgotten or, if the ascent turns out to be important, are made not a part of science but part of the history of science.[21]

Back to the issue of thinking, which is my main concern in this book, one may argue that what is good for natural science may be much less so for discourses concerned with people and people's actions. Whereas the former type of discourse deals predominantly with the human-independent world, the latter is pervaded with concerns about human will and judgments and

---

[20] To be more precise, metaphors affect source discourses as well; see, e.g., Sfard (1997). Elaborating on the intricate process of target-and-source co-constitution is beyond the scope of this book.

[21] Bruner (1986, p. 48).

may thus be considered too complex and messy to be subject to mathematization. And yet, operationalization does not necessarily mean mathematization and does not assume theoretical exclusivity. It only means *conceptual accountability*, that is, our being explicit about how we use the keywords and how our uses relate to those of other interlocutors.

To sum up, metaphors are a double-edged sword: On the one hand, as a basic mechanism behind any conceptualization, they are what makes our research discourse possible; on the other hand, they keep human imagination within the confines of our former experience and conceptions, and if not operationalized, they can lead different interlocutors to different uses of the same words. To do our job as researchers properly we need to optimize the benefits and minimize the risks of metaphor use. This means, first, eliciting hidden metaphors, and second, either barring these metaphors from further uses or turning them operational. The rest of this chapter is devoted to the first of the two tasks or, more specifically, to eliciting one special metaphor that, without being acknowledged, pervades both our everyday and scholarly discourses.

3. The Metaphor of Object

Although many figurative expressions can usually be identified in any discourse, a careful analysis would show that one particular type of metaphor may be more widely used than any other. This special kind of figurative expression is so common that one may have difficulty identifying it as a metaphor. Its very ubiquity makes it practically transparent to the discourse participants, the more so as the things they say with its help do not seem to be easily translatable into more "literal" statements. This special metaphor, one that will be called here the *metaphor of object*, has its roots in our tendency for picturing the perceptually inaccessible world of human thinking in the image of material reality. In what follows, after explaining what this objectifying metaphor is and why it is both useful and potentially harmful, I show that it plays a central role in all five quandaries listed in the previous chapter.

Consider, for example, the following keywords, randomly picked out from the former pages: *concept* (or *conception*), *learning disability*, *abstraction*. Although none of these terms is pointing to a concrete, tangible object, each one of them does seem to refer to a certain self-sustained, well-delineated entity existing at a certain location, possibly in the human head, and enjoying a permanence similar to that of material objects. The object-like effect is attained through the special linguistic forms in which the words usually appear and that are very close to forms used in descriptions of the material world. In the following, compare, for instance, the three expressions on the left that deal with mental activities, to the three on the right that speak about actions with material objects:

1a. Two of my students constructed similar conceptions of function.	**1b.** Two of my students constructed similar Lego towers.
2a. He could not cope with the topic because he has a learning disability.	**2b.** He could not help me with my luggage because he had his own bags to carry.
3a. We have to give our students a better access to mathematical abstraction.	**3b.** We have to give our students free access to the National Museum.

Although only half of the sentences deal with tangible things (Lego tower, bags, museum), in all six of them people are said to act on, or to be somehow directed or constrained in their action by, an entity that, even if perceptually inaccessible, is implied to have an independent existence of sorts.

This similarity between the discourse on thinking and that on material objects notwithstanding, one may wonder about the soundness of the claim that the keywords in the sentences on the left are metaphorical, not literal. "What is it that is figurative in the statement that a person *constructed a conception* or in an utterance about an individual who *has a learning disability?*" the doubter would ask. "Is there any other, less 'objectified' way to speak about conceptions, learning disabilities, and the like?" Such questions, however, would be a misinterpretation of what I am trying to say. The metaphor of object, I claim, is not a mere substitution for a more literal formulation of the same "things" but rather is what creates these "things" in the first place. While saying this, I posit the possibility of a discourse that, although effective in describing and organizing what we see when observing people in action, makes no reference to objects such as *concepts*, *learning disability*, or *abstraction*.

This latter claim is theoretical rather than practical, and my argument goes as follows. To begin with, the entities to which we point with the words *conception*, *learning disability*, or *abstraction* are not anything that can ever be observed directly. Instead, what we see while conducting a conceptions survey or when running learning disability diagnostic tests is *people in action*. It is only when we are describing our impressions that we turn to entities whose presence is likely to escape anybody but those who act as expert observers. Such an act of *reification* – of discursively turning processes into object – is the beginning of *objectification*, which, if completed, will leave us convinced about the mind-independent, "objective" existence of the object-like referent. Once we objectify, we no longer notice the metaphorical nature of the objectified terms; rather, we see these terms as speaking about things-in-the-world that are not any less present and real than what we can see with our eyes or touch with our hands. As with words such as *Lego tower*, *bag*, or *museum*, we feel that the use of the words *conception*, *learning disability*, and *abstraction* is a matter of world-imposed necessity, not of linguistic choices, and if the claim about the metaphorical nature of the latter notions is difficult to accept, it only shows how successful we have all been in the project of objectifying!

The process of objectification involves, therefore, two tightly related, but not inseparable discursive moves: *reification*, which consists in substituting talk about actions with talk about objects, and *alienation*, which consists in presenting phenomena in an impersonal way, as if they were occurring of themselves, without the participation of human beings. As will be explained and illustrated later, these two types of transformation are attained by different discursive means, and the occurrence of one of them does not necessitate the other.

3.1 *Reification*

Reification is the act of replacing sentences about processes and actions with propositions about states and objects. In the following examples, the propositions on the right are reified versions of the sentences on the left.

4a. In the majority of school tests and tasks dealing with function she regularly *did well* and *attained* above average scores.

4b. She *has acquired (constructed, developed) a conception* of function.

5a. He *cannot cope* with even the simplest arithmetic problems in spite of years of instruction.

5b. He *has a learning disability*.

6a. In Newton's theory, the word "force" *was used differently* than in the Aristotelian physics.

6b. The word "force" *had a different meaning* in Newtonian and Aristotelian theories.

In the first example, the reifying effect was attained by replacing the description of doing (*doing well on tests*, *attaining good scores* – see 4a) with the remark on *having a certain thing* (a conception of function – 4b). In the third example, the proposition on the *activity of using* a word (6a) was translated into one on the *existence of a certain entity* ("the meaning of the word" – 6b). In all the cases, the technique was to introduce a noun – *conception*, *disability*, *meaning* – that helped to squeeze a lengthy story of repetitive but transitory actions into a narrative on permanent, even if evolving, entities. To realize how ubiquitous this technique is, it is enough to recall such scientific terms as *energy*, *momentum*, or *speed*, all used in physics to describe motion of bodies; or terms such as *ego*, *superego*, *belief*, *intention*, or *mental schema*, used in psychology in describing and explaining human actions.

Let me add two examples of reified discourses, both of them related to our present theme and to the five quandaries presented in chapter 1. In the quest for the metaphor of object I begin with a closer look at the mathematical notion of *number* and continue with a scrutiny of the traditional discourse on *thinking*. In both cases, I consider not just the actual appearances of the focal word *number* or *thinking*, but the whole discourse in which these words play the pivotal role. In the case of number, this includes propositions that feature, among others, number-words such as *five* or *two-and-a-half*, relational adjectives and adverbs such as *more* or *bigger*, and verbs that signify numerical operations such as *add* or *multiply*; in the case of the discourse on thinking, I will also look at sentences that contain such related words as *perceiving*, *knowing*, *learning*, *remembering*, or *reasoning*. In broadening the scope, I hope to be able to show that reification, far from being a local transformation in the use of a single word, influences the whole discourse, shaping it in the image of discourses on material objects.[22]

Example 1: The Numerical Discourse

Any number-related proposition, chosen at random from either colloquial conversation or a scholarly discourse, will show that more often than not, those who speak about numbers envision them as objects in their own right, waiting there in the world to be discovered, explored, and used as tools for the betterment of human lives. This is certainly what transpires from the following sentence, taken from the popular recent book that summarizes the results of research in numerical thinking:

7. What distinguishes us from other animals is our ability to use arbitrary symbols for numbers, such as words or Arabic digits.[23]

Whatever the author's intentions, this sentence implies that numbers are mind-independent entities, exactly like humans and animals, whereas the

---

[22] Compare with George Lakoff's idea of *conceptual metaphor* – a systematic mapping from one "conceptual domain" to another, preserving some substantial interconceptual relationships characteristic of the source domain (Lakoff, 1993).

[23] Dehaene (1997, p. 73).

words and symbols that people use in numerical discourse are mere "avatars" of the real thing. A similar message transpires from dictionary definitions that describe number as

> **8.** a unit belonging to an abstract mathematical system and subject to specified laws of succession, addition, and multiplication;
>
> **9.** an element of any of many mathematical systems obtained by extension of or analogy with the natural number system.[24]

As does the author of the first example, the dictionary writers distinguish between "number as such" and the words with which we refer to numbers. This is what they seem to be trying to say when following the preceding two definitions with the other one, according to which the term *number* can also signify

> **10.** a word, symbol, letter, or combination of symbols representing a number.[25]

This additional definition makes us aware that we use the word *number* both as the signifier and the signified, the fact that is only too likely to lead to misunderstandings. To prevent confusion, some people always distinguish between the two by saving the word *number* for the signified and using the word *numeral* for the signifier.

The split between numbers and our communicational means for "expressing" them inheres not only in our colloquial talk, but also in the more rigorous research discourses. Consider, for example, the following sample of a scholarly discourse on early numerical thinking. While formulating the "cardinality principle," which is one of those facts about numbers that require some intentional, gradual learning, the authors of a book that summarizes relevant research say: "This principle . . . simply means that if we use labels in counting, say, up to 'five' (1–2–3–4–5), then there must be five objects altogether in the set that we have been counting."[26] Such formulation implies that the expression "there are five objects in the set" supplies information that is somehow different from what has already been said in the sentence "we use labels in counting up to five" (or, "when we count, we end with the word 'five'").[27] And yet, these two expressions can be seen as different only if we assume that one can be aware of the existence of

---

[24] Encyclopedia Britannica Online.

[25] Ibid.

[26] Nunes and Bryant (1996, p. 23).

[27] An alternative, disobjectified formulation of the cardinality principle would be as follows: "Repetitive counting of the same set of objects will always end with the same number-word."

numbers independently of one's ability to count. This assumption, however, may complicate matters rather than help. At a closer look, there is no reason to view numbers as anything other than *the reifications of the procedure of counting*. According to this scenario, children begin their numerical education by learning to count and, after realizing that repetitive counting of the same set always ends with the same number-word, they accept the idea that for any practical purpose (e.g., for the sake of certain comparisons and classifications) remembering this last number-word is fully sufficient. At this point, the number-words, which became shortcuts for the action of counting, may be used in sentences such as "There are five marbles in the box," where they play the role of adjectives (determiners). Some time later, these words turn into nouns and start appearing in propositions such as "Three plus five is eight" or "Five is bigger than three." When featured in this new role, they are no longer followed by the names of objects that have been counted (note the subtle difference between this last sentence and the sentence "Five is *more* than three," in which the number-words seem to appear in the role of adjectives even if they are not followed by nouns).[28] It is only at this last stage that what began as a mere procedure of ritualized chanting of number-words becomes fully reified and turns into a metaphorical object. This scenario, one that features reification as a gradual, and highly consequential, discursive transformation, is evidenced by ample empirical findings; some of them are summarized as follows by Jeremy Kilpatrick and his collaborators:

> Preschoolers... perform better in situations that require them to think about adding or subtracting actual objects (even if those objects are hidden from view in a box) than they do when simply asked an equivalent [purely numerical] question (e.g., "What's 3 and 5?").[29]

Example 2: The Discourse on Thinking

According to *Webster's Third International Dictionary*,[30] the verb *to think* may be translated into any of the following expressions, depending on context: *to form or have (as thought) in mind, to have in one's mind as an intention or desire,*

---

[28] This sentence may be regarded as an abbreviation of the proposition "Five marbles is [are] more than three marbles." Note that in Hebrew, in existential sentences such as this one, there is no distinction between singular and plural (The Hebrew original says: "Hamesh gulot ze yoter m'shalosh," where the *ze* may be treanslated into *it is*).

[29] Kilpatrick, Swafford, and Findell (2003, p. 170); for a more detailed treatment of reification in mathematics see Sfard (1991) and Sfard and Linchevski (1994).

[30] Gove (1968).

or *to have as an opinion*. *The Penguin Dictionary of Psychology* (1952) says that thinking is *any course or train of ideas*. Whether the definition mentions *ideas*, *intentions*, *desires*, or *opinions*, thinking emerges from all these descriptions as a process of emission, or as a state of possession, of certain entities. Not surprisingly, this is also the image of thinking implicit in many common everyday expressions. Let me mention just a few of them:

11. An idea popped up in my mind.
12. My mind bursts with ideas (thoughts).
13. I cannot get this thought out of my mind.
14. This idea simply doesn't enter (cross) his mind.

All these phrases clearly corroborate the vision of thinking as an activity with some special type of objects. Sometimes these objects may seem to be of an almost material quality. Consider such common phrases as

15. I finally succeeded in putting my thoughts together.
16. My thoughts are falling in place.

Nowhere does this message come through more powerfully than in what Jean-Pierre Changeaux calls "Cabains's celebrated aphorism": "The brain secretes thought as the liver does the bile."[31] While listening to all these sayings, one gets the impression that *mind* is a certain special location at which the emission and storage of the entities in question – thoughts, ideas, opinions, intentions, and so forth – take place. Consequently, the mind can be imagined as a closed space of rather limited capacity. It is therefore understandable why George Lakoff and Mark Johnson speak of the metaphor of "Mind-As-Container."[32]

One look at a few definitions collected at random from a number of scholarly texts on cognition suffices to indicate that reifying expressions related to thinking are not unique to colloquial discourses:

17. Thinking depends on how a person . . . can manipulate . . . internal representation.[33]
18. Memory is the process of storing information and experiences for possible retrieval at some point in the future.[34]

The picture is no different when one considers texts that feature the related word *cognition*. The reifying quality is clearly present in the definition of the

---

[31] Changeaux and Connes (1995, p. 155).
[32] Johnson (1987); Lakoff and Johnson (1980).
[33] Mayer (1983, p. 260).
[34] Groome (1999, p. 96).

word offered by *Webster's Third International Dictionary*: Although described as a process, cognition is said to result in the "gain of knowledge about perceptions and ideas." This is echoed by *The American Heritage Second College Dictionary*, which defines cognition as "the mental faculty or process by which knowledge is acquired." The notions we are now dealing with – cognition and knowledge – may be different from those we were considering earlier (thinking, mind), but the language of "knowledge gaining" or "knowledge acquisition" has the same metaphorical associations: It makes us think of knowledge as a kind of material, of human mind as a container, and of the learner as becoming an owner of the material stored in the container.

Learning is yet another notion featuring prominently in the discourse on cognition. It is thus not surprising that the *Collins English Dictionary* defines learning as "the act of gaining knowledge." As in the case of thinking, learning means having, or moving around, some entities, except that this time, the entity in question is knowledge. This impression is strengthened by the fact that we are used to thinking of knowledge as composed of smaller entities, which is a salient property of tangible things. Among the components of knowledge one can count such objects as *concept, conception, idea, notion, misconception, meaning, sense, schema, fact, representation, material,* and *contents*.[35] There are equally many terms that denote the action of making such entities one's own: *reception, acquisition, construction, internalization, appropriation, transmission, attainment, development, accumulation,* and *grasp*. The teacher may help the student to attain her goal by *delivering, conveying, facilitating, mediating,* and so on. Once acquired, the knowledge, like any other commodity, may now be *applied, transferred* (to a different context), and *shared with others*.

To sum up, the reifying quality of the current discourses on thinking expresses itself in the fact that all of them dichotomize the issue and present it in the dual terms of processes such as thinking, cognizing, or learning, on the one hand, and of the products of these processes, such as knowledge, concepts, ideas, on the other hand. Being denoted with nouns, the implied products emerge from these stories as phenomena more permanent than the activities that bring them into being and also as fully separable from these activities, in that each one of them is now believed to be "constructible" or "acquirable" in many different ways.

[35] Compare Lave's criticism of the metaphor of "knowledge as a set of tools stored in memory, carried around by individuals who take the tool . . . out and use them" (Lave, 1988, p. 24).

3.2 *Alienation*

Once reified, the alleged products of the mind's actions may undergo the final objectification by being fully dissociated, or *alienated*, from the actor. As can be seen from the following examples, this effect can be attained by such discursive means as the use of passive voice or the employment of the given noun in the role of grammatical subject:

19. Number is conserved as long as nothing is added to or taken away from a set.
20. There is no biggest number.
21. Every integer number greater than two is a sum of three prime numbers.
22. Two plus three make five.

By eliminating the human subject, these sentences effectively disguise the fact that numbers are discursive constructs and, as such, are human-made rather than given. With the last traces of people's agency carefully erased, even the most common arithmetical proposition, such as sentence 22, conveys the message of mind-independent existence of the mathematical object. Once reified and put into impersonal sentences, the numbers appear as to have a "life of their own." They return to their human creators disguised as exclusive masters of their own fate, whereas the participant in arithmetic discourse begins experiencing them as "happening to people" rather than caused by them, and as preexisting discourse rather than as its product.

As can be learned from the examples, impersonal discursive forms are very effective in implying the extradiscursive existence of numbers. The sentences 4b, 5b, and 6b show that the same communicational means, when applied in the discourse on thinking, are likely to produce similar effects: They turn the implied object-like products of mental activity (e.g., knowledge, conceptions) into more or less successful reproductions of some external universal models (objects-in-the-world, concepts), while also transforming features of actions (e.g., these actions' pervasive ineffectiveness) into properties of actors (learning disability). The Russian literary critic and philosopher Mikhail Bakhtin described such alienated impersonal discourse as *monological*, thus stressing that its narratives appear to be told in a single nonhuman voice – 'the voice of the life itself,' 'the voice of nature,' 'the voice of God,' and so forth.[36]

To conclude, alienation, and thus objectification, are an almost inevitable by-product of incorporating the newly created nouns into

---

[36] Bakhtin (1986, p. 163).

linguistic templates taken from discourses on material objects. The impression of permanence and mind-independence of these nouns' putative referents is produced by metaphorical entailments of such formulations. By saying this, I reverse the causal relation implied in statements such as "I have a sense of number" or "I understand the meaning of function." Indeed, the implied relation is this: First there are numbers and then, after some practice with them, one gets a sense of these objects. The relation I am claiming now is just the opposite: by practicing the numerical discourses we develop a sensation that we call, metaphorically, "a sense of number." More specifically, I argue that the sensation that we describe as a "sense of number" or "understanding of function" rather than being the primary source of the discourses on numbers and functions is the outcome of the relevant discursive practice. With experience, the stories about numbers or functions become so familiar and self-evident that we are able to endorse or reject new statements about them in a direct, nonreflective way. Such immediacy of decision, when no rationalization is necessary to make us certain of our choices, is the general defining characteristic of situations in which we say that we have "a sense of" something. In the case of decisions regarding physical activity, this immediacy results from our familiarity with the material objects on which the actions are performed. Thus, for example, we claim to have "a good sense of a terrain" if we are able to find our way through the given physical space in an instant, "without thinking."[37] The use of the expression *sense of* in conjunction with *number* or *function* is the act of metaphorical projection into a discourse on sensations that cannot be accounted for by a reference to material objects. The phrase comes to this latter discourse together with all its objectifying entailments: The implied dichotomy between the "sense" and its object makes us believe in the primacy of the entity called number or function over the experience of immediacy, familiarity, and direct recognition that underlies our talk about it.

In the rest of this chapter I argue that the reified propositions, although seemingly equivalent to their nonreified counterparts, have, in fact, some unique communicational advantages, and this accounts for the fact that reification is so ubiquitous. I will then proceed to the traps of objectification.

4. The Gains of Objectification

Summing up the last few pages, objectification is a discursive process of double elimination, which results in freeing the evolving narratives from

---

[37] Greeno (1991); Schoenfeld (1998).

the extension in time and from human agency. These two removals, which were called reification and alienation, respectively, may be implemented either successively or simultaneously. If, so far, I have sounded rather critical of our tendency to objectify human actions, I now wish to make clear that the criticism was not a plea to avoid objectifying discourses at any cost. As I argue later, such a call would be not just impractical, but also impossible to implement. We objectify because we have to.

Let me take the arithmetic discourse as the first example. The hallmark of this discourse is numerical calculation. Such calculation may be described as a discursive sequence built according to well-defined rules that, once uttered or written, counts as a confirmation of the discursive equivalence of two numerical expressions, such as *eighty-six plus thirty-seven* (or, in written symbolic form, 86 + 37) and *one hundred twenty-three* (123). Discursive equivalence, in turn, means that each of these two numerical expressions can be replaced with the other for any communicational purpose. One of the obvious reasons for our tendency to objectify arithmetical discourse is the need to account for the fact that two different symbolic or verbal strings, such as 86 + 37 and 123, count as exchangeable. Our explanation is usually constructed in the image of the substantiations we provide for claims on the equivalence of nouns signifying tangible objects. In the material reality discourse two terms such as *the lightest element* and *hydrogen* count as equivalent because they "represent (signify) the same thing." Similarly, we justify the equivalence of numerical expressions with the claim that they "represent the same number." This explanation lies at the very heart of objectification, because it implies that the latter entity, the number, is an extradiscursive, intangible object, for which the string of the digits, the numeral, is but a material "avatar."

What has just been said does not yet exhaust the reasons why it would be nearly impossible to eschew objectification altogether. The act of discursively turning our own actions into object-like entities yields at least two types of communicational gains without which much of our special achievements as human beings might not have been possible: First, it vastly increases the effectiveness of communication, and, second, it often makes the resulting discourse much more helpful as a tool for making sense of our experience and for organizing our subsequent practical actions. Let me make a case for each of these claims.

Claim 1: Reification Increases the Communicative Effectiveness of Discourse

In other words, many of the objects we speak about have been created for the sake of better communication By replacing a lengthy description of actions with a single sentence featuring a storytelling noun we not only communicate more economically, but also increase the flexibility and applicability of our utterances. Note that this claim reverses the traditional vision of the relation between talk and its objects: if, so far, we thought about discourses as secondary to the things these discourses talk about, it is now posited that at least some of the objects we talk about emerge out of our attempts to enhance the power of discourses.

A thought exercise, inspired by a story by the Argentinean writer Jorge Luis Borges, will help in making this last point clear.[38] In the imaginary town Tlön, Borges tells us, people use language that contains no nouns (the few nouns that one can find there are said to have "only metaphorical value"). Instead, there are "impersonal verbs." For example, there is no word corresponding to *moon*, but there is a verb that, to be expressed in English, would require the neologism *to moon* or *to moonate*. The lack of nouns goes hand in hand with the Tlönians' inability to view different occurrences in time, such as losing something on Wednesday and finding something similar on Friday, as related to each other by anything but "association": The thing lost and the thing found are not regarded as "the same thing," because in the absence of nouns, the people of Tlön know no objects, only processes. "The world for them is not a concourse of objects in space; it is a heterogeneous series of independent acts. It is successive and temporal, not spatial." To put it in our language, the Tlönians do not possess the faculty of reification. They cannot reify even those processes that in other people lead to the perception of material objects.

In the exercise we are now about to implement together, we shall try to put ourselves in the Tlönian frame of mind, at least as far as numbers are concerned. Let us imagine we did not yet begin reifying the discourse on numbers. This would mean that number-words such as *five* or *ten* are used only in counting sentences. These words do not even serve as adjectives yet, and this means that there is no room for expressions such as *five marbles*; rather, to convey what is usually meant by this latter expression one has to say *If you count the marbles in this box, you end up with the word "five."* Obviously, there is also no possibility of impersonal propositions such as $3 + 4 = 7$ (or, in words, *three plus four make seven*) because the number-words *three, four,* and *seven* do not function as nouns. In such a situation, how do we express the general numerical truth encapsulated in the brief symbolic statement $3 + 4 = 7$?

This latter equality can be seen as speaking about a relation between processes of counting up to three, four, and seven, respectively. More

[38] Borges (1962/1964, pp. 35–36).

specifically, the brief symbolic formula $3 + 7$ can be translated into a lengthy sentence saying that we combine two aggregates of things, one of which, if counted, would produce the word *three*, and the other of which would lead in counting to the word *four*. The expression on the right side of the equality can be unpacked in a similar way. Put together, these partial interpretations produce the following complex proposition:

- If I have a set so that whenever I count its elements I stop at the word three,
- and I have yet another set such that whenever I count its elements I stop at the word four,
- and if I put these two sets together,

then

- if I count the elements of the new set, I will always stop at seven.

After this example, there is hardly need for any further argument about the merits of reified numerical discourse: The length and complexity of the "unreified" numerical equality speak for themselves. The conciseness of the symbolic expressions made possible by reification renders the discursive products incomparably more conducive to further manipulations. Just imagine yourself trying to combine more than two numbers or attempting an operation, say, multiplication by 5, on the products of the operation already performed. Such a procedure and its result would be presented in the reified symbolic language as $5(3 + 4) = 35$, whereas the corresponding "unreified" presentation would be too long and complex even to try to record on these pages. In this context, it is important to note that the source of the special power of the symbolic expressions such as $5(3 + 4)$ lies in their ontological duality, namely, in the fact that on some occasions we may treat the formula as presenting a computational process, and on other occasions we may see it as denoting the product of this process.[39]

Claim 2: Objectification Increases the Practical Effectiveness of Discourse

Another source of our proclivity for reification is our fear of incessant change. Our relations with the world and with other people are fluid, sensitive to our every action. Reifying is an attempt to "make the moment

---

[39] For reification in mathematics as the transition from operational to structural thinking see Sfard (1991, 1992) and Sfard and Linchevski (1994).

last" – to collapse a video clip into a generic snapshot. It is grounded in the experience-engendered expectation, indeed hope, that in spite of the ongoing change, much of what we see now will repeat itself in a similar situation tomorrow. On the basis of this assumption, reification makes us able to cope with new situations in terms of our past experience and gives us tools to plan for the future. Reifying sentences are not only concise, but also reassuring. Saying *She has a mathematical gift (potential)* makes us confident that the next time this person is charged with mathematical tasks, she will perform to our satisfaction. More generally, reifying is the ongoing attempt to overcome the transitory nature of our experiences and to gain the sense of security. While reifying, we "fold up" the fourth dimension and make the absent present. Consider, for instance, sentences **4a, 5a,** and **6a** on the preceding pages. Their reified versions in the right column (**4b, 5b, 6b**), although seemingly equivalent, seem to encourage somewhat different interpretations. In the latter type of utterances, the fleeting, the passing, and the changing give way to permanent, immutable, and ever-present. This, in turn, gives rise to the reassuring conviction that tomorrow we will be able to step in the same river again.

The finishing alienating touch – the depersonification of the discourse – strengthens the effect of security. In short, while introducing the metaphor of object to the discourse that, so far, has dealt exclusively with our own actions, we use previously created islands of permanence and security in the task of "nailing down" other, more complex types of ongoing change. Considering all these gains, the importance of objectification can hardly be overestimated. Objectifying, it seems, is the very technique that gives our communication its unique power actually to shape our actions and accumulate achievements. Although Borges never actually used the word *reification*, his account of Tlön's culture and history forcefully corroborates this claim. Tlönians' programmatic refusal to reify, he tells us, made them unable to deal with their own experiences. They simply did not believe that "a later state of the subject . . . [could] affect or illuminate the previous state" (p. 34). Borges went so far as to claim that the absence of nouns, and thus of the possibility of discursively squeezing processes into objects, "invalidated all science." "There is no science in Tlön, not even reasoning," he said. His story ended with the apocalyptic vision of the linguistic habits of Tlön spreading over the globe and "disintegrating this world." One cannot help concluding that reification is not anything we could easily give up. While saying this, however, we have to remind ourselves that the spectacular gains of objectification are not without their risks and pitfalls.

5. The Traps of Objectification – the Case of the Discourse on Thinking

The objectifying techniques that may be extremely effective in natural sciences are likely to become unhelpful, or even harmful, when applied to people and their actions.[40] There are at least three ways in which excessive objectification of the discourse on thinking can undermine the utility of this latter type of discourse or even make it outright unhelpful.

First, the assumption of permanence and repetitiveness of patterns that underlies objectification, although seemingly unquestionable in mathematics and fairly well justified in physics or chemistry, *may be rather ungrounded in research on humans and their activities.* As already mentioned, the quickly accumulating empirical evidence heightens our awareness of the situatedness of human action and makes us increasingly suspicious of sweeping claims about cross-cultural and cross-situational behavioral invariants.

Second, the objectified version of one's former actions, although not easily unpackable into these actions, is usually read as a statement about the subject's future. The objectified descriptions, which more often than not take the form of claims about the person's *abilities*, tend to function as self-fulfilling prophecies. Indeed, words that make reference to action-outlasting factors have the power to make one's future in the image of one's past. As agents of continuity and perpetuation, the reifying and alienating descriptions deprive a person of the sense of agency, restrict her sense of responsibility, and, in effect, exclude and disable just as much as they enable and create. In particular, when the effectiveness of learning is seen as determined by such personal givens as *potentials, gifts, or disabilities*, failure is likely to perpetuate failure and success is only too likely to beget success.

Finally, the self-sustained "essences" implied in reifying terms such as *knowledge, beliefs*, and *attitudes* constitute a rather shaky ground for either empirical research or pedagogical practices – a fact of which neither researchers nor teachers seem fully aware.[41] I now wish to claim that it

---

[40] Caveats against too heavy a reliance on the metaphor of object could be heard, in one form or another, throughout the history of thinking about human thinking. "The fundamental philosophical question of the disobjectivation of knowledge has been with us for centuries, starting with Plato," observes Alex Kozulin (1990, p. 22), whereas Ivana Markova complains about the fact that psychology and sociology foreground stability, neglecting questions about change, and that "humans, in their desire to control and predict the world in which they live, tend to explain social and natural phenomena in terms of relatively stable attributes" (Markova, 2003, p. 5). See also Heider (1958); Schutz (1967); Woodfield (1993).

[41] Clifford Geertz is among those writers who do mention the problem explicitly while questioning the use of the term *belief*. According to Geertz, this latter term belongs

is through objectifying talk that we often entangle ourselves in controversies that have every appearance of disagreements about the "correctness" of one's worldview but, in fact, cannot be resolved by appeals to empirical evidence. The mechanism that produces the illusion of factual controversy, although simple, is also mostly invisible. After objectification, we often interpret metastatements, that is, statements about discourse, as statements about the extradiscursive world. This common category mistake may have far-reaching consequences. Consider, for example, the symbolic expression $3 + 4 = 7$, which, as I tried to make clear before, is a shortcut for a rather lengthy story about our own discursive actions of counting. As a result of objectification, the metadiscursive nature of this proposition remains invisible. Similarly, the traditional form of dictionary definitions and of the definitions found in mathematical and scientific textbooks conceals the fact that defining is a matter of human decision about the use of words. Thus, instead of saying *We shall call a polygon a triangle if and only if it has three sides*, we say *A polygon is a triangle if and only if it has three sides*. Through the very form of sentences such as the latter we "flatten" the discursive hierarchy so that the consecutive discursive layers become like a series of transparent window panes through which all the objects – discursive (words, expressions) and extradiscursive (independently existing material objects) – seem to belong to the same ontological category of "things in the world," with their mutual relations being similarly "objective" and mind-independent. This *ontological collapse* (a) may produce *illusory dilemmas*, (b) can result in *phony dichotomies* leading to tautologies disguised as causal explanations, and (c) is likely to lead us to *consequential omissions*, blinding us to potentially significant phenomena that cannot be described in the ontologically "flattened" terms. Let me illustrate each of these three types of consequences by showing that the metaphor of object might have played a major role in producing the unyielding quandaries presented in chapter 1.

to the discourse in which "extreme subjectivism is married to extreme formalism, with the expected result: an explosion of debate as to whether particular analyses...reflect what the natives 'really' think" (Geertz, 1973, p. 11). The issue at stake is that of the essentialist, objectified vision of beliefs, one that assumes their discourse-independent existence without specifying where and how one could get hold of them. A similar complaint seems to underlie the "critical assessment of the concept of attitude as a tool for study and analysis of human conduct" by Herbert Blumer. The immediate reason for Blumer's concern is, once again, a certain essentialist tenet, namely, "the idea that the tendency to act [precedes and] determines that act" (Blumer, 1969, p. 90.) The assumption about intention (or tendency) that exists in some unspecified "pure" form independently of, and prior to, the human action appears a rather dubious basis for any empirical study.

Illusory Quandaries

Illusory quandaries are entanglements that can be resolved, or rather circumvented, simply by changing the way of speaking about phenomena. More often than not, such conundrums result from unfortunate metaphorical entailments. When a word is transplanted from another discourse, the target entity thus created tends to "inherit" certain crucial features of the source entity. Thus, for example, knowledge, when objectified, is thought of as subordinated to a law of preservation similar to the one that governs the material world. According to this law, one cannot create new knowledge "out of nothing" – the new knowledge is only conceivable as a reiteration of the existing knowledge. This line of reasoning underlies one of the many versions of the learning paradox. The ontological collapse makes us defenseless in the face of such a delusion. As long as we remain unaware of the metaphorical nature of the objects we speak about, we are unlikely to bar the unwarranted transference of properties. On the other hand, all we need in order to be able to overcome certain quandaries is to acknowledge the fact that while speaking about objects such as *knowledge* or *concepts*, we speak in fact about our own discursive actions, whose rules are quite different from those that govern material objects.

A similar mechanism may be identified behind the *quandary of number*: When number-words stop being shortcuts for human discursive actions and become things-in-the-world, it is only natural to describe the development of numerical discourse in terms similar to those in which we describe the learning about material objects. We thus speak about the child's gradual "discovery of the properties of numbers" in the same terms in which we speak about her getting to know properties of exotic animals: Although the child cannot actually see any of these objects, she is expected to be able to figure out their properties from the available descriptions and from her general knowledge about the world. For example, when the teacher asks the 7-year-old Noa (see Episode 1.5) about "the biggest number," the independent existence of numbers is implied in this question in the same way in which the existence of elephants or whales is implied in nursery rhymes that talk about "the largest animals." In the next chapters I will claim that as natural as this way of talking about children's numerical activities may appear, it does have an unobjectified alternative that unravels the ontological confusion. This alternative, once adopted, will make us aware of the discourse-dependent nature of the quandary of number and will likely alleviate our puzzlement in the face of small children's special ways of dealing with requests for quantitative comparisons.

Disobjectification of the discourse on *abstraction* will help in a similar way to overcome the surprise we sometimes experience while facing considerable gaps between people's everyday ways of acting, on the one hand, and the performance that might be expected from a person well trained in school mathematics, on the other hand (see *quandary of abstraction* in chapter 1). On the basis of research findings, people are often said to be unable to "transfer knowledge" acquired in school to out-of-school situations. If this inability tends to disappoint us, it is precisely because of the objectification that accompanies the metaphor of transfer: If an object, such as a given type of knowledge, is actually present in one's mind, why isn't it used when appropriate? Having envisioned the "abstract structures" allegedly residing in different arithmetic activities, we see these structures as transferable in some disembodied form from one situation to another, in the way material objects can be moved between places. As a result, it becomes justified to speak about the possibility of performing "the same operation" either "within a familiar context" or "out of context." At this point, we lose the ability to see as different what children cannot see as the same: We become oblivious to the fact that performing symbolic multiplication such as $4 \cdot 35$ and finding the price of four coconuts with the help of banknotes and coins are two very different procedures, which will not be seen as in any way "the same" before the child gains experience with both of them and invests some additional effort in learning to discern their relevant properties. In short, only if we manage to *dis*objectify our "grown-up" discourse can we become aware that it is the difference rather than sameness that the child notices by default.

Objectification may also be the main reason for our bewilderment in the face of phenomena such as those gathered in chapter 1 under the header *The Quandary of Understanding*. The expression *grasping meaning*, often used as equivalent to the term *understanding*, reveals that our thinking about understanding also evolves around the metaphor of object. Meaning is implied to be an entity that can be "expressed" in words, carried in this verbal "wrapping" from one person to another, unpacked after being delivered, and only too often distorted in this process. These entailments lead to at least two types of claims that are persistently made in spite of their being frequently at odds with our experience. First, we think of *understanding* as a *state* – as something that is characterized by a measure of stability and invariance across time and space. And yet, as we know only too well from both everyday experience and research,[42] a person who in a certain situation

---

[42] Brown et al. (1989); Lave (1988); Nunes et al. (1993).

displays behavior we interpret as a sign of good understanding may show signs of incomprehension and helplessness while dealing with seemingly the same concept or procedure in another situation. Second, in our incessant attempts to assess our own and other people's understanding we enact the assumption that understanding is objectively diagnosable. With the meaning-based idea of understanding, such an assumption is only natural. Indeed, if understanding is a state of "having grasped the meaning," then it may vary in amount and quality, depending on the quantity and nature of what has been grasped. The very claim that meanings are liable to distortions implies the existence of the undistorted "true" version and of the objectively measurable state of understanding on which all the interlocutors would be compelled to agree. However, as evidenced by the stories told in the previous chapter, such agreement is rarely guaranteed. Just as I was unable to accept my apparently successful student's complaint about his "not understanding anything," so were Halmos's teachers likely to treat with disbelief their high-achieving student's claims about his being "stumped by the infinitesimal subtlety of epsilonic analysis." The obvious tension between these metaphor-engendered beliefs and empirical testimonies lies at the heart of all the other quandaries presented in the previous chapter as well.

Dichotomies That Result in Phony Causal Explanation

By objectifying, we often create an impression that we are saying more than we would have said in the absence of the implied entities. The discursively implied objects, the discursive origins of which remain hidden, are regarded either as a result of a certain action or as a factor that preexisted the action and that motivated or constrained it in a certain way. In each case, there is a clear dichotomy, the two elements of which, the object and the action, are considered as separate, even if related. This discursive dichotomization inevitably leads to narratives on relations between the action and the entity involved. Quite often, these narratives take the form of statements on causal dependencies. Thus, we are likely to say that this was a certain *misconception* that generated a child's strange responses to our questions, that it was a *learning disability* that obstructed another child's progress in learning, and that it was one's inability to grasp the *meaning* of a concept that should be held responsible for this person's poor results on tests and interviews. And yet, on closer look, how much value is added when one provides this kind of explanation? After all, the properties and possession of the actors, identified in this last sentence as the primary cause of the unsatisfactory course of action, are nothing other than the reified properties of the actions themselves. Having projected the property of the action on its performer, we soon fall victim to the ontological collapse and start believing that we have detected the independent cause of the particular form of the action.

Here is a brief scenario describing the course of events that may lead to such logical inversion. We begin with observing a student performing certain kinds of tasks. Seeing a girl regularly failing in calculations, we are likely to summarize:

This student has been regularly failing all tests.

Then we add:

Judging from this student's performances, she has a learning disability.

After a while, imperceptibly, we are inclined to reverse the relation and to claim the existence of the causal relation:

This student is acting this way *because* she suffers from a learning disability.

As long, however, as the term *learning disability* is not endowed with an independent operational definition that refers us to evidence other than the phenomena we are trying to account for, this latter kind of statement is hardly an explanation for the inadequacy of the student's actions. In fact, it may even be potentially harmful: By implying "objective," extradiscursive sources of the girl's poor performance, it is bound to perpetuate the failure rather than to cure it.

The discourse evolving around the notion of *understanding* seems particularly prone to delusions resulting from objectification-engendered dichotomies and the ensuing "causal" statements. The following sentence, chosen at random from a current text on the development of numerical talk, is a typical example:

When students fail to grasp the concepts that underlie procedures or cannot connect the concepts to the procedures, they frequently generate flawed procedures that result in systematic patterns of error.[43]

The message of this sentence is clear: There are two independent, although related, learning tasks that a student has to accomplish in the course of learning: She has to develop the ability to *grasp the meaning of concepts*, that is, to attain *conceptual understanding*, and she has to arrive at a *proficiency in implementing related procedures*. In the excerpt, the former is presented as a precondition for the latter: "Grasping the [meaning of the] concept" is

---

[43] Kilpatrick et al. (2001, p. 196).

a necessary condition for smooth procedural performance. As before, this seemingly informative message can be questioned, and not so much with respect to its veracity as with regard to its logical soundness: Do we really state a new fact when saying, "The student has a conceptual understanding of the concept of function," as opposed to saying, "The student performs well even on nonstandard tasks related to function"? If the answer is *no*, then many "causal" propositions that present the ability *to perform* arithmetically as the consequence of the ability to *understand*, or to "grasp the meaning," are, in fact, tautological.

Wittgenstein tried to fix the problem by replacing the metaphor of "grasping the meaning" with a description that speaks in terms of actions. According to his famous definition, *to understand means to be able to go on*, to be capable of deciding about a new step after each step already made.[44] Admittedly, this definition seems to be missing something important: It does not mention the experiential ingredient, which seems to be the primary reason for exclamations such as "I understand" or "I don't understand." As illustrated by the case of Paul Halmos, one can be perfectly able to "go on" and still feel that he or she "does not understand" the problem or its solution. Empirically speaking, there is no perfect match between the sensation that we identify as one of understanding and the ability "to go on."[45] The question whether this shortcoming of Wittgenstein's definition may be repaired without letting the metaphor of object creep back into the discourse will be addressed later in this book, after an effort is made to disobjectify the discourse on thinking.

Consequential Omissions

The thriftiness of objectification does not come without a price. When the talk about processes is replaced with the talk about objects, many different forms of actions become tied to the same noun. Hence, the differentiating power of the new talk is much lower than that of the original discourse, and, of necessity, this new talk is bound to gloss over many differences, some of which may be of vital importance. Indeed, grades and diagnoses cannot be easily unpacked into students' actual activity and they thus bar the access to the underlying diversity. Obviously, overlooking the differences largely diminishes the chances for effective interventions.

---

[44] Wittgenstein (1953/2003).
[45] The same analysis applies to the case of a mathematician who made the following confession to an interviewer: "There are things or theories that I developed myself and still, I don't understand them as deeply as I would wish to" (Sfard, 1994).

Indeed, in research on thinking and learning, stories told in the objecti-fied language of *concepts* and *skills* to be acquired, *meanings* to be constructed, and *disabilities* to be overcome obscure more than reveal. Thus, when Stanis-las Dehaene says that "a chimpanzee can compute the approximate total of a simple addition such as two oranges plus three oranges,"[46] the reader cannot help wondering about the exact shape of chimpanzees' actions that led to this highly interpretive declaration and about the elements of action that the author regards as indicative of the fact that "numerical operation" has been implemented.

6. Objectification – in a Nutshell

In this chapter I have pondered possible reasons for the researchers' inabil-ity to cope with quandaries like those presented in chapter 1. After defining research as a form of discourse, one that we develop in order to mediate and thereby improve our practical activities, I have been arguing that these dilemmas and controversies are likely a result of linguistic ambiguities. Indeed, more often than not, researchers use such words as *understanding*, *learning disability*, or *abstraction* without providing operational definitions. In so doing, they rely on the mechanism of *metaphor* – on their ability to build new discourses around familiar words transplanted into unfamiliar contexts. The use of metaphors, although indispensable in the task of inno-vating, is not without its dangers. The risk of unacknowledged differences in individual uses of words is one of its most harmful consequences.

One special metaphor that seems to pervade all our discourses, called *metaphor of object*, deserves special attention as a possible source of the irre-solvable quandaries. This metaphor is the product of the double process of *reification* and *alienation* – of turning statements about processes into impersonal statements about objects. As any other figurative device, the metaphor of object is a double-edged sword. Among its most important advantages are the thriftiness of the resulting discourse and the elimination of the temporal dimension of phenomena. This former property enhances the effectiveness of communication; the latter is crucial to our ability to cope with the fluidity of our experience. Both these features find their most extreme expression in mathematics.

Discourses on thinking are the ones to consider while speaking about hazards of objectifying. The metaphor of object enters these discourses with nouns such as *abstraction*, *meaning*, and *learning disability*. The objectifying quality of the resulting talk may be the main factor behind the quandaries

[46] Dehaene (1997, p. 52).

listed in chapter 1. Indeed, in the discourses on humans and their doings, reification and alienation may lead to *illusory dilemmas* – dilemmas that result from unfortunate metaphorical entailments, to *phony dichotomies* that engender tautological statements disguised as causal explanation, and to *consequential omissions* resulting from the fact that the "low-resolution" objectified descriptions of human phenomena gloss over important inter-personal and intra-personal differences. In addition, objectified discourses on thinking tend to produce diagnoses and evaluations that function as self-fulfilling prophecies. These and some other weaknesses of our current thinking about thinking are sufficient incentive for trying to ground the discourse of research in a more operational, disobjectified infrastructure. An attempt in this direction is made in the next chapter.

3   Commognition

Thinking as Communicating

The world does not speak. Only we do.

Richard Rorty[1]

Stamp out nouns.

Anatol Holt[2]

The rest of this book is devoted to the project of minimizing the risks, perhaps the very presence, of the metaphor of object while trying to preserve most of its advantages. The task is admittedly ambitious and far from easy. To succeed, we will have to suspend disbelief and remain patient when we slip and falter, trying to bootstrap ourselves from our present discourse into the new one, yet to be invented.

Clearly, we are not going to be the first to undertake the task of disobjectification. The necessary initial step, then, is to survey the history of earlier attempts and try to understand the reasons for their insufficiency. The subsequent move will be to identify those developments that seem to have taken us "almost there" and can thus become a basis for our own trials. Finally, a specific proposal for a disobjectified discourse on thinking will be made. All along, we will need to keep in mind that our present task is not one of establishing empirical facts about thinking but rather of finding useful ways of talking about the phenomenon.

1. Monological and Dialogical Discourses on Thinking

The numerous historical attempts to overcome the pitfalls of objectification took different forms, depending on whether they were undertaken as a part of *monological* or *dialogical* research. Let me elaborate.

[1] Rorty (1989, p. 6).
[2] Quoted in Bateson, 1973, p. 304.

According to the definition introduced by Mikhail Bakhtin, *monologically* disposed researchers view their narratives about the world as depending on the world itself rather than on the human storyteller. With their monological stories seen as verbalized versions of the reality, researchers view themselves as mere ventriloquists of these external, superhuman forces. Repeating Bakhtin's own words once again, they believe that through their impersonal, timeless monologues one can hear "'the voice of the life itself,' 'the voice of nature,' 'the voice of God,' and so forth."[3] Monological discourses thus have an in-built claim to exclusivity. They are also fully alienated, and, as such, they lead to narratives that present all their objects as being "in the world" rather than in the discourse itself. Considering the fact that this distinct objectivist flavor is their inherent property, monological discourses are naturally immune to disobjectification.

Dialogical discourse, on the other hand, is explicit about its being but a discourse. The dialogical researcher does not aspire to be any more than a participant in the "conversation of mankind," who always keeps in mind Richard Rorty's sobering reminder "World does not speak – we do."[4] Through its very syntax, dialogical discourse makes it clear that its stories have human authors and human addressees. The dialogical narrative is thus offered by its creators as but one of many possibilities, which, however, is believed to be compelling enough to be listened to and, eventually, generally endorsed.[5] Whereas monological narratives present themselves as being exclusively about the world external to the discourse itself, dialogical discourse is as conducive to narratives about the world as to narratives about itself. For the dialogical researcher, reflection about her own ways with words and about possible alternatives is an integral part of her project. Note that the discursive definition of research introduced earlier in this book was a declaration of my own dialogical vision of our investigative endeavor.

The deep epistemological–ontological gap between monological and dialogical approaches should not be dismissed as just a matter of philosophical musings. Incommensurable basic tenets lead to differing research

---

[3] Bakhtin (1986, p. 163).

[4] See note 1.

[5] A disclaimer must be added to forestall common misinterpretations of this last statement. Two views, often ascribed to dialogical thinkers, are definitely not what these thinkers themselves would endorse: Dialogism does not imply nonexistence of the "real" (extradiscursive) world, and it does not imply that "anything goes." Trying to present these two claims as a necessary consequence of the basic tenets of dialogism is as logically flawed as insisting that the statement "There is no such thing as one ultimate shirt that fits me" implies my own nonexistence or the fact that *any* shirt would fit me.

practices. Thus, whereas the monological thinker makes claims about the *correctness* or *veracity* of theories of thinking, the dialogically disposed person is likely to gauge competing theories according to their *usefulness* – according to their cogency, richness, coherence, and generative power. Consider, for example, the present exhortation to minimize reference to a certain type of objects in the discourse of thinking. For the monologist, this request is tantamount to stating the nonexistence of the objects in questions. For the dialogist, this exhortation is a call for discursive amendments. Similarly, whereas the monologist asks about facts, the dialogist often inquires about definitions. Consider, for example, questions such as *Can animals think?*, *Do animals have minds?*,[6] or *Can machines think?*[7] that have been recurring throughout history with remarkable tenacity. These queries are understood by monologists as regarding the state of affairs in the world.[8] In the dialogical discourse, they reincarnate into questions about definitions of the words *think* and *mind*.[9] The distinction between the two types of queries, those about mind-independent facts and those about definitions, is important, because each of these two kinds requires its own type of argument. It is highly implausible that a problem of one kind would be seen as resolved if treated in ways pertaining to the other type of a problem.

While urging the reader to stay always wary of the difference between the two types of discourse, I admit that the task is not easy. The borderline between monologism and dialogism is subtle. Here, as in so many other places, we are prone to fall victim to ontological collapse – we are only too likely to confuse our sentences with what these sentences are all about and to misinterpret dialogical discourse as nature's own monologue. This is, for example, what happens when we interpret the word *truth* as signifying an attribute of the world rather than of what we say about it or when we subsequently interpret the claim on the nonexistence of "the ultimate truth

[6] Dennett (1996, p. 2).

[7] Turing (p. 433).

[8] The monological interpretation of the first two questions transpires from their authors' subsequent comments on "supposedly unknowable *facts* . . . about which creatures have minds at all" (p. 14, emphasis added) and from the very fact that the questions are asked without explaining what is meant in this context by the word *mind* and without specifying criteria for deciding whether one belongs to the category of "mind-havers."

[9] The well-known query of whether machines can think, formulated by Alan Turing (1950), was, indeed, interpreted by its author as a request for a definition of thinking. More specifically, the problem Turing tried to solve was whether it was possible to *define* thinking in such a way as to capture the intuitively sensed difference between human and nonhuman phenomena. The famous Turing test was offered as a hypothetical means to find out whether there are public criteria with whose help one could define thinking as a feature existing in humans and lacking in machines.

about the world" as a claim on nonexistence of the world itself. Ludwig Wittgenstein, who may be regarded as one of the first proponents of dialogism even though he never actually used the name, made a powerful case against scholarly discourses that, at his time, were uniformly monological in nature. While fully devoted to his project, he was also aware of its inevitable limitations. His "therapeutic" philosophizing could not possibly prevent his fellow language users from straying to the edge of the linguistic abyss. The most he could hope for, he said, was that his admonitions would save them at the very last minute:

> Language sets everyone the same traps; it is an immense network of easily accessible wrong turnings. And so we watch one man after another walking down the same paths and we know in advance where he will branch off, where walk straight on without noticing the side turning, and so forth. What I have to do then is erect signposts at all the junctions where there are wrong turnings so as to help people past the danger points.[10]

This said, let us proceed to the survey of previous attempts on disobjectification, doing our best to ensure that the elusive line separating monological and dialogical discourses will never disappear from our sight.

2. Disobjectification of Discourses on Thinking – Brief History

2.1 *Objectification in Monological Discourses on Thinking*

Because the metaphor of object is omnipresent in colloquial discourses, the monological, strongly objectified vision of thinking may be seen as, in a sense, natural. In the 17th century, the French philosopher and mathematician René Descartes postulated the famous split between the material body and immaterial soul (or mind). In doing so, he laid the foundations of the dualistic discourse on thinking, which was to monopolize the Western scene for generations. The nonmaterial "half" of the Cartesian pair was said to be

> a substance, of which the whole essence or nature consists in thinking, and which, in order to exist, needs no place and depends on no material thing; so that this "I," that is to say, the mind, by which I am what I am, is entirely distinct from the body.[11]

---

[10] Wittgenstein in 1931; quoted in Richter (n.d., p. 7).
[11] Descartes (1968) in *Discourse on method* and *Meditations* II, pp. 104–107 and 111; IV, p. 132; and VI, p. 156.

Within this doctrine, the body was thus understood as an essentially lifeless machine, and the soul (or mind), the site of human awareness, was seen as what made the body alive. The vision of human existence as involving two different types of objects – the bodily and the mental, the accessible with senses and the perceptually unreachable – persisted in one form or another for centuries. So did the related split between two types of human processes, thinking and behavior. Although the present formulation of the dualist doctrine is certainly quite different,[12] the monological discourse that pictures thinking and behavior as ontologically distinct types of human doing is alive and kicking even as I am writing these lines. This said, the monological dualist discourse is also a constant source of a certain uneasiness, known as *Cartesian anxiety*.[13] Whatever form the dualist thesis takes at any given time, the slippery, indefinable character of the nonbodily component of the Cartesian duo is bound to produce a more or less explicit sense of deficiency of our thinking about thinking.

Over the last three centuries, this uneasiness led to a series of monological attempts to circumvent the pitfalls of the inherently objectifying mentalist discourse, all of them rather disappointing and short-lived. The most famous (not to say notorious) case is that of behaviorism – the movement that proposed to solve the problem simply by cutting off that part of the discourse on human doings that dealt with thinking. In this act of discursive exorcism, some phenomena were altogether lost to the scientific project. A mechanistic, reductionist vision of humans and their actions was an obvious entailment. According to behaviorists, the only type of "internal" occurrence one could reasonably imagine was the emergence of bonds between what goes into and what goes out of the black box of the human head. This, indeed, was believed to be a purely mechanical matter. The only reasonable objects of psychological study were the creation of the bond and its gradual solidification, with both these processes believed to be fully determined by external circumstances, and thus also fully observable. By throwing out the baby of human complexity with the dualistic bathwater, behaviorists impoverished their research to such an extent that nothing indicated anymore its being designated specifically for the study of humans.

Because of its inability to capture the gist of what it meant to be human, behaviorism was dumped just as decisively as it was initially embraced. By

---

[12] The Cartesian doctrine is often called *dualism of substance*, whereas its modern version has been named *dualism of property* (Searle, 2004).

[13] This latter term was coined by the biologist and philosopher Francesco Varela (1946–2001). See, for example, Varela, Thompson, and Rosch (1991).

the middle of the 20th century, the "cognitive revolution" restored mind to a state of grace. The explicit mind–brain and internal–external dichotomies returned with vengeance. And so did the metaphor of object. Terms such as *mental scheme*, *mental state*, and *mental processes* were again on everybody's lips, except that this time, the former unmentionables were no longer considered to be a threat to scientific replicability, rigor, and cumulativeness. The direct trigger for the resurgence of the unabashedly objectified dualist discourse was the advent of new information technology. With computers around, it now appeared possible to reconcile the two competing needs: the need for scientificity, on the one hand, and for the richness, breadth, and cogency of the resulting account, on the other hand. The electronic "number cruncher" was believed to be a reliable model of the human mind, and with its help at least some of the inner workings of the human "thinking machine" were now supposed to be open to public inspection. On the antibehaviorist wave, researchers became receptive to yet another brand of cognitivist endeavor, best instantiated by Jean Piaget's theory of human mental development, constructed in the image of the Darwinian theory of evolution. Once behaviorists' bans were lifted, the old idea of human intellectual development as a process of extending and perfecting one's "cognitive schemes" regained its appeal.

Considering its unrestrained objectification, it is not surprising that cognitivism did not, after all, make researchers happy ever after. Whether grounded in the computer metaphor of mind or in the vision of human development as a gradual construction of ever more complex mental schemes, the cognitivist research did not seem to be able to deliver what it was aiming at: a cogent nonreductionist account of what it meant to be human. Jerome Bruner, one of the founding fathers of the "cognitive revolution" that began in the late 1950s, admits that his and his colleagues' "all-out effort to establish meaning as the central concept of psychology"[14] did not lead to the expected groundbreaking insights into the complexities of human intellect.

Indeed, cognitivism suffers from all the usual consequences of excessive objectification: It is prone to overgeneralizations and logical entanglements, and it produces evaluations and diagnoses that act as self-fulfilling prophecies. But it has yet another serious shortcoming. Because of its objectification-engendered assumption that individual minds are the principal source of their own development, cognitivism is ill equipped to deal not just with interpersonal and cross-situational differences, but also with those changes in human processes that transcend a single life span. Within the

---

[14] Bruner (1990, p. 2).

confines of the discourse that portrays an individual development as spurred and informed every time anew by the same basically immutable factors, there is no cogent explanation for the fact that human forms of life, unlike those of other species, evolve over history and that the outcomes of the ongoing transformations accumulate from generation to generation, constantly redefining the nature and extent of individual growth and incessantly increasing the complexity of human actions.[15]

To sum up, objectification of "the mental," typical of monological discourses on humans, kept behavior and thinking separate. This was obviously true of cognitivism, but in a somewhat more subtle way it was also true of behaviorism. Indeed, rather than questioning the split between thinking and other forms of human doing, behaviorists simply banned one-half of the existing discourse on humans in action. Needless to say, in doing so they made themselves unable to do justice to the dazzling complexity of the phenomena they vowed to fathom.

2.2 *Dialogical Attempts at Disobjectification*

The idea that our helplessness in the face of human complexity may have its source in our ways of talking can be traced back at least as far as the 14th century, when the Franciscan monk William of Ockham formulated the famous principle *Pluralitas non est ponenda sine necessitate* – "Entities should not be multiplied unnecessarily." The gist of *Ockham's razor*, as the principle has been known ever since, was that scientific explanations should refer to only as many objects as genuinely necessary. True, in justifying this principle William of Ockham did not claim, as can be expected from a dialogical thinker, that the excess of explanatory entities is a purely linguistic matter, a by-product of our use of words. Rather, his argument was based on the belief that God's creation is governed by the "principle of parsimony," and thus multiplicity of entities would be contrary to the nature of the world. Still, he did conjecture that a certain tacit assumption about language may stimulate our tendency to view the universe as populated by an exaggerated amount of entities:

> The source of many errors in philosophy is the claim that a distinct signified thing always corresponds to a distinct word in such a way that there are as

---

[15] The route cognitivists usually take around this dilemma is grounded in the claim about reflexivity of the relation between activity and genes: whereas genes have an impact on human doings, the way people do things can modify the genetic blueprints in return. Although empirically corroborated and of significance, this claim, per se, does not yet explain why only humans seem capable of such genetic accumulation.

many distinct entities being signified as there are distinct names or words doing the signifying.[16]

Whatever William of Ockham's justification of his principle, the general purport of his exhortation was the same as that of my earlier admonitions: Our language does not merely describe what there is – it is responsible for what we consider as real. Proliferation of entities may be detrimental to our project of fathoming the world. Thus, avoid *talking* about intangible objects whenever you can; beware of the assumption "Each distinct word signifies a distinct entity" because only too often this belief will lead you to "all sorts of absurdities" [tautologies], such as "God . . . is good by goodness," "a suitable thing is suitable by suitability," "a blind thing is blind by blindness," or "a body is mobile by mobility."[17]

The 20th century put language at the fore and made philosophers more attentive to the problem of objectification. Groundbreaking contributions to the project of dialogization and disobjectification were made by Gilbert Ryle and Ludwig Wittgenstein. To be sure, none of these thinkers actually used the word *objectification*. Each of them tackled the issue in his own way, foregrounding a different aspect of the problem. And yet, when pulled together, the two bodies of work can be seen as a concerted frontal attack on objectification of the discourse on thinking.

Ryle was one of the first philosophers to launch a direct criticism at those who objectify discourse on thinking when speaking about the mind as an entity separate from, or additional to, the brain.[18] Although it may be legitimate to say that a whole would sometimes appear to be more than the sum of its physical parts, one commits a *category mistake* when one interprets the word *more* as implying a certain additional entity or substance, which actually exists in one form or another even if it is perceptually inaccessible (note the distinct affinity between the idea of *category mistake* and the previously introduced notion of the discursive failing called *ontological collapse*; this latter term may be interpreted as referring to the discursive mechanism that leads to category mistakes). Because of this inaccessibility, the claim that mental entities are responsible for our volitional acts has no explanatory power. Psychologists' and philosophers' first task is therefore to

---

[16] *Summula Philosophiae Naturalis III*, chap. 7; see also *Summa Totus Logicae* Bk. I, C. 51. Retrieved from http://en.wikipedia.org/wiki/Occam's_Razor. See also William of Ockham (1984, 1990).

[17] *Summa Totus Logicae* Bk. I, C. 51. Retrieved from http://en.wikipedia.org/wiki/ Occam's_Razor. See also William of Ockham (1974, 1990).

[18] Ryle (1949/2000).

exorcise the "ghost" of mind from the "machine" of brain, and this means, quite simply, a change in their ways of talking.

Wittgenstein's attack on common misuses of, and misunderstandings about, language, issued at approximately the same time,[19] is even more encompassing. In the last two decades of his life, Wittgenstein rejected the monological vision of language as a reflection of things in the world, the view for which he was arguing just a few years earlier.[20] In most cases, he now claimed, the meaning of words does not arise from objects signified by these words; rather, "for a *large* class of cases – though not for all – in which we employ the word 'meaning' it can be defined thus: the meaning of a word is its use in the language."[21] Thus, for Wittgenstein, meaning was neither a thing in the world nor a private entity in one's mind: It was an aspect of human discursive activity and, as such was public and fully investigable.

Consequently, Wittgenstein regarded the behaviorist doctrine as a gross misinterpretation of what the call for disobjectification in general, and the protest against separating thinking from other forms of human doing in particular, were all about. He distanced himself explicitly from behaviorism by engaging in a fictitious dialogue with a critic. When asked by an imaginary interlocutor, "'Are you not really a behaviourist in disguise? Aren't you at bottom really saying that everything except human behaviour is a fiction?'" he answered, "If I do speak of a fiction then it is of a *grammatical* fiction."[22] The idiosyncratically used adjective *grammatical* was meant to indicate, once again, that whatever he said referred to language and its misuses, and not to what does or does not exist in reality or what is or is not empirically investigable. For Wittgenstein, the real dichotomy was in the discourse, not in the world: It was the dichotomy between what is communicationally operative and what is doomed to remain vague and misleading. If we thus need to ban anything, it is not the study of certain phenomena; a ban, if any, should be on things that we mention but that will always result in logical entanglements.

On the other hand, Wittgenstein believed that the things that are open to investigation in a publicly accountable way are much more numerous and incomparably more complex than those included in monological research so far, either behaviorist or cognitivist. Whereas adamant in his claim "What we cannot speak about [properly] we must pass over in

[19] Wittgenstein (1953/2003, p. 86).
[20] Wittgenstein (1981).
[21] Wittgenstein (1953/2003, p. 18).
[22] Wittgenstein (1953/2003).

silence,"[23] Wittgenstein included in the category of "communicables" more than dreamed of by any monological psychologist. Rather than reducing humans to input–output machines, as behaviorists did, he posited utmost complexity of human actions. Although this claim seemingly placed him closer to cognitivists, his insistence on the inherently public nature of all this complexity made it clear that, in fact, he would not have joined the "cognitive revolution" had he lived long enough to see it. Indeed, rather than insisting that external behavior is but a "tip of an iceberg" whereas the "real action" is elsewhere, as proposed by cognitivists, he sustained that whatever matters in human activities lies open to public inspection. These activities should therefore be taken for what they appear to be: *an extremely complex network of communally established games, which are communicable by definition.* Assuming stable inner entities responsible for these intricate phenomena would be another attempt at reduction, comparable to that of behaviorists. Rather than looking for a hidden simplifying mechanism, we should deal with this complexity in its own terms. Thus, the observable phenomena that occasion the talk about thinking are not mere "windows" to another, inherently private universe. Rather, these are objects of investigation in their own right, and exclusively so. To put it in Wittgenstein's own words,

> The phenomenon is not a symptom of something else; rather, it is reality. The phenomenon is not a symptom of something else which then makes the sentence true or false; rather, it is itself that which verifies it [the sentence].[24]

This said, one should also remember that the complexity of different forms of human doing is neither modular nor describable with a finite set of rules. None of the human actions can be usefully considered separately from the "forms of life" of which they are inextricable parts and that, although public and investigable, are messy and unyielding and doomed to remain a perennial challenge to those who seek all-encompassing theories of human processes.

This latter prediction notwithstanding, Wittgenstein's doctrine gives rise to a careful optimism. Although we must renounce the hope for a neat, ultimate (monological) theory of human actions, we do seem to have a chance for creating disobjectified discourses in which the unmanageable complexity of human processes would be describable in a useful, helpful way. Wittgenstein's argument went, more or less, as follows: To disobjectify the discourse on human doings, one needs to define the keywords of this

[23] Wittgenstein (1961, p. 74).
[24] Stern (1995, p. 139).

discourse in operational terms. This means specifying the use of words such as *thinking, understanding,* or *feeling* without reference to "private" entities. And if one doubts that such operative defining is, indeed, possible, Wittgenstein offers a simple argument: If we are able to communicate about thinking (or pain, or any other process traditionally considered as inherently private) in our daily lives, there must be *public* criteria for identifying this phenomenon in its multiple manifestations. If so, there is no reason why we should not be able to use these very same public criteria, alas in a more explicit and systematic way, while trying to tell new, more insightful stories about thinking. All one has to do to operationalize a discourse is to observe how people use words and to tease out rules according to which they do so. When Wittgenstein defined *meaning* as "the use of the word in language," he both instantiated and described this simple idea of operationalization.

Of course, the actual task of specifying rules of word use may not be as straightforward as it sounds. Only rarely can defining be just a matter of observing and describing how people use words. More often than not, operationalization would require making choices and modifying. Consider, for instance, the word *understanding.* As previously illustrated with several examples, contradictions between first-person and third-person reports on one's understanding seem to be a commonplace phenomenon (see section 5 in chapter 1). It is clear that in judging their own understanding people are using different criteria than when trying to assess understanding of others. The metaphors at large, and the metaphor of object in particular, are particularly prone to lead to this kind of diversity. Words that have been transferred from one discourse to another cannot be incorporated into the new discourse without some bending of the old rules. There is no reason to expect that different users would do this bending in the same ways. In this situation, one may either give up the confusing word altogether or choose those of its competing uses that seem most helpful.[25] In the case of *understanding* there are pros and cons of each of these possibilities and, as will be shown later in this book, I have decided to opt for the latter (indeed, it is difficult to imagine the discourse about learning without the word *understanding*!).

---

[25] In fact, there is yet another thing a dialogical researcher can do in a situation like this: She can try to replace the talk about what people *are* or *have* with talk about what and how they *do.* Thus, for example, we may prefer talking about what people *mean* (that is, the way they use words) and about their actions as being more or less *meaningful* to them, rather than talking about the *meaning* they have or construct. Similarly, trying to describe the way a person *thinks* or *understands* is preferable to speaking about the *thoughts* or *understanding* one *has.*

The project of disobjectification, even if implemented in this way, has its natural limitations. It would be unreasonable to hope that we can avoid linguistic pitfalls[26] and ensure uniformity of word uses once and for all. In the best case, our efforts to disambiguate will yield only small islands of coherence. Furthermore, if operationalization is to succeed, the interlocutors must all act according to the proposed definitions. However, even the most disciplined, well-meaning person will often slip back into old discursive habits. Finally, as Wittgenstein repeatedly emphasized, our language games are simply too complex and messy to yield themselves to deterministic definitions (only mathematicians, the intrepid chasers of infallible communication, never stop believing in the possibility of such definitions). And yet, rather than renounce the hope altogether, we may think about disobjectification as a never-ending effort to minimize breaches in communication and maximize the usefulness of the resulting conversations.

3. We Are Almost There: Participationism

The last few decades generated a considerable advance toward a discourse that does not dichotomize behavior and thinking and views the latter form

---

[26] A glimpse at the numerous samples from the current research literature gathered in chapter 2 suffices to indicate that Wittgenstein's skeptical comment about the possibility of avoiding "linguistic traps" (see earlier discussion) was right on the mark: In spite of philosophers' insistence, the objectifying, dualist discourses on thinking he was objecting to continue to thrive, and not just in the vernacular, but also in academia. One cannot help wondering about what seems to be researchers' concerted resistance to philosophers' caveats. This opposition can probably be best explained with the help of the very claim that is being rejected: that about the fallibility of language users, who are only too likely to mistake disagreements about uses of language for controversies about facts-in-the-world. The following passage from Daniel Dennett's current book seems a good example of rejection stemming from this kind of misinterpretation: "Both Ryle and Wittgenstein were quite hostile to the idea of a scientific investigation of the mind, and the standard wisdom in the 'cognitive revolution' is that we have seen through and beyond their ruthlessly unscientific analyses of the mental" (Dennett, 1996, p. 169).

On the basis of my reading of Wittgenstein and Ryle, it is my conjecture that the two philosophers, were they still alive, would react to Dennett's statement with something like "Well, we could not possibly speak against *scientific investigation of mind* because for us, the expression *investigation of mind*, scientific or otherwise, is meaningless and will remain so until the word *mind* is operationalized and disobjectified. As long as the term is nonoperational, we are unable to use it and, in particular, we cannot know what should be done in order to implement the kind of investigation you are talking about. Thus, as we said, it is not that we object to the *investigation of mind* – we simply don't know what it is." They might then add with a sigh: "We are disheartened by being misunderstood, but not surprised. After all, we are the ones to alert everybody else to the common phenomenon of category mistakes – and here is a perfect example of one of them!"

of human doing as belonging to the same category as all the others. It is only now, five decades after the first "cognitive revolution," that the research community seems to be recovering from the trauma of behaviorism, while also making decisive steps in the direction of dialogical discourse envisioned by Wittgenstein. One of the earliest and most outspoken critics of behaviorism was the Russian psychologist Lev Vygotsky. His revolutionary ideas, conceived early in the 20th century but almost unknown in the West until the 1960s, played the key role in the recent antidualist turn. By the late 1980s, the disillusionment with all forms of cognitivism was widespread enough to make many ex-Piagetians a captive audience for Vygotsky's basic tenet about the inherently social nature of all human processes.

More specifically, Vygotsky was explicitly contradicting the Piagetian thesis that human intellectual growth results from the direct interaction between the individual and the world. This is what he seems to have had in mind when stating that whatever name is given to what is being learned by an individual – *knowledge*, *concept*, or *higher mental function* – all these terms refer to culturally produced and constantly modified outcomes of collective human efforts. This tenet is epitomized in his famous statement about development of an individual as a process involving "carrying" higher mental functions from the social to the psychological plane:

> Any function in the child's cultural development appears twice, or on two planes. First it appears on the social plane, and then on the psychological plane. First it appears between people as an interpsychological category, and then within the child as an intrapsychological category.[27]

In spite of reifying undertones of this metaphorical formulation, the general message was antidualist. Not unlike the American pragmatist philosophers,[28] Vygotsky seems to have promoted the vision of knowledge as "the conversation of mankind." Indeed, the issue at stake was that of the ontological–epistemological status of knowledge, with the adjective *social* functioning as tantamount to human-made, and thus as the opposite of *natural*, *received*, or *biologically determined*.

The American anthropologist Jean Lave was one of the first to criticize the then-mainstream cognitivist discourse for all the weaknesses typical of all objectified discourses.[29] This was in the late 1980s. Some time later, she followed with the "therapeutic suggestion" to replace the metaphor of

[27] Vygotsky (1987, p. 11).
[28] Rorty (1979).
[29] Lave (1988). See also Brown et al. (1989).

learning-as-acquisition with the metaphor of *learning-as-participation*. More specifically, she and her coauthor Etienne Wenger asked their readers to eschew the objectifying terms *knowledge acquisition* and *learning transfer* and to think about learning as *legitimate peripheral participation*[30] in socially organized activities. Rather than being an acquirer of goods, the learner was now to be viewed as a beginning practitioner trying to gain access to a well-defined, historically established form of human doing. The term *socially organized* was not supposed to imply that the activities in question must always be performed in collaboration with others. It only meant that processes of learning, as other human activities, are part and parcel of a patterned collective effort.

Lave and Wenger's publication was just one among many similar events that helped in the formation of a *participationist* vision of humans and of their development. As a confluence of ideas from areas as diverse as philosophy, sociology, psychology, anthropology, linguistics, and others,[31] participationism is a mélange of approaches rather than a single research discourse. Its foundational tenet is that *patterned, collective forms of distinctly human forms of doing are developmentally prior to the activities of the individual*. Whereas acquisitionists view individual development as proceeding from personal acquisitions to participation in collective activities, participationists reverse the picture and claim that people go from participation in collectively implemented activities to similar forms of doing performed single-handedly. According to this vision, learning to speak, to solve mathematical problems, or to cook means a gradual transition from being able

---

[30] Lave and Wenger (1991).

[31] Particularly relevant in this context is activity theory, which grew out of the work of Vygotsky and his associates, e.g., Engeström (1987); Leont'ev (1981); Nardi (1996). In addition, one should mention the significant influence of Wittgenstein, as well as that of two interrelated, but still distinct schools in sociology: the *symbolic interactionism* usually associated with Mead (1934), Goffman (1959, 1967), and Blumer (1969) and the *ethnomethodological* approach initiated by Garfinkel (1967). Also of relevance in this context is the *sociological phenomenology* that originated in the philosophical thought of Husserl and was founded in the first half of the 20th century by Schutz (1967). The direct influence of this latter school of thought on psychology and education can be seen in the work of German researchers, e.g., Bauersfeld (1995), Voigt (1985), and Krumheuer (1995). All these schools, as diverse as they are, share a number of basic assumptions that can also be found in most of the current versions of participationism. They all posit the inherently social nature of humans and agree that actions of the individual cannot be understood unless treated as part and parcel of collective doings and of collectively produced patterns. The patterned collective activities, in turn, are objects of sense-making efforts of their participants. The different schools begin to diverge only in their respective responses to the question of where the regularities originate and whether the observed patterns are in any sense "real," as opposed to their lying exclusively in the eyes of sense-making insiders.

to play a partial role in the implementation of the given types of tasks to becoming capable of implementing them in their entirety and of one's own accord. Eventually, a person can perform on her own and in her unique way entire sequences of steps, which, so far, she would only execute in collaboration with others.[32] The tendency for *individualization* – for gradual overtaking of the roles of others, accompanied by an increase of one's agency over the given activity – seems to be one of the hallmarks of humanness.[33]

The difference between the acquisitionist and the participationist versions of human development is thus not just a matter of "zoom of lens," as it is sometimes presented.[34] Above all, it manifests itself in the way we understand the origins and the nature of human uniqueness. For the acquisitionist, this uniqueness lies in the biological makeup of the individual. Although participationism does not deny the need for special biological prerequisites – such as special vocal cords and sound-distinguishing ability, both of which are the basis for human communication, or the newly discovered "mirror neurons" that seem to underlie human ability to imitate other people – this approach views all the uniquely human capacities as resulting from the fundamental fact that humans are social beings, engaged in collective activities from the day they are born and throughout their lives. In other words, although human biological givens make this collective form of life possible, it is the collective life that brings about all the other uniquely human characteristics. Human society emerges from the participationist account as a huge fractal-like entity, every part of which is a society in itself, indistinguishable in its inner structure from the whole.

Another notable change that happens in the transition from acquisitionist to participationist discourse is in the unit of analysis. It is this new unit that I had in mind while speaking, somewhat ambiguously, about "patterned collective doings." Other eligible candidates for the participationist unit of analysis are *form of life*, suggested by Wittgenstein,[35] and *activity*,

---

[32] To put it in Barbara Rogoff's words, children's development "occurs through guided participation in social activity with companions who support and stretch children's understanding of and skill in using cultural tools" (Rogoff, 1990, p. vii).

[33] The term *individualization* may be viewed as participationist versions of what Vygotsky and activity theorists call *internalization*. Bakhtin and Leont'ev preferred *appropriation* to internalization, believing that the former word is more effective in capturing both the active nature and the bidirectionality of the process (Cazden 2001, p. 76.) The important advantage of the present terminology is that it is free of acquisitionist undertones of both internalization and appropriation.

[34] Rogoff (1995); Lerman (1998).

[35] Wittgenstein (1953).

the pivotal idea of the activity theory. The now popular term *practice* is yet another viable option.[36] Although all these terms appear in the current literature in numerous ways, with the differences between one use and another not always easy to tell, each is good enough for my present purpose. Indeed, all I want, for now, is to describe participationist innovation according to those central characteristics that remain basically the same across different renderings. Whatever name and definition are given to the participationist unit of analysis and whatever claims about humans are formulated with its help, the strength of this unit is in the fact that it has both collective and individual "editions."

Armed with this flexible analytic focus, participationists have a chance to address the question of change that exceeds the boundaries of individual life. When speaking about human development, participationists do not mean a transformation in people, but rather in forms of human doing. This non-trivial discursive shift is highly consequential, as it removes the sharp acquisitionist distinction between development of an individual and the development of a collective. The developmental transformations are the result of two complementary processes, that of *individualization of the collective* and that of *communalization of the individual*. Individualization and communalization are reflexively interrelated: Individualization results in personally modified versions of collective activities, whereas some of the individual variations feed back into the collective forms of doing, acquire permanence, and are carried in space and time from one collective to another.

Although thinking appears to be an inherently individual form of human doing, there is no reason to assume that its origins are any different from those of other uniquely human capacities: As with all the others, this special form of human doing could only develop from a patterned collective activity. Our next task is to identify the patterned collaborative activity that can justifiably be regarded as the collective precursor of thinking.

4. Finally: Thinking as Communicating

4.1 *Defining Thinking*

To those who were "born into" acquisitionist discourses, the idea that thinking may be defined as an individualized form of a collective doing may sound somewhat implausible. After all, whatever we call thinking is usually done by each one of us alone and, by definition, is inaccessible to others in a direct manner. It is thus not readily evident which "visible" human activity

---

[36] E.g., Wenger (1998); Cobb (2002).

might be the collective version of thinking. In fact, one has good reasons to doubt whether such a collective edition can be identified at all. More than any other human activity, the phenomena we call "thinking" appear biologically determined and seem to be growing "from inside" the person. Still, participationist tenets speak forcefully against this deeply rooted image. The next thesis to explore is that thinking can be usefully defined as an individualized version of *interpersonal communication*.

A powerful, even if indirect, argument comes to mind immediately when one tries to substantiate this proposal. The ability to think in the complex way people do is absent in other species – and so is the human highly developed ability to communicate. At a closer look, communication, like thinking, may be one of the most human of human activities. This is not to say that the ability to communicate is restricted to people. At least some animals do seem to engage in activities that one may wish to describe as communication. And yet, human communication is special, and not just because of its being mainly linguistic – the feature that, in animals, seems to be extremely rare, if not lacking altogether. It is the role communication plays in human life that seems unique. The ability to coordinate our activities by means of interpersonal communication is the basis for our being social creatures. And because communication is the glue that holds human collectives together, even our ability to stay alive is a function of our communicational capacity. We communicate in order to coordinate our actions and ascertain the kind of mutuality that provides us with what we need and cannot attain single-handedly. The list of human needs that would remain unsatisfied without interpersonal communication is long and multifarious, and it includes not just the most advanced and complex cultural needs, but also the most primitive biological ones, of the kind that most animals are able to take care of by themselves, with only marginal collaboration of other individuals. In the view of all this, it is not surprising that Leontiev, one of the founding fathers of participationism, declared the highly developed capacity for communication as the hallmark of humanness: "We do not meet in the animal world any special forms of action having as their sole and special end the mastery of the behavior of other individuals by attracting their attention."[37]

All this, as important as it may sound, is not yet enough to substantiate the claim about the *usefulness* of the following definition.

> **Definition**: *Thinking* is an individualized version of (interpersonal) communicating.

[37] Leont'ev (1930, p. 59).

To ascertain usefulness, we need to show that this formulation leads to a rich, coherent, and cogent set of narratives about the defined phenomenon. This will be done, hopefully in a convincing way, in the rest of this book. For now, let me ask whether the proposed definition "covers" the same – or almost the same – set of cases as those included in the spontaneous, every-day uses of the term *thinking*. In other words, does the set of phenomena that occasion the talk about thinking coincide with the set of phenomena implied by the proposed definition? I expect little disagreement regarding the claim that self-communication (for example, in the form of "inner speech") can be considered as a case of thinking. What remains to be shown is that there is no phenomenon we consider as a case of thinking that could not be regarded as an instance of self-communicating. Because claims on nonexistence are difficult to prove, I refrain from any further argument and, instead, challenge the skeptical reader to provide examples that would show the inadequacy of the proposed definition. In my case, no such instance comes to mind. (Before you engage in this thought experiment, be reminded that we are talking about public, visible phenomena only; arguing that the proposed definition does not "cover" interactions between mental entities – for example, it does not include the process of "assimilating new pieces of information into one's cognitive schema" – would be contrary to the idea of disobjectification promoted throughout this book.)[38]

Once we adopt the claim that thinking may be usefully defined as the *individualized form of the activity of communicating*, thinking stops being a self-sustained process separate from and, in a sense, primary to any act of communication and becomes an act of communication in itself, although not necessarily interpersonal. This self-communication does not have to be in any way audible or visible and does not have to be in words.[39] In the

---

[38] Some people are likely to argue that *perception*, which we usually regard as the most elementary form of thinking, is missing from the proposed definition. I wish to claim that much of *human* perception can also count as, in a sense, a communicational act. In public terms, perception expresses itself either in an instinctive reaction or in the act of conscious recognition, that is, in an act of going back in thought to some previous experiences and to actions associated with these experiences. In humans, the associated actions include discursive responses, such as naming. If so, our present definition recognizes most of human perceiving as a form of thinking. (I am prepared to compromise and leave the more primitive form of perceiving, that which leads to immediate instinctive reactions, out of the realm of thinking; after all, in this book, our focus is on these special properties that make humans unique among species. Human perception, if defined in this way, may be one of those things we are looking for.)

[39] One of the most persistent and encompassing debates in the history of human thought has been evolving around the question of relations between *thinking* and *speech* (a brief summary of the relevant events will be presented in the next chapter). Considering the

proposed discourse on thinking, cognitive processes and interpersonal communication processes are thus but different manifestations of basically the same phenomenon.[40] To stress this fact, I propose to combine the terms *cognitive* and *communicational* into the new adjective *commognitive*. The etymology of this last word will always remind us that whatever is said with its help refers to those phenomena that are traditionally included in the term cognition, as well as to those usually associated with interpersonal exchanges.[41]

The introduction of the new keyword *commognition* is a beginning of the intricate process of building a disobjectified discourse on thinking. Operationalizing, and possibly redefining such well-known terms as *communication, language, discourse, concept*, and many others, is a part of this project.

fact that no solution, not even those offered by the most revered of thinkers, managed to bring about a durable consensus, it may be difficult to understand why the simple statement "Thinking is (can be usefully defined as) a form of communication" should now be accepted as an answer. In response, let me stress two differences between my present attempt and most of those undertaken in the past. First, what I have done has been framed as an act of *defining*, not as an attempt to find out what thinking "really is." Thus, the agreement may be possible provided I manage to convince others about the usefulness of the proposed *thinking = self-communicating* equation. The second difference stems from the fact that the time-honored dilemma is that of the relations between thinking and *language* (or *speech*), whereas the proposed definition links thinking with *communication*. The relation between thought and speech has been, indeed, a leitmotif of philosophers' musings about thinking. This is easily explicable, considering the centrality of verbal communication in specifically human forms of life and our resulting tendency to equate human communicating with talking. Speech and communication, however, although related, are not the same: The former is but a special case of the latter. There are numerous nonverbal forms of communication and all of them must be considered. Thus, the descriptions of thinking as "talking to oneself" or as "inner speech" are more restrictive than the communicational definition proposed earlier and as such, they do not do justice to the phenomenon we wish to fathom. If the attempts to capture the gist of human thinking have been invariably deemed futile, it was probably because of the fact that the problem has been restricted to the issue of relations between thinking and language.

[40] This definition resonates well with the conversation metaphor of mind to be found in Bakhtin (1981); Ernest (1993, 1994); Holquist (1990); Marková (2003); and Mead (1934). See also the idea of discursive psychology in Edwards and Potter (1992); Edwards (1997); and Harré and Gillett (1995).

[41] The act of coining my own neologism is rather daring, so I feel I owe an explanation. While trying to give a name to the just defined discourse on thinking I could, of course, follow the usual practice of employing an existing English word. In particular, I could use the word *communication* to encompass both categories – that of thinking and that of interpersonal communication. Indeed, many other human activities that begin as collective and are liable to individualization do not change their names as a result of individualization: The individually performed mathematical problem solving is still called problem solving and the task of complex data processing is called data processing whether it is implemented by a single individual or by a group. However, the word *communication* is special in that its being interpersonal seems to be its defining feature. I suspect that the association with this feature may be too strong to be removed by a mere act of redefining.

As the first step, let me complete the task of defining thinking by explaining how the component term *communication* should be understood in the present context.

4.2 *Defining Communication*

All the definitions I was able to locate in dictionaries or in professional literature present communication as an activity of two individuals, often called sender and recipient, who are said to exchange or pass *information, messages, thoughts, feelings*, or *meaning*.[42] For at least two reasons, this kind of

---

[42] According to *Collins English dictionary* (Hanks, 1986), communication is "the imparting or exchange of information, ideas, or feelings," whereas in the words of *Encyclopedia Britannica* (1998), it is "the exchange of meanings between individuals through a common system of symbols." The language of discrete movable entities corroborates Reddy's claim about the traditional discourses on communication as being driven by the "metaphor of conduit." Taking this approach, one tacitly assumes that communicating consists in transferring reified elements of human experience from one person to another. Accordingly, all one needs to do if one wishes to monitor the effectiveness of communication is to ascertain the meanings transmitted in the process and then check whether the meanings "unloaded" from symbols by a recipient are the same as those left there by a "sender." However, as in so many other cases of objectification discussed before, a researcher who follows this kind of metaphor will, sooner or later, reach a dead end: This researcher's strong sense of the existence of "things" called *information, meaning*, or *idea* cannot be matched by her ability actually to get hold of these entities and to demonstrate their invariance across contexts and interlocutors.

Even a superficial glimpse at definitions of communication adopted by communication theorists reveals similar problems. Two most widely applied models, called *code model* (Shannon & Weaver, 1949) and *interaction model* (Grice, 1975), perpetuate the same folk vision of communication as transferring entities. Dan Sperber and Deirdre Wilson describe these two models as follows:

According to the code model, a communicator encodes her intended message into a signal, which is decoded by the audience using an identical copy of the code. According to the inferential model, a communicator provides evidence of her intention to convey a certain meaning, which is inferred by the audience on the basis of the evidence provided. (emphases added; Sperber & Wilson, 1995, quoted in Horn & Ward, 2004, p. 607)

Indeed, by using terms such as *message, intention*, or *meaning*, both models build on the conduit metaphor, and they differ from one another only in the names they give to the "traveling" entities and in their respective visions of the transfer mechanism.

The inference model originated in the influential ideas of Paul Grice, who proposed to define communication as an activity of making the recipients act according to the speaker's intentions. Grice explained: " '[S] meant something by x' is (roughly) equivalent to '[S] intended the utterance of x to produce some effect in an audience by means of the recognition of this intention'" (Grice 1957, p. 58, quoted in Sperber & Wilson, 1995, p. 21).

The use of the term *intention* was supposed to help in getting around the problematic term *meaning*, but it was later criticized as being no less troublesome than the original. Like

description is inappropriate for our purpose. First, together with the metaphor of object clearly underlying the idea of communication as the activity of passing or transmitting arrive all the risks and pitfalls of this metaphor. Above all, the definition remains nonoperational as long as the entities to be passed – message, thought, feeling, meaning – are not, themselves, operationally defined. Second, the pair of communicating individuals is implied to constitute a closed system, whose activity depends on just these two actors. This stubbornly individualist, acquisitionist slant of the traditional definitions is rather striking, considering the fact that the communal nature of communication is implied in its very name. The individualistic definition cannot possibly do justice to the mechanisms that make communication possible. In most cases, it is difficult, if not utterly impossible, to understand uniquely human actions of individuals – and the actions of communicating are certainly among those – without considering the *collective* activity of which they are a part. That is, some recurrent individual ways of acting acquire their meaningfulness and effectiveness via patterns visible only at the collective level. In this global outlook, the collective is an intricate network, whereas the moves of its individual "nodes" – the members of the collective – are a part of the network's general dynamic. Metaphorically speaking, attempts to make sense of regularities in human forms of doing by focusing on an individual doer are as hopeless as trying to make sense of a football game by recording, and then analyzing, a movement of a single player.

In the present search after a definition of communication we may thus try to take one of the two directions: we may seek an operationalization of the auxiliary notions such as message or meaning, or we may adopt

---

meaning, the term *intention* was difficult to operationalize. Pragmatists, the theorists of communication who have been continuing Grice's tradition but were evidently more mindful of the metaphor of object, proposed reformulation of the inferential definition that, on the face of it, made the problematic entities disappear: "Communication consists of the 'sender' ... getting the 'receiver' to recognize that the 'sender' is trying to cause that thought or action" (Levinson, 1983, p. 16). Even if with some charity this latter definition could be regarded as objectification-free (of which I am not entirely sure, because "the sender is trying to cause that thought or action" is likely to be translated by most people into "the sender has an intention"), its nonparticipationist character is a reason why one should not trust it too readily. By presenting communication as an isolated occurrence between two individuals, such a description may be read as referring to contingent interactions in which the expected reaction is attained in an ad hoc manner. To put it differently, nothing in this description reflects the fact that specific individual interactions are communicatively effective only because they constitute a pattern *when taken together* (that is, the "carrier" of the pattern is not an individual action but the *network* of actions).

the collective perspective and describe communication as an activity of a multiagent system. The first of these two options seems inadmissible for at least two independent reasons. First, message and meaning are insiders' ideas: that is, these are notions used by communicating individuals with reference to their communicational experiences. To operationalize these notions with the help of public criteria so as to make them investigable also by an outside observer would require the use of communication as the primary concept (this is, indeed, what Wittgenstein did when he defined the meaning of a word as the use of the word in language). Second, it is difficult to keep the inherently collective nature of communication in the foreground while focusing on a single pair of communicating individuals.

We seem to have no choice but to follow the second option, that is, to describe communication as an activity of a collective. One special feature of this type of definition is that it makes reference to phenomena that are noticeable only at the level of the collective as a whole and become invisible when the focus shifts to individuals. Adopting a collective outlook means taking an outsider's perspective – the perspective of somebody who has never been exposed to human communication. We may pretend that we are trying to describe communication taking a vantage point of an alien watching the human inhabitants of Earth from another planet, but through a telescope powerful enough to observe actions of individuals. The alien observer cannot possibly see any "meanings" or "information" passed from one person to another. It is reasonable to assume, however, that he can distinguish between communicational activities and all the others. Indeed, the alien creature is likely to notice that some recurrent actions of individuals, for example, gestures, facial expressions, or sounds accompanying jaw movements, are followed, as a rule, by actions, possibly of the same type, of other individuals; and that the manner in which the action and re-actions are coupled does display certain distinct regularities when watched over time across different situations and among different individuals. This vision is in tune with the claim that communication is "the glue that holds communities together." For the participation-minded theorist, the community-coordinating role of communication is its primary, defining feature. Let me thus propose the following definition.

Definition: *Communication* is a collectively performed patterned activity in which action A of an individual is followed by action B of another individual so that

1. A belongs to a certain well-defined repertoire of actions known as communicational

2. Action B belongs to a repertoire of re-actions that fit A, that is, actions recurrently observed in conjunction with A. This latter repertoire is not exclusively a function of A, and it depends, among others, on factors such as the history of A (what happened prior to A), the situation in which A and B are performed, and the identities of the actor and re-actor.

To elaborate, individuals who participate in the activity of communicating perform actions that are customarily followed by a certain type of re-action of other individuals. The re-actions may, themselves, be communicational or noncommunicational, that is, may belong to the repertoire of communicational actions or not (in traditional language, this latter case can be presented as a case of action that is not received by the members of the collective as *signifying*). Indeed, the re-action can be a *practical action* – an action resulting in a physical change in objects in an environment (and the term *object* includes the actors themselves!). Opening a window or adding a brick to a wall when building a house is a good example of practical action. In human activities, communicational actions mediate practical actions, and both types of actions are usually simultaneously present and inextricably interwoven. Clearly, communication is what enables interpersonal coordination needed for the collective implementation of complex practically oriented activities, from preparing foods and garments to building houses, publishing newspapers, producing films, transporting goods, and so forth. This said, let me add that it is also typical of humans to have purely communicational interactions, in which every re-action is, in itself, a communicational action bound to entail yet another communicational (re-)action. In this process, the participants alternate between the roles of actors and re-actors, often playing both these parts in one communicational act.

The adjective *patterned*, appearing in the definition, refers to the fact that in the activity of communication, the actions and re-actions seem to be matched one with another in a nonaccidental, repetitive way. In other words, for each communicative action only certain types of re-actions can be observed. Furthermore, the overall repertoire of communicational actions would often constitute a *system*, in that different sets of such actions can be combined in a rule-governed way to create new communicational actions. As stated earlier, this patterned, systematic, generative nature of communication is something that can be seen only when the communicating collective is considered in its entirety. Another fact to remember is that the communicational patterns, and thus the rules of communication, are not in any sense "natural" or necessary, as nothing "in the world" can possibly necessitate the given types of associations between action and re-action. The source of the patterns lies in *historically established customs*. In other words, what makes communication possible is the fact that the community *got into a habit* of reacting to certain actions with certain types of re-actions. Indeed, an action acquires a communicational function only when it becomes associated with certain situations and re-actions, not because of its inherent properties. This contingent nature of communicational patterns may be the reason why Wittgenstein chose to speak about communication as a kind of *game*.[43]

The participationist definition of communication is probably liberal enough in its requirements to include certain types of nonhuman interactions. From now on, however, let me focus on human communication. A number of characteristic properties and communication-related phenomena are worth mentioning in this context. While reading the following list of features, keep in mind that they pertain also to thinking – the individualized form of communication – and that we could, in fact, replace the word *communication* with the term *commognition* all along.

Agency of the Participant

Because of its patterned nature and of the participants' custom-engendered commitment to participation, communication may appear as a highly constraining activity. Indeed, communication has dynamics of its own, and it reflects the human tendency for alignment. The idea of our being constrained in communicational choices has been aptly captured by Benjamin Whorf, who claimed that we communicate the way we do

> largely because we are parties to an agreement . . . that holds throughout our speech community and is codified in the patterns of our language. The agreement is, of course, an implicit and unstated one, BUT ITS TERMS ARE ABSOLUTELY OBLIGATORY.[44]

This said, it is equally important to stress that in communication, as in any other historically established activity, human players do have agency. Communicative action almost never determines a re-action. More often than not, both action and re-action are a matter of construction, to be performed according to rules that constrain but do not dictate. In other words,

---

[43] More precisely, Wittgenstein spoke about *language games* (Wittgenstein, 1953/2003). The metaphor of game, however, is clearly applicable also to nonverbal forms of communication.

[44] Whorf (1940, pp. 213–214) (emphasis in the original).

the rules do not specify a concrete action but rather a class (type) of action. For instance, the request "to do something about the noise in the room" may be responded to by shutting the window rather than the door, by asking the children in the yard to lower their voices, or even by explicitly refusing to do anything. The person greeted with "Good morning" may respond with "Good morning to you, too"; with the simple "Hi"; or with a silent gesture, all equally acceptable in this context. Finally, the student who was asked to solve a mathematical problem may propose many different solutions, all of them communicationally appropriate even if mathematically faulty. Clearly, participants' agency to choose and to change is highly relevant to one of the basic questions that gave rise to the commognitive discourse on thinking: What is it that brings about the incessant transformations in human ways of doing? What is it that allows for the constant accumulation of complexity of human action both within the confines of the individual life span and in the course of history?

Objects of Communication

Whereas practical actions are direct actions *on* objects, communicational actions are *about* objects; that is, they may *lead to* an action on an object or to another communicative action about an object.[45] In any case, *the object of a communicational act* is a thing to which the actor drives the re-actor's attention. Thus, when a person is asked to perform the practical action of closing a window, one may say that the object of exchange is (or that the exchange is *about*) the window: The actor does not perform any physical action on the window, but the re-action to her request will be deemed proper if it is an action related to the window. Similarly, when an actor

---

[45] Note the recursive nature of the definition of the relation of *aboutness*: Communicational action is *about* object O if it leads to a practical action on O or, if not, it leads to a communicational action *about* O. The assumption that this recursive sequence is always finite may be an object of controversy. Indeed, such controversy lies at the very heart of the current semiotics, and its resolution depends, to a great extent, on what is meant by *object*. I will return to this issue in chapter 6, while discussing the specific case of mathematical communication. For now it is enough to say that in human linguistic communication, the distinction between practical and communicational action is often blurred, in that communicational action about *discursive* objects may also count as practical actions on these objects. The term *discursive object* is yet to be explained (as is done in chapter 5), but just to illustrate the dual practical–communicational nature of some utterances note that if one regards numbers as objects, the sentence "3 plus 2 equals 5" may count as a practical action on such objects.

states a property of a function, this function is the object of the communicative interaction. Sometimes, deciding about the object of exchange is not a straightforward matter. The same communicational action may refer different interlocutors to different objects. Consider, for example, the case of Ari's asking Gur to look at a "zero": "you see how many is in between each, like from *zero* to what" ([13], Episode 1.3, emphasis added). Three communicational turns later it becomes clear that this utterance did not direct Gur's attention to the same object as the one Ari was looking at (see Gur's "Oh *that* zero" in [16]). Difficulties such as these notwithstanding, the idea of *object-of-communication* is an important one, and, as should be clear from our discussion so far, it is of particular significance when it comes to communication between researchers at large, and between mathematicians in particular.

Communication Mediators

Communication mediators are perceptually accessible objects with the help of which the actor performs her prompting action and the re-actor is being prompted. Mediators can have auditory, visual, or even tactile effects on individuals. Although any material object can be adapted to serve in this communicational role, communicational mediators are often artifacts produced specially for the sake of communication (the term *symbol* is often used with reference to those). More often than not, mediators create a system in the sense that these are their intricate interrelationships and the ways in which they combine one with another in every communicational interaction that let them fulfill their role effectively. In humans, linguistic exchange, which may be vocal or visual (as in the case of written exchanges), is the principal form of communication. An important advantage of linguistic communication is that it can be held at a distance, without direct physical contact between interlocutors. Many other forms of mediation, especially those that are available these days thanks to the development of wireless technology, allow for real-time interaction even if the interlocutors are thousands of miles distant from each other.

Discourses as Types of Commognition

Just as there are a multitude of games, played with different tools and according to different rules, so there are many types of communication, differing one from another in their objects, in the types of mediators used, and in the rules followed by participants. As in the case of games, individuals may be able to participate in certain types of communicational activity and be unable to take part in some others.

> **Definition**: The different types of communication, and thus of commognition, that draw some individuals together while excluding some others will be called *discourses*.

Given this definition, any human society may be divided into partially overlapping *communities of discourse*.[46] To be members of the same community of discourse, individuals do not have to face one another. The membership in the wider community of discourse is won through participation in communicational activities of any collective that practices this discourse, however small this collective may be. Of course, the boundaries of either discourses themselves or discourse communities are not as clear-cut as my descriptions may suggest; nor are discourses stable entities that remain the same in their important features over time. Still, human ways of communicating are often distinct enough to justify talking about discourses and their communities as reasonably well-delineated wholes.

While looking for examples to illustrate the preceding definitions, I recalled my own use of the terms *discourse about thinking* and *research discourse* throughout this book. Indeed, researchers dealing with a given topic and communicating with one another clearly constitute a community of discourse. In the next chapter, I speak about different academic disciplines, with mathematics among them, as distinct forms of discourse. While doing so, I specify the properties of communication that are to be attended to when one tries to distinguish one discourse from another.

5. Thinking as Communicating – in a Nutshell

In this chapter, human thinking was defined as an individualized form of (interpersonal) communication. Whether we take a historical or a single-life-span perspective, thinking can now be thought of as the type of human doing that emerges when individuals become capable of communicating with themselves the way they communicate with others. To stress the developmental unity of the processes of thinking and communicating, it was

---

[46] The idea of discourse as the communicative activity typical of a certain community is closely related to several other notions that can be found in the literature on discourses. See, e.g., *discursive formation* (Foucault, 1972); *Discourse-with-the-capital-D* (Gee, 1997); *genre* (Bakhtin, 1986; Lemke, 1993); and *register* (Halliday, 1978; Halliday & Martin, 1993).

proposed to refer to them both with the common name *commognition*. Let me briefly recapitulate the chain of reasoning that led to these ideas.

Our journey toward commognition began when we realized that the extensive objectification of discourses on thinking may be the principal reason for numerous time-honored dilemmas and controversies. The present chapter has been devoted to the question of whether and how the discourse on thinking can be *disobjectified*.

As long as one subscribes to the inherently *monological* discourses of traditional psychology, whose narratives present themselves as if they were told by nature itself, one is unlikely to deal effectively with the unhelpful metaphor of object. It takes a *dialogical* approach, one that recognizes the discursive nature of any research, to realize that some of the objects that populate our talk about thinking are but discursive constructs and, as such, may be removed or redefined. Wittgenstein, who may be regarded as one of the founders of dialogism, insisted that there is no need to refer to "intangibles" and "invisibles" when trying to account for human actions. For all their complexity, human forms of doing lie open to public inspection and thus belong to the category of "communicables." While stating this, Wittgenstein dissolved the time-honored dichotomy between thinking and behaving, two processes that, so far, have been regarded as ontologically distinct.

Taking advantage of Wittgenstein's insights, the students of human thinking may now be able to follow Vygotsky's call for putting an end to research that features "mind without behavior" or "behavior without mind."[47] The current discourses replace the metaphor of *learning-as-acquisition* with the metaphor of *learning-as-participation*. In participationist narratives, individual and collective forms of doing are presented as different manifestations of the same type of processes. Within this perspective, the historical change in forms of human doing becomes fully accountable. It now seems not unreasonable to assume that patterned, collective forms of distinctly human activities are developmentally prior to the activities of the individual. Thinking, although seemingly inherently private, should not be any different. Cognitive processes may thus be defined as individualized forms of interpersonal communication, whereas communication itself is described as a collectively performed rule-driven activity that mediates and coordinates other activities of actors. The term *commognition* was coined to encompass thinking and (interpersonal) communicating and to stress the unity of these two types of processes.

[47] Vygotsky (1982, p. 81), quoted in Minick (1987, p. 19).

More specifically, communication was defined as a patterned collective activity that involves a repertoire of permissible (communicational) actions of individual members and, for each such action, a repertoire of permissible re-actions of other individuals. Human communicational actions have several distinct characteristics: In spite of their being rule driven, they are also a function of actors' voluntary decisions; they are implemented with the help of designated perceptual mediators; and they are often *about* a certain *object*. Different types of communication, set apart by their objects, the kinds of mediators used, and the rules followed by participants and thus defining different communities of communicating actors, were called *discourses*.

To complete the answer to the question of historical change we now need to identify those properties of human communication that make the accumulation of complexity possible. In the next chapter, the case will be made for the claim that *language* may be the key to the mystery.

4 Thinking in Language

Without speech man would have no reason and no reason is possible without speech.

Johann Gottfried von Herder[1]

[Development of mathematics is] enlargement of the mathematician's self-consciousness ... a long, difficult, and extended exercise in which the human mind attempts to catch sight of itself catching sight of itself, and so without end.

David Berlinski[2]

In the last chapter, while defining thinking as individualized communication, I was careful to stress that all forms of communication need to be considered, not just verbal. Such an all-inclusive approach was necessary to ensure that the resulting definition of thinking does not leave out some of the phenomena that are commonly regarded as cases of thinking. This said, it is now time to give linguistic communication the attention it certainly deserves. This chapter is devoted to the conjecture that linguistic commognition is the primary source of perhaps the most human of our distinctively human properties: of our propensity for accumulation of complexity. More specifically, I will be arguing that this special human ability, along with many others, originates in our ability to "turn discourse on itself," that is, to *communicate about communication*. This realization will eventually make me claim that what is traditionally called human development may now be considered as almost tantamount to the development of discourses.

[1] Herder (1771/1967, V, p. 40); quoted in Marková (2003, p. 67).
[2] Berlinski (2005, p. 105).

Before addressing any of these all-important issues, however, let me take a closer look at the historical debate about relations between thinking and one particular form of communication called – *speech*.

1. The Dilemma of Relation between Thinking and Speaking

The question whether human thinking can be equated with "inner speech" has been stirring one of the most persistent and encompassing debates in the history of thinking about thinking. Generations of philosophers puzzled on queries such as *What is the place of natural language in human cognition and thought?*[3] or *Are there minds without language?*[4] The pervasive lack of resolution is hardly surprising, considering these questions' inherent blurriness. Only too often, the authors would not say explicitly, let alone operationally, what they have in mind while speaking about *thinking*, and this would make their questions inherently unanswerable. Indeed, with the meaning of the word *thinking* taken for granted, the question *Is there thinking without speech?* appears to be about facts and, as such, is interpreted as requiring an empirical answer. At the same time, the absence of an operational definition precludes the possibility of a sound empirical study. This logical entanglement is a reliable prescription for insoluble disagreements.

The situation may be further complicated by the fact that the queries are inherently ambiguous. The question *Is there thinking without language?* can be interpreted in at least two ways:

1. As the question of *extent*: Is there thinking that does not involve speech at all?
2. As the question of *separateness*: Are thinking and talking two separate processes? Is speech only the icing on the cake, and the real thing – the cake – an independent process, somehow primary to the talking? In this context, *independent* means that the same thought process could lead to different formulations, that is, thought is a "pure essence" that can be given different forms. If so, how can we get hold of this essence bypassing language?

Figure 4.1 presents these two queries more explicitly and shows their possible answers in a symbolic manner. It was rarely spelled out which of the two issues – that of separateness or that of relative extent – was meant by the inquirers. In addition, nobody would say explicitly which types of

[3] Carruthers and Boucher (1998, p. 1).
[4] Dennett (1996, p. 12).

Questions about relations between thinking and speech

Q1 (*Separateness*): Are thinking and speaking two distinct processes all along the way; that is, is there a separate process of thinking that runs in parallel to speaking even when the latter process is inner?

Q2 (*Extent*): Is there thinking that does not involve speech at all?

Possible answers

	1 The same extent — Speaking and thinking are always concomitant	2 Different extent	
		a. There is thinking without speaking but no speaking without thinking	b. There are thinking without speaking and speaking without thinking
1 dualist — Thinking and speaking are separate processes	1.1 — Thinking and speaking, although not the same, always run in parallel	1.2a	1.2b
2 nondualist — Whenever there are both speaking and thinking, they coincide (are the same process)	2.1 — Thinking and speaking are exactly the same – a single process	2.2a	2.2b

The striped bar — represents the process of *speaking* (either external or internal).

The shaded bar — represents the process of *thinking*.

The horizontal dimension represents time; points located on the same vertical line are concomitant.

Figure 4.1. Two questions on the relations between thinking and speaking and their possible answers.

phenomena counted for her or him as included in the category of thinking. As a result, what was intended as a response to the query of extent was only too likely to be mistaken as answering the question of separateness, and vice versa.

Trying to survey this inherently problematic field is thus not an easy task. Let me begin with a very brief review of theories that can be interpreted as answers to the question of *separateness*. These answers range from the doctrine of speech–thought duality to the claim on their inseparability. According to the first of these doctrines, thought and language are separate, although related and often concomitant, types of human activity, with language playing an auxiliary role of a tool for expressing thought (see cells 1.1 and 1.2 in the table in Figure 4.1). This position became known as the *expressionist*[5] or *communicative*[6] vision of what language is all about. The roots of this doctrine go back to the philosopher John Locke and the empiricist idea of human learning as the process of registering one's experience-of-the-world on the originally blank slate of her mind. The expressionist vision of the role of language entails that thought must be storable and processable in one's mind in forms other than publicly communicable linguistic expressions. This leads to the notion of *language of thought*, that is, to the idea of an inner, possibly autonomous symbolic system in which thoughts are processed. It is the result of this processing that is made public in the form of speech.[7] This idea is compatible with the vision of human communication as involving back-and-forth transformations of thoughts from one type of code to another (e.g., from "internal" to "external" – from the language of thought to a public language, such as English).[8] According to this model, a "message" or a "thought" may remain unchanged while acquiring different "verbal expressions." The language-of-thought doctrine, usually combined with the conviction about its innateness, implies that a distinctly human

---

[5] Christopher Gauker, *Language and thought*, http://host.uniroma3.it/progetti/kant/field/lat.htm.

[6] Carruthers and Boucher (1998, p. 1).

[7] The current version of this thesis, the idea of a *genetically determined* autonomous brain mechanism of which speech is an optional, separable (in that you can express "the same thought" in different words), higher-level expression, has been professed by the linguists Noam Chomsky (1957), Jerry Fodor (1975, 1983) and Steven Pinker (1994, 2003), among others. The group revives the idea of a "language of thought," the "universal mentalese" (Pinker, 1994, p. 82), which is claimed to be the same, or almost the same, for all people, regardless of the language they speak. Proponents of the thesis believe that their claim is empirically testable and that it will eventually be corroborated by evidence from brain research.

[8] Shannon and Weaver (1949) and Sperber and Wilson (1995, p. 4).

form of thinking would also be possible in a person who was separated from his parents at the day of his birth and grew up away from other people. Clearly, this thesis of the "Tarzan's [or Mowgli's[9]] thoughtfulness" goes directly against the basic participationist assumption about developmental primacy of collective forms of doing.

Wittgenstein's rebuttal of the very possibility of "distilling" thinking from speaking marks the other end of the spectrum in the thought–language separateness debate (see slots 2.1, 2.2 in Figure 4.1). Wittgenstein's critical philosophy goes hand in hand with psychological approaches that deny the primacy of thought over speech and reject the idea that there is an independent act of thinking underlying any act of speech. In other words, Wittgenstein rejects the idea of "pure thought" that can be given different linguistic (or nonlinguistic, for that matter) expressions while remaining basically "the same." Note that the statement that thought cannot be separated from speech answers the separateness query but does not yet define one's stance on the issue of extent. The claim about the unity of thought and speech does not imply that *all* thinking is verbal (thus, it admits all variants presented in row 2 of Figure 4.1). It only means that any speech act is, in itself, an act of thinking. This position found another expression in the work of Vygotsky, who supported his thesis with a suggestive metaphor: According to him, studying thinking by attending to words and thoughts as if they were separate entities would be like trying to find out the properties of water by looking at those of hydrogen and oxygen.[10] Subsequently, Vygotsky claimed that the dichotomizing vision was the reason for the unsatisfactory state of psychological research:

> The futility of most of the earlier investigations was largely due to the assumption that thought and word were isolated, independent elements, and verbal thought the fruit of their external union.[11]

This conviction originated in Vygotsky's famous debate with Piaget regarding a phenomenon known as *egocentric speech*. The fact that there is a period in every child's life when he or she frequently speaks aloud without addressing anybody in particular (this phenomenon is known as "speaking to oneself") inspired Vygotsky to conjecture that interpersonal speech precedes linguistic self-communication, a thesis that is clearly in tune with his general belief in the developmental priority of the collective over individual

[9] Kipling (1894).
[10] Vygotsky (1987, p. 45).
[11] Vygotsky (1986, p. 211).

forms of human activities.[12] It also resonates with Wittgenstein's claim that the idea of "private language" – the language a person develops on her own and for her own internal use – is untenable, as it contradicts the defining property of language as a means of social coordination. Vygotsky was also quite explicit in answering the query of extent: He was careful to stress that his rejection of the possibility of distilling thought from speech did not mean he identified thinking with "inner speech." He viewed thinking and speaking as having separate "genetic roots" and as remaining separate until the child learns a language. Later, when both interpersonal and intrapersonal communication begin to occur mainly in language, there is no point in talking about separate processes of "producing" and "expressing" thought. Vygotsky's standpoint thus belongs to the category 2.2b in Figure 4.1.

An interesting and significant event in the history of the language–thought debate was the formulation of the famous but inherently ambiguous Sapir–Whorf hypothesis:

> We see and hear . . . very largely as we do because the language habits of our community predispose certain choices of interpretation.[13]
>
> We dissect nature along lines laid down by our native languages. The categories and types that we isolate from the world of phenomena we do not find there because they stare every observer in the face; on the contrary, the world is presented in a kaleidoscopic flux of impressions which has to be organized by our minds and this means largely by the linguistic systems in our minds.[14]

Although neither of these excerpts mentions thinking directly, many interpret these statements as an expression of Sapir and Whorf's stance on the issue of relations between thought and language. The way the interpreters construe this stance depends on their own answer to the query of separateness. Those who assume a dualist position read the preceding quotes as saying that language shapes thought. In this case, the innovative aspect of the hypothesis is that it adds the dimension of reflexivity to the phenomenon that, so far, has been considered as having just one direction: Molding influences are now said to be moving not only from thought to language, but also the other way around. This thesis has been

---

[12] More specifically, Vygotsky (1978) viewed egocentric speech as an intermediate stage in the development of the "inner speech" – as a stage that follows the act of turning interpersonal talk into self-communication and precedes the process of transforming this latter kind of speech into silent and internal.

[13] Sapir (1949, p. 162).

[14] Whorf (1940, p. 213).

widely criticized on the basis of its having insufficient empirical evidence. Results of numerous studies that tried to find out whether people who speak different languages think differently have been criticized as inconclusive.[15] At a closer look, the argument seems to be flawed. In the absence of an operational definition of thinking, the very attempt to ground one's cause in empirical data appears logically untenable.

For those who hold a nondualist vision of verbal thought, the meaning of the Sapir–Whorf hypothesis is different. On the basis of the assumption that there is no point in talking about an independent process of thinking *underlying* one's speech, this conjecture can be reformulated as follows: Different languages partition the world in different ways, and thus discourses in one language may sometimes be not fully "isomorphic" with discourses in another. Indeed, differences in the ways of dissecting the world with words mean different *interrelations* between words, and this difference inevitably entails different discursive *routines* and perhaps even incompatible statements about the world. This implies that seemingly equivalent discourses (e.g., colloquial discourses about numbers) in, say Korean and English, may be somewhat dissimilar in their inner structures. Furthermore, because discourses impinge on all the other human activities, the speakers of different languages are also likely to differ in the way they do things or interact one with another. A commognitive definition of thinking allows one to translate this latter interpretation back into the statement "Language molds thinking (discourse)" (note the use of the verb *mold* rather than *determine*!) and makes this simple rendering empirically verifiable: To test how languages mold thinking one needs to check how a change in language, say from Hebrew to English, alters the structure of a discourse. This empirical study, however, would be quite unlike the one implied by the dualist interpretation of the Sapir–Whorf hypothesis. As will be discussed in detail on the following pages, discourses may differ in many aspects, and not just (not even necessarily) in the factual claims that they produce. Therefore, the term *empirical study* refers, this time, to multidimensional comparative analysis of discourses.[16]

The commognitive definition of thinking is not unlike the one given by Vygotsky: Thinking, when it occurs in a linguistic form, cannot be separated from language. This said, thinking encompasses more than just

---

[15] See, e.g., Pullum (1991).

[16] Some of the empirical studies done in the past may, in fact, be interpreted as testing this version of the hypothesis. Thus, for example, Lucy and Shweder's color memory test (1979) has shown that color recognition memory depends on color terms in the language in which a person thinks. See also Lucy (1997).

inner speech. Similarly to the nonseparatist version of the Sapir–Whorf hypothesis, this approach implies that human commognitive routines may be sensitive to linguistic idiosyncrasies and that both commognitive and practical activities may reflect the structure imposed on the world by our vocabularies.

2. Commognizing in Language

Having offered the commognitive stance with regard to the time-honored matter of the relation between thinking and speech, I am now ready to promote the thesis that linguistic communication is the primary source of human uniqueness. Having criticized past doctrines about thinking and language for the pervasive lack of clarity with respect to their pivotal notions, I am obliged to begin with clarification about what is meant here by *language*.

More specifically, what type of commognition-mediating symbolic systems should usefully be called *language* and what are the special characteristics of those among these systems that are used by humans? The term *language* can be defined in a number of ways, with the different definitions varying in their scope and emphases. Thus, according to *Encyclopedia Britannica*, language is a *"system of conventional spoken or written symbols used by people in a shared culture to communicate with each other."*[17] This definition presents language as a uniquely human phenomenon and in this sense it is quite restrictive.[18] From another point of view, however, it is fairly encompassing, as it includes in the category of languages any symbolic system, regardless of the nature and complexity of its inner relations. The definition that will guide me in this book is somewhat different.

> **Definition**: A *language* is a system, used for communication, comprising a finite set of arbitrary symbols and a set of rules (or grammar) by which the manipulation of these symbols is governed.[19]

The first advantage of this definition is that it does not attempt to limit language to humans. This said, it does provide a criterion for setting languages apart from more primitive forms of mediating systems. The distinctive property of languages is their *generativity*: Elements of the system

---

[17] Retrieved from http://www.britannica.com/search?ct=gen1andquery=language.

[18] Some writers do believe that we should reserve the term *language* for humans; the semiotician Thomas Sebeok is one of the most prominent of them. In one of his recent publications he stated explicitly that "'language' should be used only in a technical sense, in application to humans" (Sebeok, 2001, p. 14). In this book I take a less restrictive stance.

[19] Retrieved from http://en.wikipedia.org/wiki/Language.

must be combinable into more complex elements of the same system. More specifically, to be called language, the system must have a set of rules, called *syntax*, with the help of which complex communicational acts can be constructed out of simpler ones. The most remarkable feature of thus defined languages is that the user does not need to learn all possible communicational actions separately, one after another. The interlocutors will be able to create their own utterances, and, if properly constructed, these utterances will be communicationally effective even if the addressees have never encountered them before. Let me remark that the term *utterance* is used here in the broad sense of a communicational act in language, and it will thus include written communicational acts along with the spoken ones. The linguistic constructs produced throughout utterances will be called *propositions* or *sentences* (the utterance itself is an action, whereas a proposition or sentence is a durable, recordable product of such action).

Given this definition, it is no longer assumed that language is an exclusively human property. As has been known for a long time now, many nonhuman animals can communicate, that is, can make use of symbolic means while trying to coordinate their actions. In addition, recent findings indicate that in certain cases, simple symbolic systems used by nonhuman animals possess basic forms of syntax.[20] One can thus speak also about nonhuman languages. Still, according to some other empirical studies, languages used by people do have at least one feature that cannot be found elsewhere: The syntax of these languages has the potential to produce an infinity of legitimate, increasingly complex utterances.

The unlimited power to generate ever new linguistic constructs is due to our ability to construct and parse linguistic expressions in the *recursive* way, which has been claimed to be unique to humans.[21] Even more importantly,

---

[20] See, for example, Fouts (1998); Hauser, Chomsky, and Fitch (2002).

[21] Recursion is the feature thanks to which a legitimate linguistic construct may give rise to a new, more complex one, provided we replace some of its simple elements, e.g., the noun that constitutes its subject or its object, with a more complex linguistic construct, in the present context a noun clause. Thus, for example, we may expand the sentence "John loves Mary" into "The boy who teased all the girls in the class loves the girl who never let him tease her."

And here is the way the recursive parsing works. When one tries to understand a composite utterance such as the one described, rather than following the elements of a composite utterance in a straightforward linear manner, one has to identify the ingredients similar in their inner structure to the original construct, albeit not equally complex (clauses). These simpler modules must then be processed in the same manner. The cycles of decomposition repeat themselves until the atomic, nondecomposable (one-word) level is attained. Recursion, therefore, is a process in which we repeatedly suspend the implementation of a complex action in order to perform a simpler edition of this action

verbal discourses are recursively self-referential: Using language, one can talk about anything, including the discourse itself. In other words, we can turn one discursive act into the object of another – to create utterances about utterances, then utterances about these latter utterances, and so forth. Although at first glance the phenomenon of talk-about-talk, and thus the recursivity of the discursive relation of "being about," may appear rather marginal, a closer scrutiny would disclose its presence in almost any linguistic act. To use the most obvious examples of communicating-on-communicating, let me mention those utterances in which one reports on what somebody else has said, remarks on her own thoughts, or reflects on other interlocutors and their communicative actions. The utterances in Table 4.1, collected in a rather random fashion from the brief episodes presented in chapter 1, constitute just a small fraction of utterances-about-utterances that could actually be identified in the transcripts. Yet another example was presented in chapter 2, where I argued that the simple mathematical proposition $3 + 4 = 7$ is, in fact, an utterance about the acts of counting, which, in themselves, are commognitive. It is also notable that an utterance about utterance may become an object of yet another utterance. It is therefore useful to speak about *utterances of different order*. Thus, for example, the sentence "My friend told me that he calls his dog Rexie" is of the third order: The object of the utterance is what my friend told me, which, in itself, is a metautterance in relation to the discursive act of calling his dog a certain name. In this case, we can also speak about the tripartite *chain of references*: (1) my original sentence refers to (is about) *my friend's story*, (2) this story refers to *my friend's discursive action* (of calling his dog a certain name), and (3) that latter action refers to *his dog* (Figure 4.2).

Although many artificial languages, especially those used in computer programming, support recursion, the recursivity of human communication seems to be special in that it is practically *unbounded* and thus supports metautterances of any order (and hence referential chains of any length). Another feature of human communication worth mentioning in the present

---

first. Eventually, we hit the atomic level – the level of utterances that can be interpreted in the immediate manner – and there is no need for further decompositions. We perform the atomic action, then the one whose execution required this atomic action, then the next one in the sequence of suspended actions, etc., until we have returned in our implementations to the level of complexity of the original utterance.

Consonant with this vision of recursion, Hauser et al. (2002) assert that only humans possess the "language faculty" capable of such recursive processing. In this context, they speak about an "internal computational system" (FLN: faculty of language – narrow sense) that underlies linguistic activities of an individual and that, in the case of humans and humans alone, includes recursion as its "core property" (p. 1571).

Table 4.1. *Examples of communication about communication*

Episode	Utterance	What is the utterance about?
I	[6] Mother: Eynat, how do you know?	The tacit (communicational) process Eynat must have performed before she made her last statement
	[21] Mother: ... And what do you think, Eynat?	What Eynat communicates to herself
	[16] Roni: [I think] that this is too many.	What Roni communicates to herself
II	[68] Ron: Can I round the sums up?	Legitimacy of (the communicational act of) replacing one numerical expression with another
	[70] Ron: It makes 15, because I multiplied by 3.	The communicational act of finding a numerical expression (product) equivalent to another numerical expression (multiplication of two numbers)
III	[8] Gur: How'd you get that formula?	The communicational process throughout which the formula was produced (the formula is, in itself, an utterance)
	[7], [9] Ari: It's the formula, so you can figure it out ... and you replace the x by 6.	The communicational process throughout which the formula may be produced
IV	Mira: I do it silently, so that people won't see.	Mira's own communicational action of calculating with fingers
	[53] Talli: I'm not good at multiplication table.	Talli's own communicational activity of replacing multiplicative expressions with equivalent numerical expressions (their products)
V	[5] Teacher: What is the biggest number you can think of?	What Noa communicates to herself about numbers

Shadowed cells contain *discursive constructs* (as opposed to a discourse-independent object)

Figure 4.2. Recursive referential chain within the sentence "My friend told me that he calls his dog Rexie."

context is that it allows for *multilevel* utterances that draw together elements belonging to different levels of communication. Finally, this multilevelness is an elusive, mostly *invisible feature* – the fact that is directly responsible for the phenomenon of ontological collapse.[22] Let me elaborate on these three distinct properties.

The unboundedness of recursion[23] means, among other things, that we can build sentences about sentences about sentences, and so forth, with the length of this recursive chain limited only by the feasibility of the construction process. To see that this is indeed the case, it is enough to consider the simple fact that whatever has been said by an interlocutor can be subsequently reflected and commented on by either the speaker herself or others. For example, while referring to the utterance U made by her interlocutor, a person may say U *is untrue*, or she may draw the conclusion *If U then V*, with V being another self-sustained utterance. In both of these cases, the person is making metastatements, that is, statements about statements (in the symbolic form, let us say these are statements of type $[U]$ or $[U,V]$, with the brackets signaling the category of utterances that have U or U and V as their objects). When one considers the fact that the object of such metautterance may already be a product of many similar recursive cycles (for example, U may be of the type $[[[O]]]$, where O is a set of concrete objects), the claim about the unboundedness of recursion becomes clear. The most important point to remember, however, is that whatever the recursive order of a given utterance, it is always possible to ascend to the next metalevel from which to take an evaluative–interpretive look at what was said or thought before.

In fact, such ascent may be a matter of necessity rather than choice. At any point in time, we seem to be operating simultaneously at two commognitive levels at least. This appears to be true whether we are aware of this fact or not. After all, in order to respond to an utterance U we need to attend to it and evaluate it, and the act of evaluation – one that may result in saying, for example, U *is untrue* – is the act of communicating about U. If U is a complex sentence of a certain recursive depth, then in the course of evaluating (which, in itself, is a commognitive process) we attend to U

---

[22] Just to repeat, ontological collapse, first discussed in chapter 2, is the phenomenon of taking all the objects that are being talked about as belonging to the same ontological category of "things-in-the-world" that preexist discourse, with their mutual relations similarly "objective" and mind-independent.

[23] Some programming languages support recursion. I speculate that of the three features just mentioned, unboundedness of the order of metatalk, multilevelness of utterances, and invisibility of this multilevelness, only the unboundedness is uniquely human. An interesting question is whether this fact could be effectively used in trying to distinguish a human interlocutor from a computer in the way suggested by Turing.

itself – to its elements and their relations – before we attend to the objects
to which U points us.

Let me illustrate this latter claim with an example. Suppose you are
shown a polygon drawn on paper and told *This is not an octagon*. Let us
denote this latter utterance as U. To react to U you need to focus your
attention on U itself before you take a good look at the shape. When you
reflect on U (as you usually do without being aware of this fact, that is,
without climbing to yet another discursive level from which to observe the
process of reflecting!), you realize that it is a metastatement on the simpler
utterance $U' = $ *This is an octagon*. Indeed, U is the negation of U', and you
can now replace it with an equivalent, overtly higher-level statement *The
utterance U' is not true*. This makes it clear that U is about U' (U is of the
type $[U']$), and thus belongs to a higher level than U'. Endowed with this
vision of the utterance U, you may now attend to its extradiscursive object,
that is, to the shape on the paper referred to by the pronoun *this*. What you
see will let you evaluate (that is, decide whether to endorse) the statement
U'[24] and thus also the statement U. Note that to become aware of the fact
that U is a metastatement, you needed to rise to an even higher discursive
level in which to reflect on the reflection on U. This confirms the central
point I am trying to make: The recursivity of the syntax makes our thinking
processes oscillate among numerous discursive levels. The unboundedness
of the recursion stems from the fact that, regardless of the discursive level
of our present commognitive act, we always have the option of ascending
from the current discourse so as to be able to watch this discourse "from
outside."[25]

[24] This evaluation may, in fact, require yet another recursive "detour" before we attend to
the object of U: We may need to recall the definition of octagon, which is a metastatement
on when to use the word *octagon*. Following the definition, we are likely to perform the
discursive routine of counting the sides of the polygon.

[25] At this point, one may object to the claim that, for all this to happen, communication
must occur in language. Please note, however, that the very recursivity of the processes just
described makes them into *linguistic* processes *by definition*: As processes of communication
they are mediated by a certain symbolic system, and because this system has syntax (which
is even recursive), it fulfills the requirements of the definition of language adopted in this
book. Whether the language in which all those "inner" transitions from one recursive
level to another are made is the same language as the one in which we speak or some
special, inborn and universal, "language of thought" is a separate question. There are at
least two arguments that, in my opinion, speak against the language-of-thought doctrine.
First is the issue of continuity of the recursive processes: If there were another language
involved, at which point in our communicating about communicating should it appear?
The second independent argument is, basically, identical to Wittgenstein's claim against
private language, inherent also in my rendering of the strong participationist position.

The examples given suffice to justify the claim about the *multilevelness* of our utterances as well. Consider, for instance, the sentence *I think this is an octagon*, which is, simultaneously, about my commognitive activity (see the words *I think*) and about the figure at which I am pointing. This utterance, therefore, can be interpreted both as an object-level statement about the state of affairs in the world (the nature of the specific geometrical shape) and as a metalevel statement about me and my thinking.

Recursive heterogeneity is not only ubiquitous in human commognition, but is also much greater than was shown in the case just discussed. If we are rarely aware of this fact, it is because of our having recourse to grammatical forms that make the depth of the hierarchy of discursive levels practically invisible. Thus, for example, while trying to convince someone that the sentence *This is not an octagon* is a metasentence, I needed to recast it into *U′ is untrue*, with the *U′* signifying the simpler sentence *This is an octagon*. Within the original rendering, the metadiscursive nature of the sentence was not sufficiently clear. For the same reason, a rather extensive reformulation was necessary before I could show, in chapter 2, that a definition, such as *A triangle is a three-sided polygon* is not an utterance about the state of affairs in the world but rather a statement about our own commognitive activity of using the word *triangle* (as stated before, this last definition is a shorthand for the sentence *We call a polygon a triangle if and only if it has three sides*).

The activity of objectifying is one of the most effective mechanisms for camouflaging discursive levels. As has been shown in chapter 2, for example, the objects implied by our use of nouns mask the fact that the seemingly elementary mathematical propositions, such as $3 + 4 = 7$, are in fact complex statements on our own activity of counting. The use of such recursivity-flattening devices is both advantageous and risky. The gain is immediately obvious: By objectifying, we shorten the long discursive chain and flatten, often quite significantly, the complex multilevel hierarchy of sentences related one to another by the relation of "aboutness." The resulting utterances appear brief, simple, and manageable. But this simplicity does have its price: What is in fact a sentence about a sentence about a sentence, and so forth, appears to be an atomic sentence – an utterance that refers our attention directly to things-in-the-world. Clearly, ontological collapse is the inevitable outcome.[26]

---

[26] For those who feel they need a more rigorous treatment of the difficult issue of recursion and ontological collapse (and who are also convinced that they can live with the technicality and dryness of such treatment!), here is a more formal presentation. Person A tells you

Another source of ontological collapse is the fact that in recursive languages, the role of a sign is inherently ambiguous: Depending on context, a sign may be pointing us to an object that lies beyond the discourse, but it may also become an object of the discourse in its own right. In some cases it may not be easy to tell which of the two possibilities is meant by the speaker. Consider, for example, the sentence *Brahmaputra is long*. The author of this sentence is impressed by the length of the object she is talking about, but it is not clear whether the object is the Asian Brahmaputra River or the word *Brahmaputra* itself. In mathematics, objects and their names are routinely conflated in expressions such as *two-digit number*, in which the property of a symbol (in this case called *numeral*) is ascribed to the putative object signified by this name (the *number*).[27]

The overall message of the preceding analysis is that *the vast majority of human commognitive acts are about other commognitive acts rather than directly about the world*. As will be elaborated in the next section, unless the words we use are proper names signifying specific objects-in-the-world, sentences that feature these words are already a few metalevels above the most elementary level, the level of utterances that arise in immediate reactions to perceptual experiences. The sentence *This is Rexie*, uniquely identifying the dog to which its author is pointing, can serve as a good example of such *atomic* (elementary) utterance. Atomic utterances are the ultimate origins of the hidden chains of metalevels that can be found, at least in theory, in almost any of our utterances (the chain may be so long and complex that the task of recursive "unpacking" may become infeasible). The fact that the majority of our commognitive acts are metastatements of a certain order has been overlooked even by those philosophers and cognitive scientists who, in the attempt to fathom the secret of human thinking, turned to what they called *metacognition* or *thinking-about-thinking*, ideas clearly related to the phenomenon of recursivity.[28] As I will be arguing now, the unbounded

(person B) in an interview, "I am a good student." This statement belongs to the category $_A[A]_B$ (the letter in brackets is the object [person] the utterance speaks about; the left index marks the speaker and the right index the listener). You report, "A is a good student." This latter utterance belongs to the category $_B[A]_C$, with the letter C signifying your listeners. You tend to pass over in silence the fact that it is the student who told you this and that you, in fact, are telling a story of her story, $_B[_A[A]_B]_C$, not her story as such. The same can be said about sentences with even more recursive depth, such as "My teacher told me I am a good student," which belongs to the category $_A[_T[A]_A]_C$ (your subsequent story, which is in fact of the type $_B[_A[_T[A]_A]_C]_D$, is flattened – collapsed – again to just $_B[A]_D$).

27 Such conflation would be rather unlikely in a nonmathematical discourse. Indeed, the everyday counterpart of the sentence *37 is a two-digit number* would be a sentence such as *Mary is a four-letter girl.*

28 The attempts to account for the "uniquely human" with the help of the notion of metacognition (see the survey of these efforts in Clark, 1997) are substantially different from the

recursive depth of our commognitive acts may be exactly what needs to be considered if one wishes to get hold of the origins of human uniqueness.[29]

3. What Are the Properties of Commognition That Recursivity Makes Possible?

Vygotsky, pondering on the consequences of linguistic communication for other forms of human doing, remarked that "the specifically human capacity for language enables children to provide for auxiliary tools in the solution of difficult tasks, to overcome impulsive action, to plan a solution to a problem prior to its execution, and to master their own behavior."[30] The list of language-afforded forms of human actions to be proposed on the following pages is even longer, and all of them are claimed to be dependent on the recursivity of the language.

My present task is to identify those commognitive actions that could not be performed if not for the possibility of taking a discursive "look from outside" at these and other commognitive actions. The question I

present one in that they rest on the dichotomizing vision of cognitive acts and ignore the inherent multilevelness of communication. Indeed, these traditional approaches are predicated on the assumption that all human utterances can be roughly divided into two disjoint sets: the set of object-level utterances and the set of metalevel utterances. This is, clearly, quite a different vision from the one proposed here, according to which every utterance is, in itself, a multilevel structure and thus cannot be uniquely labeled as object-level or metalevel (it can only be said to be at the metalevel *with respect to* a specific other utterance and at the object level *with respect to* yet another one; moreover, the inner recursive structure of specific utterances is not uniquely defined either, and different attempts to specify such structures may lead to different results). As I am arguing in this book, it is this unboundedness of referential chains along which we incessantly "slide" up and down in our commognitive actions that may well be responsible for the human uniqueness. Let me add that the traditional approaches to thinking-about-thinking (or metacognition) are further weakened by their being grounded in yet another traditional dichotomy rejected in my present exposition – the dichotomy between thought and communication. This dichotomy is clearly implied, for example, in the otherwise insightful account by Andy Clark (1997), who admits that "'thinking about thinking' is a good candidate for a distinctively human capacity" and proceeds to the conjecture that "linguistic formulation makes *complex thoughts* available to processes of mental attention" and "enables us to 'stabilize' very *abstract ideas* in working memory" (p. 209, emphases added; note the objectified use of the emphasized nouns).

[29] The idea that the property of recursion constitutes the ultimate source of uniquely human capacities has been implied, although not in the context of communication, by Marvin Minsky (1985), in his *Recursion Principle*: "No society, however large, can overcome every limitation – unless it has some way to reuse the same agents, over and over again, for different purposes" (p. 330); or, as formulated in another place, "When a problem splits into smaller parts, then unless one can apply the mind's full power to each subjob, one's intellect will get dispersed and leave less cleverness for each new task" (p. 161).

[30] Vygotsky (1978, p. 28).

am asking may thus be formulated as follows: *Which of the human com-mognitive capacities depends on our ability to rise to ever higher commognitive levels? Which of them necessarily involve an incessant interplay between utter-ances and utterances-on-former-utterances?* Two important remarks about this query must immediately be added. First, the question is analytical rather than empirical: It requires identifying those of our activities whose defining features locate them in the universe of recursive commognition. In order to justify the claim that an activity belongs to the recursivity-dependent category, one thus needs to show that recursivity is *implied logically* by this activity's defining features. Second, the claim that a commognitive activity requires recursivity automatically implies that this activity is inherently lin-guistic (recursivity has been defined as a property of language!). This leads to an even stronger conclusion: If it is true that recursivity is unique to human languages, then any commognitive activity that requires recursivity may also be seen as uniquely human.

The claims I am now going to make should be read as conjectures, not as firm assertions. Testing these hypotheses requires more work than can be done within the confines of this book. Basically, there are two families of commognitive activities that need to be examined: those related to the commognitive *objects* and those considering commognitive *subjects*. In the present context, the word *subject* refers to the performers of the discursive actions: the thinkers or the speakers. The activities of *reasoning, abstracting,* and *objectifying* belong to the former category. My main hypothesis is that neither of these families would even be conceivable (definable) without the unbounded recursivity of human commognition.[31]

3.1 *Reasoning*

Because reasoning can be described as the art of systematic derivation of utterances from other utterances, its metadiscursive nature is implied in its very definition. In other words, recursion underlies reasoning processes because reasoning, as an activity of exploring relations between sentences, requires going beyond the sentences themselves, to metadiscourse. This observation has many important implications, of which I will mention just two. First, hypothetical thinking, that which refers to what is possible rather than actually present, is a special case of reasoning and as such necessitates

---

[31] Let me explicitly warn against interpreting the conjectures that follow as implying that the unbounded recursivity is *sufficient* for any of these phenomena; all the statements regard *necessary* conditions only.

recursion. In the absence of recursive communication we would be able to talk only about things that we can actually point to – and would thus remain "captives of our visual field."[32] Second, only recursive communication can give rise to discursive exchanges, such as conversations or "flows of thoughts," in which re-actions are new communicative actions. Indeed, such exchanges would not be possible without our being able to monitor relations between utterances, and thus without recursion.

3.2 *Abstracting*

The term *abstracting* is commonly used with reference to the activity of creating concepts that do not refer to tangible, concrete objects. Let me thus begin with clarifying the notion of *concept*. The first question to ask is whether we should tie conceptual thinking uniquely to language. The linguistic option has been favored by many thinkers, notably by Vygotsky, who defined *concept* as a word meaning.[33] I would like to make two amendments. First, let me be less restrictive than Vygotsky and relate the term *concept* to commognition at large, not just verbal commognition. Second, following Wittgenstein's lead, I would substitute Vygotsky's reference to *meaning* with the reference to *use*. Thus, in the discussion that follows, the word *concept* should be understood as follows:

> **Definition**: Concept is *a symbol together with its uses*.

(Here, I am using the word *symbol* as more encompassing than *word*.) More specifically, *conceptual commognition* may be defined as what we encounter whenever a commognitive actor re-acts with *the same word or symbol* to *an entire class of phenomena*. This is the case, for example, when an interlocutor uses the word *cat* for any member of a certain family of four-legged

---

[32] Echoing Köhler, Vygotsky (1978) uses this expression as a description for actors who can only relate to the "here and now" – to what is perceptually accessible. In this context, let me mention the famous studies by Luria conducted in the 1930s in Uzbekistan (Kozulin, 1990). Luria's findings have shown that people who do not have formal education may have difficulty with hypothetical reasoning. For example, they would refuse to answer the question "If all bears in Novaya Zemlya are white, and you meet a bear in Novaya Zemlya, what color is that bear?" saying "We do not speak about what we cannot see." This difficulty may perhaps be seen as indicative of insufficient experience with metatalk.

[33] Vygotsky (1987) states that for him, "word meaning is a unit of analysis" (p. 48), whereas "'unit' is a product of analysis that possesses *all* the basic characteristics of the whole" (p. 46, emphasis in the original). Later, this unit is called *concept*. Vygotsky asks, "Is word meaning speech or thought?" And he answers,"It is both at the same time; it is a *unit of verbal thinking*" (p. 47, emphasis in the original).

long-tailed creatures, as opposed to using specific symbols for each catlike animal that strays into her field of vision. To arrive at such symbolic "saming" of the given set of individuals one needs to perceive them as in some ways similar (as will be empirically illustrated in chapter 6, the main element of this process is learning how to disregard differences). It seems that certain basic categorization of perceptually accessible objects is a natural ability not only in humans, but also in some other species.[34] It is reasonable to assume that this natural, behavioral "saming" of phenomena is a precursor of conceptual commognition.

The concepts considered in the preceding paragraph, such as *cat* or *mouse*, may be called *concrete*, as they arise in reaction to tangible, material objects that exist independently of communication. This is not the case for concepts, which are commonly called *abstract*, such as *number* or *function*. These latter concepts cannot be regarded as a result of categorization of extradiscursive objects according to these objects' perceptual (visual, auditory, olfactory, etc.) similarities. They can, however, be seen as a product of our awareness of certain similarities *in our former commognitive acts*. Indeed, we can speak of conceptual thinking also when one symbol corresponds to a family of discursive actions or products of such actions. One example of thus defined abstracting was presented in chapter 2, where we saw how different families of the processes of counting were unified with single numerical names and symbols. Another example of the activity of abstracting is using the single word *multiplication* for discursive processes as different as repeated addition and finding a part of a quantity. In all such cases, realization of the similarity requires "looking from above" (reflecting) on discursive events in which we participated in the past. The fact that abstracting can only occur within a recursive symbolic system is thus implied by the very definition of this discursive activity.

3.3 *Objectifying*

In light of what has just been said, objectification is a special case of abstracting. As was explained and illustrated in chapter 2, reifying, which is the crucial move in the activity of objectifying, originates in the act of substituting nouns for utterances about *processes*. In the resulting discourse, the reifying nouns are featured as the results of these processes. Being a manipulation on discourse, objectification is, by definition, a result of metathinking.[35]

---

[34] See, e.g., Rosch (1978); Neisser (1987).

[35] Here, and throughout the rest of this chapter, keep in mind that the metathinking (reflection) in question does not have to be conscious; to be conscious, it would have to be

3.4 *Subjectifying*

Subjectifying (which can also be called *identifying*) is a special case of the activity of objectifying, one that occurs when the discursive focus shifts from actions and their objects to the performers of the actions. This is what happens, for instance, when we make the transition from the utterance such as

1. Ludwig writes philosophical books.

to the seemingly equivalent one:

2. Ludwig *is* a philosopher.

In the last example, a sentence about doing was replaced with the reifying sentence about being.[36] The reifying effect follows directly from the particular syntax of the "*is*-sentences," which transform the properties of the subject's actions into properties of the subject himself. Reification is as central to subjectification as it is to any objectification. Its importance lies in the fact that by shifting the focus from actions to the actor it eliminates the dimension of time and creates the sense of permanency of the subject's properties.

Of particular interest is *self-subjectification*, that is, subjectification that occurs when the subject of a reifying utterance is also its author,[37] such as

3. I *am* a bad driver.

or

4. I *have* a gift for mathematics.

Because subjectifying, as any other case of objectification, is an activity that results from reflection on discourses, it can only occur in discourses that have the property of recursivity.[38]

---

assisted by an even higher-level (third-order) commognitive activity, one that reflects on the reflection itself. This third-order commognition, although possible, does not have to be actually used.

[36] In symbolic terms introduced earlier in note 26, we are now interested in sentences of the type $_A[X]_R$, where X is a person, [X] is a sentence about X, and the indexes $_A$ and $_R$ mark the fact that the sentence is authored by the actor A and is directed to the re-actor R.

[37] According to the notation introduced in note 27, we are talking about utterances of the type $_A[A]_R$.

[38] It seems plausible that self-subjectification, or first-person subjectification, is developmentally secondary to third-person subjectification, that is, subjectification of others. Indeed, whereas even the beginning participant of the public discourse is already exposed to the processes of subjectification of others – after all, such processes happen in interpersonal communication all the time – the subjectification of oneself requires self-reference and as such can occur only as a part of the process of individualization of the interpersonal

3.5 *Consciousness*

The theme of subjectifying leads us inevitably to the issue of consciousness, which is often defined as involving "an organism's awareness of its own self and surroundings."[39] It is reasonable to expect that similarly to subjectifying, the phenomenon we call consciousness is a commognitive, recursion-dependent property. This supposition cannot, of course, be either endorsed or rejected without an operational definition of consciousness. The one presented earlier cannot count as such, because its two components, the words *awareness* and *self*, have not been defined. If I nevertheless choose to look at this definition and am not turning to descriptions proposed by other authors, it is because the formulations I was able to find in literature were not entirely free of similar weaknesses.[40] Rather than attempting to do what has been stubbornly resisting concerted efforts of specialists, I will confine myself to the preliminary question whether we should include unbounded recursivity of cognition in the definition of consciousness.[41]

Whether we accept the definition quoted earlier or not, it seems that the term *awareness* is central to any discourse on consciousness. To be *aware* of object *O* means to be able to communicate with oneself about *O*. Being conscious certainly involves awareness of one's own thinking, that is, of one's own commognitive acts. Thus, consciousness involves thinking about thinking – the ability to act intermittently as actor and as assessor of one's own commognitive action. If a person is to be conscious, metalevel discourse must be present simultaneously with any discourse in which this person is engaged. Every commognitive act must be potentially assisted by a monitoring metautterance – by an eye watching it "from outside." To put it metaphorically, our own thinking becomes visible to us thanks to this ever-present (if sometimes dormant!) "outside eye." A mere metacognitive

communication. This claim reverses the developmental order of things promoted in current literature. For example, Michael Tomasello speaks about the "ontogenetic emergence of the uniquely human social-cognitive adaptation for identifying with other persons and so understanding them as intentional agents like the self" (Tomasello, 1999, p. 7). All this is said to be happening around the age of 9 months, which implies that "the sense of self" is primary to viewing others as "intentional agents" and to the ability to actively engage in recursive (linguistic) communication.

[39] Damasio (1999a, p. 4).

[40] See, e.g., Damasio (1999a, 1999b); Dennett (1996); Searle (2002); Sperber and Wilson (1986).

[41] I am asking whether we should regard unbounded recursion as the necessary condition for consciousness. An important question, which I will not tackle here, is whether it should be regarded as sufficient as well. To answer this latter query one needs to check whether the definition that presents consciousness as the process of unboundedly recursive commognizing delineates the same class of phenomena as those to which we refer with the term *consciousness* in an intuitive manner.

capacity, therefore, does not appear to suffice when we speak about consciousness. What seems necessary is an *unbounded* recursivity that makes it always possible to rise to a higher commognitive level. Metaphorically speaking, consciousness requires the presence of unbounded reference chains, only parts of which are highlighted at any given moment, but along which the spotlight of our direct attention can be moved up and down, without restrictions.[42] It seems that of all the features of linguistic commognition, consciousness is the only one that requires the unbounded recursivity in the most genuine way (computers may well be capable of some forms of reasoning and abstracting).

Because recursivity is the property of language, the claim about the recursive sources of consciousness implies that phenomena considered as manifestations of consciousness would not be possible without language.[43] Furthermore, if it is true that consciousness is language dependent, it is also true that it is an inherently social phenomenon, that is, one that emerges as a derivative of collective forms of doing.

As impressive as the preceding list of uniquely human recursion-dependent capabilities already is, there is still one centrally important human capacity that has not been considered: the capacity for the accumulation of change. In the rest of this chapter I argue that the origins of this special property are no different from those of all the others. More specifically, I claim that it is thanks to their recursivity that human discourses gradually grow in complexity and support incessant, accruing transformations in other human activities.

4. Human Development as the Development of Discourses

According to the line of reasoning presented previously, recursive, and thus linguistic, communication underlies practically all those traits that make

---

[42] One can hypothesize that poor functioning of the recursive apparatus would result in different forms of mental handicap. Autism seems a natural candidate for this kind of explanation. One can conjecture that autistic commognition arises when recursion is blocked or when it is "broader than it is deep" (has fewer possible levels, whereas the levels themselves may sometimes be more "spacious," and thus more effective); this would explain autistic people's lowered consciousness (of themselves, of other people), as well as the possible increase in their technical skills, such as computation.

[43] Tying consciousness to language may stir controversy. The question is whether unbounded recursivity can be attained by some "inner" mechanism, not involving languages that serve in interpersonal communication. Damasio (1999a, 1999b), who also relates consciousness to a form of self-reference, claims that consciousness lies in "the unique capacity of human brain to represent itself." Thus, the latter question is whether the "bare" brain, that is, brain unequipped with higher-level language, also possesses the ability to "speak about" (represent) its own representations.

humans human. There is still one uniquely human phenomenon, though, that needs to be discussed: the phenomenon of historical change in human ways of doing. It is my aim now to show that in this case also, language with recursivity plays a decisive role. More specifically, I will be arguing for the following two theses: (1) *Changes in all forms of human doing are a function of changes in commognition, thus in discourses.* (2) *It is the recursivity of linguistic commognition that makes the growth in the complexity of discourses possible.*

To make my case, I will be looking mainly at mathematical discourses. The reason for this choice is that in these very special discourses, the general mechanisms of discursive change, while seemingly quite general, become particularly salient. Let me also remark that although it is the historical change that is of chief interest in the remainder of this chapter, most of what will be said here applies to individual development as well. Indeed, considering the self-reproducing nature of discourses, it is not unreasonable to assume that some of their inner mechanisms remain more or less the same whatever the number of interlocutors, and that these mechanisms reveal similar patterns when observed over different stretches of time.

4.1 *Why Do Discourses Change?*

One can say that discourses have change "inscribed in their genes"; they change because they must. Indeed, discourses are processes rather than static entities, and they incessantly recreate themselves in the intricate interplay of individualizations and communalization. Modification is part and parcel of the recreation. The principal source of the transformation is the inevitable heterogeneity of individual forms of participation. Individual actors, although imbued with the basic need for communication, and thus disposed to follow established discursive routines, are also independent agents, likely to modify the rules of the discursive game either intentionally or accidentally. Two conflicting human needs, the need for mutual coordination and the need for individual expression, endow discourses with inherent tension: New mismatches are constantly produced and each new appearance of the accompanying logical glitch is followed by a correcting attempt that, of necessity, produces a new mismatch. This cyclic mechanism makes human discourses in the image of Sisyphean "communicating vessels" that lose their equilibrium just as they seem to attain it.

Another site of an important developmental change are those junctures where communities meet. Different collective discourses have always been feeding into one another, and this was true even at times when the means of transferring discourses across space and time were much more restricted than in the present wireless era. Some interesting cases of such discursive crossbreeding have been carefully researched,[44] and a great many others wait to be studied.[45] The change inflicted by another discourse can be moderate or far-reaching, depending on, among other things, power relations of their participants.

Let me expand on the theme of intentional change in discourses. People are often interested in such change simply because discourses are their means for increasing the effectiveness of practical activities, and the improvement in a discourse may lead to an improvement in practical activity. When embedded properly in a practical context, mathematical explorations, such as numerical computations or geometric transformations, can be regarded as an activity of "thinking before doing": We precede an operation on discourse-independent objects with the performance of an "isomorphic" action on symbolic counterparts of these objects. Thus, for example, when asked to give change, we may first complete a series of numerical operations and only then construct the proper sum in actual banknotes and coins. At this point it also seems proper to repeat what was stated early in this book and has been built upon ever since: Research – any kind of research – is a discourse that we develop to enhance practice.

Discourses are present also in the majority of our practical activities, albeit not necessarily in an overt way. In fact, almost any routine action of contemporary humans builds on invisible discursive "scaffolding," which, throughout history, was injected into our deeds layer by layer, changing our ways of doing beyond recognition. This past discourse is now hidden in the tools we use and in the explicit instructions we are given while becoming participants of reorganized practice (in the case of computerized artifacts, this last sentence should be understood quite literally: The discourse is there, inside the tool, in the form of a program code). Historically speaking, once its effect was attained, most of this discursive scaffold could be moved out of sight. More often than not, performers of the reorganized activities would remain ignorant of what was said in the course of the reorganization. In today's knowledge-and-technology-saturated world, the discourse actually

---

[44] See, e.g., Saxe and Esmonde (2005).

[45] Striking properties of this mutual shaping are its extreme effectiveness and rapidity, indeed, its outright unrestrainability. Discourses often propagate the way fires do: A fleeting encounter with a form or function in one discourse may be quite enough to alter forms and functions of another discourse. This contagiousness of discursive features is easy to understand in view of the human overpowering need for communication. "Any utterance ... reveals to us ... words of others," says Bakhtin (1999, p. 131), thus encapsulating our natural willingness to follow in other people's discursive footsteps.

produced throughout our performances is a mere surface of the multilayered body of narratives that have been mediating the development of our
activities (and this includes tool building!) up to their present sophisticated
form.

Discourses are also the primary medium for the propagation of innovations in all forms of human doing. Although complexity accumulates in
other media as well (for example, in the material tools produced by people),
only discursive complexity is truly "unpackable" so that it can be retraced,
learned, and even retroactively modified by new generations. In addition,
discourses enable communication between individuals who are not in direct
contact, and this is true even if there are no means for rendering permanence to the things said (of course, writing and electronic recordings largely
facilitate communication at a distance). Thus, the propagation of discourses
either in time, from generation to generation, or in space, from one community to another, does not depend on direct contact between specific
individuals. This propagation happens in time scales that exceed human
life spans. Therefore, discourse is the medium and the carrier of both continuity and developmental change. And because discourses permeate and
shape all human activities, the change in discourse goes hand in hand with
the change in all other human doings.

4.2 *How Do Discourses Change?*

The main point I wish to make now is that human commognition develops
by the successive addition of ever-new discursive layers, recursive layers
of discourse about discourse. Objectification of existing discourses is part
and parcel of the construction process. Thanks to the objectification, new
generations begin the discursive building where the previous generations
left off. As the new construction goes on, the overall complexity of the system grows exponentially, and yet, because the former discursive processes
have been encapsulated in the black boxes of new discursive objects, there
is no need for a significant increase in the complexity of thinking processes.
Indeed, these latter processes remain, more or less, at the level of sophistication and complexity that was needed in order to deal with lower-level
discursive objects.

To present the cyclic mechanism of discursive change in more detail,
let me focus on mathematical discourses. The growth in complexity of
these discourses can be described as a chain of intermittent expansion and
compression.

Following is a description of the process of calculating the number of elements in a finite arithmetic progression the difference and the sum of which are given, as presented in *Aryabhatia* in the year 499 (by Aryabhata, quoted in Boyer, 1985):

Multiply the sum of the progression by eight times the common difference, add the square of the difference between twice the first term and the common difference, take the square root of this, subtract the first term twice, divide by the common difference, add 1, divide by 2.

With the help of algebraic symbolism, which was not introduced until the end of the 17th century, the same discursive procedure can be presented in the highly compressed form

$$\frac{\sqrt{8Sd + (2a - d)^2} - 2a + d}{2d}$$

where S symbolizes the sum of the first n elements in arithmetic progression a, $a + d$, $a + 2d, \ldots$

Figure 4.3. Examples of changes resulting from discursive expansion and the subsequent compression.

Discursive *expansion* happens when there is an *increase in the amount and complexity* of discursive routines or when there is a *proliferation of new discourses*. This first type of expansion, which can be called *endogenous*, is what we observe when discourses grow in volume simply because of their being in constant use. This is, for example, what happened over centuries when arithmetic procedures were successively combined one with another producing computational processes of ever greater length and complexity. One striking case of such a complex computational procedure is presented in Figure 4.3. The other, *exogenous* type of expansion may be instantiated by looking at the history of numbers. Thus, for example, two computational discourses, a discourse about the numbers that we now call *whole* and a discourse about *ratios*, which are basically *pairs* of numbers, existed side by side long before these two discourses became known as subsets of the discourse on *rational numbers*. A somewhat different example of exogenous discursive expansion is the one that happened when the discourse on nonsigned numbers gave rise to the discourse built around syntactically correct but "semantically empty" expressions such as $3 - 5$ or $15 - 23$. The term *semantic emptiness* refers to the fact that these expressions, unlike the standard $7 - 2$ or $22 - 1$, did not unpack into recursive reference chains that would link them to a discourse on concrete objects. Thanks to objectification, this new discourse would eventually be recognized as being *about negative numbers*.[46] This said, it would remain a challenge to generations of learners because of the simple fact that it did not grow from a concrete discourse about the tangible, discourse-independent reality.[47]

Reification is the key occurrence in the processes of discursive *compression*. The "compacting" effect of reification has been demonstrated in chapter 2, where I have shown that replacing counting procedures by number words greatly simplifies extremely long compound narratives about general properties of counting. More such examples will be given now, after I explain the mechanism of compression in more detail.

First, let me distinguish between the compression that occurs as a cure for endogenous expansion and the compression that takes place in reaction to exogenous expansion. The first type of compression occurs through intradiscursive saming: We rise to the metalevel to identify commonalities between different processes within the same discourse. The invention of algebra, with its thrifty notation, is a good example (*c* in Figure 4.4). Thus, when we discover that any sum of two numbers is discursively equivalent to the addition of the same two numbers performed in the reverse order, we state this fact in the form $p + q = q + p$. Although nothing in this latter proposition says so explicitly, this is, in fact, a piece of metaarithmetic. Indeed, the simple $p + q = q + p$ is a shortcut for the sentence *For every two numbers p and q, the numerical expression $p + q$ is equivalent to the numerical expression $q + p$*. Similarly, equations, say $2x + 1 = 13$, are metaquestions; in the present case the question is *What number, if doubled and increased by 1, would yield 13?*

Algebra may thus be described as *metaarithmetic* or, more precisely, as the *unification of arithmetic with its own metadiscourse*. Its power is in the names that reify and unify whole classes of computational processes and at the same time tell the exact story of the processes themselves. Consider, for example, the formula presented in Figure 4.3. This formula compactly encodes a long computational narrative while also signifying the result of this calculation: The expression that was created as a shortcut of the lengthy discursive process can now be used in new computations as if it constituted a number. This object–process duality of algebraic expressions is what makes algebra particularly effective as a tool for enhancing other forms of discursive and practical doing. At the same time, because it is outright counterintuitive

[46] See, e.g., Kline (1980).
[47] Ibid.

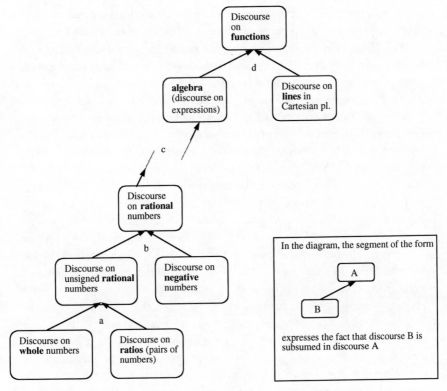

Remarks

1. The rectangles in the diagram represent sets of utterances of the discourses.
2. The relation of *subsuming* should not be confused with the relation of *inclusion* (this confusion is likely to occur because of the fact that whole numbers are a subset of the set of rational numbers). Subsuming discourse A
   - either is a metadiscourse of the subsumed discourse B, as is the case in the segment *c* of the diagram (algebra is a metadiscourse of arithmetic),
   - or contains an isomorphic reflection of the subsumed discourses (as is the case for *a*, *b*, and *d*).
3. The diagram does not reflect, at least not strictly, the historical development of mathematical discourse. It does reflect, however, the analytically derived relation of dependence: It is reasonable to assume that at least one subsumed discourse needs to be present before the subsuming discourse develops. This said, the subsuming discourse may sometimes give rise to new subsumed discourses (such a subsumed discourse would often be called "a model" for the subsuming discourse).
4. Any discourse can be compressed in several ways, thus becoming subsumed in several different subsuming discourses. For example, if in the process of compression (linear parts of) algebra combine with geometrical discourse, the discourse of linear algebra arises.

Figure 4.4. Development of computational discourses.

(how can a thing be simultaneously a process and this process's own result?), it is a well-documented source of students' difficulties and failings.[48]

Exogenous compression, that which conflates several discourses into one, also involves the rise to the metalevel and the objectification of lower-level processes (see *a*, *b*, and *d* in Figure 4.4). Consider the discourse on *algebraic expressions* and that on *graphs* (curves in a Cartesian plane; see *d* in Figure 4.4). As was noticed by Descartes, the founder of analytic geometry, certain well-defined subsets of these two discourses are isomorphic, in that whatever is said in one of them has its clear counterpart in the other.[49] To put it more precisely (and more mathematically), there is a relation-preserving one-to-one mapping from one discourse into the other. As rational beings, we have to be able to account for the fact that utterances about, say, the expression x^2 and corresponding utterances about the line called *parabola* seem to be saying "the same thing." We rationalize the "sameness" by conjuring "abstract objects" and speaking about x^2 and the parabola as "representing the same *function*." This invention leads to the emergence of a new discourse, in which the term *function*, now objectified, is the main player, whereas algebraic expressions and lines in the plane become mere "representations." The special property of this new discourse is that it *subsumes* the former, independently existing discourses, making it possible to express in the new language almost everything that can be said in any of the original discourses with their own special signifiers. Thus, in the subsuming discourse, a sentence "This quadratic function has a minimal value" replaces, simultaneously, the sentence "This parabola is like the letter *U*" in the discourse about lines and the sentence "In this quadratic expression the coefficient of x^2 is positive" in the discourse about expressions. Moreover, the new discourse will also replace parts of certain nonmathematical discourses. What we used to call "modeling real-life situations with functions"

---

[48] See, e.g., Sfard (1994, 1995).

[49] More formally, two discourses can be called isomorphic if there is an isomorphism that maps the set A of all the utterances of one of the discourses onto the set B of utterances of the other discourse. Isomorphism *i* between A and B is a one-to-one mapping that assigns to every utterance *u* from A an utterance *i*(*u*) from B and preserves the truth-value of utterances and the relations between them, that is, fulfills the following conditions: (a) Utterance *u* of A is endorsed (true) if and only if *i*(*u*) of B is endorsed, too; (b) if the utterance *w* in A is of the form "if *u* then *v*" (or "*u* and *v*" or "*u* or *v*," and so forth), then the utterance *i*(*w*) in B is of the form "*if i*(*u*) *then i*(*v*)" (or "*i*(*u*) and *v*(*u*)" or "*i*(*u*) or *i*(*v*)," and so forth, respectively. Of course, because of the blurriness of discourse boundaries and because of the context-dependence of its utterances, the relation of isomorphism is never as clearcut as required by this formal definition. Still, it is both useful and justified to think about some pairs of discourses as nearly isomorphic.

is the act of subsuming parts of the discourse about these real-life situations to the discourse on functions.

According to the definition of abstractness given earlier, the subsuming discourse is more abstract than any of those it subsumes. The subsuming discourse is also what makes the transitions between the subsumed discourses possible. The passage from the discourse about *lines* to the one about *algebraic expressions* will from now on be made via the subsuming discourse about *functions* (as in the sentence "Let's look at the *expression* of the *function* represented by this *graph*"). The subsuming discourse on numbers would have certainly been of much help to the Brazilian street vendor in chapter 1, who was so skillful in money transactions and so awkward in symbolic manipulations (see chapter 1, section 2, *The Quandary of Abstraction*).

To recap, discourses develop in pulses of expansions and compressions. The compression involves the rise to a metalevel, accompanied by objectification. The result is an immediate drop in the perceived complexity of the discourse. Another "drop" that happens thanks to reification is in the *resolution* of the discourse: Under one name, we now unify many lower-level phenomena. This means that what appears different at one discursive level may conflate into "the same thing" at the higher discursive level. Reducing the resolution yields a clear gain: The lower the resolution, the more universal our statements and the greater range of these statements' applicability. This means a substantial growth in the economy of the commognitive activity. On the other hand, lowering the differential power of the discourse does have its risks: The resulting narratives may gloss over substantial, all-important differences. When the discourse is about people, the low-resolution narratives may be particularly dangerous.

5. Thinking in Language – in a Nutshell

In this chapter, linguistic communication was identified as the primary source of sustainable, accumulable changes in human forms of doing. Let me briefly retrace the reasoning that led to this assertion.

In chapter 3, we realized that the question of historical change cannot be answered unless we view individual forms of doing as emerging from their collective counterparts. In the case of thinking, this general claim was translated into the statement that cognitive processes are individualized versions of interpersonal communication. In this context, the term *communication* was to be understood broadly, so as to include any form of interaction allowing individuals to coordinate their actions. Thinking and communicating were then united under the common name *commognition*.

In the present chapter, human linguistic communication, characterized by its *unbounded recursivity*, was shown to be the source of such uniquely human forms of commognitive doing as *reasoning, abstracting, objectifying,* and *subjectifying*. Our unbounded ability to communicate about communication was also said to play a crucial role in the phenomenon of *consciousness*.

Human discourses, with their self-referential recursive structure, may now be seen as the primary repository of complexity and as media for the propagation of change. Recursivity, therefore, can be seen as the primary factor thanks to which, in the process of evolution, the primates bifurcated into humans and nonhumans. By humans I mean the species whose members are able to shape their own activities in increasingly complex ways, as opposed to those other animals whose ways of being in the world remain basically the same from one generation to another and are almost entirely determined by external factors.

Fraught with the seeds of their own change, discourses are in a perennial flux. Cycles of expansion followed by compression bring about the accumulation of one discursive layer upon another. More often than not, discourses expand by annexing their own metadiscourses (see the case of arithmetic expanding to algebra). Such discursive expansion involves, first and foremost, a rise to a metadiscursive vantage point from which the existing discourses can be observed and examined for their intra- or interdiscursive commonalities. The next step is objectification, which begins with "mathematization" of the metadiscourse. This means formalization, but sometimes, it also involves unification of those discursive processes that can count as equivalent. Such "saming" is done, usually, by calling these processes common names and their subsequent objectification. Thus created and objectified, new discourse is said to *subsume* those in which it originated.

Because most of our practical actions are discursively mediated, the more complex the discourses, the more complex other forms of our doing. Every new discursive layer is likely to be accompanied by advancement in the effectiveness of discursive mediatio, and thus the growth of complexity in practical actions. Within a commognitive framework, research on human development becomes, therefore, the study of development of discourses. Discourses, in turn, are thought of as dynamic, time-dependent entities that preserve their identity through continuous change. In commognitive research, studying the history of mathematical discourse and studying the evolving discourse of the child become different versions of the same endeavor. The remaining chapters of this book present samples of commognitive research focusing on the development of mathematical discourse, mainly in their individualized forms.

Part II

Mathematics as Discourse

5   Mathematics as a Form of Communication

> The world for them is not a concourse of objects in space; it is a heterogeneous series of independent acts. . . . There are no nouns.
>
> Jorge Luis Borges[1]

> To think is to forget differences.
>
> Jorge Luis Borges[2]

In this part of the book, I illustrate the workings of the commognitive approach by applying it to the special case of mathematical thinking. In so doing, my intention is to show what difference commognitive analysis makes in our interpretation of observed phenomena and in our practical decisions about teaching and learning. The discussion will eventually take me back to the dilemmas presented in chapter 1. The hope is that when scrutinized with the commognitive eye, at least some of the puzzles will be solved, whereas some others may disappear.

Being interested in learning, I focus in my analysis on the development of mathematical discourses of individuals, but I also refer to the historical development of mathematics whenever convinced that understanding this latter type of development may help in understanding the former. Considering the fact that communication is inherently collective, the term *discourse of an individual* or *personal discourse* may seem to be an oxymoron. Indeed, borrowing Ed Hutchins's words, one can say that those who equate human development with the development of discourses "move the boundaries of the cognitive analysis out beyond the skin of the individual person"[3]

---

[1] Borges (1962/1964 , p. 32).
[2] Ibid., p. 46.
[3] Hutchins (1995, p. 2).

and start speaking, instead, about teams of discourse participants as "commognitive systems." Let me repeat then that thinking has been defined as self-communication. True, personal discourses, being mostly inner and silent, partly escape direct investigation. Moreover, not every participant in collective mathematical conversations is also capable of mathematical self-communication. Still, there is a point in trying to identify characteristic features of one's public discursive behavior. Although the exact shape of interpersonal exchanges is a product of collective doing, some patterns of the person's discursive actions are likely to remain relatively stable across her interactions with different interlocutors. These personal patterns are what will be meant here whenever a personal discourse is mentioned. Needless to say, focusing on the discourse of a person does not imply that the researcher can attend exclusively to actions of the individual and ignore circumstances, events, and exchanges of which these individual actions were a part (such omissions have been typical of traditional psychological assessments; reading traditional research reports is often like overhearing a person speaking on a phone – and is equally frustrating!).

In the present chapter I am asking what mathematical discourse is and how we know whether it works. To be sure, this latter question is far from trivial because the objects of mathematical discourse are famously "intangible," "elusive," and "highly abstract." Considering the fact that mathematics is a product of mathematicians' pursuit of the Holy Grail of infallible communication, there is also something truly paradoxical about this query. Indeed, if it is so difficult to specify what mathematical discourse is all about, how could this discourse possibly become a paragon of effective communication? After taking a preliminary "outsider's" look at different cases of communication that can count as mathematical, I follow in the next three chapters with a number of obvious questions that do not have obvious answers: *What are the objects of mathematics and where do they come from?* (chapter 6), *What are the routine ways of "doing mathematics"?* (chapter 7), *How do mathematical routines develop and what are the prospective gains that spur this development?* (chapter 8). For the sake of brevity, I use the word *mathematizing* to denote participation in mathematical discourse, whereas the participants of this discourse are referred to as *mathematists* (the use of the word *mathematician* would be inpropriate, because it is commonly used to refer exclusively to professional mathematicians).[4]

[4] The neologism was coined in the image of words such as *analyst* or *lobbyist*.

1. What Makes Mathematical Discourse Distinct

Seemingly the most natural way to distinguish discourses from one another is to specify their respective objects. Thus, just as zoology, chemistry, and history can be defined as discourses about animals, chemical substances, and past communities, respectively, so can mathematics be described as a discourse about mathematical objects, such as numbers, functions, sets, and geometrical shapes. The simplicity of this claim is misleading, though, because the notion of mathematical object, unlike that of an animal or chemical substance, is notoriously elusive. This fact is probably the reason why Bertrand Russell famously described mathematics "as a subject in which we never know what we are talking about, nor whether what we are saying is true."[5] Russell's pessimism about the possibility of saying anything concrete about abstract objects of mathematics (pun unintended) should not deter us, however. In the former chapter a claim was made that unlike in zoology or chemistry, where the discourse and its objects are separate entities, in mathematics the objects of talk are, in themselves, discursive constructs, and thus constitute a part of the discourse. To put it bluntly, *mathematics begins where the tangible real-life objects end and where reflection on our own discourse about these objects begins*. Indeed, mathematical discourse, especially when frozen in the form of a written text, can be seen as a multi-level structure, any layer of which may give rise to, and become the object of, yet another discursive stratum. From this description, mathematics emerges as an *autopoietic* system – a system that contains the objects of talk along with the talk itself and that grows incessantly "from inside" when new objects are added one after another.[6] Note the important implication of this last statement: The assertion that *mathematics is discourse* should not be confused with the frequently heard and oft criticized claim that *mathematics is language* (or, for that matter, that *mathematics is register*),[7] which implies that the objects of mathematics are "in the world" and preexist the talk about them.[8]

---

[5] Russell (1904, p. 84).

[6] For elaboration on autopoietic systems see Maturana and Varela (1987).

[7] According to Halliday and Matthiessen (2004), *register* is "a functional variety of language ... the patterns of instantiation [in the form of text] of the overall system [of language] associated with a given type of context" (p. 27), whereas Tannen and Wallat (1999) define the same term as referring to "conventionalized lexical, syntactic, and prosodic choices deemed appropriate for the setting and audience" (p. 352).

[8] There are additional reasons why viewing mathematics as discourse is not tantamount to saying that it is language or register: (a) Discourse and language belong to different,

For a future mathematist, the self-generating nature of mathematical discourse creates a paradoxical situation: One's familiarity with what the discourse is all about seems to be a precondition for participation in this discourse, but, at the same time, such familiarity can only emerge from this participation! The question of how people overcome this circularity is the focal theme of commognitive research on learning mathematics. For now, it is important to note that investigators of mathematical discourse are hampered by a similar dilemma. Indeed, the researcher who, for the sake of sharper distinctions and insights, tries to assume an outsider's outlook at this discourse must proceed with her investigations ignoring the question of what kinds of objects mathematists are playing with. This is quite different than in the case of, say, biology, where the "outsider" can interpret discursive moves of the participants by examining relations between these moves and independently observed objects of the discourse. Metaphorically speaking, the mission of the analyst of mathematical discourse who tries to forget her own ways with mathematical words is thus not unlike that of a hypothetical investigator of a virtual reality game who does not, herself, have access to the perceptual experiences of the players.

In spite of this difficulty, giving up the outsider's perspective would be against the commognitivist's better judgment. Indeed, it is by putting herself in the position of a perfect beginner that the researcher may hope to get useful insights into processes of learning. Although this choice entangles the discourse analyst in the same circularity that obstructs the moves of the learner, the challenge is evidently not insurmountable. After all,

---

although not unrelated, ontological categories: The former denotes human activity, whereas the latter is a symbolic system; (b) as a form of human doing, discourses are much more than vocabularies and rules of grammar and may differ one from another even when they are identical in the words they use and in the lexical combinations they support; (c) discourses, although defined by some writers as "languages in action" (Brown & Yule, 1983), include numerous forms of communication, not just verbal; (d) discourses may differ in their vocabularies the way English and Hebrew do and still be considered basically the same. Thus, we may speak about mathematical discourse without specifying whether it is in English or in Hebrew simply because Hebrew-to-English and English-to-Hebrew translations transform the relevant communicational activities one into the other in a manner that preserves the mutual relationships within the discourse and the relations among discursive and practical activities. Above all, written symbolic forms of mathematical statements, often viewed as what mathematics is all about, remain the same, whatever the natural language in which the discourse takes place. If one accepts the non-dualist version of the Sapir–Whorf hypothesis, that is, interprets it as saying that no two discourses in different languages can be fully isomorphic, this last statement should, of course, be qualified and should be understood as relative. As will be argued on the following pages, mathematical discourse seems to be less sensitive to the change of natural language than any other.

many people do manage to learn mathematics, and some of them proceed to become experts. There is no reason to think that the fate of a determined analyst should be different. In this chapter, therefore, I begin my study of mathematical discourse by asking questions that make no reference to the object of this discourse: *How well defined is the idea of mathematical communication? Can we distinguish mathematical discourse from any other just by attending to its directly observable properties?* The hope is that we may be able to identify mathematical discourse by its external characteristics just as a person may be able to recognize a language such as French or Chinese in spite of the fact that she does not speak any of them herself.

This said, delineating discourses is not a straightforward task. As collective activities whose implementers come and go and whose forms are dependent on skills and wishes of individual actors, discourses are in a constant flux, infiltrate one another, and do not have well-defined borders. On the other hand, they can be compared to Heraclitus's famous river: Although always in motion and unlikely to be the same the next time you step into them, they preserve their identities through the continuous transformations.[9] This is true even if the products of successive discursive metamorphoses appear as dissimilar to one another as adults are to babies who they were once upon a time.

Or is it? As reasonable as this last claim seems to be – after all, there must be some explanation for the fact that we insist on describing strikingly different instances of discourse with the common adjective *mathematical* – one look at the discursive samples in Figure 5.1 may rekindle one's disbelief. If a person acts as an outsider who judges discourses solely through their perceptually accessible qualities, the dissimilarities of the three pieces of text may overshadow their commonalities.

One can argue that the dissimilarity has been amplified by the differences between modalities: Whereas the first excerpt is a transcribed casual dialogue, the other two are fragments of carefully formulated written texts (and this last word refers also to the drawing!). In addition, the three excerpts are taken from contexts as different as one can imagine. The first piece is a sample of *colloquial* mathematical discourse, that is, of discourse that constitutes an integral part of everyday exchanges. It is a fragment of my conversation with Roni – the same girl whom we met for the first time in Episode 1.1

---

[9] The expression "discourses preserve their identity" refers to the way changing communicational activities appear to the observer. The continuity of the change is probably the first condition for our ability to perceive processes as staying "the same" through a series of modifications.

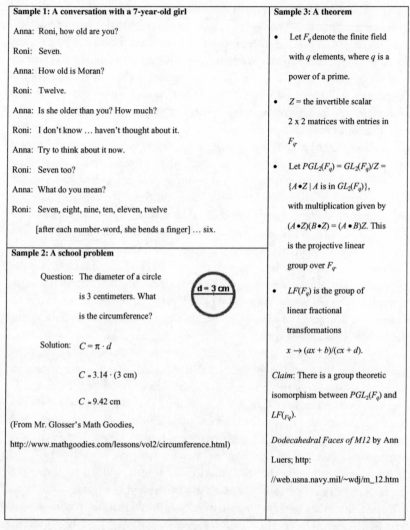

Sample 1: A conversation with a 7-year-old girl	**Sample 3: A theorem**

Anna: Roni, how old are you?

Roni: Seven.

Anna: How old is Moran?

Roni: Twelve.

Anna: Is she older than you? How much?

Roni: I don't know … haven't thought about it.

Anna: Try to think about it now.

Roni: Seven too?

Anna: What do you mean?

Roni: Seven, eight, nine, ten, eleven, twelve

[after each number-word, she bends a finger] … six.

Sample 2: A school problem

Question: The diameter of a circle is 3 centimeters. What is the circumference?

Solution: $C = \pi \cdot d$

$C = 3.14 \cdot (3\text{ cm})$

$C = 9.42\text{ cm}$

(From Mr. Glosser's Math Goodies, http://www.mathgoodies.com/lessons/vol2/circumference.html)

Sample 3: A theorem

- Let F_q denote the finite field with q elements, where q is a power of a prime.

- Z = the invertible scalar 2 x 2 matrices with entries in F_q.

- Let $PGL_2(F_q) = GL_2(F_q)/Z = \{A \bullet Z \mid A \text{ is in } GL_2(F_q)\}$, with multiplication given by $(A \bullet Z)(B \bullet Z) = (A \bullet B)Z$. This is the projective linear group over F_q.

- $LF(F_q)$ is the group of linear fractional transformations $x \rightarrow (ax + b)/(cx + d)$.

Claim: There is a group theoretic isomorphism between $PGL_2(F_q)$ and $LF(_{Fq})$.

Dodecahedral Faces of M12 by Ann Luers; http: //web.usna.navy.mil/~wdj/m_12.htm

Figure 5.1. Samples of mathematical discourse.

and who in the meantime became 3 years older. Colloquial discourses are also known as *everyday* or *spontaneous* because they often develop as if by themselves, as a by-product of repetitive day-to-day actions. The second excerpt, which is from a Web presentation intended for high school students, and the third one, which is a fragment of a scholarly publication, are samples of *literate* mathematical discourses, the salient characteristics of which are their heavy reliance on written symbols and their rich arsenal of algorithms for making use of the special notation. These common features of Samples 2 and 3 notwithstanding, a closer look would also reveal some systematic differences, reflecting the fact that literate discourses practiced by professional communities of researchers are usually several metadiscursive layers above those one encounters in schools. In addition, mathematicians' uses of words and symbols are generally much more rigorous than those to be found in classrooms.[10] The uncompromising stringency of professional mathematical discourses occurs at the expense of their accessibility. Today, discourses practiced by professional mathematicians are known for their fragmentation, and the mathematical community itself is often deplored as being pulverized into tiny subcommunities that can hardly communicate with one another.[11]

To conclude, in our attempt to categorize discourses we should probably look for family resemblance rather than for universal commonalities. As in the case of families, where each member shares one set of features with some relatives and quite a different one with some others, so in the case of mathematical discourses, probably no single uniquely mathematical characteristic could be found that would be common to all members of the category. This said, four properties can be considered as critical in deciding whether the given instance of discourse can count as "mathematical." Following is a very brief description of each of them. A more elaborate treatment of the first two properties will follow in this chapter and in the next, whereas the other two will be dealt with in detail in chapters 7 and 8, respectively.

1. *Word use.* One of the distinctive characteristics of discourses is the keywords they use. In mathematics, these are mainly, although not exclusively, the words that signify quantities and shapes. Whereas many number-related words may appear in nonspecialized, colloquial discourses, mathematical discourses as practiced in schools or in academia dictate their own, more disciplined uses of these words. Word use is an all-important matter because, being tantamount to what others call "word meaning," it is responsible for what the user is able to say about (and thus to see in) the world.

2. *Visual mediators* are visible objects that are operated upon as a part of the process of communication. While colloquial discourses are usually mediated by images of material things existing independently of

[10] Cf. the notion of *didactic transposition* (Chevallard, 1985, 1990).
[11] Davis and Hersh (1981); Thurston (1994, pp. 5–6).

the discourse, scientific and mathematical discourses often involve symbolic artifacts, created specially for the sake of this particular form of communication; think, for example, about scientific inscriptions or mathematical algebraic notation.[12] Communication-related operations on visual mediators would often become automated and embodied. Think, for example, about the procedures of scanning the mediator with one's eyes in a well-defined way. With some experience, this procedure would be remembered, activated, and implemented in the direct response to certain discursive prompts, as opposed to implementation that requires deliberate decisions and the explicit recall of a verbal prescription for these operations.

3. *Narrative* is any sequence of utterances framed as a description of objects, of relations between objects, or of processes with or by objects, that is subject to *endorsement* or rejection with the help of discourse-specific substantiation procedures. Endorsed narratives are often labeled as *true*.[13] Terms and criteria of endorsement may vary considerably from discourse to discourse, and more often than not, the issues of power relations between interlocutors may in fact play a considerable role. This is certainly true about social sciences and humanistic narratives such as history or sociological theories. Mathematical discourse is conceived as one that should be impervious to any considerations other than purely deductive relations between narratives. In the case of scholarly mathematical discourse, the consensually endorsed narratives are known as mathematical theories, and this includes such discursive constructs as definitions, proofs, and theorems.

4. *Routines* are repetitive patterns characteristic of the given discourse. Specifically, mathematical regularities can be noticed whether one is watching the use of mathematical words and mediators or following the process of creating and substantiating narratives about numbers or geometrical shapes. In fact, such repetitive patterns can be seen in almost any aspect of mathematical discourses: in mathematical

---

[12] For definition of *inscription*, known also as *immobile mobiles*, see Latour (1987).

[13] In the majority of cases, to endorse a narrative means to recognize it as describing "the real (discourse-independent) state of affairs." To use the language introduced by J. L. Austin (1962), these are the cases of constative utterances. According to Austin, only constatives can be categorized as *true* or *false*. This is not a description that can be used with respect to performative utterances, such as definitions (which are acts of baptizing). Here, one should rather speak about *felicitous* or *infelicitous* utterances. The term *endorsed narrative* is inclusive of those series of utterances that are called true and those that are described as felicitous.

forms of categorizing, in mathematical modes of attending to the environment, in ways of viewing situations as "the same" or different, which is crucial for the interlocutors' ability to apply mathematical discourse whenever appropriate – and the list is still long.[14]

2. Challenges to Mathematical Communication

Considering the circularity of the process of building mathematical discourse, it is reasonable to wonder how mathematical communication may be possible at all. Unlike in colloquial discourses on material things, where the objects of communication exist independently of the discourse and can be pointed to and scanned with one's eyes, the objects of mathematical exchange, even if already constructed, are featured as something that can perhaps be "represented" with visual means, but never really shown. Mathematical communication, therefore, more than any other, is likely to be hindered by considerable differences in interlocutors' use of words. In particular, the degree of objectification may be different for different mathematists. The issue of objectification has already been discussed in chapter 2. Let me now refresh the reader's memory with a number of examples.

Mathematical sentences often appear as if they were made of utterances on material things in which names of material objects have been replaced with mathematical nouns. Particularly relevant in this context are existential sentences typical of advanced mathematical discourses. Consider, for example, the following excerpt from Sample 3 in Figure 5.1:

- *There is* a group theoretic isomorphism between PGL2(Fq) and LF(Fq) (emphasis added).

The use of the verb *is* stipulates the existence of an entity called *group theoretic isomorphism* just as the statement "There is life on Mars" implies the existence of living creatures in addition to those to be found on Earth. A similar message is conveyed in acts of naming such as the following:

- Let Fq *denote* the finite field with q elements
- LF(Fq) *is* the group of linear fractional transformations (emphases added)

which make it clear that the word used as a name should not be regarded as a thing in itself but rather as a pointer to another entity.

---

[14] This use of the term *routine* is close to the usage proposed by Schutz and Luckmann (1973) and applied in the context of mathematics learning by Voigt (1985).

To add just one other example, mathematical equalities, such as $2/3 = 12/18$ or $2 + 3 = 5$, are most naturally accounted for by saying that the two expressions appearing on the different sides of the equals symbols "represent (refer to) the same object." After all, this is the kind of explanation we are likely to give to statements such as *"The Morning Star is Venus"* or *"The author of Romeo and Juliet is William Shakespeare."*

Being as accustomed as we are to the objectified form of mathematical utterances, we may be tempted to view this state of affairs as a matter of necessity rather than of optional, custom-sanctioned ways with words. Yet, a high-resolution analysis of different samples of mathematical talk would reveal the existence of alternatives, thereby making it clear that objectified word use, although critical to the fluency and effectiveness of mathematical communication, is not an inevitable quality of this discourse. My own empirical studies have convinced me that only a few signs of objectification can usually be found in mathematical discourses of beginners. Let me illustrate this claim with three examples.

Example 1: Incipient Numerical Discourse

Roni and Eynat, whom we saw in Episode 1.1 comparing boxes with marbles, can certainly count as newcomers to mathematical discourse. Not surprisingly, the data collected in the *Incipient Numerical Discourse* study have revealed that their numerical discourse not only was poorer in possibilities than that of grown-ups, but also differed from the latter discourse in its inner workings. Let me point out two differences that can be considered as indicative of the lack of objectification: the difference in the use of number words and in the use of the term *the same*.

Let us begin with *number-words*. Although the words *one, two, eleven,* and so on, were definitely a part of the girls' active vocabulary, they were rarely incorporated by the children into full sentences.[15] Occasions for use arose mainly when Roni's mother made an explicit request for counting or for numerical comparison. In response, the children would routinely produce canonical number-word sequences (see, for example, [11] and [12] in Episode 1.1.) Often, when the sequence ended, the girls would emphatically repeat the last number-word, as they would also do when the question "How many?" recurred after counting (see, e.g., [14]).

As long as number-words appear only in ritual number chanting, there is no room for the talk on objectification. Indeed, speaking of objectification

---

[15] See Sfard and Lavie (2005) for the full report about the study, including all the data.

is justified only when a word is used as a grammatical subject or object in certain types of sentences. In Roni and Eynat's case we were able to identify only very few relevant sentences (or rather parts of sentences), and in none of these utterances did number-words seem to appear as nouns. Rather, they served as nouns' modifiers (adjectives).

The first linguistic indicator of the use of a number-word as adjective is the appearance of this word in conjunction with a noun, as in *10 marbles*. This is, indeed, the way number-words are used in such representative sentences as "You take *four* pretty marbles" (Eynat). One may also be making this kind of use without any explicit mention of the objects that are determined by the number-words. For instance, one cannot rule out the possibility that number-words served as adjectives also in utterances such as Eynat's "There are [is] *four* here" or "I see there are [is] *four*," in which the word *four* might have been a shortcut for *four marbles*. The girl's tendency of terseness, typical of young children, might have been one reason for this lack of elaboration.[16]

More reliable differentiators of objectified and nonobjectified use are the adjectives *bigger* and *smaller* and the adverbs *more* and *less*, routinely applied in the context of comparisons. Roni and Eynat displayed a clear preference for the latter (the adverbs) over the former (the adjectives). In this respect, the following brief exchange is quite typical:

Episode 5.1. Which is more?

76. Eynat: *Ten* is more.
77. Mother: *Ten* is more?
78. Roni: Yes, and *four* too.
79. Mother: *Ten* is more than what?
80. Roni: Than *one* and *two*.
81. Mother: *Ten* is more than *one* and *two*?

When number-words are used in conjunction with *more* or *less*, they function as adjectives rather than nouns, and this implies that *sets of counters* (marbles, in the present case) rather than numbers are the objects of the talk.

[16] In English, singular and plural forms might help in deciding whether number-words are used as descriptors of sets or as signifying self-sustained objects. Thus, saying *There is 10*, in the singular, can be taken as a sign of objectification, whereas the use of the plural form, *There are 10*, entails an implicit reference to elements of a set. Unfortunately, in Hebrew this distinction is absent, so it could not be used in this study.

Indeed, it would be natural to complete an utterance such [76] as "Ten *marbles* is more [e.g., than eight marbles]." In contrast, when number-words are used as referring to self-sustained entities, the result of comparison is presented with the word *smaller* or *bigger*. This is the case with Mother's question "Is there a number that is *bigger* than 10?" and with Eynat's "When numbers don't end, then this...the number is *bigger*" uttered some time later. When one of the adjectives *small* or *big* is followed by a number-word, it is to be understood that the latter is used as a noun. In our study, the adverbs *more* and *less* dominate the conversation, and the adjectives *big* and *bigger* appear only in one brief exchange between Roni's mother and Eynat. So, although there are some objectifying characteristics in Eynat's numerical discourse, Roni's talk is devoid of any such features.

Let us turn now to the expression *the same*. Episode 5.2 took place after Roni's mother presented the children with two boxes containing two marbles each. When the conversation began, Roni had already answered the question "Where are there more marbles?" with the brief "In none." She then tried to do her best in response to her father's follow-up inquiry:

Episode 5.2. The same

42. Father:	Why? Why do you say this?	
43. Roni:	Because there is [are][17] two in one, and in [this] one there is [are] another two.	Shows two with her fingers.
44. Father:	So, this is why there is more in none of them? So, in both of them there is... what?	
45. Roni:	Two.	
46. Father:	And this is...more or less?	
47. Roni:	Less.	
48. Father:	Less than what?	
49. Roni:	Than...than...than big numbers.	
50. Father:	Than big numbers? That means...If there is [are] two in one box and two also in the other, then what is there in the two boxes?	
51. Roni:	Four.	
52. Father:	Aha. Together, there is [are] four?	
53. Roni:	Yes.	

[17] The Hebrew word *yesh*, which may be translated as either *there are* or *there is*, was used.

54. Father:	And in each box there is *the sa* ...	
55. Roni:	Because it is between ...	
56. Father:	I see. And there is *the same [thing]** in each box?	
56a. Roni:	...	
57. Father:	How many in each box?	
58. Roni:	Two	
59. Father:	Oh well ...	in the tone signaling resignation.

* The Hebrew term for *the same* is composed of two words, *oto davar*, the literal translation of which is *the same thing* (*davar* means *thing*). The first word, *oto*, cannot be used without being followed by a noun. So, one needs to specify what is (are) the thing(s) that is claimed to be "the same," as in "the same **number**" (*oto **mispar***) or "the same **child**" (*oto **yeled***). If one does not want to be so specific and just tries to say that A and B are *the same*, one says, "A and B it's the same **thing**."

Table 5.1 presents an interpretive elaboration of an excerpt from the episode (*interpretative elaboration* is a text that, utterance by utterance, elaborates on the text produced by the interlocutors). Clearly, although Roni realized that the word *more* did not apply to either of the two boxes, the expression *the same* did not occur to her as an equivalent description. The girl would rather violate the rules of grammar and change her use of words than consider the type of utterance meant by her insistent interlocutor. The simple explanation that Roni was unacquainted with the expression *the same* does not seem to work. Indeed, if her father insisted on eliciting these words, it was because he had heard his daughter using them on other occasions. The girl's imperviousness to her father's transparent hints indicated that she could see no connection between the numerical context and the situations in which the words *the same* were previously used.

One may speculate that so far, the children have been using the expression *the same* while seeing something they saw before. They might be able to say, for example, that they met *the same person* on Monday and on Friday. For them, the words *the same*, unlike the adjectives *more* and *less*, implied seeing *one thing* at different times. No wonder, therefore, that they found no use for the expression *the same* while seeing two boxes simultaneously present alongside one another. For those whose discourse on numbers has been objectified, the "one thing" that "resides" in both boxes and thus justifies the use of the words *the same* is the object called *two*; for those, however, for whom number-words are mere sounds that people make as a part of a ritual

Table 5.1. *Interpretive elaboration of an excerpt from Episode 5.2*

	What was said	Interpretative elaboration
44. Father:	So, this is why there is more in none of them? So, in both of them there is . . . what?	The father tries to elicit the use of the term *the same* with reference to the number of marbles in the two boxes.
45. Roni:	Two.	For Roni, there is no alternative to the description that says "there is more in none of them." She thus interprets her father's question "So, in both of them there is . . . what?" as inquiring after the number of marbles in the boxes.
46. Father:	And this is . . . more or less?	Father leads Roni toward the expression *the same* by trying to make her aware that neither of the alternatives, either *more* or *less*, holds here.
47. Roni:	Less.	For Roni, *the same* is not a complementary option for *more* and *less* (is not equivalent to *none has more*). Besides, according to the rules of the game that is being played, one of the two possibilities presented by the father has to be true. Roni chooses *less* because she already said that *more* is not an option. The choice makes sense if the words *less* and *more* are interpreted in the present context as *small* and *big*.
48. Father:	Less than what?	Father is surprised: To his mind, Roni contradicts herself (because if there is more in none of the boxes, none of the boxes can be claimed to have *less*). By the use of the incomplete comparative form "less than . . ." he imposes the return to the original comparative role of *less*.
49. Roni:	Than . . . than . . . than big numbers.	This statement is fully endorsable both for Roni and for her father, except that it shows that the word *less* in Roni's former utterance [47] did not express comparison between the two boxes. The present answer corroborates the preceding interpretation of [47].

chanting, nothing in the boxes warrants the talk about "the same things."[18] This delicate difference clearly escaped the father, for whom his daughter's *None-has-more* and his own *They-are-the-same* were perfectly exchangeable in the numerical context.[19]

Our other data forcefully confirm the children's inability to apply the expression *the same* in the context of numbers. Intrigued by Roni's reactions, the parents probed further. They asked the girls to change the unequal contents of two boxes in such a way as to make them "the same." They repeated this request several times, with respect to different pairs of boxes. On all these occasions, the children's strenuous efforts to meet Roni's parents' expectations resulted in much frustration and produced no solutions.

To recap, this example corroborates what was said in chapter 2 about the development of numerical discourse: Number-words, such as *five* or *ten*, known to young children as elements of counting sequences, do not begin their discursive career as "signifiers of objects." Some time must elapse after these words' first appearance in a child's discourse before the activity of counting becomes reified and the words themselves turn into nouns. However, once the project of objectification is completed, its results seem irreversible. This is why the adults seem incapable of seeing as different the things that the children cannot see as the same. As testified by the mathematician William Thurston, every mathematician is well acquainted with this inability to distinguish between the things that she or he learned, over the years, to see as "the same" and as fully exchangeable:

> Unless great efforts are made to maintain the tone and flavor of the original human insights, the differences start to evaporate as soon as the mental concepts are translated into precise, formal and explicit definitions.[20]

---

[18] A close look at the sentence evidently meant by the father – "There is the same thing [number of marbles] in each box" ([54], [56]) – reveals that the words *the same thing*, although seemingly synonymous with *neither-more-nor-less*, refer, in fact, to a different type of entity. The adverbs *more* and *less* describe a relation between two concrete things (sets of marbles), whereas the words *the same* can only be applied to something invisible that resides simultaneously in the two boxes. Thus, the transition from the talk about numerical *inequalities* to the talk about numerical *sameness* implies creation of new mathematical objects and thus a leap to a higher discursive level.

[19] More importantly, this fact might have also escaped Piagetian researchers, including Piaget himself. Because the famous conservation tasks hinge on the child's ability to describe sets of objects as either unequal or "the same," the researchers' alertness to a child's exact words is of utmost importance for their narratives about the observed events. However, until recently, researchers did not have access to electronic means of recording, and this is why one cannot be sure of the verbal fidelity of data like those collected by Piaget and his followers in their conversations with children. This uncertainty suffices to warrant treating conservation-task-based developmental research with much caution.

[20] Thurston (1994, p. 164).

Example 2: Early Numerical Discourse

Recall Episode 1.5, featuring the 7-year-old girl by the name Noa, asked by a teacher about "the biggest number?" Here is a brief reminder:

Episode 5.3. Biggest number – excerpt

5.	Teacher:	What is the biggest number you can think of?
6.	Noa:	Million.
7.	Teacher:	What happens when we add one to million?
8.	Noa:	Million and one.
9.	Teacher:	Is it bigger than million?
10.	Noa:	Yes.
11.	Teacher:	So what is the biggest number?
12.	Noa:	Two million.
13.	Teacher:	And if we add one to two million?
14.	Noa:	It's more than two million.

This conversation may serve as yet another example of mathematical communication in which the interlocutors use the same words in different ways. Commognitive interpretation of what happened in that exchange would be to say that the two participants referred to different objects while uttering the same word *number*: Whereas the teacher talked about numbers as if they were entities signified by number-words and separate from the words as such, Noa clearly used the word *number* as signifying the number-words themselves. The advanatage of this interpretation is that it allows us to account for what appeared quite puzzling as long as the conversation was analyzed in traditional, acquisitionist terms. Just to review, the bewildering aspect of that conversation was that Noa seemed unimpressed by the apparent contradiction between the belief that a given number is "the biggest one" and the claim that two million and one "is more than two million." The contradiction, however, disappears when words such as *hundred* or *million* or even *two million* are treated as things in themselves rather than mere pointers to some intangible entities. In this case, Noa's initial claim that there is a biggest number appears perfectly rational; after all, there are only so many number-words, and one of them must therefore be the last one in the well-ordered sequence of such words. Moreover, because within this conceptualization the expression *million-and-one* cannot count as a number – rather, it's a *concatenation* of numbers – the possibility of adding 1 to any number does not necessitate the nonexistence of the biggest number.[21]

Example 3: Arithmetical Discourse

Let me now return to Mira and Talli, the 18-year-old high school students whom we saw in Episode 1.4, trying to perform numerical calculations. Within the commognitive framework, the term *numerical calculation* refers to a discursive sequence that, once uttered or written, counts as a confirmation of the equivalence of two numerical expressions, such as *eighty-six plus thirty-seven* (or, in written symbolic form, 86 + 37) and *one hundred twenty-three* (123). The equivalence means that, for any communicational purpose, one can replace each of these numerical expressions with the other one.

Mira and Talli's computational discourses are instantiated with representative samples in Episodes 5.4a and 5.4b. In both cases, the girls are calculating, without writing, the sum 86 + 37:

Episode 5.4a. Mira calculates 86 + 37

15$_M$. Mira: (c) [....] let's do it this way

(d) [..] 80 and 30 [......] 80 and 30 is hmm [..] $30 + 80 = ?$

(e) one hundred [....] and ten, one hundred $30 + 80 = 110$
and ten

(f) [...] 6 and 7 is 13 $6 + 7 = 13$

(g) [....] 23. $...23$

(h) 23 and 100 $100 + 23 = ?$

(i) [...] 123. 123

---

[21] Let me remark that this interpretation of the way Noa used number-words applies only to situations in which these words are applied as stand-alone signifiers, fulfilling the role of nouns. On the basis of other observations we may claim that her use of simple and composite number signifiers as determiners, that is, in conjunction with nouns such as, say, *marbles*, was not much different from that of the experienced mathematist. In this context, it is significant that in Episode 5.3 Noa uses the adverb *more* while comparing, for example, two-million and one and two-million [14], even though the teacher's question featured the comparative adjective *bigger*. This reinforces the conjecture that in known contexts, such as that of numerical comparisons, she might tend to use number expressions as determiners.

Episode 5.4b. Talli calculates 86 + 37

23ᴛ. Talli: (a) I put the 37 down, under the 86;   She performs the
               (b) and simply added the 6 to 7, it's 13.   calcualtions without
                                                            writing.

               (c) I put the 3 down and put the 1 over
                   the 3 of the 37,

               (d) I added and it made 4;

               (e) and 4 and 8 makes 12.

               (f) 123.

I now wish to claim that Talli's arithmetical discourse was less objectified than Mira's. To show this, let me compare the two girls' typical arithmetical utterances. Four representative examples, taken from earlier episodes as well as from other parts of the interviews, are presented in Table 5.2.[22]

One can summarize the difference by saying that Mira's presentations of the calculations were predominantly *structural* and *impersonal*, whereas Talli's were mainly *processual* and *personal* (I have used the qualifying adjectives *predominantly* and *mainly* because in both girls' talk there were also utterances of the other kind). The word *structural* refers to a presentation that can be read as describing the structure of a composite number, as opposed to a *processual* utterance, which presents the calculation as somebody's action. Because each such action must have a performer, the processual rendering often goes hand in hand with *personalization*. In the case of structural presentation, in contrast, there is no need for the performing subject.

Table 5.2. *Mira's and Talli's presentations of numerical operations and their results*

	Mira		Talli	
Addition	6 and 7	[15f]	I added the 6 to 7	[23b]ᴛ
Subtraction	500 minus	[41a]ₘ	I did 5 minus 3	[37b]ᴛ
	40...is...455		I did the subtraction	[35b]ᴛ
Multiplication	9 multiplied	[70b]ₘ	I took 24 and	[125a]ᴛ
	by 2 is		I multiply it here	
Result of operation	80 and 30 *is*...	[15d]ₘ	I added and it made 4	[23d]ᴛ
	6 and 7 *is* 13	[15f]ₘ	I got	[37e]ᴛ

[22] See Ben-Yehuda et al. (2005) for the full transcription of the interviews and their analyses.

Structurality of word use, the opposite of processuality, is the result of reification, whereas the impersonal form of the discourse is the outcome of alienation. Together, these two characteristics justify the claim that the discourse is objectified. As a result of the differing levels of objectification, the two girls' brief monologues concerning the same arithmetic operations did not appear to involve the same thing: Talli focused on what *she did* with numbers, whereas Mira spoke about what *the numbers produced* as if of themselves, by force of their inherent properties. Thus, Talli's talk was framed as a story of her own actions, whereas Mira's discourse took the form of a direct report on the properties of numbers. This difference in form should not be dismissed as merely a matter of whether the calculation was presented in real time or retroactively. In the lengthy interview not even once did we hear Talli speaking about numbers in the object-level, "authorless" manner characteristic of Mira's talk, and we thus have no evidence for her ability to talk in this way. All this points to the lack of objectification of Talli's arithmetical discourse: For her, numbers did not have the permanence of extradiscursive objects that they clearly had for Mira. Rather, in Talli's talk, number-words and symbols seemed to be functioning as temporary symbolic entities, the existence of which was restricted to the highly personal computational processes of which they were a part.[23]

Let me summarize by describing all three cases, that of Roni and Eynat, of Noa, and of Miran and Talli, as involving *commognitive conflict* between interlocutors, a conflict that stems, at least in the present cases, from differing uses of words, not always acknowledged by the participants. More often than not, the speakers would resolve such conflict in an equally imperceptible manner, by gradual mutual adjusting of their discursive ways. In the next chapters, I will illustrate this last claim with examples. For now, let me just say that in the process of mutual discursive attuning, one of the participant discourses would often be privileged over all the others, that is, recognized by the interlocutors as the paradigmatic case, which sets the rules for all the interlocutors. This was certainly the case with the numerical

---

[23] These observations, as philosophical and apparently far removed from any practical aspect of arithmetic discourse as they seem, may, in fact, be informative with respect to the overall quality and effectiveness of this discourse. Even more importantly, the observed properties or word use may be related to one's ability to use the discourse whenever appropriate. We seem to have some grounds to suspect that using impersonal, alienated forms the way mathematicians do may go hand in hand with more effective arithmetical performance. Some recent empirical evidence points in this direction: Chris Bills's study with a large number of participants indicated that in computational discourse, the use of the first-person sentences in the past tense correlated with a lower achievement level than did the use of a less personal form and the present tense (Bills, 2002).

discourse of grown-ups in Example 1, with the discourse of the teacher in Example 2, and with the literate school discourse in the case of Talli in Example 3. Doubtlessly, therefore, the resulting shape of all the individual discourses involved is a function of power relations among interlocutors.

3. Visual Mediation in Mathematical Communication

In the further attempt to answer the question of how mathematical nouns fulfill their communicational role, I now wish to argue that in spite of the famous "intangibility" of mathematical objects, mathematical communication depends on what we see no less than do other, less abstract types of talk.

3.1 *Effectiveness of Communication*

My first task is to try to be operational about the term *effectiveness of communication*. One way to define this expression is to say that communication is effective if both actors and observers regard it as such. According to the definition offered earlier in this book, communication is a rule-driven activity in that discursants' actions and re-actions arise from certain well-established repertoires of options and are matched with one another in a nonaccidental, patterned way. Hence, we may say that communication is effective if we are satisfied with the match. Yet, because public criteria according to which one can make the necessary judgment are constraining rather than deterministic, different assessors may reach different verdicts. We thus have to keep in mind that communicational effectiveness is an interpretive concept: Any assessment of communication is based on personal interpretations of the discourse. In making statements about the effectiveness of a given case of communication it is therefore important to be explicit about whose perspective is being considered.[24]

Another point to remember in this context is that trying to specify indicators of a good match between action and re-action and then attempting to use these explicit criteria for actual assessments would be a dauntingly intricate task. If we succeed in sustaining our sense of effective communication in the countless conversations in which we are engaging on a daily basis, it is because for us, effectiveness is the default property of communication: As

---

[24] Remembering all of that, we may still agree to call a given instance of communication effective (just like that, without specifying whose decision it is) if there is a consensus of all the evaluating parties on its being fully successful.

with the proverbial Heideggerian hammer, we do not doubt that the work of communicating is done properly – we do not even raise the question – unless evidence to the contrary forces itself upon us. Discursants' confidence in communicational effectiveness is a necessary condition for their being able to take part in this activity in the first place.[25] All too often, if we do not interpret our interlocutor as "talking about the same thing as we are," we may not be able to continue the conversation. Consider, for instance, this brief exchange:

> **Episode 5.5. Talking about Dana's hat**
>
> 1. Ari: I like Dana's hat.
> 2. Gur: I think it is rather unbecoming.
> 3. Ari: Well, I beg to differ.

Clearly, Ari would not be able to re-act in [3] to what Gur has said in [2] if he did not interpret Gur's *it* as equivalent within the present context to his own words *Dana's hat* ([1]). Thus, in the analyses that follow, whenever trying to evaluate a discourse, I will focus on the question of what can count as an indication of *communication breaches* rather than trying to establish positive evidence of effectiveness.

3.2 *Visual Mediation*

Ari and Gur would not have been able to communicate effectively if they could not see, or just imagine, the concrete object called *Dana's hat*. As we can see from this example, images help interlocutors in making discursive decisions and in sustaining the sense of mutual understanding even in those cases when their respective utterances openly contradict one another. *Visual mediators* have been defined as providers of the images with which discursants identify the object of their talk and coordinate their communication. Thus, Dana's hat served as a visual mediator in Ari's and Gur's conversation. More generally, colloquial discourses are often mediated by images of concrete objects, which are referred to with nouns or pronouns

---

[25] Levinson (1983), inspired by Grice (1975), calls this communication-enabling principle "an assumption of topical coherence": "If a second utterance can be interpreted as following on a first utterance, in a sense that they can be 'heard' as being concerned with the same topic, then such an interpretation of the second utterance is warranted, unless there are overt indications to the contrary" (p. 51).

and which are effective in this communication-coordinating role whether they are actually seen or just imagined.

This last claim is true also of colloquial mathematical discourses. The incipient numerical talk of the young participants of Episode 1.1 is a good example. Quite understandably, the only form of visual mediation that can be found here is concrete rather than symbolic (enters from outside the discourse). The mathematical task performed by Roni and Eynat is described in terms of sets of marbles and is visually mediated by these sets. In this case, the mediators are not merely seen, but also physically manipulated – for example, the girls are touching the marbles while counting them – and this physical procedure is part and parcel of the girls' numerical discourse. In effect, this discourse is not much different from other forms of communication known to the girls from their everyday activities. The money transactions of the Brazilian street vendor (see section 1.2, *The Quandary of Abstraction*) and of Ron, the schoolboy from Episode 1.2, are similar in this respect. In both of these cases, the communication is mediated by images of banknotes and coins, and this is true even if all these concrete objects are seen and operated upon only with the interlocutors' "mind's eye."

Literate discourses, on the other hand, were defined as visually mediated mainly by *symbolic artifacts*. Along with *algebraic symbols*, symbolic artifacts include *icons*, such as conventional or individually designed diagrams, graphs, and other drawings. Students' fluency in this kind of discourse is the goal of school learning. To get a better sense of the role of different forms of visual mediation in mathematical communication, let us take a look at three additional examples.

Example 1: Symbolic Mediation in Computational Discourse

Written arithmetic computations may be the most obvious case to begin with. It is sufficient to try to calculate mentally the sum of, say, one-half and three-quarters to realize that visual mediation is present even in those cases when no mediator can actually be seen. This is also what transpires from Episodes 5.4a, b: While trying to find the sum of 86 and 37 Mira and Talli were clearly scanning numerical symbols in a complex way even though nothing had been written down. It is also noteworthy that the scanning procedures they used differed in a significant way.

In Talli's calculations, the symbolic strings were scanned and replaced by other symbols in a uniquely defined way. This manner of attending to the numerical symbol may be called *syntactic*, as it does not require more than knowing the names and order of the digits, and the rules for replacing digits with other digits. There were two distinct features of Mira's use of symbols. First, she would often assign digits names different than those given to them by Talli – see, for example, her use of the words *eighty* and *thirty* for the digits that were read by Talli as *eight* and *three*. Second, the order in which she scanned the numerical symbols was the reverse of Talli's: Mira proceeded from left to right, with the addition of 6 and 7 occurring last, whereas Talli did it from right to left, with the same addition occurring first. To sum up, this example not only demonstrates the presence of visual mediation even in seemingly most abstract mathematical activities, but also shows that the same mediators may be used in several ways even when the task and the result remain the same.

Example 2: Iconic Mediation

This example, from the *Montreal Algebra Study* mentioned in chapter 1, section 3, *The Quandary of Misconceptions*, illustrates the use of iconic mediation. Following is an excerpt from the interview with 12-year-old Jas, who has learned about linear functions but has never before tackled a linear equation. The boy is now asked to solve the equation $7x + 4 = 5x + 8$:

Episode 5.6. "Graphing in the head"

Jas: Well, you could see, it would be like.... Start at 4 and 8, this one would go up 7, hold on, 8 and 7, hold on ... no, 4 and 7; 4 and 7 is 11.... They will be equal at 2 or 3 or something like that.

Unfamiliar with algebraic procedures for solving equations, Jas nevertheless manages to implement the task thanks to his ability to imagine the two sides of the equations as two straight lines, which he then scans in such a way as to identify the x-coordinate of their intersection. Indeed, when asked by the interviewer, "How are you getting that 2 or 3?" Jas said, "I am just graphing in my head."

As an aside, let me remark that one of my studies produced much evidence in support of Jacques Hadamard's claim[26] that the majority of mathematicians use visual imagery even in the most advanced and abstract of discourses. These pictures are sometimes actually drawn and sometimes just imagined. When externalized in communication with others, they often turn out to be not more than doodles (see Figure 5.2). Although drawings

[26] Hadamard (1954).

The drawing represents "a set in a measure space" and "an increasing sequence of sets."

This drawing was used to explain Borsuk's hypothesis on the minimal number k for which any set of radius 1 in an n-dimensional space may be partitioned into k subsets of radius less than 1.

This drawing was used to explain the speaker's own proof of Van der Waerden's theorem on coloring ("For all possible integers n and c there exist an integer N such that if the set of integers $\{1, 2, 3, \ldots\}$ is c-colored, then there exists a monochromatic n-term arithmetic progression").

Figure 5.2. Drawings produced by three mathematicians explaining their ideas (adapted from Sfard 1994).

like these do not make much sense to anybody but their author, they evidently help the problem solver to keep his discourse focused and coherent.

Example 3: Visual Mediation in Interpersonal Communication

In the example that follows I try to determine the role of visual mediation in interpersonal communication the way a physiologist establishes the function of an organ: by considering a "pathological" case, in which the investigated element does not make the expected contribution. In Episode 5.7 that follows, the conversation between Ari and Gur, the participants of the *Montreal Algebra Study* who are trying to find a slope of a function given by a table, limps and stumbles and, in general, does not seem to be very effective (this episode is an excerpt from Episode 1.3 in chapter 1). In this case, visual mediation involves a whole battery of written symbols, such as numerals, tables, algebraic formulas, and perhaps even (imagined) lines.

Episode 5.7. Finding a value of a function

Function $g(x)$ is given by the table and the students are asked to calculate $g(6)$

x	$g(x)$
−1	−10
0	−5
1	0
2	5
3	10
4	15
5	20

1. Ari:	(a) Wait, how do we find out the slope again? (b) No, no, no, no. Slope, no, wait, (c) intercept is negative 5. (d) Slope	
2. Gur:	What are you talking about?	
3. Ari:	(a) I'm talking about this. (b) It's 5.	(a) points to the -5 in the right column (b) is moving his eyes to the next row
4. Gur:	It doesn't matter if it's on (mumble)	
5. Ari:	5x. Right?	Writes the formula $g(x) = 5x - 5$ on his worksheet
6. Gur:	What's that?	
7. Ari:	It's the formula, so you can figure it out.	
8. Gur:	Oh. How'd you get that formula?	
9. Ari:	and you replace the x by 6.	
10. Gur:	Oh. Ok, I...	
11. Ari:	(a) Look. Cause the, um the slope, is the zero. (b) Ah, no, the intercept is the zero.	(b) points to the 0 in the left column
12. Gur:	Oh, yeah, yeah, yeah. So you got your...	
13. Ari:	(a) And then you see how many is in between each, (b) like from zero to what	(a) points to both columns, indicating that you have to check both (b) points to the x column

Episode 5.7 *(continued)*

14.	Gur:	And the slope is, so the slope is 1.	the left counterpart of the right column 0 is 1
15.	Ari:	(a) Hum? No, the slope,	
		(b) see you look at zero,	(b) circles the zero in the x column on Gur's sheet
16.	Gur:	(a) Oh *that* zero, ok.	
		(b) So the slope is minus 5	
17.	Ari:	Yeah. And	
18.	Gur:	How are you supposed to get the other ones?	
19.	Ari:	(a) You look how many times it's going down, like we did before. So it's going down by ones.	(a) points to x column
		(b) So then it's easy. This is ah . . . by fives. See, it's going down by ones,	(b) points to the g(x) column
		(c) so you just look here	(c) and again to g(x) column

The incompatible narratives [14] and [16], more specifically Gur's "the slope is 1" and Ari's "the slope is minus 5," seem to indicate a commognitive conflict: The boys may be using the word *slope* in different ways. As instantiated by the earlier Episode 5.4, however, commognitive conflict is not the only possible reason for contradicting narratives. The controversy may be a result of differing opinions (see [2] and [3]). A genuine commognitive conflict could only be asserted on the basis of *factual* narratives, that is, narratives that are subject to consensual, rules-determined endorsement – or rejection – by the discourse community. The visual procedures to be implemented in re-action to the given word in the presence of the given mediator are among those rules of word use that should be common to all the interlocutors.

To check the origins of Ari and Gur's disagreement, let me identify procedures implemented by the boys in their search for the context-specific numerical equivalents of the terms *intercept* and *slope*. A close reading of the transcript reveals that Ari arrived at the two required numbers, -5 and 5, by scanning the table of function values in a well-defined way. Prompted by Gur's questions, he described the two procedures explicitly. Thus, his algorithm for identifying the intercept can be found in utterance [11], and the one for the slope in [13] (this latter procedure is then described again

Table 5.3. *Ari's procedures for finding slope and intercept from the table of values*

Procedure for the slope	Procedure for the intercept
1. In the left column, check the difference Δx between successive numbers, x_1 and x_2	1. Find the zero in the left column of the table
2. In the right column, check the difference Δy between the corresponding numbers, y_1 and y	2. In the right column of the table, find the number b corresponding to that zero
3. Find the ratio $a = \Delta x / \Delta y$	

in [15] and [19]). Ari's prescriptions for both of these processes are shown schematically in Table 5.3.

Gur's procedures, if any, are much less visible than those of his partner. Utterance [14], "so the slope is 1" is the only explicit statement he makes on the function. From the exchange that follows, it becomes clear that for Gur, the slope is the left column neighbor of the digit zero appearing in the right column (see [15b], where Ari points to the zero in the left column, and then [16a], where Gur recognizes his earlier mistake: "Oh, that zero, ok"). It seems that when the episode begins, Gur does not associate any discursive procedures with the word *slope* and his utterance "the slope is 1" results from an ad hoc decision made in response to discursive moves of his interlocutor. The immediate inspiration arises, so it seems, from Ari's two utterances: "the intercept is the zero," accompanied by pointing to the digit 0 in the left column of the table [11b], and "like from zero to what" [13b], uttered in the context of slope. The two uses of the word *zero*, one of them in relation to the intercept and the other to the slope, evidently gave rise to Gur's idea that the procedure for one of them is the "inverse" of the other: The slope can be found in the table to the left of the right column zero, just as the intercept can be located to the right of the left column zero.

Let me remark that although unhelpful in this interpersonal communication, the visual mediation is crucial to the success of Ari's self-communication. The image of the table, together with the well-defined realization routines, lets him proceed in a confident manner in spite of his persistent verbal confusion (see how he confuses the words *slope* and *intercept* ([1a,b] and [11a,b]). The well-defined scanning procedure leads his gaze along the proper trajectory even as he pronounces inappropriate words.

The preceding observations lead to an important practical conclusion: To prevent communication breaches, or to repair them when necessary, it may often suffice to be explicit about one's scanning procedures. This

Table 5.4. *Signifier-realization pairs in preceding episodes*

Episode	Realizator	Signifier[a]	Realization[a]
(a) 5.7	Worksheet authors	"Function g"	Table of values
(b) 5.7	Ari	"Slope of g"	"5"
(c) 5.7	Gur	"Slope of g"	"1"
(d) 5.6	Jas	"$7x + 4$"	A particular straight line
(e) 5.6	Jas	"The solution of the equation $7x + 4 = 5x + 8$"	The x-coordinate of the intersection of the two straight lines that realize $7x + 4$ and $5x + 8$, respectively
(f) 5.4	Mira	"$86 + 37$"	"123"
(g) 5.5	Ari and Gur	"Dana's hat"	The piece of clothing on Dana's head

[a] The quotation marks in the examples were used to stress that the intention is to focus on the written word as a physical object rather than on its function, use, or interpretation.

said, we also need to remember that articulating the process of scanning is, in itself, an act of communication and, as Ari and Gur's case has shown, this communication-improving communication may fail as well!

4. Visual Realizations of Mathematical Signifiers

As instantiated by the preceding examples, mathematical communication involves incessant transitions from signifiers to other entities that, from now on, will be called *realizations* of the signifiers. *Signifiers* are words or symbols that function as nouns in utterances of discourse participants, whereas the term *realization of a signifier S* refers to a perceptually accessible object that may be operated upon in the attempt to produce or substantiate narratives about S. To put it more precisely:

> **Definition**: *Realization of the signifier S* is a perceptually accessible thing S′ so that every endorsed narrative about S can be translated according to well defined rules into an endorsed narrative about S′.

Table 5.4 shows some of the signifier–realization pairs we have seen in the preceding episodes.

Realizations can take the form of spoken or written words, algebraic symbols, drawings (icons), concrete objects, or even gestures (see the summary in Figure 5.3). Often, the signifier and its realization are entities of

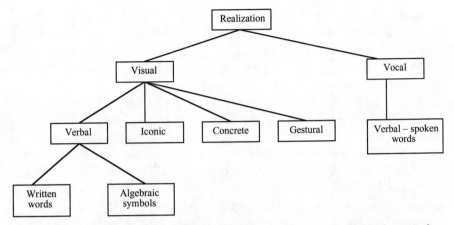

Figure 5.3. Different types (modalities) of signifiers' realization in mathematical discourse.

the same kind and the signifier–signified relation is symmetrical. This is the case, for example, for the pair (f) in Table 5.4, the elements of which could be distributed "in reverse" between the "signifier" and the "realization" columns. The discursive transition from signifier to its realization may be immediate – as is the case with the signifier–realization pair (a) in Table 5.4, or *mediated* by an elaborate realizing procedure, as is the case with all the other pairs. Inspecting or manipulating the structure of realizations of S is one of the principal methods for constructing endorsed narratives about S.[27]

Realizing signifiers in *visual* media is of particular importance, because what we get in this process is most liable to investigation and manipulation and may thus lead to endorsed narratives in the immediate way. Thus, the piece of clothing on a girl's head, which was Gur's realization of Ari's signifier "Dana's hat," made him able to formulate and endorse a new narrative (opinion) about the hat. Similarly, Jas's realization of the "solution of $7x + 4 = 5x + 8$" via the graph enabled him to construct narratives about the approximate value of the solution. Often, the realization of one signifier may be necessary for the realization of other ones. Thus, to realize the

[27] In some cases, for example, in those marked as (a) and (d) in Table 5.4, there is some deceptive similarity between the pair <signifier, realization> and <representation, the represented object>. The difference is in the implied ontology of the component terms. Whereas in the case of mathematics, representation is to be understood as but a material "incarnation" of a basically intangible *abstract* entity (mathematical object), realization belongs to the same ontological category as signifier – the category of perceptually accessible entities.

signifier "Dana's hat," Gur had first to realize the signifier "Dana." In the same vein, once Ari realized "function g" as "$y = 5x - 5$," he became able to realize other related signifiers, such as "$g(6)$." Finally, once Mira realized "$86 + 37$" as "123," she could go on and realize this new signifier as a point on the number line or as a set of coins and banknotes.

It is notable that the same signifier may be realized visually in a number of ways, in different media. In the case of "function g," for example, one may use a table, algebraic formula, and graph. Subsequently, one can apply several different procedures to realize the signifier "slope of g," each one of them implemented via a different realization of "function g," but each of them leading to the same result "5." A phenomenon such as this is one of the reasons why we say that all the realizations of the same signifier, although rather dissimilar, can be treated as equivalent, at least in certain contexts.

Realization of a signifier would often involve a transition from one medium to another – for instance, from the algebraic–symbolic signifier to an iconic realization. Because each medium has its own discourse that supports its unique set of narratives, the multiplicity of visual realizations broadens communicational possibilities. More often than not, a given narrative may be constructed and substantiated in a number of ways, via different realizations of the component signifiers. Some of these alternative processes may be easier to perform than some others, depending on the type of "materials" in which they are implemented. Relative advantages of the basic visual modalities – symbolic, iconic, concrete, and gestural – depend on particularities of the task at hand and on what is expected from its implementation. For example, although iconic and concrete realizations would often facilitate *production* of factual narratives, mathematicians still regard symbolic realizations as necessary to warrant these narratives' general *endorsement*. Thus, although Jas was able to assess the numerical value of his solution by scanning the imagined graphs of $7x + 4$ and $5x + 8$, he would have to revert to the symbolic realization if he wanted to ensure that experienced mathematists regard the task as properly implemented.

Each process of realization entails a particular combination of verbal actions, visual scanning, and physical manipulations, and the proportions of these three elements vary with the medium within which the process takes place. Whereas operating on symbols is a version of the inherently linguistic activity of reasoning, iconic and concrete procedures require a relatively small amount of verbalization. Unlike in the case of symbols, realization processes of this latter type are implemented predominantly with one's eyes, sometimes also with one's hands. Thus, icons would "give an answer" simply by being systematically scanned, whereas concrete realizations can bring

The following definition introduces the terms *promenade* and *stroll*. Read the definition and the example, and then try to implement the following task. When you are finished with tasks 1 and 2, or just tired of thinking about them, proceed to Figure 5.5 (but do make a sincere effort to implement tasks 1 and 2 before you continue).

DEFINITION: *Promenade* is the set of all the integers between 1 and 25 in which one can *stroll* from one number to another using combinations of the following steps:

$S(x) = x + 5$, provided $x \leq 20$

$N(x) = x - 5$, provided $x > 5$

$E(x) = x + 1$, provided $x \neq 5n, n \in N$

$W(x) = x - 1$, provided $x \neq 5n + 1, n \in N$

EXAMPLE: The stroll $S \circ W^3 \circ S^2$ leads from 5 to 17:

$$S \circ W^3 \circ S^2(5) = W^3 \circ S^2(10) = W^2 \circ S^2(9) =$$

$$W \circ S^2(8) = S^2(7) = S(12) = 17$$

YOUR TASKS:

1. Give an example of a stroll leading from 11 to 3.
2. Find all the numbers that one can stroll to them from 9 without using N or E.
3. Proceed to Figure 5.5

Figure 5.4. *Promenade – Part 1.*

about the required results by being physically transformed. For instance, all one needs to do in the case of addition is to put together two sets of objects and count the elements in the resulting set. In the case of division, the necessary action is partitioning of the set into a given number of equipotent subsets. As a result of these concrete manipulations, certain numerical equivalencies "reveal" themselves to the implementer rather than being actively produced through a discursive process. Symbolic realizations, on the other hand, entail sequential discursive procedures, only partially supported by visual means. Such procedures put much more demand on one's memory than their iconically or concretely mediated counterparts. To experience this difference or, more specifically, to see to what extent iconic realizations may facilitate problem-solving processes, the reader is invited to perform a two-stage experiment, introduced in Figure 5.4.

It is noteworthy that frequently repeated realization procedures may become embodied and automated. In the present context, *embodiment* means that as in swimming, bicycling, or typing, the necessary scanning and physical actions are remembered "by our bodies" as a series of body physical movements, rather than "by our minds," as a series of discursive moves.

Automation implies the ability to perform all the components of the procedure one after another without having recourse to verbal prescriptions – without an explicit thought about the connection and without asking oneself what comes next. A person who has embodied and automated a realizing procedure may have as much difficulty trying to explain her actions as did the proverbial centipede when asked how it coordinated the movements of its multiple legs. For any given signifier, some realizations are more conducive to embodiment and automation than some others. Naturally, these embodied–automated realizations are the ones that we tend to evoke spontaneously upon hearing or seeing the respective signifier. As such, they may be called the *leading* realizations of the signifier. For a beginning mathematist, the leading realization may appear as the signified object itself, whereas all the others would count as this object's mere "representations" (the common tendency to identify functions with their algebraic realizations expresses itself, among others, in the use of such expressions as "a graph of function x^2," where the x^2 is featured as "the function itself" and the graph is talked about as its mere "representation").

In colloquial mathematical discourses, embodiment and automation of realization procedures are common phenomena. One such case has been described in Sylvia Scribner's study on dairy warehouse workers who appeared impressively skillful in mental arithmetic. One of these workers testified to visualizing containers of different shapes and sizes whenever trying to decide about how to implement clients' orders for a certain amount of milk. He said, "I don't never count when I'm making the order; I do it visual, a visual thinking, you know."[28] The Brazilian street vendor in the study by Teresinha Nunes and her colleagues operated on coins and banknotes the way Scribner's workers operated on milk containers – with only a very scarce amount of discursive scaffolding. Embodiment and automation are not entirely absent from literate mathematical discourses either. To see that this is indeed the case, the reader is invited to pause for a moment and try to add two fractions, which, instead of having the usual vertical form, are given as horizontal pairs:

$$(3, 5) + (7, 12)$$

Let me guess: To perform the task, you probably felt the urge to revert to the traditional vertical form, $3/5 + 7/12$. Through years of practice, the sequence of eye movements that need to be performed on this canonical vertical symbol became your "second nature," and a/b turned into your leading realization of simple fractions.

[28] Scribner (1997, p. 362).

The present discussion would remain incomplete without a few words about unique features of algebraic symbolic realizations, which are the hallmark of literate mathematical discourse. Unlike icons or concrete realizations, compound symbols such as $134/29$ or $2x - 5$ are shortcuts for verbal expressions. And yet, there is an important difference between spoken and symbolically implemented talk. The spoken medium is sequential and no two sounds can be experienced at the same time – we stop hearing one before being able to hear another. With the help of symbolic records, the inherently transient spoken discourse acquires permanence and the different discursive elements become simultaneously present. Although this is also true about discourses recorded in the form of written texts, the usual phonetic writing is linear and bulky, whether symbolic notation, which is ideographic in nature, turns substantial discursive segments into concise, timeless wholes, with their patterned internal structure readily visible. Because of this, the introduction of the symbolic mediation brings about a considerable increase in the *generative power* of the discourse. Indeed, if mathematics is discourse about discourse, and if noticing discursive patterns is the name of the game, then turning the audible, ephemeral talk into visible permanent text is a turning point in the development of mathematics. The symbolically encoded mathematical discourse is even more likely than its spoken or even written counterpart to become an object of metadiscursive activity. In the symbolic encoding discursive regularities express themselves pictorially, as visible patterns.[29] In this context, I am reminded of a story of a mathematician-turned-juggler who constructed a symbolic system for recording juggling moves. Unexpectedly, this invention broadened his juggling repertoire, as it made him aware of "unfilled" slots within the table of juggling combinations he was now able to construct. Finally, when implemented in the symbolic medium, *processes of realization* turn into their own outcomes. As a result, a single symbolic discursive construct, say $2 \cdot 3 + 5$, begins to serve as both a description of a series of actions and as a noun that constitutes this process's realization. As such, symbolic realizations are "a tremendous labor-saving device."[30]

---

[29] It is probably for this reason that introduction of writing at large and of symbolic encoding in particular is seen by some writers as a landmark event in the development of cultures and in the emergence of modes of thinking typical of these cultures. For example, according to Jack Goody (1977), "Logic, 'our logic,' in the restricted sense of an instrument of analytic procedures ... seemed to be a function of writing" (p. 11). Not only "the development of mathematical thinking," but "the growth of individualism and the rise of bureaucracy were closely connected with the long and changing process of introducing graphic symbols for speech" (p. 19). On the role of writing and other graphic symbolizing in the development of culture see also Donald (1993).

[30] Thurston (1990, p. 847).

As in Figure 5.4, the definition in Figure 5.5 introduces the terms *promenade* and *stroll*, but in a different way. The first two tasks are the same as in Part I. The additional final task is to reflect on the two problem-solving processes, the only difference between which is the nature of visual mediation that has been employed.

DEFINITION:

YOUR TASKS:

Promenade is the scheme presented here. The *stroll* in the promenade is a function composed of N, E, S, and W, whereas

1	2	3	4	5
6	7	8	9	10
11	12	13	14	15
16	17	18	19	20
21	22	23	24	25

$N(x)$, $E(x)$, $S(x)$, and $W(x)$ are the squares **n**orth, **e**ast, **s**outh, and **w**est to x, respectively.

1. Give an example of a stroll leading from 11 to 3.

2. Find all the numbers that allow one to stroll to them from 9 without using N or E.

3. Note the present use of an iconic realization of *promenade*, as opposed to its purely symbolic appearance in Part 1 (Figure 5.4). Compare the degree of difficulty of the solution processes in the two cases. Try to account for the difference by analyzing the proportion of verbal (symbolic) and visual actions in each of them.

Figure 5.5. *Promenade* – Part 2

One last advantage of symbolic realizations over iconic and concrete ones comes to the fore when the *effectiveness* and *applicability* of the resulting discourse are considered. The reliance on concrete realizations makes discursive procedures highly situated: One can only perform these procedures when appropriate materials (e.g., milk containers) are present and when one is able to associate the tasks at hand with the corresponding realizations (such association would be unlikely to happen, for instance, if the available materials were milk containers, but the task was about the amount of rug needed to cover a triangular area). Symbolic systems, on the other hand, are our universal portable "realizing kits," which make us our own persons wherever we go.

5. Mathematics as a Form of Communication – in a Nutshell

After having disposed in chapter 3 of the split between thinking and doing (behavior), and in chapter 4 of the idea that one can "distill" thought from speech, in the present chapter I did away with yet another time honored divide – that between mathematical discourse and its objects. Mathematics has been presented here as an autopoietic system – a system that produces the things it talks about. Indeed, mathematics is a multilayered recursive structure of discourses-about-discourse, and its objects therefore are, in themselves, discursive constructs. This is the main reason why the claim that *mathematics is a discourse* is quite different from the often heard and equally often criticized statement that mathematics is a language. The autopoietic feature is a challenge to both mathematists and outside observers of mathematical discourse: Some familiarity with the objects of the discourse seems a precondition for participation, but at the same time participation in the discourse is a precondition for gaining this familiarity. One of the main tasks of the student of mathematical thinking is to answer the question of how mathematists manage to overcome this inherent circularity of processes of learning and of investigating.

Trying to characterize mathematical discourses according to their external features rather than their objects is the researcher's way out of the entanglement. Although there is probably no single external feature common to all instances of communication that we would like to call mathematical, the *family resemblance* among these special activities is strong enough to justify the talk about *mathematical discourses*. These discourses are made distinct by their tools, that is, *words* and *visual means*, and by the form and outcomes of their processes, that is, the *routines* and *endorsed narratives* that they produce. Unlike *colloquial* discourses, which are visually mediated mainly by concrete material objects existing independently of the discourse, *literate* mathematical discourses make massive use of *symbolic artifacts*, invented specifically for the sake of mathematical communication.

Mathematical communication counts as *effective* if the interlocutors have no reasons to suspect a breach. The effectiveness is constantly being threatened by the circularity of the process of development of mathematical discourse and by the pervasive vagueness as to the nature of its objects. No wonder, then, that *commognitive conflict* – the encounter between interlocutors who use the same mathematical signifiers (words or written symbols) in different ways or perform the same mathematical tasks according to differing rules – is a common phenomenon. For example, one mathematist may use such words as *number* or *function* in the objectified way, that is, as if it signified another, basically intangible entity; whereas others may treat these signifiers as objects-in-themselves.

An effective way to examine the coherence in an interlocutors' use of words and symbols is to try to find out how they *realize* those signifiers.

Realizations of the signifiers are perceptually accessible objects that may be operated upon in the attempt to produce or substantiate mathematical narratives. Visual realizations may be *simple* or *composite* and can be linked to their signifiers either by *immediate* association or through a mediating *realizing procedure*. Some of the realizations that one learns as mediated may become immediate as a result of *embodiment* and *automation* of the realization procedure. Visual realizations may be *symbolic, iconic,* or *concrete.* The special strength of iconic and concrete mediators is that they may lead to new endorsed narratives with only a relatively small number of verbal manipulations (reasoning actions). The symbolic means, on the other hand, are basically verbal and thus sequential and as such exert greater demands on one's memory. And yet, what is lost in simplicity is gained in generalizability and applicability. The process–object duality of symbolic mediators is a basis for compression and the subsequent extension of mathematical discourse, and it renders this discourse independent of external, situation-specific visual means. All this ensures a very wide applicability of the discourse.

By taking a close look at processes of realization and their results, I have tried to show that visual perception plays as fundamental a role in mathematics as in any other discourse, except that the manner in which the sense of sight is employed is more complex and less obvious. Armed with some basic observations about the relations between mathematical signifiers and their realizations, I will proceed in the next chapter toward operationalization of the notion of *mathematical object*. In doing so, I hope to answer the question of what mathematical discourse is all about and how it can possibly mediate our practical actions.

6   Objects of Mathematical Discourse

What Mathematizing Is All About

I close my eyes and see a flock of birds. The vision lasts a second, or perhaps less; I am not sure how many birds I saw. Was the number of birds definite or indefinite? The problem involves the existence of God. If God exists, the number is definite, because God knows how many birds I saw. If God does not exist, the number is indefinite, because no one can have counted. In this case I saw fewer than ten birds (let us say) and more than one, but did not see nine, eight, seven, six, five, four, three, or two birds. I saw a number between ten and one, which was not nine, eight, seven, six, five, etc. That integer – not-nine, not-eight, not-seven, not-six, not-five, etc. – is inconceivable. *Ergo*, God exists.

Luis Jorge Borges[1]

I remember as a child, in fifth grade, coming to the amazing (to me) realization that the answer to 134 divided by 29 is $^{134}/_{29}$ (and so forth). What a tremendous labor-saving device! To me, "134 divided by 29" meant a certain tedious chore, while $^{134}/_{29}$ was an object with no implicit work. I went excitedly to my father to explain my discovery. He told me that of course this is so, $^a/_b$ and a divided by b are just synonyms. To him, it was just a small variation in notation.

William Thurston[2]

The "content" of mathematics does not exist in the material world; it is created by the activity of mathematics itself and consists of ideal objects like numbers, square roots and triangles.

Michael A. K. Halliday[3]

---

[1] Borges (1998, p. 294).
[2] Thurston (1990, p. 847).
[3] Halliday (2003, p. 140).

Mathematicians and philosophers have been grappling with the idea of a mathematical object for ages, always recognizing its inherent blurriness, but never considering the option of simply giving it up. After all, if there is no such thing as mathematical reality, why should one bother to engage in mathematical investigations? In their most extreme forms, the claims about the nature of mathematics implied that mathematical objects have an independent existence of sorts. Those who objected have been reproached by their platonically minded colleagues:

> Everything considered, mathematicians should have courage of their most profound convictions and thus affirm that mathematical forms indeed have an existence that is independent of the mind considering them.[4]

If I opt for operationalizing the time-honored idea of mathematical object rather than trying to do without it, it is only partly out of reverence for its long history, and certainly not because of any platonic leanings. My main reason is the hope that this special notion, with its deep metaphorical roots, will help us in understanding the developmental connection between mathematical discourses and discourses on material reality.

1. Mathematical Objects

1.1 *Discursive Objects*

While mathematizing, we are in the incessant chase after the objects of our activity. True, in this "object hunt" we proceed from one tangible entity to another, but I have called these latter entities *realizations* rather than *mathematical objects*. There are a number of reasons for this lexical restraint. First, realizations are characterized by being perceptually accessible – a property that one does not expect to find in a genuine mathematical object. Second, one signifier would usually have many visual realizations, and determining which of them deserves to be singled out as "the" object would be difficult. Finally, as already mentioned, the distinction between signifier and realization is relative. Symbolic artifacts are often exchangeable in these two roles. For example, one can use a table of function values as a signifier and realize it in a formula, and vice versa – the formula may be realized in a table. Thus, whether a word, algebraic symbol, or icon should count as a signifier or as a realization of a signifier is a matter of use, not of any intrinsic property of these artifacts.

---

[4] Thom (1971), quoted in Davis and Hersh (1981, p. 319).

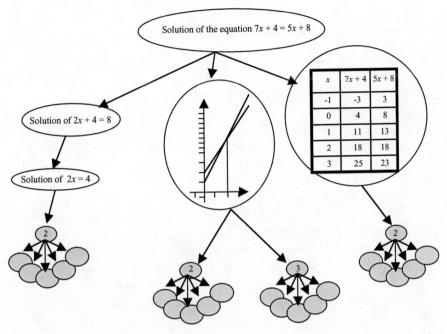

Figure 6.1. A realization tree of the signifier "solution of the equation $7x + 4 = 5x + 8$."

Basically, therefore, almost any mathematical realization may be used as a signifier and then realized even further. From here it follows that any signifier can be seen as a "root" of a "tree" of realizations. In this tree, each node fulfills the double role of a realization of the node just above it and of a signifier realized by the nodes just beneath it. Figure 6.1 presents a schematic beginning of a possible realization tree for the signifier "Solution of $7x + 4 = 4x + 8$." The nodes featuring "2" and "3" can be unpacked even further, showing that each of these signifiers may be realized, for example, as equipotent sets of objects. On the basis of what we saw in Episode 5.6 it is justified to claim that at least the middle subtree reflects Jas's realizing capacities. I have supplemented the scheme with the other two subtrees so as to present my own realizations that correspond to "solution of $7x + 4 = 4x + 8$."[5] The notion of a realization tree will now help me to define *discursive object*.

[5] The term *tree of realization* is reminiscent of the notion *chains of signification*. This latter notion was introduced and extensively dealt with (under differing names) by the prominent semioticians Peirce (1931–1935; 1955) and Lacan (1966); recently, it was explained and instantiated in Walkerdine (1988) and in Cobb, Gravemeijer, Yackel, McClain, and

Definition: *The (discursive) object signified by S* (or simply *object S*) in a given discourse on *S* is the realization tree of *S* within this discourse.[6]

A few remarks about thus defined mathematical objects are now in order. First, realization trees, and hence mathematical objects, are *personal constructs*, even though they originate in public discourses that support only certain versions of such trees. As researchers, we may try to map personal realization trees and present them in diagrams such as the one in Figure 6.1. Inclusion of a specific realization – the graph of a function, for instance – in the tree would mean that in certain situations the person has been observed implementing this realization.

Second, the realization trees are a source of valuable information about the given person's discourse. Making skillful transitions from one realization to another is the gist of mathematical problem solving. In addition, a person's tendency to apply mathematical discourse in solving practical problems depends on her ability to decompose signifiers into trees of realizations with branches long enough to reach beyond the discourse, to familiar real-life objects and experiences. Hence, one method to gauge the quality of one's discourse about, say, function, would be to assess the richness, the depth, and the cross-situational stability of the person's realization tree for the signifier "function."

This last statement leads me to the third point. While analyzing transcripts of conversations in the attempt to map discursive objects, one needs to remember that *these personal constructs may be highly situated* and, in particular, can be easily influenced by interlocutors and by other specifics of the given interaction. For example, some realizations, although well known to the person and likely to be used in a skillful manner whenever such use is initiated by others, may never be evoked by the person on her own accord (in this case, we may say that the person did not fully individualize the use of the given signifier – a fact that escapes our eyes if we never have the opportunity to observe the person trying to solve problems on her own). Realization trees of an individual, as mapped by a researcher on the basis of a finite number of observations, may thus change from one set of observations to another. In particular, as shown time and again in cross-cultural and cross-situational studies, processes of realizations of a given signifier, say "four times thirty five," evoked by a person in school or in a research

---

Whitenack (1997). If I am reluctant to use this term, it is because the word *chain* implies linearity rather than a complex hierarchical structure, which is better captured by the term *tree*.

[6] To put it recursively, the discursive object signified by *S* is the *S* itself together with all the objects signified by its realizations.

interview may be quite different from those that arise spontaneously while the same person is implementing everyday activities.[7]

Finally, *different interlocutors may realize the same signifier in different ways.* Unacknowledged differences between personal realizations harm the effectiveness of communication and may even lead to a breach. The conversations between Ari and Gur, between Noa and her teacher, and between Roni and her father are good illustrations of this claim. In each of these cases realization trees of the two interlocutors differed not only in the amount of components and their mutual arrangement, but also in the nature of these components. Identifying individuals' discursive objects may thus help in assessing the effectiveness of interpersonal communication. While analyzing Ari and Gur's conversation about the slope I tried to do exactly this: I scrutinized the conversation for accessible parts of their realization trees "growing" from the root (signifier) "slope of *g*." According to my interpretation, Gur's realization tree was practically nonexistent, even though the boy did try to create it ad hoc. The result of my analysis of Ari's discourse appears in the rightmost column of Table 6.1 under the heading *object*. I assessed Ari's realizations for "slope" as equivalent to my own. Of course, in stating this equivalence I relied on the absence of negative evidence no less than on the presence of the positive. In mapping people's mathematical objects one needs to remember that trying to specify *all* the elements of one's realization tree is not a viable research task. In our analyses, rather than asking whether interlocutors' objects are "the same," we should be trying to see whether there is a reason to suspect that they might be different.

1.2 *How Discursive Objects Come into Being*

Let me now turn to the processes of construction of discursive objects. The task is, in a sense, the reverse of what I did in the preceding sections. So far, we have been looking at processes of realization employed by the mathematist in the attempt to interpret familiar signifiers. I am now going to look at realization trees in the reverse direction: Rather than "unpacking" them from their roots, I will now proceed from the "leaves" of the trees to their roots. This is the direction in which realization trees, and thus discursive objects, are being constructed in the first place. The main question I will be asking may be formulated as follows: Why and how does a signifier of an

---

[7] Consider also the example offered by Lave (1988), a participant of her study constructed two-thirds of three-quarters of a cup of cottage cheese simply by spreading the cheese evenly on a plate, dividing it with two cuts into four equal parts, taking three of them, and then removing one.

Table 6.1. *Object analysis of Ari's talk in Episode 5.7*

Utterances	Object signifier	Realizing procedure	Realizations	Object[a]
[1a], [1b], [11a], [1c]	"the slope" "the intercept" "the zero"	In table 1. Find the zero in the left column of the table 2. In the right column of the table, find the number b corresponding to that zero	Written: −5 Spoken: *minus five*	The intercept
Writes: $5x + -5$		In algebraic formula Locate the free coefficient in the formula $5x + -5$	Written: −5 Spoken: *minus five*	The intercept
[1d], [13], [15], [19]	"slope"	In table[b] 1. In the left column, check the difference Δx between successive numbers, x_1 and x_2 2. In the right column, check the difference Δy between the corresponding numbers, y_1 and y 3. Find the ratio $a = \Delta x/\Delta y$	Written: 5 Spoken: *five*	The slope
[3], [5]	"slope"	In algebraic formula[b] Locate the coefficient of x in the formula $5x + -5$	Written: 5 Spoken: *five*	The slope

[a] This is, of course, my interpretation of Ari's signified object (in this case, interpretation is the signifier that the interpreter uses exchangeably with the singfier that is being interpreted). Because Ari's use of the signifiers *slope* and *intercept* was rather confusing (see his hesitation between these two words in [1] and [11] in Episode 5.7), I needed to attend to his realizing procedure and the resulting realizations before I could come up with my interpretation of this signified object. In the first row, for example, I concluded that his object is the one I myself evoke when I use the signifier *slope*. My interpretation, like any other, is tentative, and I will regard it as the best available hypothesis as long as no contradicting evidence is found.

[b] This table-based procedure can also be described in structural terms as "locating the right column counterpart of the left-column zero."

168

existing object become a realization of another signifier? Or, to put it in a somewhat different way, what is it that makes people collapse a number of dissimilar things into one – into realizations of a new signifier? To translate it into a concrete example, how do entities as different as the canonical parabola, table of numbers paired with their squares, and the formula x^2 come to be seen, one day, as similar enough to become realizations of the same signifier, "the basic quadratic function"?

Let me begin by dividing all the objects into *primary* and *discursive*, or *p-objects* and *d-objects*, for short. Discursive objects have already been defined, and one way to define the term *primary object* is to say simply that it refers to an object – a perceptually accessible entity – that cannot be called discursive. More specifically,

> **Definition**: The term *primary object* (*p-object*) refers to any perceptually accessible entity existing independently of human discourses, and this includes the things we can see and touch (material objects, pictures) as well as those that can only be heard (sounds).[8]

In other words, primary object is a real-life tangible thing that has not yet been signified and thus did not become an object of communication. The process of construction of discursive objects may now be described recursively, as follows: *Discursive object* (*d-object*) arises by "signifying" a set of *p*-objects or of previously created *d*-objects with a single *p*-object, that is, by replacing these sets with a single *p*-object for the sake of communication. To explain why and how such signification occurs, let me first define the simplest, "atomic" *d*-objects and then show how compound *d*-objects are built from those that have been constructed previously.

> **Definition**: *Simple (atomic) discursive objects* arise in the process of *proper naming (baptizing)*: assigning a noun or other nounlike symbolic artifact to a specific primary object. In this process, a pair <noun or pronoun, specific primary object> is created. The first element of the pair, the signifier, can now be used in communication about the other object in the pair, which counts as the signifier's only realization. For example, assigning my dog

---

[8] One can even go further and say that the primary object is a set of images or sounds that are associated one with another and recognized as "the same" (the criterion for the "saming" is that a person reacts to the different images or sounds in the same way) primary to (independent of) naming. According to Piaget, people are not born with even this most basic form of saming (objects) but rather construct the primary objects – learn to treat the different images as the images "of the same thing" – in the first few months of their lives. It is this initial saming that Piaget had in mind in speaking about children's acquiring the principle of "permanence of objects." The empirical support offered by Piaget to corroborate this hypothesis has been challenged by others (see Dehaene, 1997).

the noun *Rexie* (or the words *my dog*, for that matter) is an act of creation of the discursive object Rexie (my dog). *Compound discursive objects* arise by according a noun or pronoun to extant objects, either discursive or primary, in one of the following ways:

- By *saming*, that is, by assigning one signifier (giving one name) to a number of things that, so far, have not been considered as in any way "the same" but are mutually replaceable in a certain closed set of narratives[9]
- By *encapsulating*, that is, by assigning a signifier to a set of objects and using this signifier in singular when talking about a property of all of the set members taken together
- By *reifying*, that is, by introducing a noun or pronoun with the help of which narratives about processes on some objects can now be told as "timeless" stories about relations between objects.[10]

Let me elaborate on each one of these constructions.

The process of *saming* can be seen as the act of calling different things the same name. Thus, we create a new *d*-object when we assign the signifier *finger* to all the elongated objects growing from human palms, when we pair the signifier *fraction* with all the symbols of the form $^a/_b$ where a and b are sequences of digits (numerals), or when we use the expression *basic square function* in communicating about both parabola and the expression x^2. Saming is thus the act of associating one signifier with many realizations. The necessary basis for such saming is the fact that whatever is said with the common signifier (e.g., *basic quadratic function*) and turns out to be endorsable when translated into a narrative about any of this signifier's realizations (the parabola) will be endorsable also when translated into a narrative about the other realization (the expression x^2). To state it more simply, the basis for calling two objects the same name is the fact that a certain closed subset of endorsed narratives about one of these objects is isomorphic to a certain closed subset of endorsed narratives about the other object. While reportedly describing mathematics as "the art of calling different things the same name" Henri Poincaré stressed the fact that although the process of saming-with-names is not unique to mathematical discourses, it plays a particularly prominent role in this discourse. The range and depth of the resulting realization trees are much greater than in any other discourse.

---

[9] A set of narratives is called closed if it contains all the narratives that can be logically derived from those already in the set.

[10] Some writers (e.g., Dubinsky, 1991) use the word *encapsulation* as exchangeable with the word *reification*. In this book the two are used in distinct ways, as described here.

Encapsulation is the act of assigning a noun or pronoun (signifier) to *a specific set* of extant primary or discursive objects, so that some of the stories about the members of this set that have, so far, been told in plural may now be told in singular. Encapsulation, therefore, is the creation of the pair <noun, specific *set of* objects>, which turns a number of objects into a single entity for any communicative purpose. For example, when we speak about the *Addams family*, we may continue and say "The Addams family *is* rich," and this is discursively equivalent to saying, in plural, "Members of the Addams family, when taken together, *are* rich." Similarly, when we say, "Three-quarters *is* bigger than two-thirds" (rather than saying that the three-quarters *are* bigger, as seems to be suggested by the plural form of the *three-quarters*) we encapsulate the set of three parts, each of them called *quarter*. Finally, when we speak about *basic quadratic function*, we encapsulate the set of ordered pairs of numbers such as $(1, 1), (2, 4), (3, 9)$.

It is notable that the preceding number-pairs are, in themselves a product of *reification* of the squaring operation. Much has already been said about this latter type of process, so let me add just a brief reminder. Basically, reification involves replacement of talk about processes with talk about objects. This is what happens, for instance, when the signifier $5/7$ is introduced and the utterance "I divided the whole by 7 and took 5 of the parts" turns into "I have 5/7 of the whole." Or to use another example, reifying the operation of squaring 2 leads to the ordered pair <2, 4>, which can also be realized as a point in the Cartesian plane. Combined with encapsulation of all such pairs created by letting the left element of the pair range over all possible numerical values, the reification leads to the discursive object called *basic quadratic function*. To give another example, the object we use to refer to as "number five" arises from sets of objects that, when counted, lead to the final number word *five*. This happens in two steps. First, the term *five fingers* is used to reify the process of counting the fingers of one's hand, then the phrase *five apples* replaces the discursive process of counting apples up to five, and so on. This assignment reifies the process of counting in that the noun phrase *five apples* replaces the processual description that says, "When I count these apples, I invariably end with the word *five*." At a later point, the discursive object "number five" arises when we decide to use the common name *five* in order to same all the instances of "five *somethings*."[11]

---

[11] To put it still another way, the relation between the noun *five* and its realizations in the form of specific sets of five objects is that of reification: Endorsed narratives that feature the noun *five* can be translated into endorsed narratives about the process of counting of the members of these sets.

Note that all three constructions that create a new object S – saming, encapsulating, and reifying – turn the component p-objects and the signifiers of the component d-objects into realizations of S. Indeed, according to the definition of these three constructions, whatever endorsed narrative is now created on S, this narrative is a translation of a narrative on its component subobject. Such translation is performed according to well-defined rules, the exact nature of which depends on whether the new object was created in the act of saming, encapsulating, or reifying. The discourse on S is thus isomorphic to certain closed subdiscourses about component objects.

1.3 *Mathematical Objects as Abstract d-Objects*

Let me now revisit the time-honored dichotomy between concrete and abstract objects. The term *concrete objects* can be defined as including all primary objects and all those discursive objects that arise through saming or encapsulating familiar primary objects. The realization trees of concrete objects are thus free of reifications. In contrast, abstract objects may be defined as d-objects that originate, among others, in reification of discursive processes.[12] According to this definition, a good example of a concrete d-object is *animal*, which is the product of saming *fish*, *bird*, *mammal*, and so forth, whereas each of these component objects is, in itself, a product of saming of concrete d-objects. The d-objects signified by *number* or *5* are abstract. The relations among the different types of objects, primary and discursive, concrete and abstract, are presented in Figure 6.2.

Having made all these distinctions, I may now say that *mathematical objects are abstract discursive objects with distinctly mathematical signifiers*, that is, signifiers regarded as mathematical. The claim made in the beginning of this chapter about the importance of perceptual elements in mathematical discourse can now be put in an even stronger form. Mathematical objects are not any less material than the primary objects, except that rather than being a single tangible entity that predates the discourse, they are complex hierarchical systems of partially exchangeable symbolic artifacts. A number of practical implications immediately follow.

[12] This definition corresponds to Jean Piaget's claim that what he called concrete and abstract thinking develop, respectively, through empirical and reflective abstraction. Lev Vygotsky would speak, in this context, about empirical and theoretical conceptualization. Of course, one needs to remember that neither Piaget nor Vygotsky regarded concept construction as a discursive process.

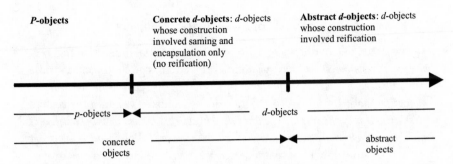

Figure 6.2. Mutual relations between categories of objects.

First, the need for teaching "mathematical formalism" in schools has always been a moot point. Those who object to "formalization" clearly assume that one can distinguish between "mathematical objects" and their "representations." This dualism of content and form or of object and tool-of-description is stated quite explicitly by the mathematician Alain Connes:

> The mathematician fashions what may be called *thought tools* [symbolic artifacts] for the purpose of investigating mathematical reality. These are not to be confused with mathematical reality itself.[13]

And yet, I have just argued that symbolic artifacts, far from being but "earthly incarnations" of the inherently intangible entities called mathematical objects are, in fact, the fabric of which these objects are made.

Another issue worth attention is the current tendency to engage schoolchildren in the activity of inventing their own symbolic systems. Although this is certainly a highly educative type of task, it does not eliminate the child's need to become acquainted with commonly endorsed realizations of generally adopted signifiers. Once again, far from being just optional proxies of the "real thing," the consensual, publicly endorsed signifiers and their realizations are the very thing that is being learned. To communicate with others and build on their ideas, one needs to use the same means as those endorsed by his or her interlocutors.

Finally, because mathematical communication does not differ from any other in its reliance on the senses, impairments of one's vision, hearing, or bodily movement may stand in the way of becoming a fluent mathematist.

---

[13] Jean-Pierre Changeaux and Alain Connes (1995, p. 13).

2. Historical Development of Mathematical Objects

Having stated that mathematical discourse is an autopoietic system that creates its own objects, and having defined the latter type of objects as those that originate in discursive *processes* on concrete objects rather than in the objects as such, I am now in the position to address yet another related question. *Historically speaking, what is it that spurred the emergence of different mathematical objects as well as their further evolution?* The issue is of great interest to philosophers of mathematics who wish to fathom the nature of mathematical discourse, and it is crucially important to students of human development and to educators who care about processes of learning – of individualization of mathematical discourse. The topic requires theoretical as well as empirical studies, and many monographs would have to be written to deal with it properly. Here, I will limit myself to a brief outline of the history of one mathematical object and to some general reflections on processes of individual object-making that are part and parcel of mathematical learning.

Creation of the discourse on function was the act of exogenous compression in which at least three different discourses were joined and subsumed in a new one. These discourses were, respectively, about algebraic formulas, about curves in the Cartesian plane, and about physical processes, such as the movement of falling bodies or of vibrating strings. The focal object called *function* was thus a product of saming of three types of discursive objects. An opportunity for this type of saming arises when mathematicians become aware of an isomorphism between different, seemingly unrelated sets of endorsed narratives. Identification of two such isomorphisms was crucial to the emergence of the discourse on functions. The first step was taken in the 17th century by René Descartes (1596–1650), the founder of analytic geometry, who is credited with the idea of matching curves in the plane with newly introduced algebraic symbols (formulas). This invention was grounded in his awareness of one-to-one relation-preserving correspondence between sets of algebraic and geometric narratives. A few decades later, in the work of Johann Bernoulli (1667–1748), Isaac Newton (1643–1727), Gottfried Leibniz (1646–1716), and many others, algebraic narratives were also associated with physical processes.

Of course, the set of all the generally endorsable stories one can tell about function is more restricted than the set of generally endorsable stories about any of its visual realizations – graphs, algebraic formulas, tables, and so forth. One can say that the stories about function that we endorse are those narratives that are true about all three of its realizations – the

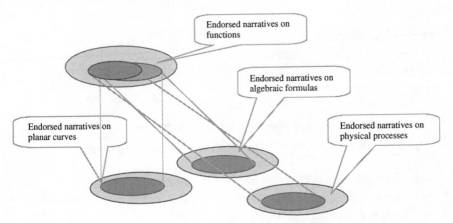

Figure 6.3. Discourse on function subsumes discourses on algebraic formulas, on curves, and on physical processes.

formulas, the curves, and physical processes – and they clearly do not exhaust all the true things that can be said about any of the latter objects (see Figure 6.3). Thus, some endorsed narratives about algebraic formulas – for instance, those that regard syntactic rules for constructing formulas – do not have an isomorphic equivalent in the discourse about curves, whereas some narratives about curves do not correspond to endorsed narratives about formulas (think about a curve representing the change of temperature over time). Some general truths about formulas will not make it to the new subsuming discourse on functions, and the same may be said in the case of curves or physical processes. What is lost in the amount of endorsable narratives is gained, however, in the remaining narratives' expressive power. One such narrative reveals "the truth" about more aspects of reality than the corresponding narratives on any of its realizations.[14]

The preceding explanation also implies that the discourse on functions is inherently unrealizable in just one mode, symbolic, iconic, or concrete. After all, if there were just one type of realization, say formula,

[14] At a certain point, the new subsuming discourse may also start producing narratives that have no counterpart in any of the discourses that gave rise to it. Think, for example, about nonnumerical functions that have no graph and no formula or about numerical functions that do not have a counterpart in one of the subsumed discourses, that on formulas of that on curves in the plane. The function that assigns to each natural number a value between 1 and 6 obtained by throwing a die is an example of function without a formula. The Dirichlet function, defined as the mapping that assigns the value 1 to every rational number and 0 to every irrational number, is a function without a graph (or, at least, its graph is not a single line in the Cartesian plane).

Johann Bernoulli, 1718	Leonard Euler, 1748
One calls a function of a variable a quantity composed in any manner whatever of this variable and of constants.	A function of a variable quantity is an analytical expression composed in any manner from that variable quantity and numbers or constant quantities.

Figure 6.4. Early definitions of function. After Kleiner (1989).

mathematicians would have no incentive to introduce a new signifier – we would simply speak about formulas.[15] This is why the first definitions of function, which associated the new signifier exclusively with a combination of "variables and constants" or with "analytic expressions" (see Figure 6.4), were short lived: They failed to capture the subsuming aspect of the new discourse (after all, even this early idea of function was already a response to the awareness of isomorphic correspondence between narratives on "analytic expressions" and on curves). The insufficiency of the definition that identified function exclusively with what we now view as its algebraic realizations became obvious when, after his famous debate with Jean-le-Rond d'Alembert about the problem of vibrating string,[16] Leonhard Euler became aware that his original rendering excluded the possibility of viewing certain types of physical movements as realizations of functions. These movements were not describable by a single formula but rather required what we now call a *split-domain* function. After this observation, Euler proposed a new definition of function, one that made no explicit reference to any specific visual realization. From now on, he said, "a quantity should be called function only if it depends on another quantity in such a way that if the latter is changed, the former undergoes change itself."[17] He went on to formulate a new definition: "If . . . x denotes a variable quantity then all the quantities which depend on x in any manner whatever, or are determined by it, are called its functions."[18] This time, rather than being a mark on paper, function presented itself as a disembodied abstract entity, existing independently of its perceptually accessible "avatars." This formulation made it clear that functions could not be identified with any specific primary object, but at

[15] Many people, especially students, do express themselves in this way. They say, for example, "function x^2" rather than "function expressed by the formula x^2." One needs, however, to distinguish between the cases when this phrase is just a convenient abbreviation and the cases when a person cannot see the difference between the two formulations.
[16] Kleiner (1989).
[17] Ruthing (1984, pp. 72–73).
[18] Ibid.

the same time it blurred the fact that they were a complex composition of such objects.

The benefits of the definition that made no reference to visual realizations showed themselves when the hegemony of iconic realizations (curves) ended as a result of further attempts at bridging between algebraic and geometric discourse. As a result, the new subsuming discourse made the category of objects recognized as functions even more inclusive.[19] Generalizing from this example, we may say that the inherent indispensability of multiple visual mediation is one of the defining characteristics of mathematical discourse.

3. Individualization of Mathematical Objects

A child who is being introduced to mathematical discourse is faced with other people's objectified uses of words or symbols. The order of things in the processes of discourse individualization is thus different from that in historical processes of object-creation. Think, for example, about such signifiers as number-words in the case of Roni and Eynat or "the slope of g" in the case of Gur. Initially, neither of these expressions signifies much to young learners; however, the need to communicate with those for whom the signifiers are but tips of rich realization trees will fuel the children's interpretive efforts. Their unwritten aim will be to connect the new with the old – to find a way to realize the novel signifiers in possibly unusual combinations of discursive constructs with which they are already familiar.

Only rarely will the realization effort be a mere guessing game. To begin with, the learners' attempts may be guided by examples and explicit definitions offered by more experienced interlocutors. Indeed, exemplifying and defining are what mathematics teachers usually do while introducing a new signifier. As straightforward and promising as this strategy may appear, however, it may not be the first priority of the newcomer. More often than not, the learner would opt for a gradual immersion in the new mathematical discourse – the process in which she may be able to take advantage of learning techniques that have been working for her in colloquial discourses. One such technique is based on the mechanism of metaphor, that is, of inserting the new signifier into familiar discursive templates. To see how it works, you are invited to pause for a moment and implement the sequence of tasks presented in Figure 6.5. This self-experiment will give you the opportunity to learn from firsthand experience that a single, very

[19] Any single–valued mapping, not necessarily numerical, is now a function.

You have never heard the word *krasnal* before, but you have just read the sentence

A krasnal woke up and got up from his bed.

This sentence does not tell you what a *krasnal* is (it is not a definition), but after you read it you may still be able to answer many questions about *krasnals*. Just try the following:

1. Which of the following syntactically correct propositions seem to you to be meaningful sentences about krasnals, and which of them do not?
   - *Yesterday, a krasnal went to a supermarket.*
   - *A krasnal was divided by three and then squared.*
   - *Some of the krasnals were cheerful, some of them sang.*
   - *This krasnal is raised by public subscription.*
   - *A krasnal begins at 5:30 p.m.*
   - *This krasnal is younger than this one.*
2. Now, can you complete the following sentence in a meaningful way?
   - *Krasnal A is cheerful,* whereas *krasnal B is . . .*
3. Finally, try to construct a possibly meaningful sentence about *krasnals* yourself. Build one you believe cannot be meaningful.
4. And now, reflect on what you did and try to tell what made you able to
   - disqualify the utterance about "squaring *krasnals*" as senseless
   - complete the sentence about *krasnals* in a sensible way
   - create a new sentence about *krasnals*

Figure 6.5. The mechanism of interpreting new signifiers according to familiar discursive templates.

brief exposure to the use of a word would often be enough to turn a person into a beginning participant in a new discourse. It is thanks to the spontaneous metaphorical projections that we manage to break the inherent circularity of the process of object-creation and engage in the new type of talk while still unable to realize the new signifier in any way. The workings of metaphor are pretty straightforward. The familiar discursive form into which the unfamiliar signifier has been inserted produces an association with other familiar forms and evokes an awareness of what may be proper or improper as an utterance about the new object, which, in itself, is yet to be built.

Repetition of what was done before in new situations that, for one reason or another, seem to invite a similar sequence of actions is the very gist of learning. Such repetitions may be quite crude – they may be too indiscriminate or altogether out of place. Be they as rough as they may, however, these first awkward word uses are the indispensable beginning. They will be fine-tuned in further interactions with more experienced mathematists.

These and other processes have certainly contributed to the changes that we were able to observe in the numerical discourse of Roni and Eynat when we returned to them after a 7-month-long break with the battery of comparison tasks from the first series of interviews. This time, the children's use of number-words and words of numerical comparisons was not so different from that of the grown-ups as it was 7 months earlier. To begin with, Roni and Eynat were now using number-words in full sentences, such as "Six is less than eight."[20] This is a considerable step forward to a more variegated, more flexible use of these words. Having said this, I should also stress that the girls still displayed a preference for the adverbs *less* and *more* over the adjectives *smaller* and *bigger*, and this indicated that they used number-words mainly as descriptors of sets, and not as signifiers of self-sustained objects. Another point to note is that they were now using the generic word *number* – a word that had never appeared in their former utterances and that, in their earlier conversations, Roni's mother seemed to avoid deliberately[21] so as not to expose the children to terms with which she did not expect them to be able to cope. Thus, for example, after having counted the contents of a box, Eynat pointed to that box and said, "Look at the *number* that it gave me," thereby urging Roni's mother to check for herself that the number she found was correct. On another occasion, while faced with an empty box, Roni declared, "There is no number." Even if rather nonstandard, both these utterances belong to the category of objectified uses of the word *number*.

As the conversation proceeded, the children also became able to use the word *number* in conjunction with the expression *the same*. To be sure, they did not seem to be capable of such use when the new meeting began. Their enduring resistance to the term *the same* in the numerical context is readily visible in the following exchange, which took place after the children discovered two marbles in each of the two boxes.

---

[20] Because of idiosyncrasies of Hebrew, the literal translation should be "Six is more-little than eight," with the *more little* not entirely standard but easily understandable as equivalent to *less*.

[21] For example, here is the way she formulated the request to make the contents of two boxes equal: "Can it be done so that there be the same [thing]? That there be the same marbles in both boxes [....] the same amount of marbles in the tw...." Obviously, without the word *number* (or the word *amount*, for that matter, which the mother eventually did utter) the efforts could not be very successful.

Episode 6.1a. *The same – 7 months later*

125.	Mother:	If there is 2 here and 2 here, in which is there more?	
126.	Roni:	In none.	Shows two with her fingers.
127.	Mother:	And where is there less?	
128.	Roni:	In none.	
. . . . . .		And this is . . . more or less?	
132.	Roni:	It is not more and not less.	
133.	Mother:	Neither more nor less? So what?	
134.	Roni:	In the middle.	

In the view of all the advances made during the 7 months that passed since the first meeting, we found this persistent confusion quite striking. The puzzlement was aggravated by the fact that the girls were using the words *the same* in other contexts. For example, Roni declared on a number of occasions that she and Eynat "did the same thing." It was thus extremely interesting to see the sudden breakthrough that happened just moments after Episode 6.1a. Frustrated with the children's persistent inability to say what she considered obvious, Roni's mother eventually decided to make her intentions explicit:

147.	Mother:	Roni, so what does it say about the number of marbles? That it is. . . . *the same*?

Also in Episode 5.2, which took place 7 months earlier, the words *the same* were offered to the girls explicitly in a similar context (see Roni's father's utterance [56]). At that time, however, this offering had no effect on the girls' discourse. Now, the result was immediate. The children's next task was to compare boxes with two and four marbles, respectively. The following exchange took place after they successfully completed the assignment:

Episode 6.1b. *The same – 7 months later*

288.	Mother:	Can you do it so that there will be the same amount of marbles in the two boxes?

289. Roni:	Yes.	
290. Mother:	How?	
291. Roni:	(a) One moment.	(a) Empties both boxes.
	(b) It is *the same* number now.	

Later, Roni was also able to implement her mother's request "to make the same amount" differently, by distributing the marbles evenly (three and three) between the two boxes.

Although the sudden jump in discursive possibilities is certainly impressive, interpreting it as the ultimate evidence of reification of counting processes and of the emergence of a new discursive object may be premature. Rather, we have been witnessing the creation of a bond between the words *the same* and a certain type of situation, namely, a situation in which counting marbles ends with the same number-word in both boxes. Thus, all that can safely be claimed at this point is that the expression *the same* has been successfully associated with the procedure of evenly distributing marbles in boxes.

To sum up, Roni and Eynat are in the midst of creating their first mathematical signifier–realization pair. For all the advances already made, they still have a considerable way to go. Let me venture a general hypothesis about how their word uses are likely to change in the process of individualization. In the first phase, although not yet able to use a word in her own speech, the child may nevertheless be capable of certain routine reactions to other people's utterances containing the given word. This is the case, for example, when she does not yet incorporate the word *number* in her sentences but begins counting upon hearing the question "What is the *number* of marbles in this box?" With respect to the word *number*, Roni and Eynat were at this stage of *passive use* when we met them for the first time. Seven months later they were already beyond it; they were now actually uttering the word. This active use, however, occurred only in a restricted number of specific routines, as a part of constant discursive sequences. This type of use can be called *routine-driven*. The next step in the development of word use will be witnessed when words become linked with constant phrases rather than with whole routines. At this stage, which can be called *phrase-driven*, the entire phrases rather than the word as such constitute the basic building blocks of the child's utterances. In the case of words such as *number*, the process of individualization is completed when the word "gets a life of its own" as a noun. One can now insert this word in any proposition in which there is a slot for this particular grammatical category.

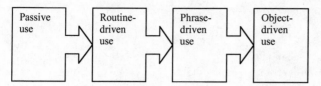

Figure 6.6. Four-stage model of the development of word use.

It is at this stage that the word becomes linked to a unique realization tree that remains relatively stable across contexts. Another characteristic phenomenon is the *transparency of the signifier*. When used, the signifier evokes immediate association with its realizations so that realizations rather then the signifier itself become a focus of attention. The use of the word is now guided by the signified object – by the user's awareness of the availability and contextual appropriateness of different realizations of the word. We may thus start talking about *object-driven* use of the word. The development of word use is schematically summarized in Figure 6.6.

4. Challenges of Object Construction

The hypothetical four-stage model of the gradual change in word use constitutes only a top-level description of the development. This development may also be described in terms of object construction. As explained previously, this construction would usually involve many interrelated acts of reification, saming, and encapsulation, each of which faces the learner with its own challenges. Let me survey some of these challenges briefly.

4.1 *The Challenge of Reification and the Anxiety of Unrealized Signifiers*

The very same process–object duality of algebraic symbolism that constitutes the source of its special advantages may put many students off simply because of its being at odds with universally endorsed narratives about things in the world. Recall, for instance, that composite symbolic expressions, such as $4 + 5$, $^{134}/_{29}$, or $2x + 1$, may be used both as prescriptions for processes and as the products of these processes.[22] Thus, we may treat

---

[22] The process–object duality is not unique to algebraic symbolism. Many colloquial words, such as *solution*, may be used in two roles – as signifiers of processes (in the present case, the process of solving), and signifiers of objects (the result obtained at the end of the solution process). However, the dualism of algebraic symbols is more difficult to accept,

$^{134}/_{29}$ as an *operation* of division or as the *result* of the division. This latter interpretation is involved when, for instance, one incorporates the expression $^{134}/_{29}$ into other symbolic expressions, such as, say, $(^{134}/_{29})^2 + 7$, thus treating $^{134}/_{29}$ as a realized object, ready to be operated upon. And yet, in the extradiscursive world, the notion of process that also serves as its own product sounds as implausible as the idea of eating the recipe for a cake instead of the cake itself. The confusion a participant in algebraic discourse may experience in having to deal with what appears to be a prescription for action but must be treated as the result of this action is well instantiated in the following conversation with Guy, a 15-year-old student who has nearly 2 years of algebra behind him. In Episode 6.2, Guy tries to solve the parametric equation $kx - x = -2$ for x. His momentary bafflement clearly stems from the difficulty of treating $k - 1$ as its own realization.

Episode 6.2. Guy solves $kx - x = -2$

1. Guy:	There is a multiplication here, so what can I do?	*points to kx*
2. Interviewer:	And if I wrote $3x - x$, would you be able to proceed?	
3. Guy:	$3x - x$? It's $2x$.	
4. Interviewer:	So? Isn't $kx - x$ similar?	
5. Guy:	But this... but this doesn't work... I don't know what k is.	
6. Interviewer:	What have you done here to get $2x$? What did you do to the 3?	*points to 3x – x*
7. Guy:	I subtracted 1... So what? Shall I subtract 1 here? I don't know... If I subtract 1 from k I will be left with the same mess... see, I don't know how to write it... How do I subtract 1 from k? How do I write it? $k - 1$?	

The "anxiety of unrealized *d*-objects," instantiated in this episode, may be explained in yet another way. As was argued earlier, the main advantage of

---

because, first, these are compound symbols that *read* as descriptions of processes; and second, whereas the word *solution* is realizable in two distinct separate forms, as a process (the description of a procedure) and as an object (the product of the solving procedure), this is not the case with algebraic expressions such as $2x + 1$ (there is no separate product of multiplying x by 2 and adding 1).

realizations is that they generate new endorsed narratives. This added value is made possible by the naturally occurring merge of the present discourse with the more familiar one, from which the realization was taken. Thus, when the *promenade*, which was initially but a bunch of intricately interconnected algebraic symbols, is realized as a 5×5 lattice (see Figures 5.4 and 5.5), one starts capitalizing on her ability to create and endorse narratives about geometric shapes just by scanning these shapes visually and without any symbolic manipulation. This example may suffice to conclude that to be truly helpful, processes of realization need to yield forms different from the original signifier. One can hardly see how anything new can be asserted about $k - 1$ without its being first worked out into a familiar object that can be combined with other familiar objects of the same kind.[23]

A close look at the history of mathematics reveals that the worry about unrealized algebraic expressions did not pass over mathematicians. This difficulty could well be the reason why computational discourse was much slower to develop than geometrical discourse. It was probably the reason why the third-century Greek mathematician Diophant, who was among the first to use combinations of letters and numerals in dealing with computational procedures, did not enter history as the father of symbolic algebra.[24] For Diophant the idea of using a prescription-for-a-process as the ready-made result of this process must have been as foreign as it was for Guy, who balked at the sight of the "unrealized" expression $k - 1$. A similar difficulty might have prompted Newton's declaration that "algebra is the analysis of bunglers in mathematics."[25] The autobiographical testimony of the mathematician William Thurston that appears at the beginning of this chapter is a rare case of retroactive documentation of the experience of coming to terms with the process–object duality of mathematical symbols.

At this point it is natural to ask how one can help students who have not yet reconciled themselves with unrealized expressions. One such method

---

[23] The related common phenomenon, students' tendency to "simplify" expressions such as $3x + 2$ as $5x$ or even just 5 is known in the literature as "the need for closure" (Chalouh & Herscovics, 1988). One can view this type of action as additional evidence for students' inability to use what appear to be prescriptions for a sequence of operations as if they were already realized as objects.

[24] Diophant's mathematical discourse that involved a mixture of verbal and symbolic expressions is known as *syncopated algebra*. Until his time, and for more than a millennium afterward, algebra was mainly rhetoric, that is, practiced in words only, without any symbolic mediation. The algebraic symbolism, as we know it, was introduced only at the end of the 16th century, and although proposed in one form or another by many individuals simultaneously, it is credited mainly to the French mathematicians François Viète (1540–1603) and René Descartes (1596–1650).

[25] Kline (1980, p. 124).

would be to replace compound symbolic expressions with simple ones, thus according them the appearance of an accomplished, full-fledged "thing." This ploy, however, cannot be truly effective. Historically speaking, this is what was done by mathematicians in the case of negative and complex numbers when expressions such as $3 - 8$ or $\frac{1}{2} - 1$ were replaced with -5 and $-\frac{1}{2}$, respectively, and when $\sqrt{(-1)}$ was substituted with i. This mere renaming did not result in any real breakthrough, though. One explanation may be that the new symbols did not entail any new discursive possibilities, as icons and concrete objects usually do. In both cases, it was discourse-enriching iconic mediation that eventually did the job. For negative numbers, the discourse-enhancing realization was the number line extended infinitely to the left of the origin; for complex numbers, it was the complex plane organized by "real" and "imaginary" axes.[26] Iconic and concrete realizations seem thus indispensable also in mathematics classrooms.

Another issue to consider in the present context is the remedial potential of practice. That practicing a discourse on, say, negative and complex numbers may, indeed, help in getting used to the counterintuitive duality of algebraic symbols has been repeatedly noted by mathematicians. For instance, Girolamo Cardan (1501–1576), who could see the usefulness, although not "the inner logic," of "unrealizable" formulas such as $3 - 8$ or $\sqrt{(-1)}$, urged his fellow mathematicians to persist in using these expressions while "putting aside mental tortures involved."[27] A few centuries later, the French historian and philosopher of mathematics Philip E. B. Jourdain justified this advice as advice that, in hindsight, obviously proved itself:

> For centuries mathematicians used "negative" and "positive" numbers, and identified "positive" numbers with signless numbers like 1, 2, and 3, without any scruple, just as they used fractionary and irrational "numbers." And when logically-minded men objected to these wrong statements, mathematicians simply ignored them or said: "Go on; faith will come to you." And the mathematicians were right.[28]

4.2 Challenges of Saming

The first challenge facing those who wish to create a subsuming discourse by saming hitherto unrelated objects with the help of a single signifier is

---

[26] This iconic mediator is also known as the *Argand plane* and is sometimes called the *Gauss plane*. The real number line was introduced in the 18th century and the complex plane in the 19th (Kline, 1980; Boyer & Mertzbach, 1989).

[27] Kline (1980, p. 116).

[28] Jourdain (1956, p. 27).

the resulting loss of certain deeply entrenched endorsed narratives. This difficulty is particularly acute when the saming signifier is taken from one of the subsumed discourses. As a result of the new saming, a considerable change will occur in this signifier's use. The amount of its realizations will grow whereas the amount of relevant endorsed narratives will decrease. Consider, for example, one's first encounter with the discourse on rational numbers. This discourse subsumes two seemingly unrelated forms of talk: the discourse on objects such as *one*, *two*, *three*, and so on – and the discourse on objects called *ratios* – 1:2, 3:5, and so on. So far, the word *number* has been reserved for the first type of object, but in the subsuming discourse the ratios will also count as its realizations, that is, as numbers (see the schematic presentation of this transition (a) in Figure 4.4). After this growth of the realization tree, a narrative such as "Multiplication makes bigger" (or, more precisely, "A product of two numbers is bigger than either of the numbers"), so readily and obviously endorsable as long as the word *number* is reserved for *one*, *two*, *three*, and so on, will have to be given up. The concession may not be easy to make. The lingering of old discursive endorsements and their reappearance in discourses in which they are bound to lead to contradictions are the well known phenomenon that gave rise to the theory of misconceptions discussed in chapter 1 (section 3).

Another challenge that accompanies first attempts to use a common signifier for objects that did not count earlier as in any way "the same" is the counterintuitive nature of this process. The primary source of saming lies in visually performed routines: We speak about different-looking things as "the same" if we can transform one of the images into the other in a continuous manner. It is such transformability that underlies our claim that the person who speaks to us now is *the same person* as the one who was talking to us a minute ago, even though the image before our eyes has changed. Indeed, either we actually witnessed this continuous transformation of the former image into the present one or, on the basis of our previous experience, we are aware that such a transformation must have taken place.

In abstract discourses, the mechanism of saming is different. Consider such an endorsed narrative as "$5 + 3(x + 2) = 3x + 11$ for all x," according to which the two component expressions, $5 + 3(x + 2)$ and $3x + 11$, are equivalent (and thus, in a sense, "the same"). As in the case of primary objects, one way to substantiate this narrative is to show a certain kind of transformability. For instance, we may manipulate the first expression by applying the distributive law and then grouping similar terms. And yet, this operation is quite unlike the one that allows us to transform one image of a person into another. First, the chain of operations performed according to the laws of algebra does not result in a visible *continuous* transformation of the image we see. What we get is a discrete sequence of intermediary images (e.g., $5 + (3x + 6)$, and then $3x + (5 + 6)$), none of which resembles its predecessor in an immediately obvious way. Second, identity-preserving transformations of concrete images, such as an image of a person, do not leave behind them the visible "history" of the transformation in the way symbolic artifacts do. Indeed, when we transform a formula, all the intermediary expressions can be seen simultaneously written on a page alongside each other. Algebraic saming may thus be seen as contradicting the experiences underlying our sense of sameness in the case of primary objects. After all, we cannot see a person simultaneously as she is now and as she was 3 minutes ago (unless helped by a camera, of course). If we did see these two images together, we would have said we were seeing two different people.

For reasons of mathematical consistency and elegance, which I will not discuss now, transformability is not the preferred textbook substantiation of algebraic equivalence. Rather, textbook authors would explain that two formulas such as $5 + 3(x + 2)$ and $3x + 11$ count as *equal* or *equivalent* because they may be realized with the help of the same table of values or the same graph. This kind of substantiation, as elegant and desirable as it is in the eyes of the mathematician, may have little appeal for the student. Data from several studies have shown that although the symbolic transformations deviate considerably from the transformations of concrete objects, the argument of transformability may still appear more acceptable than the claim about shared graphs or tables. Thus, for example, in the *Montreal Algebra Project* the students were introduced to the notion of equivalent expressions after they discovered that different-looking linear expressions could have the same graph. A few days passed during which the class engaged in solving problems such as "Among the given expressions, which are equivalent to $3x + 11$?" Following are excerpts from the classroom conversation that took place some time later.

Episode 6.3. Equivalence of algebraic expressions

1. Teacher: What does it mean that two expressions are equivalent? .... If two expressions are called equivalent, what do you, what does that mean? Sam...

2. Sam: That they *equal the same*.

3. Teacher: What do you mean when you say that?

....

Episode 6.3 *(continued)*

7. Sam:	They *are the same*.
. . . .	
. . . .	
35. Jas:	They, *they're basically the same thing*, but they look different.

The debate went on for a long time; the preceding excerpts convey its gist. It is remarkable that the existence of a common table or a common graph, which had been discussed in the class as the defining feature of equivalent expressions, was never mentioned in this conversation, and that the students spoke in terms of *sameness* rather than equivalence ("equal the same" [2], "are the same" [7], "they are . . . the same thing" [35]). The language of sameness is yet another indication of their preference for transformability as the required defining property. Indeed, this language imposes itself whenever the present image appears as a transformation of what was seen before. This is clearly the way one tends to think when a new formula is connected to the former one with the equality symbol.

Resistance to the loss of endorsed narratives and the preference for the criterion of transformability can be hurdles to mathematical saming. These may well be the reasons why beginning mathematists would often be unable to see as the same what grown-ups cannot see as different. On the basis of what has been learned from cross-cultural and cross-situational research, saming may be most problematic when it is supposed to bridge between colloquial and literate discourses. If such cross-discursive saming does not occur, the two discourses will function as mutually exclusive rather than exchangeable. In particular, everyday situations will evoke only colloquial forms of mathematical talk, whereas institutionalized educational settings will be dominated by literate discourses. In the traditional language, this phenomenon is described as the "lack of transfer." The case of the Brazilian street vendor, M, who did not associate the school signifier 4·35 with the money transaction that he had implemented so skillfully just a few days earlier is a good example. In this context, I also recall a successful psychology graduate, Rinat, who, when asked to recount her story as a mathematics student, wrote: "[In elementary school] I could not understand why they told us to solve '¼ of 5' as '¼ ·5.'" In the conversation that followed she explained: "I was perfectly able to find a quarter of five cups of flour, and I could multiply ¼ by 5; what I didn't know was what made these two operations in any way 'the same.'" M's and Rinat's literate and colloquial realization trees were fully disjoint: The signifiers $4 \cdot 35$ and $\frac{1}{4} \cdot 5$ failed to work for them as the "kingpins of sameness" through which two realization trees combine into one.

An important point to remember is that the ability to see sameness in different-looking things may be highly situated. A person who realized a signifier in a given way in one context may be incapable of the same association in another context. To put it in a metaphorical way, some paths down or up one's realization tree may be open in some situations and blocked in others. Once again, this phenomenon is most common for those links that connect colloquial and literate realizations of mathematical signifiers. In our interviews we often saw students who seemed unable to realize mathematical signifiers in colloquial ways until explicitly assured that it would be "perfectly okay" to do so. This is what happened in the case of Mira, who had no difficulty realizing literate signifiers such as $7 \cdot 16$ via icons and concrete objects but who would not reveal this ability without a great deal of probing by the interviewer. Clearly, the link between the literate signifier and the colloquial realizations remained blocked as long as she interpreted the interview as a classroom situation in which such a realization would often be deemed improper.

Finally, one needs to remember that different people may use the same signifier while saming across different sets of objects. Roni's and Eynat's inability to see as "the same" the things that the grown-ups could not see as different is one manifestation of this phenomenon. A similar example can be found in Lewis Carol's famous character Humpty Dumpty, who could see only as the same what most people could see as different:

> "I shouldnt know you again if we *did* meet," Humpty Dumpty replied in a discontented tone, giving [Alice] one of his fingers to shake: "you're so exactly like other people." "The face is what one goes by, generally," Alice remarked in a thoughtful tone. "That's just what I complain of," said Humpty Dumpty. "Your face is the same as everybody has – the two eyes...nose in the middle, mouth under. It's always the same."[29]

4.3 *Challenges of Encapsulation*

Encapsulation – replacing the plural form with the singular when referring to a collection of objects – faces the learner with challenges of its own. The mere grammatical change may be not enough to bring about the consolidation of a collection into a single entity. Some students would thus continue

---

[29] Carroll (1998, 1982, p. 196).

referring to individual elements even when asked about the set as a whole. In a study on school students' discourse on infinity, the interviewees were asked to "tell which of the two sets, the set of odd numbers or the set of even numbers, [was] bigger."[30] The following excerpt is representative of solutions offered by a sizable proportion of interviewees:

Episode 6.4. Which set is larger?

1. Interviewer: Given the set of all the even numbers and the set of all the odd numbers, which set is bigger?

2. Rona: The evens.

3. Interviewer: The evens is bigger? *[Note the teacher's use of the singular in spite of the plural form of the subject]*

4. Rona: Because . . . one . . . one and . . . one is odd and two is even. And so it goes.

The "so it goes" in utterance [4] seems to say that for each subsequent odd number the corresponding even number is bigger. This latter inequality is translated into the relation between "all the odds" and "all the evens." Thus, rather than trying to compare the numerosity of the two sets by constructing one-to-one mapping from one of the sets to the other, as could be expected from an experienced mathematist, the interviewee compared single elements with respect to their numerical values.

Another related phenomenon was observed in a study in which a class was just introduced to the set-theoretical operation of *unifying* sets.[31] In the problem-solving activities that followed, the most common student error was the confusion between the connectives *and* and *or* (conjunction and disjunction) in presenting the defining conditions of the unification of two sets. Thus, for example, the student would write:

$$\{x: x < 3\} \cup \{x: x > 5\} = \{x: x < 3 \text{ and } x > 5\}$$

or even in the "simplified form"

$$\{x: x < 3\} \cup \{x: x > 5\} = \{x: 5 < x < 3\}$$

instead of the required

$$\{x: x < 3\} \cup \{x: x > 5\} = \{x: x < 3 \text{ or } x > 5\}.$$

[30] Caduri (2005).
[31] Sfard (1987).

This common confusion seems, indeed, indicative of the difficulty with the transition from plural to singular (or, in this case, from the talk about numerous objects to the talk about a single representative that epitomizes them all): The connector *and*, which would have been appropriate if the condition had been put in plural ("all the elements of *A and* all the elements of *B* belong to the union") becomes inadequate when applied to a single element of the set.

4.4 *Pedagogical Remark*

The upshot of what has been said here is that those who wish to come to terms with new signifiers face many challenges. The obvious question is how a novice mathematist can be helped in the task of object construction. This query merits its own studies, and several such studies are already under way. For now, let me mention just one general principle.

All the hurdles of object-construction mentioned in this chapter contribute to, and are in turn aggravated by, the self-generating (autopoietic) nature of mathematical discourse and by the resulting inherent circularity of construction processes. The fundamental question, therefore, is how the circle of discourse-building can be broken. The principle "Practice makes meaningful," previously mentioned as a possible cure for the anxiety of unrealized objects, may be of help also in this more general case. This principle is certainly in tune with the teachings of Wittgenstein, for whom the meaning of a word (or mediator) was no other than this word's use in discourse, and who, in fact, endorsed this maxim openly while offering the following "instructional" advice: "Let the use *teach* you the meaning."[32]

Earlier I remarked that unlike the historical process of signification, the processes of individualization are grounded mainly in attempts to realize new signifiers to which one is exposed while particiapting in the discourse with more expereinced interlocutors. Metaphorically, we can thus say that the historical and individual developments stress opposite directions: The former are predominantly upward oriented, that is, aim at creating ever higher realization trees; the latter are mainly attempts to connect a new signifier to familiar objects. Such linking, if successful, will turn the new signfier into a top of a new realization tree, with the familiar objects constituting this tree's lower layers. This said, let me stress that neither historical creations nor the processes of individualization are unidirectional. Indeed, both types of construction involve up and down zigzagging along

---

[32] Wittgenstein (1953/2003, p. 181).

the branches of realization trees, from one layer of mathematical objects to another. In the processes of learning, the proportions of significations – of the upward movement from existing objects to new ones – and of realizations – of the downward movement from a new signifier to its realizations in the existing objects – are a matter of the pedagogical philosophy of the teacher.[33]

5. Objects of Mathematical Discourse – in a Nutshell

While trying to pinpoint the gist of famously impalpable mathematical objects one is likely to feel as if she is chasing a phantom. In this chapter, after having shown that perception – the sense of sight, of touch, and of hearing – plays as fundamental a role in mathematics as in any other discourse, I engaged in the project of operationalizing this elusive idea. To implement the task, I focused on the question of how signifier–realization pairs come into being in the first place.

The first thing to note in this context was that more often than not, realizations can also serve as signifiers and thus a realization of a signifier can be realized even further. If the process of "unpacking" of a given signifier is reiterated, its *tree of realizations* results. The signifier S together with its realization tree is called *discursive object*, or *d-object*, for short, as opposed to *primary objects* (*p-objects*), which are unnamed perceptually accessible things. To put it recursively, S is a *d-object* if S is an atomic *d-object* of the form <proper name, specific primary object>; or S is a compound object created through the processes of *saming, encapsulating,* or *reifying* of other *d-objects* with the help of S. Saming is attained by giving one name to many different objects. This can be done whenever the samed objects share a closed set of endorsed narratives (that is, every narrative about one of the objects has an isomorphic counterpart in the form of an endorsed narrative about the other object). Reification consists in associating a noun with a discursive process and replacing narratives about those processes with equivalent narratives about the object signified by the noun. Encapsulation is the act of replacing talk about numerous objects, in the plural, with talk in the singular, in which one signifier refers to all these former objects taken together as one entity.

---

[33] These days, the tendency is to keep processes of learning close to those of historical invention. In such processes the element of signification – of inventing new signifiers and creating one's own mathematical objects as a prelude to being introduced to those taken from existing public discourses – is strongly recommended (e.g., National Council of Teachers of Mathematics, 2000).

An object is called *concrete* if it is either a *p*-object or a *d*-object constructed by saming or encapsulating primary objects. *Abstract objects* are *d*-objects originating in reified processes on *p*-objects. *Mathematical objects* are abstract objects with distinctly mathematical signifiers. These objects are personal constructions, and different mathematists may associate different objects with the same signifier. If they do, their ability to communicate is impaired.

A number of conclusions about mathematical objects immediately follow. First, although regarded as inaccessible to senses, mathematical objects are in fact complex combinations of visible realizations. Second, a special property of literate mathematical discourses that sets them apart from many others is that no one type of visual mediation – symbolic, iconic, or concrete – would suffice to realize this discourse in its entirety. Metaphorically, one can say that mathematics resides in relations between visual realizations, not in the realizations as such. Third, mathematical communication apparently reverses the developmental order known from colloquial discourses: Whereas these latter discourses are created for the sake of communication about physical reality, in mathematical discourse objects are created for the sake of communication. True, mathematical communication is also supposed, eventually, to mediate practical activities, and thus to pertain, in one way or another, to the world of primary objects that predate the discourse. However, this fact may easily escape one's attention. The realization trees of mathematical signifiers, although likely to have primary objects or processes on such objects as their basis, may be too rich and complex to be embraced at a glance. Leaving the concrete foundations of such trees out of sight may thus be the condition for the proficiency of mathematical communication.

Processes of individualization of the use of mathematical nouns are of particular interest to those who seek pedagogical applications of research on human development. A model has been suggested according to which learners proceed from the *passive* use of such signifiers to *routine-driven*, to *phrase-driven*, and eventually to *object-driven* use. As one advances through these stages, the use of the word becomes broader and more flexible. In this process, the increasingly skillful "peripheral participant" overcomes multiple hurdles inherent in the processes of saming, reifying, and encapsulating. First, creation of subsuming discourses involves loss of some of the previously endorsed generalizing narratives. Second, saming processes in mathematical discourses may often appear counterintuitive, as they do not match our everyday experience. Two properties make them quite different from the identity-preserving transformations of concrete discourses:

the discreteness of the symbolic operations that transform one realization into an equivalent one and the fact that they leave behind them a trace of visible intermediary forms. With relation to reification, the learner may suffer from the anxiety of unrealized signifiers and be baffled by the counterintuitiveness of process–object duality. The action of encapsulation faces learners with yet another type of difficulty, one that finds its expression in their frequently observed inability to translate the properties of elements into properties of the set, and vice versa.

On the top of all these obstacles, there is the already mentioned inherent circularity of the process of individualization: Participation in mathematical discourse is both a result of and a precondition for our ability to construct mathematical objects. This dilemma is yet to be dealt with in a detailed way. In the meantime, the principle "Practice makes meaningful," consonant with Wittgenstein's theory of meaning as words' use in discourse, has been proposed as an alternative to the idea of "meaning before practice."

Although by operationalizing the notion of mathematical object I seem to have answered the question of what mathematical discourse is all about, many important queries are yet to be tackled. One of them concerns the way mathematical objects mediate our practical actions. We shall deal with this issue in chapter 8. In the meantime, in the next chapter, we will take a closer look at the way mathematists perform their discursive actions and decide when to perform them.

7   Routines

How We Mathematize

We are what we repeatedly do. Excellence then, is not an act, but a habit.

Aristotle

The rules of formation operate not only in the mind or consciousness of individuals, but in discourse itself; they operate therefore, according to a sort of uniform anonymity, on all individuals who undertake to speak in this discursive field.

Michel Foucault[1]

If the meaning of words is in their discursive use, Wittgenstein's exhortation "to let use teach us meaning" makes perfect sense and may even appear tautological. It is by reproducing familiar communicational moves in appropriate new situations that we become skillful discursants and develop a sense of meaningfulness of our actions. The all-important regularities to be found in any discourse are the focus in this chapter.

1. Meaningfulness from Repetition

In chapter 4, communication was defined as a collectively implemented activity that, when observed over time in its diverse manifestations, displays repetitiveness, and thus patterns. The repetitiveness is the source of communicational effectiveness. If I know how to react to a given action of an interlocutor, it is because I was exposed to a similar situation before and am now able to implement an action quite similar to the one that was performed then.

[1] Foucault (1972, p. 63).

Figure 7.1. Two patterns created by a rhythmic multilevel (recursive) reiteration of the same doodle.

Discursive patterns are multifaceted and intricately interrelated. Words and symbols are combined into utterances; the utterances, through their structural commonalities and through their recurrent coappearance in discourse, solidify into stable associations of communicational actions and re-actions; these latter associations, in turn, are coupled with sets of situations and practical deeds that, from now on, will occasion their use. The communicative power of tools such as words, graphs, or algebraic symbols, therefore, does not inhere in these objects but is rather a result of habitually created links between their different uses and situations in which the uses are made. To put it metaphorically, in communication, the effect of a systematic rehearsal is much like that of a rhythmic repetition of an accidental doodle (Figure 7.1). Both turn the originally "meaningless" item into a communicational artifact, one we are able to re-act to in a nonarbitrary manner.[2]

---

[2] In fact, we have the propensity to view any regularity as a product of somebody's intentional doing and as an act or result of communicative action. In consequence, whenever witnessing a pattern we tend to suspect an "intelligent intervention." The term *intelligent intervention* may be defined as referring to an act by an agent with intention, capable of communicating, and thus of thinking, about things in the world. The tendency to ascribe commognitive purport to repetition and patterns finds its expression, among others, in the popular belief that the regularities known as "laws of nature" are the product of the "intelligent design." Some psychological examinations, such as the Rorschach test, in

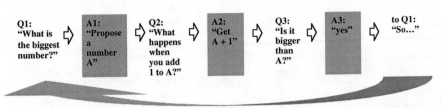

Figure 7.2. Ad hoc routine course of action in Episode 1.5.

Regularities can, indeed, be seen in every aspect of communication. A greeting that evokes another greeting is perhaps the simplest example of a discursive pattern. The use of logic in construction of meaningful discursive sequences or of certain problem-solving heuristics is another. Regularities can also be seen in the way we match our discourses with situations, the way we take turns in different kinds of conversations, the way we act as interviewers or as interviewees, and so on, and so forth. In chapters 5 and 6 we had an opportunity to take a close look at a number of discursive patterns specific to mathematical discourse. Some of these regularities were *standard*, that is, would be recognized as proper by any experienced mathematist; some others were *idiosyncratic*, forged by the participants of a specific conversation in an ad hoc manner. The lexical regularities that we identified in Mira's and Talli's talk went beyond purely grammatical, but the two girls' uses of specifically mathematical words, such as *eighty-six* or *plus*, were rather standard. In contrast, Roni's and Eynat's use of numerical discourse keywords, although not arbitrary, was certainly idiosyncratic, that is, quite unlike the standard uses one may observe in discourses of experienced mathematists. In Episode 5.7, Ari implemented a standard procedure to realize the signifier "the slope of function *g*," whereas Gur was quite helpless because of his inability to come up with any predesigned sequence of steps.

In situations that do not automatically evoke standard routines, an ad hoc pattern would often settle in from the very first exchange. This is particularly true of educational settings. There is a salient rhythm to interactions involving newcomers to a discourse, trying to become its full-fledged participants. For example, in the conversation about the biggest number (Episode 1.5), the sequence of actions schematically presented in Figure 7.2 repeated itself four times in the span of less than 2 minutes (see Table 7.1).

Closer examination of this last example will shed more light on what it means that communication is a patterned activity. First, what we see here

which a person is shown a symmetrical inkblot, utilize this human propensity for viewing regularities as "communicating something."

Table 7.1. *Episode 1.5 as four implementations of the same ad hoc course of action*

Iteration		1	2	3	4
conjecture	Q1	[5] T: What is the biggest number you can think of?	[11] T: . . . what is the biggest number?	[15] T: Can one arrive at the biggest number?	[19] T: . . . what is the biggest number?
	A1	[6] N: Million	[12] N: Two million	[16] N: Yes	[20] N: There is no such number.
				[17] T: Let's assume google is the biggest number.	
test	Q2	[7] T: What happens when we add one to million?	[13] T: And if we add one to two million?	[17] T: Can we add one to google?	
	A2	[8] N: Million and one	[14] N: It's more than two million.	[18] N: Yes, there are numbers bigger than google.	
	Q3	[9] T: Is it bigger than million?			
	A3	[10] N: Yes			
evaluation	to Q1	[11] T: So. . .	[15] T: So. . .	[19] T: So. . .	

shows with clarity that communicational patterns are dynamic structures rather than perfectly invariant schemes of action. Indeed, although the repetitiveness of the exchange between Noa and the teacher is unquestionable, it is also notable that subsequent cycles involve modifications. Whereas the general structure of the sequence *conjecture–test–evaluation* is preserved, the details change. For example, in the second and third implementations of the course of action, the middle element of the tripartite pattern, the one called *test*, is much shorter than in the first round; this time, Noa is able to perform the testing actions singlehandedly, without the teacher's "scaffold."[3] The change, therefore, can be seen both in what is being done and in who does it. This kind of change is typical of interactions involving participants who are in the process of individualizing a discourse.[4]

Another point to make is that ad hoc repetitive sequences, although idiosyncratic, do not arise from nowhere. They are made possible by certain standard discursive patterns, already known to the interlocutors. Thus, the unique cyclic configuration that emerged in Noa's conversation with the teacher was constructed on the basis of the famous initiation–response–evaluation (IRE) pattern, which is the hallmark of teaching–learning interactions.[5] It was clearly because of the fact that the teacher's "so..." and her ensuing repetition of the initial question appeared in the discursive slot reserved for evaluation that Noa interpreted her interlocutor as requiring a revision of her former answer.

In this context, it is proper to recall the all-important recursivity of discursive patterns: Such patterns can usually be decomposed into smaller modules, each of which is a discursive unit in its own right, applicable in many additional contexts; or, to put it "in reverse," existing patterns may be combined to create ever more complex ones. This claim can be illustrated with two of our former examples. In Episode 1.1 we saw the standard comparing-by-counting procedure embedded in the larger discursive pattern that emerged when Roni and Eynat were faced with the question "In which box are there more marbles?" In Episode 1.3 (see Table 7.2), Ari's standard procedure for constructing the equation of a linear function given

---

[3] I call this subsequence a *test* because this name reflects the role it plays in the task implementation, at least according to the teacher (it is not clear whether this role is acknowledged by Noa).

[4] Following Vygotsky one can say that such interpretations are typical of interactions that happen within the "zone of proximal development" of the child.

[5] This pattern is, indeed, pervasive in traditional classrooms and, more generally, in any interaction in which there is intentional teaching (Mehan 1979; Sinclair & Coulthard, 1975). In Table 7.1, the third element, that of evaluation, does not appear explicitly at any stage, but this does not prevent Noa from interpreting the teacher's reactions as fulfilling the evaluative function.

Table 7.2. *Ari's course of action for finding the equation of a quadratic function from a table of values (in case there is a zero in the left column)*

Find equation from the table	1. Find slope	1.1 In the left column, check the difference Δx between successive numbers, x_1 and x_2
		1.2 In the right column check the difference Δy between the corresponding numbers, y_1 and y_2
		1.3 Find the ratio $a = \Delta x / \Delta y$
	2. Find intercept	2.1 Find the zero in the left column of the table
		2.2 In the right column of the table, find the number b corresponding to that zero
	3. Write equation	Write the equation $y = ax + b$

by a table consisted of three independent modules, including the subprocedure for realizing the slope, and another one for realizing the intercept.

The quest for discursive patterns is the gist of commognitive research. Repetitions may be occurring in different aspects of discourse and across different fields and ranges. Sometimes, we are searching for what stays invariant across the whole community, and sometimes we scrutinize only discourses of newcomers. On other occasions, we search for patterns typical of mathematical discourses in schools, and in yet other cases we satisfy ourselves with what remains constant over time in the mathematical discourse of a certain classroom or even just in the discourse of an individual student. As in any other type of research, familiarity with what stays the same through incessant change is the basis for our understanding of phenomena and for our ability to extrapolate beyond the present set of data into a range of future situations.

2. Rules of Discourse

Human communication has been defined in chapter 4 as a rule-regulated activity, and the preceding observations about the repetitive, patterned nature of discourses convey the same message.[6] Any pattern, including

---

[6] In the last few decades, the theme of the rule-governed nature of human activities has been dealt with by many authors and has been presented and explained with the help of numerous theoretical constructs. Thus, Wittgenstein (1953/2003) speaks extensively of human communication as an instance of rule-following activity. Similarly, at the heart of Foucault's theory of discursive formations lies the assumption of the existence of rules

discursive, can be described as resulting from rule-governed processes. In this context, it is important to distinguish between *metadiscursive* and *object-level* rules. For example, the law of gravitation or Newton's laws of motion, all of them expressing patterns in the behavior of material bodies, are object-level rules of physics, because they regard the properties of the objects of this discourse and take the form of *narratives on these objects*. Similarly, mathematical narratives on geometric shapes, such as "The sum of the angles in a polygon with n sides equals $(n-2) \times 180°$," are object-level rules of geometry. Metarules are involved when we look at the patterned activity of formulation and substantiation of these object-level rules. These higher-level rules speak about the actions of the discursants, not about the behavior of mathematical objects. In physics, the metadiscursive rules define, among others, what counts as empirical evidence and how this evidence is used in the production of endorsable utterances about object-level rules. In mathematics, the relevant metarules are those that govern the activity of proving. More generally, *object-level rules are narratives about regularities in the behavior of objects of the discourse*, whereas *metarules define patterns in the activity of the discursants trying to produce and substantiate object-level narratives*. In our present context, that of the patterned nature of discursants' activity, we are interested mainly in this latter type of rule.

This said, it is important to stress an inherent relativity of the distinction between object-level and metalevel rules of mathematics. As was repeatedly noted, mathematics is an autopoietic system that grows by annexing its own metadiscourses, and this means, among others, that what counts as a

---

that regulate the discourse both "from outside" and "from inside," and without which the different discourses would neither be possible nor have their distinct identities (see the quote in the beginning of this chapter). The motif of activity-regulating rules, often hiding under different names and referring to a wide range of related phenomena, recurs in the seminal work of the French sociologist Bourdieu (1999). Without making an explicit reference to communicative activities, Bourdieu contributes to our present topic when speaking of *habitus*, "systems of durable, transposable dispositions, structured structures predisposed to function as structuring structures, that is, as principles which generate and organize practices and representations [thus discourses]" (p. 108). In research concerned specifically with learning–teaching interactions, one finds much attention to the regularities in classroom discourse. This is true of the work of Bauersfeld (1995), Voigt (1985, 1994, 1995, 1996), Krummheuer (1995), O'Connor and Michaels (1996), and Forman (1996), to name but a few. Notions such as *routines, patterns of interaction, obligations* (Voigt, 1985); *participation structures* (O'Connor & Michaels, 1996); and *discursive practices* (O'Connor, 1998), although not tantamount to the idea of metadiscursive rule, are clearly related to the same phenomena. The related notions *social norms* and *sociomathematical norms*, introduced by Cobb, Yackel, and their colleagues (Cobb, 1996; Cobb et al., 1993; Yackel & Cobb, 1996), have been picked up by many other researchers as a useful tool not only for analyzing mathematical learning in a classroom, but also for thinking about practical matters, such as instructional design and improvement of learning.

metarule in one mathematical discourse will give rise to an object-level rule as soon as the present metadiscourse turns into a full-fledged part of the mathematics itself. For example, the utterance "To multiply a sum of two numbers by a third number one can first multiply each addend and then add the products," which is a metarule of arithmetic, turns within algebraic discourse into the object-level rule "$a(b + c) = ab + ac$," expressing the relation among three algebraic objects, the variables a, b, c (the variable is the product of saming of all the numbers in a certain domain, in this case, in the domain of all real numbers).

The word *rule* has many connotations, only some of which would be proper in the present context. Thus, for example, although the word implies constancy, metadiscursive rules may *evolve* over time (as opposed to the object-level rules of mathematics, which, once formulated, remain more or less immutable). Metarules are also made distinct by being mainly *tacit*, and by being perceived as *normative* and value-laden whenever made explicit. Finally, metarules are *constraining* rather than deterministic and are *contingent* rather than necessary. Let me elaborate on each of these five characteristics one by one.

Variability

The stress on repetitiveness implies relative stability of the discursive rules. Although the repetitiveness and constancy are our point of departure, it is also important to stress the variability of metadiscursive rules in both space and time. Indeed, discursive patterns, incessantly created and recreated in ongoing interactions, are likely to undergo substantial transformations as time goes by. This is certainly true from the historical point of view: Metarules regulating the activities of defining, substantiating, recording, and so forth, have been evolving through the ages, often changing beyond recognition. Gradual modification of metarules that govern the student's mathematical discourse is one of the goals of school learning.

On the face of it, in the classroom, the rules of mathematical discourse are established by the teacher, the person whose expertise in the discourse creates a position of relative power and authority. The teacher's discursive ways are supposed to be privileged, and the attainment of mastery in this privileged type of discourse is the official goal of learning. And yet, this unidirectional vision is an oversimplification. The incessant process of discourse modifying that takes place in any community is reflexive. Discursive rules of the mathematics classroom, rather than being implicitly dictated by the teacher through her own discursive actions, are an evolving product of the teacher's and students' collaborative efforts. Or, in Heinrich

Bauersfeld's words, "Teacher and student(s) *constitute the reality* of classroom *interactively*."[7] This does not mean that the discursive principles in question are created in the classroom from scratch; nor does it imply that the class and the teacher are fully autonomous in their choices. After all, mathematical discourse is a historically established activity practiced and extended by one generation after another and taught in schools for the sake of further continuation. Mathematics students are thus supposed to join this activity rather than invent their own, idiosyncratic version. However, whenever a new teacher and a new class start their work together, variations are inevitable.

Tacitness (Interpretive Nature)

Discursive rules are not anything that would be followed by discourse participants in a conscious, intentional way. The rules for creating utterances and for matching them with situations are no more in interlocutors' heads than the law of gravitation is in the falling stone. As is the latter law, the rules of discourse are observers' constructs, retroactively written into interlocutors' past activities and expected to reappear, possibly in a slightly modified version, in these interlocutors' future actions. To use Pierre Bourdieu's formulation, although we deduce the existence of regulating principles from visible regularities in human activities, the patterned structures we see are not "in any way the product of obedience to rules, they can be collectively orchestrated without being the product of the organizing action of a conductor."[8]

More often than not, articulation of metarules is nothing the discursants themselves would care to do. This said, the claim about the tacitness of metarules should be qualified. People, unlike falling stones, are capable of reflecting on their own actions. It is thus not rare for a person to make explicit comments on principles that guide her actions.[9] This is particularly true of mathematists, who develop their discourse through constant reflection on the patterns in their own actions and by turning these patterns into

---

[7] Bauersfeld (1988, p. 37). Compare Cobb (1996).
[8] Bourdieu (1999, p. 108).
[9] In fact, some writers maintain that reporting, interpreting, and scanning one's own and other people's actions for regularities is a rule rather than exception. This claim is the basic assumption of ethnomethodologists, who view themselves as regular participants ("members") of social phenomena under study, using the very same sense-making methods as any other member. If so, their own method is, in a sense, the focus of their investigations: rather than examining social phenomena (structures) "as such," they explore the manner in which members impose rational schemes on what is going on around them, and this includes constituting patterns and regularities that retroactively inject order in the everyday and the common. See Garfinkel (1967) and Sacks (1992).

new mathematical objects. Indeed, explicating its own metarules is one of the fundamental activities of mathematics. Defining is a good example of such rule-articulating activity.

The rules that are explicitly recognized as a person's own will be called *endorsed*, whereas the adjective *enacted* will be used with reference to rules that regulate this person's actions according to an observer. Endorsed metarules may be deduced from interlocutors' direct or indirect metaremarks about the discourse. From the observer's perspective, enacted metarules describe the discourse as it actually *is*, whereas the endorsed metarules state the way it *should be* according to the discursants themselves. Enacted and endorsed rules need not be identical. For example, in our *Learning Disabilities Study*, we had several opportunities to observe Mira's silently counting fingers or little strokes on paper while multiplying two numbers. We could thus infer one of her enacted metadiscursive rules: "Use concrete materials while calculating." However, when asked to show how she counted fingers, Mira refused, saying, "I do it silently, so that people won't see." This reaction can be interpreted as showing that she regarded counting fingers as opposing proper arithmetic behavior; that is, her endorsed metarule collided with the one she enacted. Probably the most common reason for such observed discrepancies between what is done and what is endorsed is the students' inability to live up to rules that, on the basis of their former experience, they regard as norms.

Value-Ladedness (Normativeness)

In the present context, this last term, *norm*, well known from the current literature in mathematics education,[10] requires some elaboration. Not every metarule, whether enacted or endorsed, is a norm. To be considered as a norm of a given discourse community, the rule must fulfill two conditions. First, it must be widely enacted within that community; second, it must be endorsed by almost everybody, and especially by those within the community who count as experts. If discussed by experts, this metarule must be explicitly presented as one of the defining, indispensable characteristics of the given type of discourse.

A norm becomes explicit and most visible when violated. Violation evokes interlocutors' spontaneous attempts at correction, often accompanied by a condemnation of the transgressor's illegitimate behavior. For

---

[10] For example, see the notions of social and sociomathematical norms in Yackel and Cobb (1996).

example, the ongoing controversy over mathematics teaching in American schools has been initiated by mathematicians who believed that new curricula deviate from the norms of mathematical discourse.[11] Some of these mathematicians claimed that the new curricula "redefine what constitutes mathematics."[12] It is interesting to reflect on the question of why the violation of some rules stirs such passions. Frequently, interlocutors have no justification for the norms, and their only explanation for the resistance to change is the fact that the rule is generally practiced and, in particular, is observed by those who count as authority. Thus, strangely enough, the reverence for norms would often result from their being widely practiced rather than being the primary reason for sustaining this practice![13] The usual, the ordinary, and the dominant tend to acquire the quality of the desirable, whereas anything that deviates from the common is described as pathological, as wrong, and sometimes even as unethical. This fact expresses itself, for example, in the well-documented resistance, so common among teachers, to changes in their professional routines, and in the students' characterization as *not fair* of teachers' requirements that cannot be implemented in routine ways. In short, norms of discourse are a self-perpetuating phenomenon: They are widely followed because of their being valued, but they are often valued because of their being widely followed.

Flexibility

The very mention of rules may bring to mind stringent control, that is, something that determines our actions, leaving no space for individual variations. True, metarules may sometimes reduce all the possibilities to just one option. This happens when a routine procedure is describable algorithmically, as is the case with the routine for numeric calculations and the one for constructing the equation of linear function presented in Table 7.2. Given such a deterministic dictate, the performances of any two competent discursants are practically indistinguishable and have the same outcome. It is important, however, to remember that more often than not the rules of

---

[11] Sfard (2005).

[12] Wu (1997, p. 954).

[13] This is true of metarules, not of the object-level rules of mathematics. The latter rules, which describe relations between mathematical objects (and are thus part and parcel of mathematical discourse) are constant and deterministic. It is when one "climbs" to the metalevel and studies the rules governing the activities of those who investigate object-level rules that the observed rules stop being a matter of necessity.

discourse do not tell us what to say or think any more than the rules of traffic tell us where to go. If anything, they make us aware of what would not be a proper thing to do in a given situation. By constraining rather than determining, metadiscursive rules make communication possible just as traffic regulations make collision-free traffic possible. This enabling effect results from the fact that the rules eliminate an infinity of possible discursive moves and leave the interlocutors with only a manageable number of reasonable options. Without this preselection, we would probably be deprived of the ability to participate in any discourse at all. Just imagine that a student is required by a mathematics teacher to "investigate the function $f(x) = 3x^3 - 2x + 5$" and he is not sure whether to list the properties of the graph (yet to be drawn!) or to admire its aesthetics, to count the characters with which the function has been recorded on the paper or to express his opinion about them, explore the effects of real-life applications of the formula $3x^3 - 2x + 5$ or to check possibilities of transforming it, and so on, and so forth.

Let me remark that this last example also shows that discursants' patterned re-actions to their interlocutors' utterances are discourse-specific and are by no means a one-to-one function of the utterances as such. One thus needs to be an insider to the given discourse to understand why people are doing what is not uniquely implied by what is said. On the other hand, one also needs to be able to adopt the outsider's perspective in order to notice the possibility of alternative interpretations, and thus see logic in the moves of participants who do not act as expected. For instance, one has to think as an outsider in order to foresee the possibility that the student would answer the request "Find x" by simply pointing to the letter x and saying, "Here it is!" rather than solving the equation in which this letter appears. Later in this chapter, I will adopt the outsider's perspective while trying to make sense of Roni and Eynat's nonroutine reaction to the request to compare boxes with marbles.

Contingency

As explained earlier, discursive regularities, and thus metadiscursive rules, are the result of custom-sanctioned associations rather than a matter of externally imposed necessity.[14] The contingency of the rules was noted

---

[14] This statement is likely to be contested by those who speak about the innateness of grammars.

by Wittgenstein, who, to make this point, chose the instance of metarules seemingly least likely to appear in this context – the metarules involved in the activity of mathematical proving. To put it in his own words:

> For it is a peculiar procedure: I *go through* the proof and then accept its results. – I mean: This is simply what *we* do. This is use and custom among us, or a fact of our natural history.[15]

It is important to understand that the claim of contingency does not regard the proof as such but rather the metadiscursive rules that govern the activity of proof construction. It is the inevitability of the discursive ways of acting that is questioned, not the inner consistency of object-level inferences. Moreover, saying that the metadiscursive rules of proving cannot themselves be proved (that is, cannot be shown to be necessary) does not mean there are no reasons for their existence. It only means that, contrary to the platonic view of mathematics, the reasons that can be given are nondeterministic and have to do with human judgments and choices rather than with the "ruling of nature." Mathematics, which, when watched from inside, appears to be fully governed by logical necessity, becomes a product of historical contingencies when scrutinized from outside.

Wittgenstein is equally explicit in his warning against attempts to justify metarules that govern mathematical calculations:

> The danger here, I believe, is one of giving a justification of our *procedure* where there is no such thing as justification and we ought simply to have said: That's how we do it.[16]

For all that has been said so far, and with all due respect to Wittgenstein, the claim about contingency of mathematical metarules may raise a brow or two. To insiders – to those who live embedded in a given discourse – this discourse is an organic part of the world as well as of themselves. To everybody, both insiders and outsiders, human communication appears to be working with the world in unison – and what could be stronger evidence against the claim about the contingency of discursive routines? I wish to claim that both the apparent objectivity and necessity of communicational rules and their effectiveness in mediating practical actions are the result of discursive evolution and adaptation. Rules of communication develop gradually, through intermittent elimination of what does not work to our satisfaction and subsequent alienation of the remaining patterns. The elimination can

[15] Wittgenstein (1978, p. 9).
[16] Wittgenstein (1978, p. 10).

be metaphorically described as a process of "natural selection" in which only "the fittest," the most useful of our communicational activities, survive.[17] Alienation gives the remaining rules the appearance of being "natural" and unquestionable. Through incessant rehearsals, the bonds between words and situations, actions and re-actions, and things said or actions performed solidify and become unbreakable: The name of an object is experienced as an inextricable aspect of the object itself and a given type of communicative re-action is conceived as a natural consequence of the preceding action. What began as a chance association becomes necessary and inescapable: We are now impermeable to other possibilities and we protest when another option is suggested. These protests are reinforced by the fact that once a communicational pattern sets in, words and symbols appear to have a life of their own: Time and again, their novel combinations prove communicationally effective even if they were never seen or heard before.

3. Routines

A *routine* may be defined as a set of metarules that describe a repetitive discursive action. This set of pattern-defining rules may be divided into two subsets:

- The *how* of a routine, which is a set of metarules that determine, or just constrain, the course of the patterned discursive performance (the *course of action* or *procedure*, from now on) and
- The *when* of a routine, which is a collection of metarules that determine, or just constrain, those situations in which the discursant would deem this performance as appropriate.

Many routines can be regarded as general, in that they can be found in the majority of discourses. Other discursive patterns may be specific to a restricted, well-delineated community of discourse.[18] One goal of the commognitive researcher is to make routine-defining metarules explicit. When it comes to the rules of *how* the pattern works, the task is often quite straightforward. Tables 7.1 and 7.2 present the *how* of the routines observed

---

[17] This idea is in tune with Stephen Toulmin's "evolutionary analysis of intellectual development" (Toulmin, 1972, p. 140), supported with his claim that "Darwin's populational theory of 'variation and natural selection' is one illustration of a more general form of historical explanation; and that this same pattern is applicable also, on appropriate conditions, to historical entities and populations of other kinds" (p. 135).

[18] Many types of social studies – anthropological, ethnographical, and sociological – may be seen as concerned with investigating community-specific metadiscursive rules.

in Episodes 1.5 and 1.3, respectively. In both of these cases, metarules delineate categories of discursive actions that should be performed one after another in reaction to a given request or question. Presenting the *when* of routines, that is, constructing exhaustive lists of conditions under which given patterns tend to appear in a discourse of a given group or person, is more complicated, if not altogether unworkable. In this case, we will usually be watching for deviations from common uses rather than trying to compile an explicit list that defines these uses.

As is generally true of metadiscursive rules, the *how* and *when* of personal routines are the observer's construct, deduced from patterns the researcher was able to notice in the given person's discursive activities to date. Thus, these rules are descriptions of past actions rather than of those to come. This said, the past observations are the best basis we have for making predictions about one's future actions and, in particular, about when the person would be likely to turn to a given routine course of action. Treated with caution, thus constructed metarules allow us to map the trajectory of one's discursive development.

The routine *when* may be further subdivided into applicability and closure conditions. *Applicability conditions* are rules that delineate, usually in a nondeterministic way, the circumstances in which the routine course of action is likely to be evoked by the person. The set of metarules called *the closure* defines circumstances that the performer is likely to interpret as signaling a successful completion of performance. Applicability rules specify, among others, routine *prompts*, that is, those elements of situations whose presence increases the likelihood of the routine's performance. The prompts, which may be verbal or environmental and can be provided by others or self-presented, occur in clusters. Only some combinations of prompts suffice to spur routine performance. When a person seems to be following a given course of action restrictively, showing a greater dependence on situational clues than would be proper in the eyes of an experienced mathematist, we say that her discourse (or just the given course of action) is *situated*. An important, but only too often overlooked, point teachers and researchers need to remember while trying to assess one's mathematical discourse is that one's capability to perform a given procedure is not yet a warranty that this person will choose this course of action when, and only when, this choice would seem proper to any experienced mathematist. Let me give a number of examples illustrating the diverse ways in which routine performances may be coupled with situations, for better or worse.

Some of the prompts associated with a given course of action function as *discourse framers*, that is, as factors that activate certain discourses while inhibiting some others. The framers are the first to act whenever a person needs to decide which course of action to follow. The effect of framers is obvious, even if their action remains imperceptible. This is what transpires, for example, from the fact that even well-educated people are often reluctant, if not altogether unable, to apply schoollike computational courses of action in real-life situations. Sometimes, this reluctance may be explained by the fact that another course of action may be more efficient in the given situation. In other cases, however, the unavailability of the potentially useful procedure may stem from the fact that this course of action has been framed as a part of school discourse and of this discourse alone.

According to research findings, the reverse is true as well: Certain computational procedures would be marked as colloquial and would thus be barred from a mathematics classroom. In the eyes of an experienced mathematist, presenting a person with the incomplete equality "$4 \cdot 35 =$" should be enough to evoke *any* procedure for quadrupling 35, which this person happens to know. But in the study by Nunes and her colleagues, the symbols failed to prompt the use of the money-mediated calculations with which the young Brazilian street vendor was incomparably more familiar than with the school algorithm. Further investigation would be needed to answer the question whether this failure was the result of discursive framing that, in the given circumstances, inhibited the colloquial routine (the child might have felt that he was tested for his proficiency in schoollike computational procedures rather than merely supposed to tell the result) or, as conjectured in chapter 6, of the fact that the equation, per se, was insufficient as a prompt for the money-based routine. In this latter case, the child would not even realize the equivalence of the money-mediated and symbolic calculations.

The dependence of discursive procedures on specificities of situational prompts may be observed also inside the school, where literate mathematical discourse is institutionally marked as the default option. For example, a question that invites calculations may be answered differently, depending on whether it is asked in a mathematics classroom or in any other.[19] In one of our studies,[20] the following query has been presented to two seventh-grade classes with 72 students of the age 12 to 13: "Fourteen balloons were divided among four children. How many balloons did each of the children get?" To one class, the question was presented during their mathematics lesson and to the other, during Hebrew language lesson. The

[19] Säljö and Wyndhamn (1993).

[20] The study was conducted in Israel, together with Maya Gurnik and Adi Saban (Gurnik & Saban, 2003).

classes were comparable in terms of their mathematical achievement. The written response "Each child will get three balloons" or "Two children will get four balloons and two others will get three balloons each" prevailed in the language classroom – they constituted 86.1% of all the answers. In the mathematics classroom, however, these responses appeared only in 55.6% of cases. In the remaining cases, the students wrote, "Each child will get 3.5 balloons" or simply left the number 3.5 as the final answer, without any additional explanation. This example shows, once again, that a mathematics classroom may immunize the learner to everyday considerations. Indeed, for many mathematics students, the procedure as such, rather than the results, is the gist of the classroom game.

Individual variations in ways students associate procedures with tasks may also be observed *within* a mathematics classroom. Mathematics teachers are often disheartened to see their students using procedures they learned in either too liberal or too restrictive a manner. Thus, on some occasions a learner would react to quadratic expressions, such as $x^2 - 3x + 5$, by performing the calculation $(-b \pm \sqrt{\Delta})/2a$, even though the experienced mathematist would not find any indication that this action, or any action at all, was required. In one of our studies on secondary algebra,[21] this widely enacted metarule was also explicitly endorsed, at least by some of the participants. When the students were asked to draw a graph of the function $y = x^2 - 5x + 4$, the following exchange took place between two of them:

> **Episode 7.1. If there is *x* squared**
>
> 1. Student 1: Everytime you see an expression, doesn't matter which, and there is the *x* squared, this is the sign that you must use this formula...
> 2. Student 2: You mean...?
> 3. Student 1: You know, the "*x* one, two [$x_{1,2}$] equals..."

In this example, the applicability condition was not restrictive enough. The opposite case was observed in the *Incipient Numerical Thinking* study: In Episode 1.1, as well as in the three subsequent trials (see Table 7.3), the question "In which box are there more marbles?" though likely to prompt any grown up to open the boxes and to count the contents, failed to stir the action of counting in the 4-year-old children. Evidently, in this latter case the actual visibility of the marbles was the additional condition necessary for associating the question with the compare-by-counting procedure.

[21] Kristal (2005).

Table 7.3. *Four episodes of comparing boxes with marbles revealing the same choose – compare – [evaluate] pattern*

Case (the numbers show the amounts of marbles in boxes 1 and 2)	6 × 8	2 × 2	2 × 4	8 × 10
1. *Choosing (guessing)* 1.1 Prompt	1. M: I want you to tell me in which box there are more marbles.	34a. M: I am putting two boxes with marbles here. Where…in which one of them are there more marbles? Tell me [*puts one box next to Roni and another next to Eynat; both boxes are closed*]. 35a. M: Where are more marbles? What do you think?	62a. M: What do you say? Where are more marbles?	213a. Mother: Let's see whether you are able to discover how many…no, where is there more marbles? I now put a lot, so let's see. One moment, who thinks… Where, where do you think there is [are] more … 214a. M: Where do you think there is more, Roni?
1.2 Direct choice	3c. E: *Points to the box that is closer to her.* 3d. R: *Points to the box Eynat is pointing to.*	34b. R: *Exchanges the placement of the two boxes. Then changes her mind and reproduces the original arrangement of the boxes.* 35b. E: *Points to her box without opening it.*	62b. E: Points to one of the boxes. Eynat points to the box on the left side. 62c. R: *Points to the box Eynat is pointing to.*	214b. E: *Points to the box next to her.* 214c. R: *Points to the box next to Eynat.*
2. *Comparing (checking)* 2.1 Prompt	10a. M: Do you want to open and see? Let's open and see what there is inside. Take a look now.	35a. M: Where are more marbles? What do you think? 37a. M: Eynati, do you want to open yours?	63. M: Both of you say it is here? How do you know? What makes you think so?	215a. M: Do you want to check?

2.2. Count marbles (find N_1 and N_2)	Finding N_2	Finding N_1	Finding N_2	Finding N_1	Finding N_2	Finding N_1	Finding N_2
	12. E: *[opens the box]* 1, 2, 3, 4, 5, 6.	11. R: *[opens the box]* 1...1.... 1...2, 3, 4, 5, 6, 7, 8.	37b. E: *[Opens her box and closes it immediately]* Two	64a. E: I want to open *[pulls the box to which she pointed before]* 64c. E: *[Takes the box to herself and opens it.]* 66a. E: 1, 2, 3, 4.	64b. R: *Starts pulling the box too.* *Takes the other box and opens it.* 65. R: *[Takes the other box and opens it.]* Two	215b. E: Here *[opens the box]* 219. E: 1, 2, 3, 4, 5, 6, 7, 8, 9 *[As she counts, the marbles roll and she errs]* 226. E: 1, 2, 3, 4, 5, 6, 7, 8...eight	216. R: *[opens the box next to her]* 218. R: 1, 2, 3, 4, 5, 6, 7, 8, 9, 10
		36a. R: *[Opens and closes her box]* Two					
2.3 Compare N_1 and N_2 and point to the box corresponding to the bigger number	13. M: So, what do you say? 14. R: 6. 15. M: Six what? You say 6 what? What does it mean "six"? Explain. 16. R: That this is too many. 17. M: That this is too many? Eynat, what do you say? 18. E: That this too is a little. 19. M: That it seems to you a little? ... 19. M: Where do you think there are more marbles? 20. E: I think here.	38. M: Two...Indeed? Where are more marbles? 39. R: In none				231. M: She said that she has eight, so where is there more? In this box or in this one? 232. E: In this one *[points to the box next to Roni]*. 233. M: Roni, what do you think? 234. R: In this one *[points to the same box and closes it]*.	
3. Evaluating (verifying the guess)				67. R: We were right.			

Note: As can be seen from the numbering of the turns, some parts of the four episodes have been omitted in the table. These utterances were additions to the basic structure presented earlier (such as the mother's request for explanations and the girls' trials' to respond). These additions were "neutral" in that they did not seem to change the basic sequence of events or the way the component actions were performed (this, of course, is my interpretation, but other readers of the episodes agreed that the removed parts were independent modules). Another feature of the presentation is that some parts are presented in parallel along parallel channels (e.g., mother–Roni vs. mother–Eynat). These parts were deemed as presenting interaction in spite of the fact that they occurred sequentially.

Different mathematists may associate the same procedure not only with different applicability conditions, but also with different closures. For example, some students regard a routine equation-solving performance as completed only if they are convinced that they found all the numbers that, when substituted for the "unknown," turn the given equation into a tautology. For some other learners, the mere appearance of an expression of the form "$x = $ number" would suffice as a "halting signal." This difference is not easy to notice because more often than not, the observable performances would be indistinguishable. In one of our studies on secondary algebra, however, we did hear a student describe this latter closing condition explicitly. This happened in an interview with Naomi, the 15-year-old student presented with the singular system of simultaneous equations, $2(x - 3) = 1 - y$ and $2x + y = 7$.[22] While trying to solve the problem, Naomi substituted $7 - y$ instead of $2x$ in the first equation and obtained the equality $1 = 1$. She then commented:

Episode 7.2. When x disappears...

Naomi: We did all this...we isolated $2x$, etc...to arrive at y. We substituted this [*points to the expression* $7 - y$] and we were left without x, only with y. And then there was no y either. Our goal was to find y and we didn't succeed. So I think that there is no solution.

To summarize these last few paragraphs, there is much more to human discursive decisions than meets the ears. Verbal prompts, such as questions or requests, often regarded in school as holding the exclusive responsibility for students' choices of discursive procedures, may, in fact, be only the tip of an iceberg. What many people would deem "the same" questions, tasks, or problems may spur different re-actions, depending on such additional factors as seemingly negligible variations in wording, the "social marking"[23] of settings and interlocutors, the availability and salience of potential visual mediators, the placement, and thus the function of the required discursive action within the larger discursive pattern, and this is but the beginning of the long list. In situations in which verbal and visual prompts do not suffice to guide a person toward a specific course of action, the history of the exchange and the "generic" metarules associated with the given setting will have a decisive impact. Thus, for example, the student would tend to solve

---

[22] For a fuller description of the study see Sfard and Linchevski (1994). The brief fragment of transcript that follows was slightly modified in comparison to the original publication as a result of a more careful translation from Hebrew.
[23] De Abrau (2000).

any new mathematical problem with the help of procedures that have been applied in the problems the class has just worked out. According to the universally enacted rules of school discourses, once a "technique" is demonstrated, it becomes the default choice for the tasks that immediately follow.

The important point to remember, therefore, in investigating discourses is that routines are not uniquely defined by their *how* – by the course of actions that they prescribe, or just enable. The awareness of this simple but often overlooked truth should alert teachers and researchers to the inherent weaknesses of most traditional assessment and research methods. While looking through the narrow window of an interview or written tests, we may be getting a misleading picture of the students' discursive competence. Tests and interviews can examine the respondents' acquaintance with the *how* of mathematical routines, but they are quite useless when it comes to assessing people's ability to follow the relevant course of actions whenever appropriate. Two students acting in identical, seemingly satisfactory ways on a written test may be enacting different routines, a fact that would have become visible only if the students were faced with nonroutine situations, devoid of typical school clues about the required course of action.

In short, although the devil is in the *when* of routines, this all-important aspect of mathematical discourse escapes the traditional lens. To realize how misguided it can be to focus exclusively on the question of *how*, it suffices to think about the image of Roni's and Eynat's numerical skills likely to emerge from evaluation based solely on the second part of Episode 1.1 (see the row titled *Comparing* in Table 7.3, where the girls perform the comparing-by-counting procedure almost without a glitch.)[24] This said, let me add that if the *when* has been neglected by teachers and researchers for such a long time, it is probably not without a reason. Identifying situations in which a given routine course of action is likely to be spontaneously evoked is a self-defeating endeavor. The very presence of a teacher or a researcher "institutionalizes" the context and increases the likelihood of schoollike interpretations. Thus, even if students are faced with tasks modeled on what is known to them from everyday life, the real-life flavor of the assignment

---

[24] Guy Brousseau (1997) seems to have referred to this phenomenon when he coined the terms *Topaze* and *Jourdain Effects*. In commognitive terms, the gist of these two related effects is the observer's tendency to interpret students' performance as evidence for their mathematical competence. In other words, people tend to see students as mathematically competent on the basis of the mere fact that in certain situations, and as a result of teachers' direct prompting, the students display behavior that is in concert with the rules of that discourse. Whoever ventures such an overgeneralization ignores the fact that the students are rarely tested for the *when* of mathematical routines and that there is usually no indication that they could relate their specific performance to other discursive objects and other procedures.

may well be lost in this life-to-school translation. Because of this inherent difficulty, not only the assessment, but also school teaching, often seems guided by the principle "Take care of the *how* of routines, and the *when* will take care of itself."

4. Routines and Creativity

Many of us would shrug at the vision of ourselves as irrevocably entangled in routines. Because of its common colloquial uses, the word *routine* is often associated with a lack of imagination, boredom, and insipidity. The goal of the next few paragraphs is to deconstruct the conviction that repetitive patterns leave no space for novelty. Human routines, far from being the opposite of agency and creativity, are fluid and changeable and, in fact, constitute the medium in which creative contributions are made. Paraphrasing Lucy Suchman, who spoke about "plans," one can say that in most cases, routines do not dictate a fully predesigned sequence of steps but rather "orient you in such a way that you can obtain the best possible position from within to use those embodied on which, in the final analysis, your success depends."[25] Considering the strong elements of variation and unpredictability inherent in the task of implementing routine tasks, it is justified to claim, together with Courtney Cazden, that "descriptions of human behavior require both searching for repeated patterns and acknowledging, even with admiration, the inevitable improvisation."[26]

Individual variations are, indeed, part and parcel of any discursive activity, and thus constitute the "other side" of any repetition. To begin with, most discursive routines do not determine our actions but only constrain what we can reasonably do or say in a given situation. Quoting Cazden again, we live within "negotiated conventions," which are "spontaneous improvisations on basic patterns of interaction."[27] Routines, therefore, do not strip discursants from agency. On the contrary, implementation of routines usually requires a measure of creativity. To realize how great the demand for creativity may be, it suffices to think about mathematical proving, which, although certainly constrained by well-defined metarules, is often believed to be unworkable without a "spark of genius." Contrary, therefore, to what is usually expected when one hears the word *routine*, much inventiveness may be needed if one wants to be a skillful rule follower.

---

[25] Suchman (2007, p. 72).
[26] Cazden (2001, p. 39).
[27] Ibid.

A different type of creativity is involved in violating the rules of the game, that is, in introducing metalevel modifications. Some of these modifications may be ephemeral: They would occur in an ad hoc manner; would count as inadvertent deviations, indeed, errors; and would disappear with equal abruptness. Some others, although initiated by specific individuals, may endure and may eventually change the discourse of others in a lasting way, contributing to its historical development.[28] Innovations can also be categorized according to their source. Some discursants may deviate from regularity simply because of the imperfection of their discursive skills; others would do this purposefully, as a result of reflection followed by a conscious decision. More often than not, the accidental deviation would be dismissed as harmful rather than useful. The deliberate innovation stands a better chance to be deemed truly creative and worth sustaining. All along history, purposeful and serendipitous modifications of routines have been ceaselessly revolutionizing science and art, as well as colloquial discourses.

To fathom the mechanisms of discourse variation, let us consider two discursive occurrences that can count as acts of deviating from commonly practiced routines. The stories I am about to tell are anecdotes rather than meticulously documented pieces of data. Even so, I find them informative and eye opening.

Example 1. Odd One Out

Five-year-old Emi has been asked the following question: "Which of the numbers 2, 3, 4, and 10 does not belong with the others?" Thanks to her kindergarten experience, Emi was well acquainted with this kind of task and needed no further explanation to produce an answer. At this point in the story, you are urged to pause and to think about the girl's possible response. After this brief exercise, you are probably not surprised that Emi pointed to 10. She explained that this number stood out as one that was "not according to the order" (she could also say that 10, unlike the other ones, was a two-digit number; if this did not happen, it was probably because of the fact that the numbers were presented to her orally, not in writing). The girl went on and offered another possibility: She pointed to 3, saying it was the only odd number among the four. Although these two choices were already more than the problem poser asked for, she did not stop here. Her next choice was number 4, which she justified by saying: "4 is the only one that does not begin with the 't.'" If this choice brings a smile

---

[28] For a rare longitudinal study of such development see Saxe (2005).

to your face, it is probably because it is not a possibility that you would consider yourself. This unexpected selection is exactly where the departure from the unwritten rules of the game seems to have occurred. In a grown-up school-educated person, the appearance of numerical signifiers evokes mathematical routines, and considering the sound of number names while looking for differences between numbers is not one of them.[29]

Example 2. Measuring Height with a Barometer

The anecdote that follows is attributed to the well-known physicist and recipient of the Nobel Prize Sir Ernest Rutherford. The hero of his story is another physicist and Nobel Prize winner, Niels Bohr.[30] According to Rutherford's account, Bohr, when still a student, was asked to solve the following problem: "How can you tell the height of a tall tower if the only measuring instrument you have is a barometer?" "I would climb to the top of the tower, tie the barometer to a long rope, lower it to the ground and, eventually, measure the length of the rope thus used" was the student's answer. When accorded zero points for this solution, Bohr protested. Subsequently, he volunteered several alternatives. Among others, he suggested throwing the barometer from the top of the tower, measuring the time it would take it to reach the ground, and using this latter number to calculate the height from the formula of free fall. Another idea was to transform the barometer into a pendulum and to measure with its help the difference between the values of the constant of gravitation at the foot of the tower and on its top. Finally, the young man claimed that one can get the necessary information from the janitor of the tower, in exchange for the barometer. When asked to explain his unwillingness to give the expected answer, Bohr reportedly responded that he was just fed up with "being told how to think."

There is a clear similarity between these two stories of the departure from rules. In both cases the nonroutine solutions made perfect sense, and in both stories the outsider's perspective on the relevant discourse was necessary to see these special options. But there is also an important difference: For the 5-year-old child being an outsider was the default option, whereas

---

[29] To complete the story, Emi's initial answer was that all the numbers can count as the ones that "did not belong." I have already reported on how she justified this claim with respect to 3, 4, and 10. In the remaining case of 2 she did not initially volunteer any explanation. When urged to finish her story, she said: "Can't you see? 2 is the only one which is not an exception – so it *is* exceptional!"

[30] This story can be found all over the Internet; see, for example, Rutherford (n.d.), http://epmalab.uoregon.edu/weird/Rutherford%20Story.pdf.

for young Bohr it was a matter of conscious choice. If Emi was able to notice the dissimilarity between the sounds of various number-words, it was because for her, these words were not yet transparent – they did not yet function in her discourse as object names. Bohr, on the other hand, although able to be an outsider, was a skillful insider in the first place. Thus, what for the young child was possible simply because of the lack of alternatives, for the future reformer of the discourse of physics was an act of conscious rebellion against old routines – and an act of creativity. Curiously enough, the innovation was attained by the nonstandard application of other routine procedures.[31]

If creativity is not a commonplace phenomenon even among the most skillful of insiders, it is because expertise is a double-edged sword. On the one hand, an intimate acquaintance with established routines is necessary if one is to be able to distance oneself from the discourse, so as to reflect on it, to compare it to others, and to notice both commonalities between them and distinctive features of each. It is in the recognition of the importance of the insider's perspective that Picasso reportedly claimed that it is necessary to be a skillful realist before one can become an abstract painter. It is also what transpired from Wittgenstein's declaration that "doubt comes *after* belief."[32] On the other hand, being an insider is a self-perpetuating condition. Too deep an immersion in a specialized discourse may close problem solvers' eyes to promising routes leading through other discourses.[33]

In sum, repetition is as indispensable for a useful innovation as it is for sustaining of traditions, except that to be creative, one needs to be able to apply routines in nonroutine ways. Innovation may express itself merely in modification of an established routine course of action, but it may also go much further than that; it may involve metaphorical projections, that is, applying familiar routines in unfamiliar discursive contexts. To give a recent example, "finding deep connections between what were unrelated

---

[31] Of course, the claim about Bohr's creativity may be supported with more serious evidence than the preceding anecdote. It is enough to recall his insightful model of an atom, his counterintuitive claims about electrons making quantum leaps between constant orbits, or his unearthly idea of a subatomic entity that is a particle and a wave at the same time.

[32] Wittgenstein (1969, p. 23e).

[33] The *"aha" phenomenon*, known also as the phenomenon of *insight*, often reported by mathematicians (Hadamard, 1954) and first studied by Gestaltists, may well be due to sudden transitions from one discourse to another. Mathematics educators have identified a whole assortment of "insight" problems that are particularly difficult to solve not because of the intricacy of the required mathematical techniques, but because their solutions cannot originate in the discourse that imposes itself when these questions are first presented (for examples of such problems and research about them see, e.g., Perkins, 2001).

fields of mathematics"[34] is what reportedly allowed the Russian mathematician Grigory Perelman to make a paramount contribution to mathematics by proving the famous Poincaré's conjecture.[35] Such interdiscursive "borrowing" of scripts for action would often mean a literal upheaval in the *when* of discursive routines and would end up in the emergence of a whole new discourse. Indeed, in the majority of cases, a nonstandard application of a familiar discursive pattern would require certain far-reaching procedural adjustments. The ability to make such adjustments is yet another feature we tend to admire in those whom we deem creative.

Creativity, therefore, requires the ability to alternate between insider's and outsider's perspectives: One needs to be able intermittently to step in and step out of discourses. The question of how such perspective switching, and thus the creative act, becomes possible is one of those long-standing, vexing puzzles that many have tackled but nobody seems to have given a satisfactory account of. At a closer look, the reason for this pervasive failure may lie in the inherent unanswerability of the query. Those who inquire are looking for rules that govern the phenomenon under study; alas, the defining property of creativity may well be that it defies any rules!

5. Routines – in a Nutshell

After having discussed, in chapter 6, the questions of what mathematical discourse is all about, we turned in the present chapter to the "anatomy" of mathematizing, that is, to the ways in which mathematical communication is performed. Because communication is a patterned activity – indeed, our ability to act in new situations hinges on our capacity for recycling previous behavior – our task was to fathom the nature of and inner structure of mathematical *routines*.

In the present context, routines are sets of metadiscursive rules that describe recurrent discursive patterns. As opposed to object-level rules, which depict regularities in the behavior of discursive objects, metarules reflect the structured, regular nature of discursants' actions (considering the fact that mathematical discourse develops by annexing its own

---

[34] Quote from the University of Columbia scholar John Morgan in the *New York Times* article "An elusive proof and its elusive prover" by Dennis Overbye (2006).

[35] The discovery of the structure of DNA is another good illustration. According to existing historical studies (Olby, 1974), as well as to the discoverers' own account (Watson, 2001), Watson and Crick might not have been able to figure out the double-helix configuration if not for the fact that they were relative outsiders to the prior research in this field (at that time, they were both at the beginning of their careers and they both specialized in domains only partly relevant to the problem of DNA structure).

metadiscourse, the distinction between object-level and metalevel rules is, of course, relative; in local contexts, however, when it is clear which layer of mathematical discourse is being considered at any given moment, the ambiguity is easy to disentangle). One should bear in mind that metadiscursive rules have some characteristics that may seem at odds with what is usually associated with the word *rule*. To begin with, they are dynamic structures that are constantly created and recreated in the course of interactions. Modifications in metarules occur as a result of unintended deviations, of other interlocutors' influences, and of intentional redesigning. Further, metarules are mostly tacit – they are observer constructs rather than explicit principles that the discursants would follow in a conscious, intentional way. Many of these rules are value laden. Those of them that are widely enacted and endorsed within a given community of discourse, and are thus called norms, set the standards of behavior for all the community members. Some metarules are strictly deterministic. This is the case, for example, with the rules that define mathematical algorithms. In the majority of cases, however – and mathematical proving and recording are good examples – these rules are merely constraining. Finally, metarules are time-honored conventions rather than a matter of externally imposed necessity.

The set of metarules that define routines can be divided into three subsets that specify, respectively, the applicability conditions, the course of action (procedure), and the closing conditions of the routine. The first and the last of these sets constitute the *when* of the routine and the middle defines its *how*. Two people whose particular performance may seem identical may, in fact, be implementing different routines, set apart by their applicability and closing conditions. Whereas learning a routine *how* is often a fairly straightforward task, learning its *when* may be a lifelong endeavor.

Routines are both confining and indispensable. Although too much rigor is paralyzing, so is a complete lack thereof. Rather than stifle creativity, routines are its indispensable basis. Routines are the thing to be creative about. This is particularly true of mathematics, where new layers of discourse emerge from reflections on the existing layers. Mathematicians sculpture in routines just as artists sculpture in marble. Sometimes, the creative innovations regard the *how* of the routine. True breakthroughs, however, result from changes in the routine *when*. This kind of change occurs when a familiar course of action is transplanted into new discursive contexts. In short, creativity, like anarchy, involves deviation from rules; unlike anarchy, however, creativity changes rules rather than simply rejecting them. In the next chapter, this observation will help us in addressing the question of what people mathematize for and in formulating conjectures about how routines develop in history and in learning.

8   Explorations, Deeds, and Rituals

What We Mathematize For

It is so much a part of "thinking philosophically" to be impressed with the special character of mathematical truth that it is hard to shake off the grip of the Platonic Principle [according to which differences in certainty must correspond to differences in the objects known]. If, however, we think of "rational certainty" as a matter of victory in argument rather than of relation to an object known, we shall look toward our interlocutors rather than to our faculties for the explanation of the phenomenon. If we think of our certainty about the Pythagorean Theorem as our confidence, based on experience with arguments on such matters, that nobody will find an objection to the premises from which we infer it, then we shall not seek to explain it by the relation of reason to triangularity. Our certainty will be a matter of conversation between persons, rather than a matter of interaction with nonhuman reality.

Richard Rorty[1]

The word did not exist in the beginning. In the beginning was the deed.... The word is the end that crowns the deed.

Lev Semionovitch Vygotsky[2]

Rituals help us... to connect deeply with people.... The repetition that ritual always involves sets the present moment in a larger context and infuses it with wider meaning. It's difficult to invent rituals.

Huston Smith[3]

To use Walter Fisher's expression,[4] humans are "storytelling animals" and mathematizing is just one special type of storytelling activity.

[1] Rorty (1979, pp. 156–157).
[2] Vygotsky (1987, p. 285).
[3] Smith (n.d.), retrieved from http://www.brainyquote.com/quotes/quotes/h/hustonsmit220777.html.
[4] Fisher (1984).

Unlike practical routines, which produce change in discourse-independent objects, mathematical routines aim at producing narratives about mathematical objects. Of course, most mathematists, if asked, would probably state that as abstract as their narratives are, they are supposed to help, one day, in attaining practical goals. Nevertheless, mathematical routines can count as *explorations*, in that they end with narratives rather than with tangible environmental changes.

I wish to argue now that explorations are not the only type of mathematical routine and that the production of endorsable narrative is not necessarily the ultimate goal of every performer. Even if one's performance seems to end with a narrative and thus appears as exploration, it may, in fact, be an implementation of a *deed* or a *ritual*. In this chapter, after defining these three types of mathematical routines, I make a case for the claim that deeds and rituals are developmental predecessors of explorations. I also hypothesize that as long as school teaching focuses on the issue of *how* routines should be performed to the almost total neglect of the question of *when* this performance would be most appropriate, it is more likely to result in the discourse of rituals than of explorations.

1. Explorations

The overall goal of mathematizing is to produce narratives that can be endorsed, labeled as true, and become known as "mathematical facts." The word *narrative* is used here to denote any sequence of utterances, spoken or written, framed as a description of objects, of relations between objects, or of activities with or by objects.[5] In colloquial mathematical discourses, narratives are often endorsed on the basis of empirical evidence. Thus, we endorse the equality $2 + 2 = 4$ because whenever we put together two pairs of objects and count, the counting ends with the word *four*. At more advanced levels of the colloquial discourse, and at any level of scholarly mathematical discourses, a narrative counts as endorsable if it can be derived according to generally accepted rules from other endorsed narratives. Some of the widely endorsed mathematical narratives are known as *axioms*; some others are termed *definitions*. Still others, called *theorems*, are endorsed by

---

[5] According to the classical definition by Labov (see e.g. Labov and Waletzky, 1967), *narrative* is "one method of recapitulating past experience by matching a verbal sequence of clauses to the sequence of events which (it is inferred) actually occurred" (p. 20). Here, this definition has been extended to include any sequence of declarative utterances related by their common objects and by logical interrelations rather than by chronological order (as is the case with stories about events).

the community after being derived from the initial set of axioms and definitions according to well-defined rules of inference. Together, closed sets[6] of different types of endorsed narratives combine into well-organized systems called *mathematical theories*. The following paragraphs are devoted to routines that bring mathematical theories into being.

1.1 *More about Endorsed Narratives*

A routine will be called *exploration* if its implementation contributes to a mathematical theory. In other words, exploration is a routine whose performance counts as completed when an endorsable narrative is produced or substantiated. The term *endorsable* signals that the narrative can be endorsed or rejected according to well-defined rules of the given mathematical discourse.[7] Realization routines, such as numerical calculations or equation solving and routines of defining or proving, are representative examples of mathematical explorations.

Different mathematists may, of course, endorse different narratives, but whenever this latter expression is used in this book without an explicit reference to an endorser, it is to be understood that the narrative fulfills the generally accepted rules of endorsement and can thus count as endorsed by the whole mathematizing community (or at least by those who count as authoritative mathematists, that is, mathematicians). Mathematics is not the only discourse that produces generally endorsable narratives, but mathematical terms of endorsement are special. In our times, scholarly mathematical discourse, which is the result of mathematicians' centuries-long pursuit of infallible communication, is often believed to be impervious to any considerations other than purely deductive relations among narratives.[8]

---

[6] A set of narratives is *closed* if it contains all the narratives that can be derived from any of its subsets.

[7] Not every well-formed mathematical utterance is endorsable, and its status in this respect depends on its discursive context. Thus, for example, the equation $2x + 1 = 5$, when treated as arithmetic utterance (that is, as one in which x stands for a given number that is currently unknown), is not endorsable because of the fact that x is not realized as a number. When treated as an algebraic equation, though – as one in which $2x + 1$ signifies a function with the x ranging over all real numbers – this equation is an endorsable narrative, except that the attempt to endorse it is deemed to fail (and this shows that it is its negation, $\sim[2x + 1 = 5]$, that should be endorsed).

[8] Volumes have been written about mathematicians' ambition to attain ultimate endorsability and about the inherent untenability of this goal. Lakatos's celebrated volume *Proofs and Refutations* (Lakatos, 1976) was a milestone in this respect. Both themes – that of longing for universally endorsable narratives and that of the subsequent disillusionment – are aptly summarized in the following confession by Bertrand Russell: "After some twenty years of very arduous toil, I came to the conclusion that there was nothing more that *I* could do in the way of making mathematical knowledge indubitable" (1956).

Any two mathematicians charged with the task of determining the endorsability of a narrative are expected to arrive at the same conclusion. If they don't, at least one of them is suspected to have deviated from the rules of mathematical endorsement. These special rules, unlike those governing, say, discourses of historians, politicians, sociologists, or even scientists, have been believed, at least until recently, to determine the set of all endorsed narratives fully and unambiguously.[9] This pursuit of perfect, infallible communication has been conducted at the price of the constant increase in the complexity of endorsement procedures and the irrevocably platonic flavor of mathematical discourse.

Endorsement of narratives is the gist of discourses cultivated in schools. All the exploratory routines can be divided into three types: *construction*, which is a discursive process resulting in new endorsable narratives; *substantiation*, the action that helps mathematists decide whether to endorse previously constructed narratives; and *recall*, the process one performs to be able to summon a narrative that was endorsed in the past.

1.2 *Construction of Narratives*

Because of mathematicians' pursuit of perfect communication, mathematical discourse stands out among all the other discourses as particularly rigorous. This, however, does not mean that rules of construction or substantiation of mathematical narratives are uniquely defined. Thus, for example, there are important differences between construction and substantiation routines practiced in colloquial and literary mathematical discourses, and these routines change again in the transition from school discourse to the scholarly discourse of mathematicians. Each personal enactment of any of these discourses may also have its own distinctive traits (except that in this case, narratives endorsed by the individual may not be endorsable in the eyes of other mathematists). Endorsement-related routines change not only across discourses, but also in time; they evolve historically as well as during individual learning.

Most of the endorsed narratives that have appeared in this book in various learning episodes were constructed with the help of realization procedures. Among representative examples let me list Mira's and Talli's numerical utterances such as "$86 + 37 = 123$," Gur's claim "The slope of function g given by the table is 5," and even Roni and Eynat's statement that a certain box deserves the label "the one with more marbles." There is an

[9] This belief was shattered in 1931 when the Czech-born mathematician Kurt Gödel proved his famous theorem about the incompleteness of arithmetic.

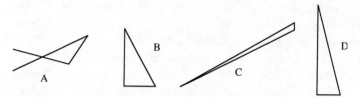

Figure 8.1. Which of these shapes is triangle?

interesting difference between this last narrative and the former two. Unlike number facts or assertions on properties of functions, all of which arise from intradiscursive manipulations, Roni's and Eynat's narratives belong to the "interface" between mathematical discourse and "real-life" talk. These latter narratives speak about concrete objects and reflect children's perceptual experiences rather than their vision of logical relations among narratives. Realizations of this type, residing at the very "edge" of mathematical discourse, may be simple or compound. In Episode 1.2 Ron's construction of the narrative about the sum to be paid was a multistep procedure, whereas Roni and Eynat produced the narrative about the bigger box in a one-step, direct manner, without any discursive mediation, such as counting. Literate mathematical discourses, such as those practiced in school, do not admit of direct realizations. Replacing direct realizations with discursively mediated ones is among the aims of school learning. To have a better grasp of the required change, let us consider an example.

Example 1. Direct versus Mediated Realizations.[10]

In Episode 8.1, two first-graders are required to identify triangles among the many shapes appearing in the picture before them (see Figure 8.1 for a representative sample). The conversation with the teacher takes place after the girls have completed the task to the best of their understanding.

Episode 8.1. Identifying triangles

| [42:05] Ela: | This is a triangle but it also has other lines. | Pointing to shape A |
| [42:08] Teacher: | Well, Ela, how do you know that triangle is indeed a triangle? | |

[10] The excerpt is taken from the study conducted with Orit Admoni. The interviews were conducted in Hebrew.

[42:12] Ela:	Because it has three . . . aah . . . three . . . well . . . lines.	
. . . . . .	. . . . . .	
[44:00] Teacher:	This one also: one, two, three . . .	Pointing to shape B
[44:02] The girls:	Yes	
[44:03] Teacher:	So, *is* it a triangle? Why didn't you mark it in the beginning?	
[44:05] Ela:	'Cause then . . . I did not exactly see it . . . I wasn't sure.	Starts putting a circle also around shape C
. . . . . .	. . . .	
[44:10] Shira:	Hey, this is not a triangle. Triangle is wide and this one is thin.	Looking at shape C, which Ela is marking
[44:16] Ela:	So what?	While saying this, she stops drawing the circle
[44:30] Teacher:	Why? Why isn't this a triangle? Shira said it is too thin. But haven't we said . . .	Points to shape C
[44:35] Ela:	There is no such thing as too thin.	While saying this, she erases the circle around shape C
[44:37] Teacher:	Triangle – must it be of a certain size?	
[44:41] Shira:	Hmmmm . . . yes, a little bit. . . . It must be wide. What's that? This is not like a triangle – this is a stick!	Points to C

The children were supposed to produce identifying narratives of the type "It is [is not] a triangle." The set of narratives they actually constructed did not fully coincide with the one expected by the teacher: Shira disqualified any shape that seemed to her "too thin"; Ela, though apparently convinced that "there is no such thing as too thin" (44:35), still could not decide whether the sticklike shape in the picture was a triangle or not. The criterion of three-sidedness, repeatedly recalled, or at least hinted to by Ela and the teacher (see, e.g., [42:08], [42:12], [44:00], [44:30], [44:35], [44:37]), did not manage to change Shira's mind about the sticklike shape. Clearly, Shira identified shapes as triangles spontaneously, in one decisive step: Upon seeing certain two-dimensional figures, she uttered the word *triangle* spontaneously, without any former reflection, just as one identifies people's faces. The teacher, however, expected the children to split the task into two: into the act of *recognition*, involving a recall of certain past experiences associated with the present one, and the act of *naming*, of attaching a word to the recognized shape.

School discourse is supposed to supersede the direct identification procedure with the discursively mediated one. From now on, when the child tries to decide whether a polygon is a triangle, she will have to count its sides. More precisely, the primary recognition will have to be followed by the discursively mediated assignment, or just verification, of a name. The change will not be easy. The direct and mediated identification routines differ not only in their procedural aspects, but also in their ontology and in their objectives, as conceived by the participants. The statement "This is a triangle" made as a result of the direct identification is an object-level utterance expressing "the truth about the world": The person asserts that the shape is triangle by the law of nature, not because of what anybody says. When the identification is discursively mediated, the utterance "This is a triangle" becomes equivalent to the metadiscursive sentence "This shape may be called a triangle," and it thus turns into an assertion about the discourse rather than about the world. The difficulty of the transition from narratives determined by the world itself to discourse about discourse has been theoretically and empirically corroborated: research has shown that this change is invariably slow to occur.[11]

Within literate mathematical discourse, new narratives are constructed mainly through operations on previously endorsed narratives. In this respect, the discourse of professional mathematicians is rather extreme: After endorsing a number of seemingly "arbitrary" narratives, which from

---

[11] None of these is surprising to those who are familiar with the seminal work done by Pierre and Dieke van Hiele (van Hiele, 1959/2004; van Hiele, 1985). Using van Hiele's language, one may say that the resistance to the idea that the elongated shape may be called *triangle* shows that the children are still at the level of *analysis*, with their ability to "take a figure apart" and speak about its separate elements and features not yet accompanied by the ability to distinguish between necessary and sufficient conditions for a figure to be a member of a given category. The ability to formulate and use definitions in the activity of identifying is a hallmark of the next level in the development of geometrical thought, known as the level of *abstraction* or of *informal deduction*. This description can be easily translated into commognitive terms, whereas van Hiele levels would be presented as types of geometric discourse. In the present discussion, my intention is to heighten the resolution of van Hiele's portrayal by comparing the children's and teacher's routines for construction of narratives. For a more detailed account, see Sfard (in press).

now on will be known as *axioms*, the mathematicians would endorse only those narratives that can be derived from this initial set according to well-defined rules.[12] The rules of narrative construction include three metadiscursive manipulations, known as *deduction*, *induction*, and *abduction*. Let me say a few words about each one of them.

Deduction takes place when a new narrative is obtained from previously endorsed narratives with the help of well-defined inferring operations. The basic form of such operation is *modus ponens*: If you already endorsed the narratives $P \rightarrow Q$ (in words: "If P then Q") and P, then Q can be endorsed as well. As an example, you can derive "The diagonals of the quadrilateral *ABCD* are perpendicular" (Q) from the endorsed narrative "If the quadrilateral *ABCD* is a square then its diagonals are perpendicular" ($P \rightarrow Q$) and "*ABCD* is a square" (P).

Induction is a process in which a new narrative on any object of a given type is obtained from a finite number of already endorsed narratives on specific instances of this type (that is, narratives on lower-level objects from which the object of the new narrative arose by saming); think, for example, about the narrative "$1 + 3 + \cdots + (2n - 1) = n^2$," which one can construct after examining the following first cases: $1 + 3 = 4 = 2^2$, $1 + 3 + 5 = 9 = 3^2$, $1 + 3 + 5 + 7 = 16 = 4^2$. In mathematics, thus created narrative is endorsable but not yet endorsed. For the endorsement, and independent substantiation is necessary.

Abduction[13] is a process in which endorsability of a new narrative appears highly plausible because what is known to be its necessary consequence has been endorsed. A good example of abductive thinking is taken from my own recent experience. My printer began smudging the pages, and in order to fix the problem, it was necessary to find out the reason. The technician whom I asked for help said, "This kind of phenomenon [smudging the pages] is what happens when the toner cartridge malfunctions." We thus proposed

---

[12] Let me add that if I qualified the term *arbitrary*, it was because mathematicians' choices of axiomatic systems do have rational reasons, and no such choice is regarded as finalized until the consistency of the system has been demonstrated. The way axioms are chosen changed in the course of history. At the time of Euclid, an axiom was understood as a narrative expressing self-evident "truth about the world." The idea that any consistent set of narratives may be regarded as the axiomatic basis for a mathematical theory is relatively new. The resulting axiomatic systems are sometimes called arbitrary because rather than stating facts about already existing objects, they define these objects in the first place.

[13] The inclusion of abduction along with deduction and induction among the basic routines of narrative construction is due to Charles Peirce and his work on semiotics and scientific inquiry (Peirce, 1955).

the plausible narrative that needed yet to be substantiated: The cartridge may be the source of the problem. Because abduction can be presented as inferring P ("The cartridge is the problem") from P → Q ("If the cartridge malfunctions then the printer smudges the pages") and Q ("The printer smudges the pages"), it is sometimes described as "erroneous deduction." Of course, no error was committed as long as one does not endorse the thus derived narrative without an additional substantiation.

Of the three rules, only deduction produces narratives that do not require additional substantiation to be endorsed. Both inductively and abductively constructed narratives will have to be either refuted or confirmed in a separate, deductive procedure (the product of abduction may be also preliminarily tested in the inductive way). The routines of induction and abduction are nondeterministic and their implementation, therefore, is a highly creative act.

Whereas the strictly intradiscursive procedures of narrative construction are typical of scholarly mathematical discourse, they are much less prominent in colloquial mathematical discourses. What the mathematician views as inherently intradiscursive, metalevel activity, less experienced mathematists would often replace by an object-level, quasi-empirical procedure. This claim may be illustrated with the following example, in which the participants of a conversation refrain from discourse-on-discourse (from manipulations on narratives) and construct narratives about extradiscursive reality on the basis of what they know from their direct, everyday experience.

Example 2. Bypassing Metadiscourse

The example is not really mathematical, but it aptly illustrates the phenomenon in question. Sylvia Scribner, in her study on syllogistic reasoning conducted in Liberia, presented her interviewees with the following problem:

> All people who own houses pay a house tax.
> Boima does not pay a house tax.
> Does Boima own a house?[14]

Many of the respondents gave answers such as "Boima does not have money to pay a house tax." Obviously, the interviewees ignored the first sentence

[14] Scribner (1997, p. 131).

and never considered the possibility of performing a metalevel operation on the first two utterances together. They simply elaborated on the second utterance on the basis of their direct real-world experience: They added an utterance ("Boima does not have money") that their experience associated with "Boima does not pay taxes." "This appeal to real world knowledge and experience . . . is the single most prominent characteristic of villagers' performance," stated Scribner.[15]

In mathematics, endorsed narratives logically derived from other endorsed narratives are called *theorems*. Creation and endorsement of *definitions* constitute yet another type of theory building activity. For a mathematician, definitions, just like theorems, are products of intradiscursive manipulations; the only difference between the two types of narratives is that definitions are merely *constrained* by the existing endorsed narratives, whereas theorems constitute their necessary entailments. Thus, today's mathematician introduces negative numbers by offering a new set of symbols (e.g., assigns the new symbol -2 to expressions such as $3 - 5$ or $21.5 - 23.5$) and then endorsing *in advance* a number of narratives about thus created new objects. In the extended number set, for example, these latter narratives are known as *the axioms of numerical field*, and they state that addition and multiplication must be commutative, associative, distributive, and endowed with the neutral element, just as they were in the familiar set of unsigned numbers. Any other definition regarding negative numbers – for example, the definition of multiplication, according to which "minus times minus is plus" – is then logically derived from the axioms. The idea of intradiscursive substantiation of definitions, however, may seem inadmissible to the student, for whom, so far, definitions were statements about the world rather than claims about discourse and were thus constrained by empirical evidence, supplied from outside the discourse.[16]

1.3 *Substantiation of Narratives*

Substantiation of a narrative is a process through which mathematists become convinced that the narrative can be endorsed. Being dependent on what participants find convincing, routines of substantiation are probably the least uniform aspect of mathematical discourses. The very term

[15] Ibid., p. 132.
[16] This claim was empirically corroborated in the study described in Sfard (in press).

endorsement may be interpreted differently by different people. For the mathematician, endorsement means simply that the narrative has become a part of a theory. For those who use mathematical narratives in everyday life, it means that the narrative reflects "the real state of affairs" and can thus safely be used as a guide for attaining practical purposes. The question of when substantiations are required and how they should be performed has been answered differently by mathematists of different historical periods, and even today, the answers vary greatly across communities and discourses.

For today's mathematician, the only admissible type of substantiation consists in manipulation on narratives, and it is thus purely intradiscursive. In some cases, the process of construction, if correctly performed, is already the act of substantiation. This is certainly true of all algorithmic realization procedures, such as those for numerical and algebraic computations, for solving linear or quadratic equations, and for finding derivatives and certain types of integrals. Other types of narratives will have the status of mere conjectures until they are separately *proven*, that is, until they undergo the process of substantiation independent from the process of construction. To substantiate, one produces a proof – a sequence of endorsed narratives, each of which is deductively inferred from previous ones and the last of which is the narrative that is being endorsed.[17] Thus, for example, inductively created narratives about properties supposed to hold for every natural number may be substantiated in the deductive process known as *mathematical induction*. Abductively created narratives would often be inductively tested and then deductively proven (or disproven). Narratives defining new mathematical objects will be examined for their consistency – the activity that often involves identification (possibly construction) of a specific object that actually fulfills the requirements of the definition (that is, the signifier of the object, if substituted in the definition's utterances, would result in an endorsed narrative).

Colloquial discourses mark the other end of the spectrum of possibilities. Substantiations practiced in schools not only are much less exacting than those that govern professional mathematical discourse, but may also be qualitatively different. School learning is supposed to transform gradually both the *when* and the *how* of the substantiation routines with which children arrive in school. Let me illustrate these two types of change with examples.

---

[17] Note that the activity of substantiating is recursive: It may always expand, because the substantiation itself is a narrative that may become an object of substantiation.

One attempt to change young learners' ideas about *when* substantiation is needed could be seen in Episode 8.1, in which the children treated utterances such as "This is [is not] a triangle" as grounded in the immediate perceptual experience, and thus as self-evident, whereas the teacher expected a substantiation. So far, the only thing the children were able to say when asked for substantiation was something like "Because it *looks* [does not *look*] like a triangle." From now on, they will have to perform a certain discursive procedure (counting) and to conclude, "It has [does not have] three sides." For this change to occur, the latter narrative will have to reincarnate from the merely necessary entailment of being a triangle to the necessary-and-sufficient condition for the triangularity.[18]

As could already be seen from this last example, the question of *what kind* of discursive action counts as a satisfactory substantiation may also be a source of serious communicational mismatches. Above all, mathematists are likely to differ on the question of *where* the substantiation should originate. Whereas for a mathematician, substantiation is a purely discursive activity, with all the evidence arising from the discourse itself, children are likely to seek substantiation beyond the discourse. Here, intradiscursive operations are rare and the empirical argument is dominant. By *empirical argument* I mean one that speaks about concrete realizations of the focal signifiers and relies on their perceptually accessible features. In school, teachers are trying to narrow the gap between the two extremes, and although not altogether opposed to the import of extradiscursive considerations, they attempt to replace some of the colloquial substantiation routines with literate ones, thus introducing a strong element of purely discursive manipulation.

The question "Where should substantiation come from?" may also evoke a controversy regarding the role of the human agent. While the platonically minded mathematicians view substantiations as, in a sense, "humanproof" because of their "being already there in the discourse," children are likely to view substantiation as ultimately depending on people. Rather than fully relying on her own substantiations, the child would always seek the approval of a more experienced person and, in the case of controversy, would treat this person's verdict as overriding her own. The following example aptly illustrates this phenomenon.

---

[18] The claim that three-sidedness is for the children but a necessary condition is grounded in the fact that the visually based narratives clearly override any other consideration: Although anything that looks like a triangle necessarily has three sides, what does not look like a triangle is not a triangle even is it is three-sided.

Example 3. The Teacher as Ultimate Substantiator[19]

Ori, 12 years old, was asked to calculate $7935 + 96$. The child thought for a moment, then gave the answer: 8031. When asked how he did it, he said:

> Ori: See, it's difficult. I made 7996 and 35 was left. So 7996 . . . I took 4 and made 8000. I was left with 31, so together, it's 8031.

The interviewer now asked Ori to implement the same calculation again, in writing. Ori wrote:

$$
\begin{array}{r}
7935 \\
+\,96 \\
\hline
17535
\end{array}
$$

(Note the way Ori aligned the two addends: according to the first digit rather than the last.) The following conversation then took place:

Interviewer:	Which of the two results is correct, 8031 or 17535?	
Ori:	It's 17535. See, the way I did it is difficult, and the teacher did it this way.	Points to what he has just written
	So it must be 17535.	

The upshot of this story is that for the child, mathematical decisions might have been not much different from any other resolutions he needed to make in life: All of them depended, ultimately, on people and on power relations between them.

1.4 *Recalling*

Because explorations build on previously endorsed narratives, remembering a certain amount of those former narratives (e.g., number facts) is important for one's discursive fluency. Some previously endorsed narratives may be immediately available; some others may have to be reconstructed. Such mediated recalls involve special routines that are likely to depend on the way

---

[19] The excerpt is taken from a study conducted with Liora Linchevski. The interview was conducted in Hebrew.

the recalled narratives were memorized in the first place. To illustrate, let us take a look at the following example, taken from our *Learning Difficulties Study.*

Example 4. Memorizing the Multiplication Table

In our interviews with Mira and Talli, neither of the girls could recall much of the multiplication table. We found it revealing to examine the girls' behavior in situations in which their progress was stymied by the inability to summon previously endorsed narratives.

In Mira's case, some of our data permit the claim that the girl, in spite of her obvious difficulties with the multiplication table, was capable of performing some reconstructing derivations. Thus, Mira translated the operation $6 \cdot 7$ into a repeated addition:

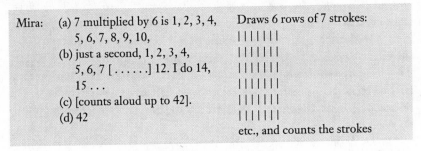

Mira: (a) 7 multiplied by 6 is 1, 2, 3, 4, 5, 6, 7, 8, 9, 10,

       (b) just a second, 1, 2, 3, 4, 5, 6, 7 [. . . . . .] 12. I do 14, 15 . . .

       (c) [counts aloud up to 42].

       (d) 42

Draws 6 rows of 7 strokes:

etc., and counts the strokes

On another occasion, she derived $4 \cdot 9$ from $9 + 9 = 18$:

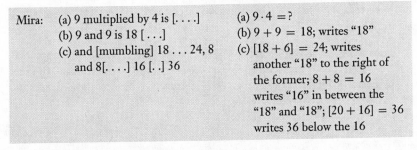

Mira: (a) 9 multiplied by 4 is [. . . .]

       (b) 9 and 9 is 18 [. . .]

       (c) and [mumbling] 18 . . . 24, 8 and 8[. . . .] 16 [. .] 36

(a) $9 \cdot 4 = ?$

(b) $9 + 9 = 18$; writes "18"

(c) $[18 + 6] = 24$; writes another "18" to the right of the former; $8 + 8 = 16$ writes "16" in between the "18" and "18"; $[20 + 16] = 36$ writes 36 below the 16

In yet another case, she tried to obtain $9 \cdot 6$ from $10 \cdot 6$:

Mira: (a) The 9 multiplied by 6, say . . . say

       (b) we will add 1 to the 9 and it makes 10.

(b) $9 + 1 = 10$

(c) 6 multiplied by 10 makes 60	(c) $6 \cdot 10 = 60$ [instead of $9 \cdot 6$]
(d) Now I have to take off all the parts because it is not really 10.	(d) $9 \cdot 6$ is less than 60; one has to take away all that has been added
(e) So I got something like that, approximately.	(e) She previously said that 9.6 is "more than 50."

Thus, thanks to her recalling routines, Mira was never entirely stymied in the face of a request for a number fact that she did not remember. We never saw Talli engaged in this type of reconstructive activity. Whenever challenged with a simple multiplication, the girl would either wait for the interviewer's help ("6 multiplied by 7 is 36. Okay? [laughingly] I am asking you") or simply try to "excavate" the table from memory by visually recalling its different rows. This is, at least, the way we interpreted several events, and, in particular the one in which Talli was trying to find $9 \cdot 6$. Here, she said that she might take "the 6 and 7 from the other exercise" (the $7 \cdot 6 = 42$ has been mentioned in one of the former tasks) and then asked the interviewer, "What is the next number in the . . . multiplication table?" This did not seem to be an attempt to derive $9 \cdot 6$ from $7 \cdot 6$, but rather a trial to recall the missing table entry by visualizing its surroundings. On several occasions, the interviewers did try to stimulate a derivation, but to no avail.

The way one tries to recall endorsed narratives is, no doubt, revealing. It can indicate a lot not just about how the narratives were memorized, but also about how they were constructed and substantiated originally. The aim of every teacher may well be to arrive at the kind of learning that would eventually make the learner say what Poincaré said about himself:

> I can perceive the whole of the [lengthy mathematical argument] at a glance. I need no longer be afraid of forgetting one of the elements; each of them will place itself naturally in the position prepared for it, without my having to make any effort of memory.[20]

2. Deeds

In chapter 3, the distinction was made between discursive (communicational) and practical action, with the latter defined as *an action resulting in a physical change in objects (environment)*. Routines that involve such practical actions will be called *deeds*. Deed, therefore, may be defined as a

---

[20] Poincaré (1952, p. 51).

set of rules for a patterned sequence of actions that, unlike explorations, produce or change objects, not just narratives. The following example sheds additional light on the similarities and differences between deeds and explorations.

Example 5. Monetary Transaction

Let me compare the syntactic calculation of $86 + 37$ (see, e.g., Episode 5.4) with the one performed by Talli in Episode 8.2, when the girl engaged in a monetary transaction.

Episode 8.2. Talli pays for three cookies, each of which costs 75 agoras		
Interviewer:	Now you have to pay me. You bought three cookies from me; each one costs 75 agoras. Please pay me.	
Talli:	Each one is 75 agoras . . .	While saying this, hands to the interviewer one coin of 50 agoras ($\frac{1}{2}$ shekel), two of 10 agoras, and one of 5 agoras.
Interviewer:	What did you give me?	
Talli:	75.	
Interviewer:	Yes, you mean half and?	
Talli:	20 agoras and 5. Ok. And a shekel	Passes a coin of 1 shekel.
	One shekel and 75. Inside the shekel there is a 75, so there is 25 more. So, here is half a shekel more.	Passes the coin of 50 agoras.
	And that's it.	

Let me now argue that unlike the simple numerical routines, such as those, say, in Episode 5.4, the one in Episode 8.2 is a deed rather than exploration: In the insider's terms, its goal is to transform objects, not to tell a story. Indeed, whereas in the former episode the narrative $86 + 37 = 123$ is constructed, in the latter conversation hardly any story is told. This dissimilarity is evidenced, among others, by the differing compositions of the two texts: Whereas Episode 5.4b is full of words signifying mathematical operations (e.g., *add*) and mathematical relations (e.g., *makes*, *equals*), the only specifically mathematical words appearing in Episode 8.2 are number-words. The almost complete absence of full sentences in this latter text is another relevant feature. What is being said here sounds as if it is a series of announcements about the coins that are being successively passed to the interviewer. In fact, in this latter case Talli does not seem to be performing any calculations – she does not add or multiply the number of agoras while composing the different sums. She simply *knows* that some combination of coins, for example, $\frac{1}{2}$ shekel (50 agoras), two coins of 10 agoras, and one coin of 5 agoras, produces a particular amount of shekels and agoras, in this case the sum of 75 agoras (notice that the coin she calls "half a shekel" is never explicitly converted into 50 agoras). In addition, in Episode 8.2, unlike in 5.4, Talli is clearly not interested in any "final answer." She deems the routine action as successfully completed the moment she and her inter-locutor can feel satisfied with their respective shares of coins. This latter situation is attained not by stating their final possessions but by the very manner in which the paying procedure was implemented.

This one example suffices to indicate that mathematical explorations and those everyday practical actions in which mathematical explorations are supposed to be of help are two very different types of activities. Educators may be underestimating this difference when assuming that what has been learned in school will be spontaneously evoked in everyday situations, in which learned procedures could be applied.

Let me now use examples to substantiate the following two claims:

- What for adults is an invitation for exploration may prompt a child to perform a deed.
- A sequence of actions that for one person is an implementation of exploration for another person may be an implementation of a deed.

Example 6. What for Adults Is an Invitation for Exploration My Prompt a Child to Perform a Deed

When asked numerical questions about the boxes with marbles, a grown-up person is likely to implement an *exploration*, that is, a procedure that she regards as complete only when a new endorsed narrative results. As could be seen in the episodes in Table 7.3, a similar numerical query may lead young children to a different re-action: In Episode 1.1, for example, Roni's mother's question "In which box is there more marbles?" led Roni and Eynat to touch one of the identical boxes, which, after a while, they also tried to grab. Evidently, when the question was first asked, it was not received as a prompt for a conversation on numbers but rather as an invitation to what the children usually do of their own accord and willingly: to choose one of the boxes for themselves.

Unlike numerical comparisons, choosing one object from a set is the kind of activity that Roni and Eynat have already individualized. For them, choosing seems to be an act of taking for oneself, even if only symbolically. According to the definition given earlier, therefore, it is a *deed* rather than an exploration: a practical action that produces a change in objects, and not just in narratives.[21] This interpretation seems helpful, because it accounts for those aspects of the girls' behavior that we found puzzling while discussing Episode 1.1. It is certainly in tune with the fact that throughout this and three additional episodes of comparing boxes (Table 7.3) the children acted as if they intended to take possession of the boxes deemed to have more marbles. The word *more* was likely to be the direct prompt for this action: It is reasonable to assume that, so far, the children have heard this word mainly in utterances such as *Take [eat, have] some more*, and that they thus also read it as an invitation to "take for oneself" in the present context. And because the aim of choosing is *to have* rather than *to know*, one feature that sets *deeds of choosing* apart from explorations is that the former type of routine action always has a definite resolution: When a person chooses in order to have, one option will be chosen even if it seems indistinguishable from the other. Indeed, nobody is likely to consider the lack of a difference as a sufficient reason to remain empty-handed.

Let me turn now to the claim that what for one person is an implementation of exploration may be an implementation of a deed for another. The difference between deeds and explorations becomes elusive in those cases when the objects on which the deed is performed are, in themselves, discursive rather than primary. Considering the progressive objectification of mathematical discourse, the same performance may be indicative of either exploration or deed, depending on what the performers are trying to achieve. In the case of numerical calculations, for example, the same procedure may be employed by a person who wishes to tell a story about numbers (formulate a numerical fact) and by one whose aim is to combine

---

[21] The term *deed*, in the context of discourse, brings to mind the Austinian idea of *performative utterances* – utterances that do not merely describe, report, or constate what one is doing but are actually doing it (Austin, 1962); we may similarly say that deeds are performative routines.

a few numbers into a new one, so as to prepare the ground for further numerical operations. The difference between the two routines can be identified by the manner in which the performers speak about their actions.

Example 7. What for One Person Is an Implementation of Exploration Is an Implementation of a Deed for Another

In Example 3, Ori's account of what he was doing while calculating 7935 + 96 seems indicative of his being engaged in a deed rather than an exploration. This interpretation is supported by his use of the words *make, leave,* and [taken] *together,* which are all reminiscent of physical actions on material objects; by his deft transition from the numbers 7935 and 96 to 7996 and 35, which brings to mind the activity of recombining pieces of Lego; and by his exclusive focus on the new number he got, as opposed to the focus on the equivalence between 8031 and 7935 + 35 (which would be stressed if he said something like "7935 plus 96 equals 8031").

This latter difference, although delicate and amenable to alternative interpretations, seems worth attention because it may be indicative of the student's fluency in the discourse and of his readiness to proceed to the next discursive layer – to the metadiscourse, where the reified deeds performed in the present discourse will turn into an object of exploration. In order to make this next step, one needs to be able to think about the calculation not only as a deed – as an operation resulting in new numbers – but also as an exploration – as a storytelling activity, producing new endorsed narratives about the deeds and their results. These are the narratives that will have to be scrutinized for their commonalities and thereby give rise to claims about general properties of numerical deeds, such as their associativity or distributivity. Note that the two modes – that of deed and that of explorative storytelling – belong to different discursive levels (object-level and metalevel, respectively). As a metadiscursive activity, the storytelling (explorative) mode can count as more advanced. Indeed, some students – and Ori may well be one of them – can perform numerical calculations as deeds but are not yet able to see these procedures as explorations. This latter inability is signaled, for example, by their use of the equals symbols as a *prompt for implementation* of an operation rather than as a *symbol of an equivalence relation.*[22] Considering all this, it is reasonable

---

[22] This phenomenon has been reported by many researchers (for a summary, see Kieran, 1981; Sfard & Linchevski, 1994). One of the indicators of the use of the equals symbol as a prompt for calculation is the phenomenon of *didactic cut* (Filloy & Rojano, 1989): the

to assume that one of the indications of the students' fluency in numerical discourse is their ability to alternate between the modes of deeds and of explorations.

3. Rituals

I now wish to argue that for many children, some mathematical routines begin their life as neither deeds nor explorations but *rituals*, that is, as sequences of discursive actions whose primary goal (closing conditions) is neither the production of an endorsed narrative nor a change in objects, but creating and sustaining a bond with other people.

Example 8. Roni and Eynat's Routine of Comparing-by-Counting as a Ritual

Let me show that Roni and Eynat's routine of comparing-by-counting, as demonstrated in the episodes in Table 7.3, was a ritual.

Because in all the episodes choosing one of the boxes invariably preceded the implementation of the comparing-by-counting procedure, it is clear that for Roni and Eynat the latter action was not a deed. After all, the only change in objects one can think of in this case had already been completed when the counting began. This subsequent action was not an exploration either: A person for whom comparing-by-counting is deeds-enhancing exploration would have had recourse to this routine before making her choices of a box with marbles. No such relation, however, seemed to exist for Roni and Eynat in Episode 1.1. Not only did they implement the comparing-by-counting *after* making their choice, but they also did not seem bothered by the question whether the two performances – the two independent acts of singling out one of the two boxes – led to the same result. Producing an endorsed narrative, therefore, was clearly not their goal.

For Roni and Eynat, chanting number-words while touching the marbles one by one was not unlike the repetitive incantation of invented words that are often a part of children's play. In both cases, the routine performance is a way of getting attention and approval of others and becoming a part of a social group. This social concern can clearly be seen throughout the conversations with Roni and Eynat. The way Roni monitors her mother's face,

---

fact that a child who can deal with equations of the form $ax + b = c$ is stymied when facing an equation with the "unknown" appearing on both sides. It seems that this child can interpret the former type of equation as a story of an operation performed on number x, and this is what makes her able to solve the equation by "undoing" what was done to x.

talks to her, and follows her lead clearly indicates that getting the parent's attention and approval is the girl's main focus. This wish competes and is successfully combined with an equally strong need to belong with the peer. While making their choices, Roni and Eynat are careful to stress that their decisions are shared (in the further parts of our transcripts, this need for solidarity with the friend is further evidenced by Roni's repetitive use of the word *we*, through which she asserts the joint ownership of solutions). While counting-and-comparing, the children are in fact preoccupied with the delicate social fabric of their little group, and the conversation on boxes with marbles is as good an occasion for interpersonal engineering as any other. The counting-and-comparing operations of the young participants are therefore a form of community-building activity.

In trying to distinguish rituals from deeds and explorations, we need to remember that the difference in the goals (closing conditions) entails differences in many additional features of the routine performance. Some of these differences have been summarized in Table 8.1. Here, let me say just a few words about each of the distinctive features of rituals, while also encouraging the reader to use Roni and Eynat's comparing-by-counting performances for illustration.

To begin with, the social bond that is the main concern of rituals' performers is constructed and sustained by acting with others in harmony, that is, by doing *exactly* what these other people do. More often than not, therefore, rituals would be performed with others, for the sake of others, and according to these other performers' rules.[23] Second, applicability conditions of rituals are incomparably more restrictive than those of explorations. The only criterion for the application of an explorative procedure is whether this particular course of action is likely to lead to the proper type of outcome (narrative); therefore, the decision whether to apply the procedure does not depend on other people, at least in theory. In the case of ritual, the prompt needs to be produced by a person or be imagined as originating from a person. In addition, because it is the whole performance that counts, the implementation depends on specific situational attributes, such as the availability of particular mediational means. Rituals, therefore, unlike well-developed explorations, are highly *situated* and associated with prompts, which are very specific and thus extremely restricting. Third, rituals stand out among the

---

[23] Of course, ritual may be "turned at oneself." Thus, a person may develop "private" rituals that she would practice without the participation of others. Still, the main property of this kind of ritual would be the same as that of the rituals implemented in a team: Its goal would be to express the adherence to a certain inherently social "form of life" rather than to arrive at a new truth about, or a change in, the world.

Table 8.1. *Deeds, explorations, and rituals – comparison*

	Deed	Ritual	Exploration
Closing condition/Goal	A change in environment	Relationships with others (improving one's positioning with respect to others)	Description of the world (production of endorsed narrative about the world)
By whom the routine is performed	No special requirements	With (scaffolded by) others	No need for scaffolding – can be performed individually
For whom the routine is performed	No special requirements	*Others* (authoritative discourse)	*Others and oneself* (internally persuasive discourse)
Applicability (changing the *when*, keeping the *how* constant)		Restricted – the procedure is highly *situated*	Broad – the procedure is applicable in a wide range of situations
Flexibility (changing the *how*, keeping the *when* constant)		Almost no degrees of freedom in the course of action	The procedure is a whole class of equivalence of different courses of action
Correctibility	By tinkering	Cannot be locally corrected – has to be reiterated in its entirety	Parts can be locally replaced with an equivalent subroutine
Acceptability condition	The *result* – the change in environment – must count as adequate; no need for human mediation of the acceptance – it depends on the environment	The activity has to be shown to adhere strictly to the rules defining the routine procedure – the acceptance depends on other people	The narrative produced through the performance must be *substantiable* in such a way that the acceptance is independent of other people
Words' and mediators' use	Possibly no active use of keywords	Phrase-driven use of keywords – as descriptors of extradiscursive mediators	Objectified use of keywords – as signifying objects in their own right

three types of routines in their relative rigidity – in the lack of permissible variations. Indeed, rituals attain their goal through their very performance. No part of such a performance is more important than any other. After all, the whole point of the ritual action is that it is strictly defined and followed with accuracy and precision so that different people can perform it in an identical way, possibly together. Unlike in the case of exploration or deed, different ritual performances cannot be seen as interchangeable just because they generate the same end product.[24] To sum up, in rituals, the name of the game is high-fidelity reproduction, constancy, and homogeneity – the exact opposite of the innovation, variation, and diversity that characterize genuine explorative behavior. Fourth, in contrast to the other two routines that admit of local repairs, rituals that "go wrong" must simply be repeated. Fifth, rituals and the other two types of routines are also set apart by the criteria according to which their performance is evaluated and deemed proper. The acceptability of exploration is ascertained by substantiating the closing narrative. In the case of ritual, which is about *performing*, not about *knowing*, there is no room for substantiating. In this case, the precise, accurate performance of the routine procedure is the only requirement.[25]

At this point, the reader is invited to begin practicing the task of diagnosing different types of routines by taking a look at Mira's and Talli's

---

[24] The property in question may be called *flexibility*, as it denotes the degree of variability in the routine course of action. In the box-with-marbles comparison task, the flexibility would mean the child's ability to perform the task in many different ways, but to the same final effect.

[25] In the case of ritual, the request for substantiation would often lead to a story about the way the task was performed. The absence, indeed impossibility, of substantiating their outcomes was a salient feature of Roni's and Eynat's performance. Throughout the four episodes Roni's parents made numerous requirements for substantiations. By asking questions such as "How do you know?" or "Why there is more here?" they tried to see whether the children were capable of justifying their performances. The girls responded with utterances composed of the word *because* followed by one of the assertions made as a part of the original performance. This was the case, for example, when Roni said, "Because this is the biggest than this one. It is the most" ([5]), although nothing indicated that the box she pointed to might, indeed, contain more marbles. It was clear that at the moment, the children's use of the connective *because* was ritualized: If Roni and Eynat answered the mother's *why* questions in a seemingly rational way, it was obviously not the result of their awareness of the relations between boxes but of their familiarity with the *form of talk* that was expected by the grown-ups in response to this kind of question. At this point, the children were already aware of *how* to talk when answering a request for an explanation but were not yet fully aware of *when* – under which circumstances – it was appropriate to apply it. The mere appearance of the word *why* in the interlocutor's question might be enough to prompt an utterance that begins with *because* and then simply repeats, in a somewhat modified form, what the question was asking about.

numerical performances, as demonstrated in Episodes 5.4a and 5.4b, and at Ari's routines related to functions, as shown in Episode 5.7. Our own analyses have revealed that Mira and Ari implemented explorations, whereas Talli's performances were ritualized. You may be interested to see whether your analysis verifies this result. Of course, this diagnosing exercise allows for only very tentative answers. Because the difference between ritual and exploration lies in their *when* rather than *how*, to diagnose the nature of one's routine fully, the diagnostician needs to attend to more than one performance and analyze the different implementations in a wider discursive context.

4. Development of Routines

How do new discursive routines emerge and how do they later evolve? The *Incipient Numerical Thinking Study* provided us with an opportunity to watch early stages in the development of the comparing-by-counting routine. As argued earlier, in this initial phase, the routine was clearly a ritual rather than an exploration. I now wish to argue that this one case may count as representative of a more general phenomenon: Far from being an unintended result of an unsuccessful learning–teaching process, ritual is often a natural, mostly inevitable, stage in routine development. This vindication of rituals is a necessary consequence of our recognition of the inherently social nature of human knowing and learning. Let us take a closer look at this latter claim before discussing possible trajectories of routine development.

4.1 *The Road to Exploration Must Sometimes Lead through Ritual*

Because mathematical explorations are developed to enhance deeds, it is reasonable to assume that mathematists' concern about deeds should be the starting point for any discursive development. Thus, the transition from the deed of direct choice to the choice mediated by the explorative procedure of comparing-by-counting is certainly beneficial to the choice maker. Similarly, syntactic numerical calculations may greatly enhance all practical deeds that require quantitative evaluations, of which monetary transactions are a paradigmatic example. Discursive deeds, that is, deeds concerned with abstract rather than concrete objects, such as identification of geometric figures, seem to be an equally plausible starting point for new explorative routines. This time, the beneficial effects of the exploration – of the procedure of naming that follows counting of polygons' sides – express themselves in the fact that geometric figures can now be organized into a hierarchical structure,[26] thereby becoming objects of a concise, elegant theory – of a set of interconnected endorsed narratives of differing generality.

For all its didactic appeal, the idea of "growing" explorations directly from deeds may not always be feasible. For one thing, a child who is skillful in the performance of the deed would usually have no reason to look for improvements – the good is known to be the worst enemy of the better. The more skilful the child is in performing a deed, the less inclined she may be to look for, or even just to accept, an alternative procedure. The direct jump from deed to exploration is particularly unlikely in those cases in which new metarules are involved. This follows directly from the participationist vision of learning. The argument goes as follows. Metarules of mathematical discourses, rather than being "laws of nature," are historically established customs which survived because of their usefulness. This is the case, for example, with the rules for mediated identification of geometric figures, as well as with the metarule for conjuring new mathematical objects from sets of axioms, as opposed to deriving them from concrete models. One cannot expect a child to learn the corresponding routines by independent reinvention. Rather, the individualization of new metarules occurs through the engagement in a discourse that already features these rules. First attempts at individualization of other people's discourse, however, are more likely to result in rituals than in explorations, and this is true even if the learner is already familiar with deeds that the new discursive routine is supposed to enhance. This was certainly the case with Roni and Eynat's implementations of comparing-by-counting, with Shira and Ela's performances of mediated identifications, and with Talli's syntactic calculations. In all these instances, the learner did not manage to combine the new routines with the respective deeds – that of choosing a box, of identifying triangles, or of operating with money. As argued before, the inevitability of this initial ritualization stems from the inherent circularity of the development process: The child could not possibly appreciate the value of the new routine until she was aware of its advantages; such appreciation, however, could only emerge from its use.

---

[26] The basis for the hierarchical categorization of geometrical figures is the hierarchical organization of the discursive procedures of identification. These procedures can be ordered according to the relation of inclusion. For example, the procedure for identifying a square may be presented as including a procedure for identifying a rectangle: It would begin with counting the sides of the polygon and checking its angles, a method that is sufficient to find out whether the polygon is a rectangle, and it would continue with comparing the lengths of the sides, an action that is necessary to identify squares.

Yet another known circularity may hinder explorations in certain cases: As illustrated in the following, the deed-enhancing mathematical explorations would sometimes involve new abstract objects, objects that can only emerge through implementation of this very routine.

Example 9. New Mathematical Objects as a Prerequisite for New Exploration[27]

Eydan, a 7-year-old second-grader, is asked by the interviewer to split a number of cookies between two plates, so that there will be "the same amount of cookies" in both. In Episode 8.3, the splitting is not performed physically, just imagined.

Episode 8.3a. Eydan splits sets of cookies into halves

4. Interviewer: Say, you have four cookies
5. Eydan: Two and two
6. Interviewer: Two and two. And six?
7. Eydan: Three and three

So far, so good. However, when an odd number appears, Eydan becomes stymied.

Episode 8.3b. Eydan tries to split five cookies between plates

8. Interviewer: And five?
9. Eydan: One and one?
10. Interviewer: One and one. . . . How many would it amount to?
11. Eydan: Three, and then . . .
12. Interviewer: One and one is not enough, right?
13. Eydan: I know; it is two.
14. Interviewer: It is two. Two, in each one two. And then, how many is it together?
15. Eydan: . . . I need to get the same thing. . . .

---

[27] This excerpt is taken from the study conducted with Bina Langmantz. The interview was held in Hebrew.

To help the child out of the deadlock, the teacher provides an alternative description of the assignment – she presents the task as sharing the cookies among friends:

Episode 8.3c. The teacher reframes the task

16. Interviewer: Say your friend is with you in this room, you have five cookies, and you need to share them with the friend. To share evenly. Each one of you needs to get the same amount. You need to use all the cookies.

The reframing results in the immediate the breakthrough: Eydan suddenly appears to know what to do. However, his words puzzle the interviewer.

Episode 8.3d. The change of the deed – from splitting into halves to equal sharing

17. Eydan: I would take four and four and then half and another half.
18. Interviewer: Four and four and then half and another half? But you have five . . .
20. Eydan: But . . .
21. Interviewer: So how many . . . Aha, you would take four whole cookies and then half and half. How much would you get?
22. Eydan: Four and a half.
23. Interviewer: And your friend?
24. Eydan: Four and a half.
25. Interviewer: And how much is this together?
26. Eydan: Four and four?
27. Interviewer: Each gets four and a half. But you only have five!
28. Eydan: So it is eight . . .
29. Interviewer: But you have only five!
30. Eydan: So, each gets four . . .
31. Interviewer: But this will be too much! If each of you gets four, so how many cookies. . . .
32. Eydan: No! Half of this cookie for me, and half the cookie for him, half for me, half for him . . .
33. Interviewer: Oh, I got it. You split each cookie into halves!

The child's seemingly improbable use of numbers – somehow, he manages to produce "four and a half and four and a half" out of just five cookies – becomes justifiable when it turns out that the "four" expresses the number of cookies' halves. The deed of fair sharing ("one for me, one for you" – see [32]), evidently well known to Eydan, may be regarded as one from which the exploratory routine of halving whole numbers can now begin to grow. The first step would be the demonstration of this new explorative routine by the teacher. This, however, will have to be accompanied by the introduction of fractional numbers, such as $4\frac{1}{2}$, which do not yet exist for the boy. Even the term *half*, already well integrated into Eydan's discourse, does not yet function as a number-word, but rather as a signifier of a piece obtained by splitting an object into two parts (even his awareness of the request of congruency of these parts cannot yet be taken for granted). Thus, if the boy is to individualize the routine of halving *numbers* (rather than halving material things), he will have to participate in the performance of this routine even before his new discourse is objectified, that is, before the new signifiers, such as $4\frac{1}{2}$, turn into full-fledged discursive objects (numbers). As long as the objectification remains incomplete, his routine of halving numbers will remain a ritual.

It is interesting to remark that what was said here about individual learning might also be true of the mathematicians who were the first to introduce new mathematical objects and metarules. The inherent circularity of discourse development hindered practices of the first inventors of mathematical routines just as they hinder those of today's children who learn the same routines from others. In the absence of objectification, the new routines often felt like rituals rather than explorations. The previously quoted remark by the sixteenth century mathematician Cardan about "the moral suffering" involved in applying the "impossible" routines[28] aptly illustrates the sense of uneasiness with which mathematicians often practiced new discourses.

4.2 *Thoughtful Imitation and the Ritualized Beginnings*

The upshot of the preceding observations is that on their way to new routines involving new metarules or new mathematical objects, learners must pass, if only very briefly, through the stage of ritualized performance. At this transitory stage, they may become quite familiar with the *how* of the new routine, but will be much less aware of its *when*. It is now natural to ask how the child who does not yet have a clear idea of when the routine can be

---

[28] Kline (1980, p. 116).

implemented or why it works can still be able to collaborate in its collective implementations and may eventually be even capable of implementing it independently. The answer, it seems, lies in the child's propensity for imitation. Imitation, which evidently is a natural human property, is the obvious, indeed, the only imaginable way to enter new discourse. The tendency to imitate others occurs hand in hand with the need to communicate, a need so strong that it would often lead to what may appear as the reversal of the "proper" order of learning. The learner would be prepared to follow a rule enacted by another interlocutor as a prelude to, rather than a result of, her attempts to figure out the inner logic of this other discourse. Although acts of mimicking that take place in the course of learning are often disparaged as a mere attempt to "please others," the participationist vision of human development compels us to do what Vygotsky urged us to do: to "reevaluate the role of imitation in learning."[29] Without the instinct to imitate, children might never be able to enter any of the uniquely human forms of life, including communication in their first language.

Imitation is not as simple a process as it may appear. No imitation is an exact reproduction of the model. To put it in Michael Bakhtin's words:

> The unique speech experience of each individual is shaped and developed in continuous and constant interaction with others' individual utterances. This experience can be characterized to some degree as the process of *assimilation* – more or less creative – for others' words (and not the words of a language).... These words of others carry with them their own expression, their own evaluative tone, which we assimilate, *rework*, and *re-accentuate*.[30]

I have highlighted the terms *reword* and *reaccentuate* to stress that modifications are inevitable in the process of individualization of routines. Knowing what to change and what to keep constant in the successive implementations is the secret of successful learning. By speaking about *thoughtful* imitation, I mean the process in which one is constantly monitoring her decisions about the variable versus invariable elements of performance.

Be the process of imitation as thoughtful as it may, it rarely succeeds in the first trial. The very idea of invariance implies the necessity of a wide range of experiences from which the child could deduce which aspects of the performance constitute the permanent "skeleton" of the routine and which are situation-specific. More often than not, young children's

[29] Vygotsky (1978, p. 87).
[30] Bakhtin (1999, p. 130) (emphasis added).

imitations of other people's routines replicate more than would be appropriate. The phenomenon, which Piaget called *egocentricity* and which expresses itself in a child's inability to fine-tune her discursive actions to the needs of her interlocutor, is a good example of such inflexible, communicationally inadequate, replication. Another example of indiscriminate routine imitation is Roni and Eynat's way of answering the "why" questions.[31] The following example from the *Montreal Algebra Study* shows that imitations may sometimes miss the point altogether.

Example 10. What to Preserve and What to Change?

As a prelude to the *Montreal Algebra Study*, the participants, beginning seventh-grade students, were tested for their arithmetic and algebraic skills. One of the tasks was to "write a good story (word problem) that could be solved by performing the following calculation: $7 \cdot (3 + 5)$." Knowing that the children were all well acquainted with this type of task – a fact that was confirmed by the results of the test – the researchers were startled by one student's response:

> Tim went into a store to buy chocolate bars. It turned out that if he calculated the total of $7 \cdot (3 + 5)$ in his head, he would get that number of chocolate bars. What was the answer?

4.3 Transforming Ritual into Exploration

Transforming ritual into exploration is not a separate process that occurs only after the child has attained full mastery of the routine course of action. The thoughtful imitator, while constantly fine-tuning her performance to that of others, is also pondering the expert mathematists' reasons for doing what they do. The growth of proficiency is accompanied by gradual deritualization. Ideally, the routine will eventually be transformed into full-fledged exploration. To illustrate, let me revisit Roni and Eynat 7 months after we saw them implementing comparing-by-counting as a ritual in Episode 1.1.

Example 11. Coalescence of Deeds and Rituals – from the Incipient Numerical Thinking Study

In this phase of the study, Roni and Eynat were presented by Roni's mother with exactly the same comparison tasks they tackled 7 months earlier. Our

---

[31] See note 25.

first impression was that not much change occurred in their performance. The sequence

direct choosing → comparing-by-counting → evaluating

which appeared four times in the first round of conversations (see Table 7.3), was also observed four times in the present case. And yet a closer inspection of the children's actions did disclose some significant differences.

First, it was now clear that the rather accidental routine that developed 7 months earlier reincarnated into a guessing game. The metamorphosis had already begun in the first phase and was evidenced by the seemingly marginal addition of the evaluative move (see "We were right!" [67] in Table 7.3) in the third reiteration of the sequence. This move indicated that what was initially implemented as a quite arbitrary concatenation of two independent procedures – that of taking-for-oneself and that of comparing-by-counting – evolved in a matter of minutes into an integrated procedure, the goal of which was to arrive at the same result in two different ways. Seven months later, the children not only evaluate, but also explicitly speak about "guessing" on several occasions. For example, in one of the second-round episodes, the children and the grown-ups exchanged roles, so that it was now Roni mother's task to answer the question "In which box are there more marbles?" After a few moments of silence, Roni prompted her mother, "Go on, Mom, guess!"

Second, as can be seen from the following episode, the deed of choosing was no longer direct.

Episode 8.4. Choosing a box with marbles

Roni's mother presents the children with two closed opaque boxes and asks them, *"In which box are there more marbles?"*

84. Roni:	Hold on . . .	Lifts the two boxes and holds each one in one hand
85. Roni:	This one . . .	Puts down the two boxes and points to the box next to her
86. Mother:	Eynat, and what do you say?	
87. Eynat:		Points to the other box, the one next to her
88. Mother:	How do you know?	
89. Eynat:	By the noise	
90. Mother:	How do you know, Roni?	
91. Roni:	Because this one is heavy	Lifts the box next to her

Obviously the deed of choosing is now mediated by two new, mutually independent procedures: In Eynat's case, it is the procedure of comparing the *noise* made by the marbles ([89]), and in Roni's case, it is the comparison of the *weights* of the boxes ([91]).

Third, the difference expresses itself in the children's ability to answer the "why" question. Unlike 7 months earlier, when they constructed their response by concatenating the word *because* with a modified version of the question itself ("this is a bigger/more huge one"), they are now giving independent reasons: the greater weight or the greater noise.

These three differences indicate that after 7 months, the process of deritualization of the comparing-by-counting routine is already quite advanced. The procedure is now clearly seen as equivalent to comparing-by-weight and comparing-by-noise, and this fact affects all the aspects of the routine performance listed in Table 8.1. The success of comparing-by-counting is now independent of other people – it can be judged against the results of other comparisons. The procedure was thus relocated from the interpersonal sphere to the space between the child and the world. The fact that the procedure is replaceable by others makes its performance potentially more flexible and more corrigible. Finally, its role (and thus its acceptability) in the deed of choosing became substantiable. In short, by being integrated with the deed of choosing along with several other procedures, comparing-by-counting has been transformed into a choice-enhancing exploration.

To summarize what has been said so far, new mathematical routines that begin their life as rituals may eventually evolve into explorations. This latter transformation can happen quite abruptly, so that the stage of ritualization is hardly noticeable, or it can last for a long time, perhaps even forever. The transitory phase of ritualization corresponds to the period of individualizing – the period during which the learner can participate in the collective implementation of the routine but is not yet capable of independent performance. Using Vygotsky's language, ritual is the form routines take in the *zone of proximal development*.

Let me now take a broader look and consider the change that occurs in the discourse as a whole when new routines evolve from rituals to explorations. Before the deritualization occurs, the routines in question constitute a loose collection rather than an integrated discourse. The loosely assembled routines may not appear to be related one to another even if they feature the same words and similar actions. In the discourse of explorations, in contrast, many different routine ways of acting may be grouped according to the relation of possibly partial equivalence (exchangeability under the certain set of constraints). Discourse with such a well-developed network of interlacing, partially overlapping routines can be described as *consolidated*. One of the characteristics of routines' development, therefore, is their coalescence into a highly consolidated discourse.

4.4 *Spurring and Cultivating Learning: The Principles of the Continuity of Discourse and of the Commognitive Conflict*

As stressed time and again throughout this book, the participationist vision of human development implies that any substantial change in individual discourse, one that involves a modification in metarules or introduction of whole new mathematical objects, must be mediated by experienced inter-locutors. The mediation may take many different forms, and the question that now should be asked is which of these forms are potentially most effec-tive. Although there is no general answer – the success of the learning–teaching process depends on too many factors to be captured in a single, universal formula – at least two basic conditions for effective mediation can be deduced from what was said earlier about the mechanism of discursive change.

Continuity of Discourse

Introducing a new discourse by transforming an existing one is certainly more effective than trying to build the new discourse from scratch.[32] More specifically, it seems that the safest way to new explorations is to intro-duce them as (prospective) enhancements of familiar deeds. According to this principle, comparing-by-counting will be introduced as an enhance-ment of the deed of choosing, mediated identification of geometric figures will be introduced as a replacement for the deed of immediate identifica-tion, syntactic calculations will be developed from manipulations on sets of concrete objects, and the routines of endorsement grounded exclusively in intradiscursive argument will evolve from those that appeal to extradiscur-sive evidence. As argued before, the presence of the deeds will not neces-sarily prevent the new routines from taking the form of rituals rather than explorations, at least initially. In some cases, familiarity with a deed may hinder the attempt at modification of the discourse altogether. However, when the necessary discursive evolution does take place, the familiar deed

---

[32] In fact, new discourses are never built from scratch. After all, our everyday discourses serve as a basis for any new discourse we may wish to learn. Still, the distinction can be made between introducing new vocabularies and routines as modifications of those that are already in place and the attempts to impose the innovation "from above," without any explicit connection to the existing discourse.

would help in ensuring that the new routine does eventually turn into a genuine exploration. This claim is corroborated by what we saw in the case of Roni and Eynat's comparing-by-counting routine, which evolved from ritual to exploration thanks to its being consolidated with the deed of choosing, and through this deed with several other mediating routines. The principle of continuity can also be analytically substantiated: The deed that waits to be enhanced by a new procedure bequeaths to this new procedure its own applicability and closure conditions, thus taking care in advance of the *when* of the new routine – and the *when* is exactly the aspect of routines that remains underdeveloped in the phase of ritualization.

It is important to stress that deeds on the basis of which explorative routines can be developed do not have to be practical; that is, they do not have to consist in transforming concrete objects. The deeds may be purely discursive, as is often the case with transformations of numbers (calculations) and with differentiating functions. Let me repeat that a discursive routine counts as a deed when the implementer's discourse is fully objectified and when from her point of view, the routine is one of producing objects rather than narratives. True, many discursive developments supposed to happen in mathematics classrooms can be grounded in practical deeds. Many, but not all. For example, because there is no concrete model for the routine of multiplying a negative number by a negative number, no practical deed would fully support the transition from unsigned to signed numbers.[33] This disclaimer is of particular importance in view of the current exhortations to teach mathematics "from everyday context," implying that mathematical discourse should be "grown" exclusively from *practical* deeds. This seems to be the misinterpretation of the principle of continuity with familiar discourses, discussed earlier.

Commognitive Conflict as a Trigger of Meta-Level Learning

If learning mathematics is a change of discourse, one can distinguish between two types of learning:

- *Object-level learning* that expresses itself in the expansion of the existing discourse attained through extending a vocabulary, constructing new routines, and producing new endorsed narratives; this learning, therefore, results in endogenous expansion of the discourse (see chapter 4); and

---

[33] For the substantiation of this claim and elaboration on the issue of learning–teaching processes related to negative numbers, see Sfard (in press).

- *Metalevel learning*, which involves changes in metarules of the discourse and is usually related to exogenous change in discourse. This change means that some familiar tasks, such as, say, defining a word or identifying geometric figures, will now be done in a different, unfamiliar way and that certain familiar words will change their uses.

Considering the contingency of metadiscursive rules – the fact that these rules are a matter of a useful custom rather than of necessity – it is rather implausible that learners would initiate a metalevel change by themselves. The metalevel learning is most likely to originate in the learner's direct encounter with the new discourse. Because this new discourse is governed by metarules different from those according to which the student has been acting so far, such an encounter entails *commognitive conflict* – a situation in which different discursants are acting according to different metarules. Usually, the differences in metarules that are the source of the conflict find their explicit, most salient expression in the fact that different participants endorse contradicting narratives. Of course, some cases of conflicting narratives may stem from differing opinions rather than from discursive conflict. Discursive conflict should be suspected only in those cases when the conflicting narratives appear as factual, that is, as endorsable according to well-defined metadiscursive rules, and the possibility of an error in their construction and substantiation has been eliminated. As simple as this last claim may sound, the presence of commognitive conflict is not easy to detect. Only too often, commognitive conflicts are mistaken for factual disagreements that can be resolved according to a certain well-defined set of criteria.[34]

The notion of *commognitive conflict* should not be confused with the acquisitionist idea of *cognitive conflict*, central to the well-known, well-developed theory of conceptual change.[35] At least three substantial differences can be listed. First, acquisitionists and commognitivists do not agree about the locus of the conflict. Cognitive conflict is defined as arising in the encounter between one's beliefs and the world: A person holds two contradicting beliefs about the world, and one of these beliefs is, of necessity, incompatible with the real state of affairs. In one's attempt to resolve

---

[34] The majority of the well-known incompatibilities between scientific theories may, in fact, be resulting from commognitive conflicts rather than from correct versus incorrect factual beliefs. Thus, for example, what appears as a straightforward contradiction between Aristotle and Newton – between the former thinker's claim that a constant force applied to a body results in the body's constant movement and Newton's assertion known as the second law of dynamics that constant force results in constant acceleration – may, in fact, be the outcome of the two men's differing uses of the word *force*.

[35] Vosniadou (1994); Schnotz et al. (1999); Vosniadou, Baltas, and Vamvakoussi (2007).

the conflict, the person will try to employ *the world itself* as an ultimate arbitrator. The idea of commognitive conflict, on the other hand, rests on the assumption that learning, as a change of discourse, is most likely to result from *interactions with others*. According to this latter approach, the main opportunities for metalevel learning arise not from discrepancies between one's endorsed narratives and certain external evidence, but from differences in interlocutors' ways of communicating. The commognitive framework, therefore, questions the traditional relation between the world and the discourse: Rather than assuming that what we say (think) about the world is determined by what we find in the world, it claims a reflexive relation between what we are able to say and what we are able to perceive and endorse. Most of the time, our discourses remain fully consistent with our experience of reality. We need a discursive change to become aware of new possibilities and arrive at a new vision. We thus often need a change in how we talk before we can experience a change in what we see.

The second difference between the two types of conflict is in their significance for learning: Whereas creating cognitive conflict is considered an optional pedagogical move, particularly useful when the students display "misconceptions," the commognitive conflict is the most likely, often indispensable, source of metalevel mathematical learning. Without other people's example, children may have no incentive for changing their discursive ways. From their point of view, the discourse in which they are fluent does not seem to have any particular weaknesses as a tool for making sense of the world around them.

Finally, the commognitive and acquisitionist versions of the learning-engendering conflict differ in their respective implications regarding the way the conflict is to be resolved. The acquisitionist vision of conflict resolution is grounded in the principle of noncontradiction – in the assumption that any two narratives that sound mutually contradictory are also mutually exclusive, and that there is a common criterion for deciding which of them must be rejected and which should be endorsed and labeled as true. Preferrably, such conflict is resolved by appeal to empirical evidence. Commognitive conflict, in contrast, is defined as the phenomenon that occurs when seemingly conflicting narratives are originating from different discourses – from discourses that differ in their use of words, in the rules of substantiation, and so forth. Such discourses are *incommensurable* rather than incompatible; that is, they do not share criteria for deciding whether a given narrative should be endorsed.[36] Unlike in the case of conflicting narratives

[36] By *commensurable*, says Rorty (1979), "I mean able to be brought under a set of rules which will tell us how rational agreement can be reached on what would settle the issue on every

Table 8.2. *Comparison of concepts: Cognitive conflict versus commognitive conflict*

	Cognitive conflict	Commognitive conflict
The conflict is between:	The interlocutor and the world	Incommensurable discourses
Role in learning	Is an optional way for removing misconceptions	Practically indispensable for metalevel learning
How is it resolved?	By student's rational effort	By student's acceptance and rationalization (individualization) of the discursive ways of the expert interlocutor

from the same discourse, two narratives that originate in incommensurable discourses cannot automatically count as mutually exclusive even if they sound contradictory. This kind of conflict, therefore, cannot be resolved with decisive empirical evidence, confirming one of the conflicting claims and refuting the other. Rather, one resolves the problem by choosing one of the two conflicting discourses and abandoning the other. Thus, whereas acquisitionists view conflict resolution as making sense of the world, commognitivists regard it as making sense of other people's thinking (and thus talking) about this world.[37] This means a gradual acceptance, "customization," and rationalization – figuring out the inner logic – of other people's discourses.

The differences between the concepts of cognitive and commognitive conflict are summarized in Table 8.2.

point where statements seem to conflict" (p. 316). In other words, incommensurability means there is no supertheory that would provide criteria for proving one framework right while refuting the other. "Incommensurability entails irreducibility [of vocabularies], but not incompatibility" (Rorty, 1979, p. 388).

[37] Commognitive conflict is often involved also in mathematical invention (or any other scientific invention, for that matter). In this case, the conflict is likely to occur *within* a person, between two partially overlapping discourses in which the person is embedded. Indeed, in the transition from a familiar discourse to a new one the mathematician may find himself endorsing conflicting narratives. One famous case of such inner conflict is that of George Cantor, the inventor of set theory, who in his letters to another mathematician, Richard Dedekind, complained about his inability to overcome the contradiction between the well-known "truth" that a part is smaller than the whole and the conclusion he reached on the grounds of his new theory, according to which a subset of an infinite set may be "as big as" the whole set (Cavaillès, 1962).

5. Explorations, Deeds, and Rituals: What We Mathematize For – in a Nutshell

In this chapter I divided discursive routines into three types differing from one another mainly by the types of tasks they accomplish (their closure). Two identical performances by different mathematists, or even by the same mathematist at different stages in the development of her discourse, may be implementations of different types of routine. Both deeds and explorations are geared at extradiscursive reality; they are, respectively, about changing the world (transforming concrete objects) and getting to know it (producing endorsed narratives). In contrast, rituals are socially oriented: These are acts of solidarity with coperformers. Other questions that need to be addressed when one tries to distinguish between ritual and exploration are when the routine is most likely to be applied, whom the performance involves as actors or addressees, how flexible and corrigible the routine is, and whether the implementer is capable of substantiating the routine in an acceptable way.

All three types of routines play a role in the development of discourses. In the case of *metalevel* learning, when the routine to be learned involves new metarules or new mathematical objects, its reinvention by the learner is highly unlikely. In this case, the learning would typically occur through scaffolded individualization, that is, through interaction with mathematists who are already insiders in the target discourse. When the process of individualization begins and the child makes her first steps in collective implementations of new routines, her performance is ritualized. The *how* of the routine is usually individualized well before the *when*. Thus, far from being the unintended result of an ineffective learning–teaching process, ritual is a natural, mostly inevitable, stage in routine development. This vindication of rituals is a necessary consequence of our recognition of the inherently social nature of human knowing and learning.

Our ability to act in new situations hinges on our capacity for recycling either our own or other people's previous behavior. Becoming a participant of a new discourse is made possible by our propensity for thoughtful imitation. It is the child's readiness to follow in other people's footsteps that powers the process of individualization, at least in its initial stages. Later, through gradual rationalization, the ritual will ideally be transformed into a full-fledged exploration.

The best, perhaps the only, workable way to develop a new discourse is by gradual transformation of a discourse in which the child is already conversant. One way to preserve the discursive continuity is to "grow" new routines in conjunction with familiar deeds that the new routines are supposed to enhance. The main opportunity for metalevel learning, that is, for the evolution of metarules, arises when the learner is exposed to *commognitive conflict*. Such conflict appears when one encounters a discourse *incommensurable* with one's own – when familiar routines are confronted with other people's alternative ways of implementing the same discursive tasks, grounded in different metarules.

At this point, the mission of presenting the basics of the commognitive vision of mathematical thinking seems completed, at least for now. In the next chapter I take stock of tasks already accomplished and present some of those that are yet to be done.

9 Looking Back and Ahead

Solving Old Quandaries and Facing New Ones

It is venturesome to think that a coordination of words (philosophies are nothing more than that) can resemble the universe very much. It is also venturesome to think that of all these illustrious coordinations, one of them – at least in an infinitesimal way – does not resemble the universe a bit more than the others.

Jorge Luis Borges[1]

The fact that Newton's vocabulary lets us predict the world more easily than Aristotle's does not mean that the world speaks Newtonian.

Richard Rorty[2]

We (the undivided divinity operating within us) have dreamt the world. We have dreamt it as firm, mysterious, visible, ubiquitous in space and durable in time; but in its architecture we have allowed tenuous and eternal crevices of unreason which tell us it is false.

Jorge Luis Borges[3]

We have come a long way since we first puzzled upon a bunch of persistent quandaries on human thinking. That early encounter led us to question the traditional acquisitionist discourse and resulted in the attempt to modify our thinking about thinking. It is now time to ask where we are at the end of this long journey. In this final chapter, after a brief summary of what has been done so far, I ponder about the implications of the shift to a commognitive outlook for research on human development and for educational practice. My first move, however, is to revisit the old quandaries, one

---

[1] Borges (1962/1964, p. 207).
[2] Rorty (1989, p. 6).
[3] Borges (1962/1964, p. 208).

by one, asking whether the change in our discourse has yielded the desired resolutions.

Throughout this process of stocktaking let us keep in mind that what has been done on these pages is only a part of the story that waits to be told. The focus, so far, has been mainly on the inner dynamics of discourses. A look "from outside" is now necessary in order to address such questions as *What is it that makes people engage in a given discourse – mathematical, for example – in the first place? What shapes one's participation? How do different discourses interact with one another and how does a person steer a course among them?* In the last part of this closing chapter I will try to outline a proposal on how the project of answering these new queries could be approached.

1. Looking Back: What Has Been Done

Let me retrace our trajectory. Five long-standing quandaries regarding mathematical thinking – the quandary of numerical thinking, of abstraction, of misconceptions, of learning disabilities, and of understanding – triggered the attempt to rethink thinking. The commognitive approach developed gradually, as we were trying to disobjectify and operationalize the existing discourses on thinking. The basic commognitive tenet, according to which thinking is a form of communication, was derived from the more general participationist claim that human development is the process of individualization of historically established, collectively implemented forms of life. The term *commognition* was coined to stress that interpersonal communication and individual thinking are two faces of the same phenomenon. Although it was stated time and again that commognition does not have to be verbal, it was also noted that language and linguistic forms of discourse may well be the key to one of the most persistent conundrums regarding humans. It is probably thanks to the recursivity of human languages – to our ability to turn communication into its own object – that people, in contrast to other species, are able systematically to increase the complexity of their activities from one generation to the next.

Because it is in mathematics that this capacity for accumulation of complexity finds its strongest expression, it was natural for us to focus on mathematical discourse while trying to fathom the mechanisms of discourse development. Easily recognizable by virtue of its special vocabulary, visual mediators, and routines, mathematical discourse constitutes an autopoietic system, a system that stirs its own incessant growth and develops in "pulses" of intermittent expansions and compressions. As mathematical discourses grow and multiply, they are also constantly scrutinized for differences and commonalities. Every so often, this scrutiny generates a new discourse that subsumes, and thus partially replaces, all those lower-level discourses that inspired its birth. New mathematical objects produced in such a transition are the result of saming and encapsulating of lower-level objects and of reifying lower-level processes. The compression of the discourse resulting from objectification triggers a new expansion that will be eventually followed by new attempts at compression. This is, basically, how mathematical discourses evolve throughout history.

In the process of individual learning, discourses develop by individualization of historically established discursive patterns. It has been hypothesized that students' use of new mathematical vocabulary proceeds from passive to routine-driven, then to phrase-driven, and, eventually, to objectified. The learner can develop some discursive routines directly from the deeds that these routines are supposed to enhance. Some other routines can be derived from simpler ones. Yet others would become a part of one's discourse only with the help of more experienced mathematists, through the process of individualization. This latter process would usually begin with the phase of ritualized performance, even if only imperceptibly brief. As stated by Vygotsky, "The path from object to child and from child to object passes through another person"[4] (p. 30), and rituals seem to be an integral part of this path. As the rituals gradually turn into explorations, they combine into a tightly interwoven network of partially equivalent discursive routines. In this way, what began as a bunch of unrelated procedures turns into a well-consolidated, objectified full-fledged mathematical discourse.

2. What Happened to the Old Quandaries

Let me now return to the old conundrums in an attempt to find out what happens to the puzzling phenomena when we look at them through the commognitive lens.

2.1 *The Quandary of Number*

Our brief encounters with samples of early numerical thinking and its descriptions in current literature left us with a number of questions:

1. Why is it that children who can count without a glitch do not use counting when asked to compare sets of objects?

---

[4] Vygotsky (1978, p. 30).

2. How can we account for what they actually do?
3. More generally, where does numerical thinking begin?
4. How is the incipient version of this thinking different from our own and how does it become, eventually, just like that of any other adult persons?

In the preceding chapters, questions 2 and 4 have been answered in detail once the term *numerical thinking* has been replaced with the expression *numerical discourse*. I now wish to claim that question 1 should be dismissed as stemming from ungrounded acquisitionist assumptions, whereas question 3 has a clear commognitive answer.

The problematic assumption underlying the first question is part and parcel of acquisitionist discourses on thinking and learning. For a person who views numbers as self-sustained, discourse-independent entities, getting acquainted with numbers is much like learning about material tools: One becomes aware of the tool's existence through a direct exposure and then becomes acquainted with the tool's use while seeing it in action. This is, for example, the way one learns about spoons or pencils. In the case of numbers, a child's counting is interpreted by acquisitionists as her direct encounter with the tool (number), whereas comparing-by-counting is a basic, indeed, self-imposing, form of this tool's use. Within this perspective, therefore, it is natural to be puzzled by the fact that a person seemingly "endowed" with numbers may systematically ignore this potent instrument when asked, "In which box are there more marbles?"

Within the disobjectified commognitive discourse, there is no room for this kind of surprise. Commognitivists view numbers as particular forms of language use and thus reject the idea of number as a tool existing independently of its specific uses. In the process of individualization, prior to the objectification of numerical discourse, each numerical routine is learned separately, as an activity in its own right. At this point, a child's engagement in the numerical rituals is motivated by her wish to gain and sustain her membership in a valued community. Indeed, whereas grown-ups count to get closer to the truth about the world, children count to get closer to the grown-ups. It is only after objectification and deritualization that the child becomes a flexible user of numerical discourse, capable of building novel numerical routines. Thus, rather then being puzzled by children's initial reluctance to use counting for comparison, the commognitivist marvels over how quickly and infallibly young learners become aware of this routine's advantages.

As was repeatedly stressed in this book, answering the question *When does numerical thinking begin?* is not a matter of empirical discovery but of semantic decision, that is, of one's explicitly presented stance about what should count as numerical thinking. Because commognitivists view numbers as discursive constructs, it would be senseless to talk about numerical thinking that precedes one's ability to engage, if only peripherally, in the communication on numbers. True, even very young children may display sensitivity to differences in cardinality, and this sensitivity is crucial for their future success in the numerical discourse.[5] These early abilities should thus be of interest to anybody who wishes to study the genesis of numerical thinking because they are what will one day make this thinking possible. And yet, the advantage of leaving these early sensitivities on the other side of the mathematical–nonmathematical divide is that this decision allows us to focus on the "uniquely human," that is, on those forms of activity that are typical of humans and cannot be found in other species. Although discursive skills do seem to belong to this latter category, the sensitivity to the cardinality, as described earlier, probably does not: Much evidence has been collected showing that some animals, exactly like human babies, are visibly startled by changes in the number of elements in small sets.[6]

2.2 *The Quandary of Abstraction (Situatedness)*

The ample research literature on abstraction and transfer of learning led me to pose the following questions:

> Why is it that even well-educated people do not apply abstract mathematical procedures in situations in which such use could help them with problems they are trying to solve? More generally, why does people's thinking appear so much dependent on particularities of the situations in which it takes place? Are there any teaching strategies that could be used to counteract this situatedness?

We seem to have good reasons to wonder. If mathematical explorations are such a powerful way of enhancing our practical deeds, why do we see them so rarely in people's everyday activities? One answer seems pretty straightforward: Everyday deeds, such as money transactions, which are firmly grounded in familiar manipulations on familiar objects, are preferable because of their superior effectiveness resulting from the embodiment and automation of the required course of action. And yet, people tend to shy away from literate mathematical discourse also in situations in which they can recall no familiar practical routine. Why is it that they remain stymied

---

[5] Wynn (1992, 1995).

[6] See anecdotes and research-based stories about "talented and gifted animals" summarized in Dehaene (1997, pp. 13–40).

rather than turning to appropriate exploration with the help of which a useful practical action might be designed? Whereas this phenomenon is natural in a person who does not possess the required discursive experience, it may appear puzzling in school-educated people, who were introduced to the potentially relevant explorations in the past and demonstrated reasonable mastery of these procedures in all kinds of tests and examinations.

As in the case of the former quandary, the commognitive perspective compels me to reverse the question. Rather than wondering about the fact that people do not associate familiar routines with situations in which these routines would be useful, one should probably wonder how it happens that they are ever able to act in apparently the same way in situations that, at the first sight, do not seem to have much in common. If the same routine is to be applied, one must see two situations as in a sense the same (e.g. visually similar), or at least as describable with the same discursive means. And yet, it is the difference rather than sameness that we seem to be perceiving by default, without learning. As remarked by Luis Jorge Borges, "To think means to forget differences."[7] "Forgetting differences," in turn, is tantamount to deritualization and objectification of the discourse in which we engage to deal with the different situations. For example, to have the idea of applying the same computational routines in school, in the marketplace, and in a diary warehouse, one must be able to use the numerical discourse as one that subsumes the discourse on money transactions and the discourse on milk containers, at least partially. This will not happen unless the numerical discourse becomes deritualized and objectified, that is, unless number-words are being used as signifying intangible entities for which coins and milk containers are but physical "avatars." It is only in thus objectified numerical discourse that computational procedures count as a means for producing endorsable narratives about a wide variety of different-looking objects.

As already explained, creation of subsuming discourse, its objectification, and its deritualization are not straightforward processes. These processes involve frequent alternating between object-level and metalevel discourses, and they require time and effort. Moreover, one cannot simply skip deritualization and objectification altogether. As argued in the last chapter, subsuming discourses introduce new mathematical objects and more often than not change at least some of the existing metadiscursive rules. One develops such discourse with the help of more experienced mathematists rather than through independent invention. Of necessity, the process

---

[7] Borges (1962/1964, p. 66).

of individualization begins with loosely related rituals. Because ritualization means a considerable dependence on situational clues and thus very restricted applicability, situatedness is a natural, unavoidable stage in the development of new mathematical discourses.

In the view of this, the phenomenon of situatedness stops being a puzzle: It is a necessary, if only transitory phase in the process of individualization of mathematical discourse. The fact that a school-educated person does not utilize literate mathematical routines in real-life situations simply means that the school learning stopped short of attaining its goal: It did not take her beyond the stage of ritualization. This does not mean, however, that overcoming ritualization, thus minimizing the situatedness of learning, is impossible altogether. Whenever the conversion to the full-fledged explorative discourse fails to occur and what was supposed be but a transitory stage gains permanence, teaching methods are the immediate suspect. A handful of ideas about what can be done to encourage objectification and deritualization of mathematical discourse have been presented in the preceding chapters. Some others will be discussed in the next part of this chapter. In the end, however, I will claim that teaching methods, as such, are definitely not the only possible reason why the process of individualization of mathematical discourses often fails to arrive at its completion. The other reasons originate outside the mathematics classroom rather than inside, and although more elusive, they may be equally, or even more influential.

2.3 *The Quandary of Misconceptions*

Two questions were asked in chapter 1 after the brief review of current literature on phenomena called misconceptions:

1. How can one explain the fact that a child who learned a mathematical concept from a teacher or a textbook "errs" about this concept in a systematic way? How can we account for the fact that some of these mistakes are shared by a great many children all around the world? Even more puzzlingly, how is it that students' "misconceptions" are often very much like those of the scientists or mathematicians who were the first to think about the concepts in question?
2. Most importantly, because the theory of misconceptions, even if perfected, does not seem likely to suffice as a framework for studying learning of mathematics or science, what is it that this theory is missing?

Researchers who profess the theory of misconceptions, or of *conceptual change*, as this theory is currently known, speak in terms of *concepts*, *conceptions*, and *misconceptions*, but they rarely provide any of these terms with operational definitions. As was explained earlier in this book, one can operationalize the notion of *concept* as a word (or other symbol) together with its discursive uses.[8] This operationalization yields the immediate answer to the second question: The element that seems to be conspicuously missing from studies on misconceptions is the attention to the systemic nature of our use of words and thus to the fact that a concept, as such, is an unlikely unit of analysis. If a concept is a word together with its discursive uses, one cannot get a sense of a person's concept of number without considering the totality of this person's discursive activities in which the term *number* may appear. In research on development of numerical thinking, therefore, nothing less than the entire discourse on numbers must be considered.

The focus of the theory of conceptual change is on recurrent, systematically nonstandard ("misconceived") ways in which mathematics learners often solve certain types of problems. These phenomena can be observed, for example, each time a new kind of number – rational, negative, and so forth – is introduced. Endowed with the commognitive definition of concept and with the whole discourse on numbers as the unit of analysis, we can now explain these phenomena as stemming directly from the systemic nature of discursive development. Indeed, uses of words are tightly interconnected, and so are different discursive rules and routines. If so, one cannot change any of these elements without changing all the others. Such complex change, however, is unlikely to happen in one decisive move. The difficulty of the transition stems, among others, from the fact that the new discourse is going to be incommensurable with the one from which it evolves: The two discourses, the old and the new, will be producing conflicting narratives, and there will be no common set of criteria with which to resolve the apparent contradictions. This incommensurability will be the result of a change in the use of familiar words. Thus, the use of the word *number* is modified each time new types of numbers are added. In the transition from whole to fractional numbers, for example, one can no longer endorse the claim "The product of two numbers is at least as big as the bigger of these numbers," whereas in the transition from real to complex numbers one has to give up even such a seemingly self-evident story

---

[8] This definition was first proposed in chapter 4. It is in tune with the work of Vygotsky, who defined concepts as referring to words together with their meaning, and of Wittgenstein, who claimed that meaning is the use of a word in language. Indeed, when combined, these two descriptions, Vygotskian and Wittgensteinian, define the term *concept* as referring to a word together with its discursive uses.

about numbers as the one that says that numbers can be ordered and that they answer the question "How many?" or "How much?" As a result of the objectification of the previous discourse on numbers, however, the narratives that are now questioned appear as if they were laws of nature rather than a mere product of human ways with words.

Thus, at these special developmental junctures where "misconceptions" are most likely to appear, the required change in discourse runs as deep as the basic ontological and epistemological assumptions inherent in its metarules. Their invisibility makes these assumptions highly resilient. The transition to the new discourse may thus be a slow process, full of lapses. It will likely happen in leaps and bounces. Some new rules will be quick to arrive, and some old ones will refuse to leave. This will sometimes result in a hybrid: in a discourse that is not yet the way it should be, but also not the way it was before. This discourse will systematically produce seemingly contradictory narratives – and the emphasis here is on the adverb *systematically*. Indeed, if the hybridity does not seem accidental, and if it recurs in the same form in different places and at different times, it is because the source of the phenomenon is always the same: any given hybridity is a side effect of an attempt to modify a certain historically established discourse in a certain well-defined, historically imposed way. The "misconceived" narratives that the learner endorses at this stage originate in those deeply rooted, seemingly self-evident rules of the old discourse that do not fit with the new one. It is therefore the inner mechanics of discourses that injects a method into the "madness" known as "misconceptions."

2.4 *The Quandary of Learning (Dis)abilities*

The brief survey of recent literature on learning disabilities, combined with the story of two 18-year-old students with extremely shaky arithmetical skills, left us wondering about a number of issues:

1. If the condition known as "learning disability" is supposed to originate in "natural" rather than environmental factors, why does it seem so tightly related to life stories of those who are diagnosed as learning disabled? Which of the two occurs first: learning disability or life hardships?
2. Besides, without direct access to physiological factors, how are we supposed to distinguish between learning disabilities and "normal" learning difficulties?

These ponderings seem to originate in the assumption that learning problems reside exclusively "beneath [the learner's] skin and between his ears."[9] The claim about the exclusivity of individual determinants disappears from the commognitive account. Although commognitive tenets do not concradict the claim that physiological factors have an important, often decisive impact on a child's learning, they also imply that physiology alone cannot tell the whole story. After all, according to commognitivism, school learning is the process of individualization of historically established discourses, whereas discourses, at least in the early stages of individualization, are collective activities. Such activities are by no means simple sums of individual performances. Whatever is done by the learner constitutes a response to a discursive move of interlocutors and an invitation to yet another move on the interlocutors' part. Moreover, one's participation in mathematical discourse may be informed by this person's experience as a participant of other discourses. All this implies that failure and success in learning are shaped "from outside" not any less, sometimes even more, than they are shaped "from inside."

One can imagine many ways in which the history of one's discursive participation may inform this person's mathematical learning. For instance, considering the fact that the development of mathematical discourse involves frequent transitions from discourse to metadiscourse, it is reasonable to conjecture that the student's familiarity with talk-about-talk would prove an advantage in the mathematics classroom. Previous nonmathematical experience with symbolic saming or with different types of reasoning techniques gives the student a significant head start. Because patterns of participation have a tendency to repeat themselves, one's early performance may have a decisive impact on this person's future learning. Highly dependent on interpersonal dynamics and on the mechanism of reiteration, discourses do not leave much space for individual change. After an initial false start, the child may not be entirely free to modify her performance: Her interlocutors, the insiders to the discourse, are only too likely to reproduce the initial pattern of interaction time and again; their expectations from the child have been formed in the very first encounter. In this way, the newcomer's initial failings would solidify into a lifelong failure. The process of rendering permanency to what might have been just a passing experience is particularly effective if accompanied by labeling with reifying descriptors such as *below average* or *learning disabled*.

We can also conjecture that this self-perpetuating effect of discursive performances is amplified by the tendency of discourses to occur in clusters: Some of them keep company and invite joint participation, whereas some

[9] Mehan (1996, p. 268).

others do not appear to belong together. Thus, a person who is easily recognizable as an insider to a colloquial working-class discourse may be given little credit as a prospective participant in the literary discourse. Conversely, a person who shows competence in, say, mathematical discourse is often seen as one who will have little difficulty gaining participation in any other discourse. Some combinations of discourses may appear not just possible, but also desirable, whereas some others would be thought of as not just unlikely, but also illegitimate. These perceived interdependencies may play a role, sometimes quite central, in enabling or barring one's access to new discourses.

To sum up, except for clear-cut cases of extremely impaired functioning, individual success or failure should always be suspected of being a product of collective doing. In spite of impressive developments in brain research, it is not yet easy to make clearcut distinctions between learning problems originating primarily in physiological, possibly genetically determined deficits and those that result from particularities of one's discursive trajectory. Much better diagnostic tools will have to be developed before we are ready to discontinue our current labeling practices and stop seeing as "disabled" those students whose pervasive learning difficulties are a result rather than the cause of this labeling.

2.5 *The Quandary of Understanding*

Although the notion of understanding is ubiquitous in educational discourse, it is also elusive and, in many cases, not quite helpful. Our initial reflections on this issue left us with a question that, considering the centrality of the talk on understanding, seems to be of much theoretical and practical importance:

> Although we do not seem to hesitate in deciding whether we understand something or not, and although we are only too quick to diagnose other people's understanding, we have considerable difficulty in articulating our criteria for this kind of judgment. What is it that we do not yet understand about understanding?

In response, I argued in chapter 2 that the phenomena that gave rise to this question are due to the nonoperational, objectifying use of the term *understanding*. The overall consequences of such use can be so serious and pervasive that some writers propose to purge educational discourses of any mention of understanding. Yet, the talk on understanding is a prominent, potentially consequential phenomenon in discourses of those who teach and those who learn. First- and third-person comments on understanding that accompany – in real time or in retrospect – the processes of individualization and communalization are too central to these processes to be ignored. The students' and teachers' discourse on understanding interwoven with other classroom activities deserve as much of researchers' attention as any other aspect of the processes of teaching and learning.

At this point, I urge the reader to note the subtle difference between the use of the term *understanding* in traditional, monological research and the kind of use I am proposing now. An endorser of the commognitive approach is not supposed to make direct statements on participants' understanding but rather to investigate the talk on understanding that pervades the discourse of teaching and learning. This means refraining from monological, impersonal statements on the learner's understanding; it also entails abstention from claims on understanding made in the researcher's own name; it does imply, however, the talk about participants' talk on understanding.

Those who study human thinking have, indeed, every reason to be interested in the question of when, how, and to what effect students and teachers produce talk on understanding. Because understanding, as featured in everyday discourse, seems to be like the proverbial Heideggerian hammer that remains unnoticed until it breaks, complaints about the lack of understanding may be more frequent than the explicit claims to the contrary. This disturbing experience, the sense of incomprehension,[10] is likely to have a major impact on the process of learning. It may lead to an emotional reaction that would hinder any further progress, but it may also create a powerful incentive for learning. Just to illustrate: Commognitive conflict, which is sometimes indispensable for learning to begin, is also likely to produce an initial sense of incomprehension. Turning incomprehension into a stepping stone rather than a hurdle to learning is often a matter of appropriate handling of the interaction. Those who wish to help people learn, therefore, need to be able to identify situations in which the student is likely to claim incomprehension, and those who want to improve teaching need to be able to tell why teachers' claims about students' understanding are often different from students' own.

In our studies, while comparing situations of manifest incomprehension to those in which discursants seemed to be at peace with their own actions, we noticed that the difference was not so much in the question

---

[10] The expression "one has a sense of incomprehension" is used here as tantamount to the statement that "one is communicating to oneself, and possibly to others, that she suffers 'the lack of understanding.'"

of whether the learner acts according to standards as in the availability of a discursive routine that this learner considered as matching the situation. This observation is in tune with Wittgenstein's definition first quoted in chapter 2, according to which understanding means knowing "how to go on." Sometimes, just knowing what *kind* of result is going to count as a solution to the task at hand (what kind of closure the solution routine should have) may be enough to give one a sense of command over that situation. In our studies, a particularly striking confirmation of this conjecture arose from the realization that ritualized participation was not necessarily accompanied by signs of incomprehension in the performer. The same phenomenon repeated itself in all our studies: As long as the participants dealt with familiar questions that invited standard routine performances, they seemed fully satisfied with their actions. From their point of view, nothing was missing in their performance. Not only did they follow the procedure in an impeccable manner, they were also able to arrive at what counted for them as the proper closing: They were rewarded with the approval of their interlocutors. This was certainly true for Roni and Eynat as they engaged in the ritual of comparing-by-counting in the first phase of our study. It was only in the face of requirements that failed to evoke familiar routines that the children became visibly frustrated and desperate for help. This happened in two types of situations: when the girls were asked to produce sets "with the same number" of marbles and when they were required to substantiate their statements on relations between boxes with marbles. In both cases, their helplessness obviously stemmed not just from the unavailability of ready-made routines for halving and for substantiation, but also, and more seriously, from their inability to identify what kind of outcome would have to arise from such routines. In effect, they lacked second-order routines for constructing the appropriate object-level routines.

These observations on why and when people make claims – to others or to themselves – about their understanding help to explain the frequent disparities between first-person and third-person assessments of understanding. These two types of evaluations are likely to involve different kinds of criteria: Whereas the participants' self-judgments are based on their sense of being able "to go on," the observers are likely to ask themselves, in addition, whether the routines used by the participants can count as appropriate. Thus, in the well-known study by Stanley Erlwanger[11] about Benny, the sixth-grader who participated in the individualized instruction on fractions and invented his own idiosyncratic procedures for fractional operations,

[11] Erlwanger (1973).

the typical judgment of an inquisitive observer would be that the learner "lacked understanding" of fractions; the learner himself, however, would be unlikely to make any such claim.[12]

To account for the opposite type of disparity between first- and third-person assessments, we need to remember that one's thinking at large, and one's sense of understanding in particular, is shaped by what is considered by the relevant community as full-fledged participation. As observed previously, a person whose mathematical discourse is a collection of rituals but who was never exposed to situations in which this discourse would prove insufficient has no reason to complain about the lack of understanding. Her sense of understanding would be shaken, however, as soon as substantiations, versatility of performance, and ability to derive new procedures for solving new types of problems became required features of the discourse. Recall the case of the American mathematician Paul Halmos, who, as a student, passed examinations without difficulty but nevertheless complained of a "lack of understanding." It is reasonable to assume that this latter complaint was a product of Halmos's failed attempts to answer self-posed questions modeled on those that he expected the expert discursant to ask. In particular, having individualized the rules of professional mathematical explorations, he could not satisfy himself with his discourse of "epsilonic analysis," which, at that time, was for him but a bundle of unrelated rituals: "I could read analytic proofs, remember them if I made an effort, and reproduce them, sort of, but I didn't really know what was going on."[13] Thus, although there was probably no disparity between the criteria young Halmos was using to assess his own understanding and those employed by the external assessors, his self-evaluation differed from that of others because his self-testing was more thorough and more exacting than the examination implemented by others.

These remarks complete our attempt to apply a commognitive lens to this quandary, as well as all the other old quandaries. In all the cases, the transition to the commognitive discourse on thinking dissolved, rather than solved, the long-standing problems. More specifically, some of the outstanding questions (those on *numerical thinking*, *abstraction*) simply disappeared after their keywords were operationalized in accord with the basic commognitive tenets; some others were removed simply by deleting a problematic notion (e.g., *misconception*) from the researcher's vocabulary; yet

---

[12] To be sure, Erlwanger used the expression "incorrect understanding" rather than "lack of understanding," and his description thus does not contradict the claim that the boy himself might have had a sense of understanding.

[13] Halmos (1985, p. 47).

others dissipated when certain words (*learning disability, understanding*) were suspended in their role of the researcher's own linguistic tool but were given new attention as an important component of activities under commognitive study.

3. What Happened to Research on Thinking and Human Development

The transition from cognition to commognition is not a mere replacement of one theory of human thinking with another. Commognitive research differs from both its predecessors, behaviorism and cognitivism, in its epistemology, ontology, and methods: It is dialogical rather than monological; it makes away with time-honored splits between thinking and behavior, between thinking and speaking, and between discourses and their objects (or at least some of the objects); and it translates research on human development into the study of the growth of discourses. The choice of discourse as the principal object of attention is what sets this approach apart from other types of participationists' research.[14] At the same time, it blurs many of the traditional disciplinary divides. As the repositories of complexity and generators of change in all other human activities, discourses become the object of study not only for the developmental psychologist, but also for the anthropologist, the sociologist, the historian of human culture, in short, for anybody who is interested in distinctively human forms of life. Commognitivism, therefore, may be expected to have a positive impact on the quality of interdisciplinary communication.

Revision of the traditional distinction between *development* and *learning* is another consequence of the choice of discourse as the principal object of study. For cognitivists, development means growth that arises "from inside" the person – one that would happen even if the person lived in total isolation from human communities. This type of growth is seen as bearing exclusive responsibility for at least some of the basic types of human doing, such as speech and reasoning. Within the cognitivist framework, learning is the process in which these basic activities receive their culture-specific forms through "outside" stimulation. For commognitivists, on the other hand, no uniquely human form of activity, not even human thinking, can be seen as growing from inside the person. True, one's biological makeup is a necessary condition for his or her ability to develop uniquely human

---

[14] Some other participationist frameworks focusing on human development evolve around such constructs as *practice* and *culture*.

forms of activity, but it is certainly not sufficient.[15] When watched from
the commognitive perspective, transformations in discourses of individuals
and the historical evolution of discourses are simply different facets of one
phenomenon – the phenomenon of growth in the complexity of communication. From the mouth of an endorser of commognitivism, therefore, the
word *development* refers to discourses, and it encompasses both historical
change and individual learning.

Let us now take a look at methodological consequences of putting discourse in the center.

Unit of Analysis

Having adopted discourses as the principal object of inquiry, the student
of human development is left with a wide choice of possible research questions. Discourses may be analyzed with respect to their inner dynamics,
to the factors that make them change, to the roles of interlocutors, and so
forth. The phenomena under study may differ in their time scales, in their
participants, in the context of their occurrence – and the list is still long. In
this book, I have been focusing on mathematical discourses and analyzed
the developments that take place in the course of individual lives. Because,
however, mathematical self-communication may be difficult to observe, I
have been using as my data things said and done by individual learners
in direct interactions with others. The work done on these kinds of data
can be compared to that of an archaeologist who reconstructs an ancient
vessel from its remnants. Indeed, as presented in Figure 9.1, conversation
is an act of multichannel communication, only parts of which are publicly
accessible. Commognitive researchers' analyses complete the perceptible –
visible or audible – discourse to form a more comprehensible, plausible
whole, the way the parts added by a restorer complete the ceramic pieces of
a vessel. Of course, neither the restorer nor the interpreter makes claims to
the "authenticity" or to the ultimate "correctness" of the final product, and
this is true even if both of them tend to believe that the original producer,
if asked, would confirm the fidelity of the reconstruction.

Data

Once the researcher decides to investigate transformations in discourses
rather than "in people," the questions asked, the data gathered, and the

---

[15] Nor is biological change seen as primary, by default, to the change in activity. According
to current research, change in activity may transform our biological makeup.

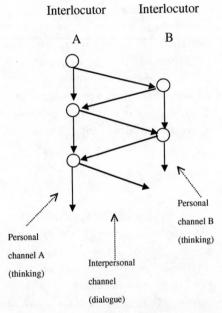

Interlocutor   Interlocutor

A   B

The circles symbolize interlocutors' successive utterances. The solid arrows mark the flow of attention along both private and interpersonal channels.

Personal
channel B
(thinking)

Personal
channel A
(thinking)

Interpersonal
channel
(dialogue)

Figure 9.1. Dialogue as multichannel communication.

analytic lens applied change considerably, often beyond recognition. On the face of it, there is not much difference between data typical of commognitive research, and those colleted in any other kind of study: They are human talk, either vocal or written. And yet, commognitive ways of collecting and documenting these data have some distinct features. In commognitive research, the data collectors must observe the principle of utmost verbal fidelity: They have to pay uncompromising attention to the verbatim version of the interlocutors' utterances and document interactions conducted for the sake of data collection in their entirety (as opposed to attending only to interviewees' parts of oral or written exchanges, for example). The commognitive researcher is to begin her report with showing what was done and said, rather than with her own story about it. Instead of revoicing the actors, she must let them speak in their own voice,[16] and even when interested in a voice of an individual, she must not forget the other voices to which this person responds or that he tries to evoke. Throughout, she has to remember that whatever is said, although uttered by a specific

---

[16] Of course, even transcribing is an act of interpretation (to begin with, the choice of symbol in which to record what is said is already interpretive). With some training, however, one can learn to produce transcriptions that would be accepted by the actors themselves as reflecting their activities in a nonbiased way.

individual, is the work of many. This remains in stark contrast with most quantitative and some qualitative studies in which the basic form of data is the researchers' rendering of the participants' written or oral responses to the researchers' questions.[17] Such selective, highly interpretive presentation of the data results in "low-resolution" images of activity, in which diverse forms of actions hide under the same descriptions and some telling differences between individuals practically disappear. Obviously, overlooking the differences largely diminishes the insightfulness and usefulness of the subsequent analyses.

The Researcher's Role in Data Production

While the monologist researcher believes in the possibility of her being "just an observer," the endorser of commognitive stance is fully aware of her being also a *participant* of the observed activity. The only dimension to play with in commognitivist data gathering is the degree of a researcher's proactivity. Thus, an observer may try to be "noninterventional" and may never perform an intentional instructional action. This said, she keeps in mind that those whom she observes are only too likely to interpret anything she does as evaluative and corrective. This is true even if she refrains from any verbal or gestural responses and re-acts to what study participants are saying with a prolonged silence.

The Researcher's Perspective in Data Analysis and Interpretation

In her analyses, rather than treating one's words as mere proxies of discourse-independent objects, the commognitivist is interested in the utterances as such, accepting them for what they appear to be: words that shape one's actions. Mapping the intricate relations between things said and deeds performed is the principal focus of this researcher's attention. To be able to keep an eye on these relations, she needs to alternate between being an *insider* and an *outsider* to the discourse under study. To understand the difference between these two perspectives, you may compare the way you listen to conversation in your native tongue, where you are an insider, to a

---

[17] Many studies ignore linguistic differences that, according to the analysts, do not change "the meaning" of one's statements. To use one illuminating example, the transcriber would often write the symbol 1/4 whether the interlocutor said "a quarter," "one-fourth," or "one over four." And yet, in our studies we had an opportunity to notice that the different verbalizations may sometimes lead the user to different actions, showing that for him or her the three expressions do not denote "the same thing."

conversation in a language you never learned, where you are an outsider. Or, to use a different metaphor, think about outsiders as visitors from Mars who can notice and record only the palpable surface of things, and whose later report to their fellow-Martians contains descriptions of images and sounds but is free of any reference to what the insiders call *meaning, idea, information, intentions*, and so forth.[18]

An outsider's perspective, with its stress on the perceptual accessibility supposed to enable "objective testability," counted for a long time as the only admissible approach in the traditionally conceived scientific research. In contrast, an insider's perspective may appear much more appropriate to anthropologists or ethnographers. The endorser of commognitivist stance is well aware of the importance of both these outlooks. Insiders, relying heavily on the contextual dimension, narrow down the set of possible interpretations, thus greatly increasing the efficiency of their sense-making efforts. But narrowing the range of options also has obvious pitfalls. An insider's sense making is effective only as long as the participants adhere to the rules of the given discourse. In the face of participants' unexpected moves, the insider becomes helpless. You need to step out from that present discourse to see that an utterance insiders find surprising can, in fact, make sense in another discourse. Thus, you need to be an outsider to your own well-developed numerical discourse to realize that choosing one of two identical opaque boxes in response to the question "In which boxes are there more marbles?" does not have to be a statement of quantitative inequality, and you need to forget all you know about arithmetic operations if you want to be cognizant of the difference between the actions people perform while calculating the price of coconuts and those they implement while manipulating written numerical symbols, a difference so huge that seeing these two procedures as completely unrelated may, in fact, be more natural than seeing them as instances of "the same operation." Indeed, what is senseless or inexplicable in the insider's eyes may become meaningful for an outsider, if only because from the outsider's perspective, the rules of the discourse in question do have alternatives. Or, as stated by Mikhail Bakhtin, "In the realm of culture, outsideness is a most powerful factor in understanding. It is only in the eyes of *another* culture that foreign culture reveals itself fully and profoundly."[19]

---

[18] Note that disobjectification means attaining an outsider's perspective; this is why the definition of *communication* offered in chapter 3, unlike those to be found in current literature, describes the activity of communicating with the help of only those characteristics that would be accessible to an outside observer of the human kind.

[19] Bakhtin (1986, p. 7).

In commognitive research, therefore, an outsider's and an insider's perspectives complement each other. To arrive at a truly informative interpretation of data, one must incessantly step in and out of discourse. Such stepping in and out requires special training. The insider's perspective is the obvious default – it imposes itself on the observer even if the discourse under observation is, in fact, quite different from her own (of which she is then doomed to remain unaware). To adopt the outsider's outlook, one must focus on what is directly visible while trying to disregard the context. This is the exact opposite of what needs to be done to sustain an insider's perspective (note also that this "stepping out" exercise would not be possible without the verbatim, all-inclusive data of the type described earlier). Listening to familiar words while barring their spontaneous interpretations is as difficult as focusing your sight on a very clean, very clear windowpane and trying to ignore what can be seen through it. Even for the most experienced among commognitive analysts, the task of becoming an outsider to their own discourses will always be challenging, and their performances will invariably leave something to wish for.[20] This said, the technology of audio and video recordings can help: With the unlimited possibility of revisiting past events, the outsider's perspective becomes more affordable. Recurrent scrutiny of high-fidelity records is an opportunity for stepping back from events and finding interpretations that are not the ones we instinctively produce in real time while acting as participants.

Table 9.1 summarizes the salient features of commognitivist research and, for the sake of greater clarity, contrasts them with those of its two immediate predecessors, behaviorism and cognitivism.

4. Some Implications for the Practice of Teaching and Learning

It is through communication with others that a person develops uniquely human forms of life and turns into an integral part of the human community. Individualization of different historically established ways of communication extends, strengthens, and diversifies the individual's bonds with others, while also increasing her ability to cope with the environment. If that is so, studying the way people learn mathematics is more than just trying to get a

[20] Note that behaviorists simply refused to deal with those phenomena that they were unable to approach as outsiders, whereas cognitivists might have deluded themselves with respect to their own perspective. If cognitivists regarded themselves as outsiders to the discourses they observed, it was only because they objectified these discourses and thus treated such central constructs as conceptions, meaning, and intentions as external to the discourse, and thereby accessible to every outsider.

Table 9.1. *Behaviorist, cognitivist, and commognitivist research on human development*

	Behaviorism	Cognitivism	Commognitivism
Discourse of research	Monological	Monological	Dialogical
Position on the issue of thinking and behavior	Nondualist by reduction (by exclusion of thinking as object of study); cryptodualist?	Dualist	Nondualist (no more split between thinking and behavior)
Vision of human change	Acquisitionist (the object of developmental change: the individual)	Acquisitionist (the object of developmental change: the individual)	Participationist (the object of developmental change: human activity)
Unit of analysis	Skill	Concept (mental scheme), skill	Discourse (as practiced by a certain community)
Data	Researcher's rendering (categorization) of individuals' stimulus–response pairs; very-low-resolution data	Researcher's rendering (categorization) of things said or done by individual actors; low-resolution data	Verbatim rendering of discourses involving the individual actor; high-resolution data
Researcher's role in data production	Observer	Observer	Participant and observer
Researcher's perspective in data analysis	Outsider	Insider who regards herself as an outsider	Insider and outsider, intermittently

deeper insight into the question of how we become participants of this particular discourse. Much of what one finds here may be true also of getting access to other discourses, and thus of all those processes through which individuals become who they are and with the help of which discourse communities are being sustained over time. Let me devote the next few paragraphs to the idea of *learning-teaching agreement*, which seems to be a necessary condition for the effectiveness of these processes.

4.1 *Learning-Teaching Agreement as a Condition for Learning*

What does it take to turn outsiders to a discourse into insiders? In the preceding chapters I argued that the process of scaffolded individualization is the only way for a "newcomer" to enter a discourse governed by rules different from those that regulated her communicational activity so far. Individualization, by definition, requires proactive participation – and help – of this discourse's "oldtimers." To put it in James Gee's words, one gains access to a discourse "through scaffolded and supported interaction with people who have already mastered the Discourse."[21] I can thus reformulate the question as follows: What kinds of relationship and what kinds of interaction between newcomers and oldtimers are most conducive to learning? Note that the term *newcomer* is very broad, and it includes, among others, students in formal and informal educational establishments, interns, novices to a profession or craft, immigrants whose future depends on their ability to enter dominant discourses of their new country, and those who climb or descend the social ladder. Depending on context, the term *oldtimer* may refer to a teacher or a competent student, to a highly skilled professional, to a recognized member of an artistic community, to a native of a given country, or to a person who is a typical representative of her social class.

In the last chapter I argued that whenever further development of a discourse requires a change in metarules, the learner needs to be exposed to a commognitive conflict. The situation of conflict, however, is not without its dangers. As was argued earlier, the main challenge is the somehow contradictory nature of the requirements that must be met if the conflict is to be resolved. Thus, if commognitive conflict is to become a gate to the new discourse rather than a barrier to communication, both the newcomer and the oldtimers must be genuinely committed to overcoming the hurdle.

---

[21] Gee (1989, p. 7). In Gee's writings, the term *Discourse, with the capital D* has a special meaning, which is not far from the one the word *discourse* has within the commognitive framework.

This kind of collaboration requires a voluntary alignment of the discursants. Such alignment, in turn, can succeed only if accompanied by a certain set of mutual understandings. In most general terms, *learning-teaching agreement* is what is needed to ensure the kind of interaction that was presented by Hans-Georg Gadamer as "true conversation":

> It is characteristic of every true conversation that each opens himself to the other person, truly accepts his point of view as worthy of consideration and gets inside the other to such an extent that he understands not a particular individual, but what he says.[22]

Learning-teaching agreement regards those aspects of the teaching–learning process that are essential to its success. On the basis of the commognitive vision of learning it is reasonable to assume that the discursants, to attain their respective goals, need to be unanimous, if only tacitly, about at least three basic aspects of the communicational process: the *leading discourse*, their own respective *roles*, and the *nature of the expected change*. Let me elaborate on each of these requirements.[23]

Agreement on the Leading Discourse

In the case of commognitive conflict, interlocutors are facing two seemingly conflicting (and in fact incommensurable) discourses. It is clear that the conflict will not be resolved if each of the participants goes on acting according to his or her own discursive rules. Agreement on a more or less uniform set of discursive routines is the condition for effective communication. Although this agreed set of rules will be negotiated by the participants and will end up being probably somehow different from each of those with which each individual entered the interaction, the process of change may be ineffective if the interlocutors are divided over the question of which of these initial discourses should be regarded as setting the standards.

The issue of leadership in discourse is, of course, a matter of power relations. In a traditional classroom, the leadership was, in principle, predetermined and undisputable. Within the institutional context, the discourse of teachers and of textbooks counted, by default, as the leading form of communication. According to the principles of current child-centered

---

[22] Gadamer (1975, p. 347).

[23] The notion of *learning-teaching agreement* can be seen as a communicational counterpart and elaboration of Brousseau's idea of *didactic contract*, that is, of "the system of [students' and teachers'] reciprocal obligations" (Brousseau, 1997, p. 31).

curricula,[24] the power relations in a mathematics classroom should now be subject to negotiation and the learners are invited to make their own choices. In particular, the leadership in discourse is supposed to be attained through mutual agreement rather than by means of institutional coercion. In other words, the leaders should be accepted and understood, not just mindlessly obeyed; they should be chosen, not imposed. To retain their leading role without compromising other participants' agency, the leaders need to be trusted and the membership in their discourse community must be valued and desired.

Agreement on the Discursants' Roles

Once the choice of the model discourse is made, those who are given the lead must be willing to play the role of *teachers* – of welcoming usherers and facilitators – whereas those whose discourses require adaptation must agree to act as *learners*. The acceptance of roles is not a formal act. Rather than expressing itself in any explicit declaration, this role taking means an unflinching commitment to the communicational rapprochement. Such agreement implies that those oldtimers who agreed to act as teachers feel responsible for the change in the newcomers' discourse, whereas those newcomers who agreed to learn show confidence in the leader's guidance and are genuinely willing to follow in the oldtimers' discursive footsteps. It is important to reiterate that this acceptance of another person's leadership does not mean readiness for mindless imitation. Rather, it signals a genuine interest in the new discourse and a strong will to explore its inner logic. It is also important to remember that the consent to act as teacher or as learner can never be taken for granted, not even in seemingly the most favorable of situations, when there is no visible dissent about whose discourse should be given the lead. As widely documented in research literature, cases of student resistance are not infrequent these days.[25]

Agreement on the Course of the Discursive Change

Agreeing about the discourse to follow and the readiness to shape one's own discourse in its image are important factors in learning, but more seems necessary to help the newcomers in the "impossible" task of bootstrapping themselves out of the circularities inherent in commognitive conflicts. In the

---

[24] See, e.g., National Council of Teachers of Mathematics (2000).
[25] Forman and Ansell (2002).

initial stages of the process of learning, their participation is possible only if heavily scaffolded by the oldtimers. For some time to come, the newcomer cannot be expected to be a proactive user of the new discourse: In her eyes, the new form of talk is but a *discourse-for-others*, that is, a discourse used for the sake of communication with those to whom it makes sense and in spite of the fact that it does not yet fully make sense to her. Ideally, the goal of further learning will be to turn this discourse into a *discourse-for-oneself*, that is, into the type of communication in which the person is likely to engage of her own accord, while trying to solve her own problems.[26] If learning is to succeed, all the participants – those who are willing to learn and those who agreed to teach – need to be of one mind as to the final goals of the process of learning and as to the manner in which the learning is likely to occur. Disparate visions of the expected results of learning preclude fruitful collaboration, whereas unrealistic expectations with respect to the nature of the learning processes may backfire, leading to practices that stymie learning.

The three components of a learning agreement, although interrelated, do not depend on one another, and any of them can be missing even if the others are present. To get a sense of the range of possibilities, let us return for a moment to the empirical studies described in this book.[27] The case of Roni and Eynat, the 4-year-old newcomers to the numerical discourse, may serve as a paradigmatic example of full-fledged learning-teaching agreement: The children's readiness to engage in the ritual of comparing-by-counting reflected their strong need to communicate with grown-ups, as well as instinctive recognition of the fact that this could be done only on the grown-ups' own terms; Roni's parents' insistent attempts to induce proper performance of standard numerical routines showed their strong commitment to the role of teachers. In the case of Mira and Talli, the adolescents with the long history of failure in mathematics, the situation seemed somewhat different. Although there was no visible controversy with regard to the leading role of the literate mathematical discourse, there were

---

[26] The term *discourse-for-oneself* is close to Vygotsky's idea of *speech-for-oneself*, introduced to denote a stage in the development of children's language (see, e.g., Vygotsky, 1987, p. 71). These ideas also bring to mind the Bakhtinian distinction between *authoritative discourse*, a discourse that "binds us, quite independently of any power it might have to persuade us internally," and *internally persuasive* discourse, one that is "tightly woven with 'one's own world'" (Bakhtin, 1981, pp. 110–111).

[27] In this paragraph, I restrict myself to a brief summary of the findings of the respective studies. For the presentation of data and analyses on the grounds of which these conclusions were formulated, see Sfard and Lavie (2005); Ben-Yehuda et al. (2005); Sfard and Kieran (2001a).

signs of a tacit dissent with respect to the other two elements of learning-teaching agreement. Talli's exclusive adherence to symbolic algorithms and her readiness to satisfy herself with the ritualized performance was likely to be at odds with the teachers' idea of successful learning. It is the third element of the communication agreement, therefore, that might have been lacking throughout her school years. It is the second one that might have well been missing in Mira's case: Less keen than Talli to abide by the rules of the literate discourse, Mira was explicitly hesitant to accept teachers' help.[28] The case of Ari and Gur, the seventh-graders making their first steps in algebra, exemplifies yet another type of situation. Whereas Gur seemed to agree, if only grudgingly, that Ari should take the lead and that he himself should act as a learner, Ari was clearly reluctant to serve as a teacher.[29] As in Mira's case, it was the second element of the learning-teaching agreement that seemed to be missing, except that this time, the violation expressed itself in the refusal to teach rather than to learn.

The claim that commognitive conflict and learning-teaching agreement are the basic conditions for meta-level mathematics learning provokes second thoughts about some common pedagogical beliefs. For instance, it casts doubt on the current call for "learning with understanding," at least insofar as this call is interpreted as the exhortation for "understanding before practice" – for never letting the student engage in routines that she cannot properly substantiate. According to the commognitive analyses, students' persistent participation in mathematical talk when this kind of communication is for them but a discourse-for-others seems to be an inevitable stage in learning mathematics. Of course, this acceptance of the initial ritualization, to be pedagogically sound, must be assisted by the general understanding that the ritualization is but a transient stage in learning, which should be as brief as possible. The license to become a "peripheral participant" in other

---

[28] Here is a relevant excerpt from Mira's testimony: "She [the teacher] tries to explain. Say, there is an exercise. She asks me to do it and then tries to explain. 'Now, let's take an example, and then another example.' And I already feel confused. And then suddenly she shows me several different ways and this is already too much. . . . 'Alright, leave me alone, I don't want to hear anymore.' It's a waste of time and I am unable to keep grappling with this."

[29] To quote Sfard and Kieran (2001a, 2001b): "Ari's wish to communicate with Gur was evidently not just insufficient; it might even be somehow negative. Indeed, not only did he make satisfactory progress on his own, but he would probably work quicker and more effectively weren't he obliged to communicate with Gur at the same time. In addition, it seems that even if Ari did want to help Gur, he did not have the appropriate means. All these findings cast doubt upon the common belief that working with a 'more knowledgeable partner' speeds up one's development *as a rule*" (p. 71).

people's discourse is to be read as the invitation to the fascinating inquiry: inquiry into the inner logic of the new discourse and into oldtimers' reasons for using it. Thus, rather than dismissing the newcomers' readiness to participate in a discourse-for-others as resulting from the mere wish "to please the teacher," one should keep in mind that this kind of participation may actually boost students' agency and creativity. The process of individualization, if grounded in a proper learning-teaching agreement, naturally acquires the characteristic of learning by inquiry, one that is supposed to result from the learner's own explorations. This special type of inquiry, the object of which is a historically established form of discourse, requires at least as much interest and originality as any other. Indeed, making sense of other people's discourse is not any less creative than, say, "reading the codes" of nature or trying to reconstruct the past from historical sources. As in any exploration, the student needs to raise and test one conjecture after another. If successful, she may soon be able to make her own innovative contributions to the discourse.

There is also an important ethical dimension to the learning-teaching agreement. If genuine and unwavering, this agreement promotes such values as respect of others and openness to difference. The newcomer who in the face of unfamiliar discourse accepts her role as a learner may be seen as saying to herself: "If these people are talking the way they do, they must have good reasons. After all, they have been doing this for a long time now. Thus, why shouldn't I suspend disbelief and do my best to fathom the inner logic of their discourse?" In a complementary manner, the oldtimer who willingly assumes the role of a leader makes it understood that the newcomer is welcome and her developing communicational skills are taken seriously and appreciated even when only partly conforming to those of the oldtimer. Learning-teaching agreement, therefore, entails tolerance and solidarity. Its value, it seems, goes well beyond its contribution to the processes of learning of a particular discourse.

4.2 *Factors That Shape Learning*

The claim that learning-teaching agreement is a basic condition for learning and for one's eventual full-fledged participation in a new discourse raises an immediate question of how to cultivate such agreement in classrooms and beyond. At a closer look, orchestrating newcomers' and oldtimers' preferences appears to be a complex matter. For one thing, the institutional context of school blurs the delicate distinction between democratic leadership and forced dominance. What is intended by the teacher as a plea for confidence may be interpreted by students as an attempt to exert power. In addition, whether the teacher is accepted as a leader or not – whether she is trusted and her discourse is valued – is not just a simple function of what happens in the school. When it comes to issues of voluntary alignment versus resistance, cultural factors may be of principal importance. In the special case of mathematics, classroom norms that seem most conducive to learning may turn out to be not entirely compatible with the norms of the "outside" world.[30]

This leads us to the more general question of factors that shape the nature of discursants' collaboration: *Why are some newcomers genuinely interested in turning a given discourse into a discourse-for-themselves whereas others are not, and why are some oldtimers welcoming and helpful to newcomers whereas others would rather keep their discourse to themselves?* One cannot answer this query without taking into account the fact that any given form of commognition is just one of many, that each individual belongs to numerous discourse communities, and that the various discourses that the person employs on an everyday basis interact with one another, coshaping this individual's participation in each one of them. Indeed, each of us may be seen as residing at a particular nexus of many possible ways of commognizing. Some of the visible paths are enticing and accessible; some others remain closed, even though desired. Some discursive routes have little allure on their own but are nevertheless traveled by almost anybody simply because there is no other way to reach one's coveted destination. For example, in the world where all the roads to valued careers lead through a mathematics classroom, many learners of mathematics are but passengers in transit, hurrying to catch the connection to where they really want to be. The question of what place mathematical discourse occupies among the totality of discourses of a given society is thus of principal importance for our understanding of processes that shape individual learning.

More generally, to get hold of the mechanisms that shape personal discursive preferences one needs to fathom intricacies of the politics of discourses – of the complex power relations among diverse discourse communities. Once again, let me turn to mathematics as an illustrative example. In the modern society, dominated by the discourse of rationality, objectivity, and progress, it is only natural to view mathematics as the pinnacle of

[30] For example, mathematicians are likely to claim that if mathematics is to fulfill its mission as the paragon of infallible communication, it needs to be spoken in one impersonal voice. As a result, mathematical discourse may appear as irreducibly monological, and its learning may thus collide with the current striving toward dialogical classroom discourse.

human achievement. The privileged status conferred on mathematics as reward for its decisive contributions to science and technology extends well beyond the area where the contributions were made. These days, mathematical vocabulary and its unique forms of substantiation infiltrate, and if necessary overwrite, almost any other type of justifying and convincing. In particular, they pervade discourses on people and their actions. The popularity of quantifying discourses is easily understandable: Once phenomena are translated into numbers, narratives about them appear objectively imposed rather than human-made. The impression of rigor, objectivity, and glitch-free communication engenders the comforting sense of the practical effectiveness of the narratives and of the reduced responsibility of the narrator. After all, numbers speak for themselves and nobody can argue with what they say. Moreover, with the transition to mathematical discourse, decision making becomes easy. When all the options disguise themselves as numbers and order themselves along a single scale, the question of which one of them should be chosen is answered even before being asked. No wonder, therefore, that contemporary societies are preoccupied with counting, weighting, and evaluating, and that only too often the guiding principle of these quantifying activities seems to be "Take care of the measurement and what is being measured will take care of itself." And when the talk on quantities occupies center stage, it is also not surprising that insiders to mathematical discourse are welcomed as honorary citizens in almost any other. The dominance of mathematics and, above all, its role as other discourses' gatekeeper may affect individual learning in multiple ways, for better and for worse.

The more general question of how the wider cultural context influences the development of specific discourses may well become one of the central foci of commognitivists' research in the years to come. In the rest of this chapter, and as the closing message of this book, let me sketch a few ideas about the direction that this future research may take.

5. Looking Ahead: Facing New Questions (and New Quandaries?)

The commognitive vision of thinking emerged through the attempts to account for those aspects of human development that cannot be found in other species. Within this framework, the question of how our unique characteristics come into being has been translated into the query about the emergence of unique forms of interpersonal and intrapersonal communication. In studying this issue, I have been considering, so far, mainly the inner mechanisms of discourse development. The complementary topic of the interdiscursive aspects of the phenomenon, without which the story of "the uniquely human" remains less than half-told, is yet to be addressed. I would thus not end this book without sharing some thoughts, be they preliminary and tentative as they may, about the possibilities of commognitive research on the subject.

Tackling the question of how discourses interact and how wider cultural messages find their way into individual learning requires a dedicated conceptual apparatus. Many of those who have been pursuing the topic for some time now speak about the notion of *identity* as a potential conceptual link between what is happening at the collective and individual levels.[31] The term *identity*, however, although promising and seemingly a good match for its designated role, has been criticized for its being pervasively unclear and undefined.[32] Within the commognitive framework, it can be operationalized through the notion of *subjectifying*. This latter term, introduced in chapter 4 and left dormant ever since, refers to a special case of the activity of objectifying, the one that takes place when the discursive focus shifts from actions and their objects to the performers of the actions. More specifically, subjectifying is the process of constructing *d*-objects signified by such personal pronouns as *I*, *you*, and *she*. Let me outline the way in which the commognitive discourse of subjectifying and identity can help in investigating interdiscursive forces influencing the development of individual discourses.

The activity of subjectifying runs parallel to all other human processes. Indeed, at a closer look, every human action is an opportunity for telling stories about the actors themselves. These stories may sometimes begin as a description of deeds and actions, but they almost invariably end up as narratives about permanent states. Thus, for example, a mathematist may say that she "always succeeds in school tests," but in the longer run, she is likely to claim to "be a successful mathematics student" or to "have a mathematical gift." A student unsatisfied with her progress in mathematical discourse is likely to call herself a "terrible mathematician" or a "slow thinker." The records of learning–teaching interactions collected throughout our numerous studies reveal a plethora of such reifying comments, spontaneously made by discursants in the attempt to account for the quality

[31] See, e.g., Bauman, 1996, 2001; Hall, 1996; Holland, Lachicotte, Skinner, and Cain (1998); Lemke (2000); Gee (2001). For the commognitive take at the issue of identity as an interface between sociocultural influences and individual learning, see Sfard and Prusak (2005).

[32] For a critical survey of these discourses see Sfard and Prusak (2005).

of their actions. Some of these subjectifying narratives are self-referential; some others refer to those who interact with the narrator. Indeed, throughout our lives we are the constant objects of first-, second-, and third-person stories about ourselves.

Taking the ubiquitous phenomenon of subjectifying as a point of departure, we may now operationalize the term *identity* as signifying the products of this activity. According to this definition, identities are to be understood as reifying narratives about a person, endorsed by their authors as reflecting the actual or expected state of affairs. Two features of identifying narratives are of particular relevance in our present context. First, by translating the stories of processes into stories of states, identities create the sense of stability and permanence that the processes themselves are lacking. As such, they are likely to function as self-fulfilling prophecies: Rather than being a mere reflection of reality, these narratives are also what makes things happen. The descriptors that outlast an action become agents of continuity and perpetuation. They may exclude and disable just as much as they enable and create. The second important point regards materials of which the identifying stories are made: These narratives emerge as joint products of personal and communal storytelling, and of the constant mutual fine-tuning of the personal and collective versions. To put it differently, identities are products of discursive diffusion – of our proclivity to recycle, usually unknowingly, strips of things said by our interlocutors. Paraphrasing Mikhail Bakhtin, we may say that any narrative reveals to us stories of others.[33] Identities originating from different narrators and addressed at different audiences are in a constant interaction and feed one into another.

These two salient properties of identities – their power to shape human actions and their location at the crossroads of multiple discourses – make the narratively defined notion of identity naturally predestined for the role of a conceptual link between the general and the specific, between the collective and the individual. If carefully defined and immunized against essentialist interpretations, this notion may thus help in explaining how intradiscursive forces shape individual discourse. As such, it may also play a central role in accounting for the interrelated processes of ontogenetic and historical transformations. Its dynamic dimension, its susceptibility to collective molding, on the one hand, and its effectiveness in shaping individual doings, on the other, makes identity the principal transmitter of the relevant changes from one form of activity to another, and from discourse to discourse.

---

[33] Bakhtin (1999) spoke about utterances and words rather than stories.

To make the notion of identity truly useful in answering the outstanding questions about human development, we need to be more knowledgeable about the mechanisms of subjectification. Along with the task of mapping developmental trajectories of diverse discourses, building a commognitive theory of subjectifying should feature most prominently in the commognitivists' research program for the years to come. The work that lies ahead is as urgent as it is plentiful. For all that has already been done, we cannot expect the sign "under construction" to be removed from the commognitive framework any time soon.

6. Looking Back and Ahead – in a Nutshell

The commognitive vision of human development offered in this book is a product of a concentrated effort to deconstruct the numerous dichotomies that populate all our discourses, and the discourse on thinking in particular. After the claim that the acquisitionist "ghost in the machine" had been responsible for many of the unanswered questions about human uniqueness, the commognitive discourse was built so as to allow for a nondualist vision of human processes. This vision grew out of the participationist assumption that collective implementations of historically established forms of activity are the primary source of individual growth. The claim that human thinking develops through individualization of interpersonal communication imposed itself as a logical entailment. Other assertions about human development made in this book followed from this one.

The transition to commognitive discourse impacts the research on human thinking in a substantial manner and has important implications for the practice of teaching and learning. First, when human processes are observed from the commognitive perspective, many long-standing quandaries, and in particular those presented in the first chapter, become tractable or simply dissolve. Second, the commognitive research is quite different from both its behaviorist and cognitivist predecessors in a number of ways: In addition to its being nondualist, it is dialogical rather than monological and looks upon the discourse as the primary unit of analysis. The researcher who adopts commognitive perspective makes a commitment to act both as an observer and as a participant of the discourse under study. In her analyses, she alternates between the insider's and outsider's perspectives. Third, according to the commognitive vision, learning that aims at the resolution of a commognitive conflict requires tripartite learning-teaching agreement among all the participants of the learning–teaching process. More specifically, the discursants need to be in consensus with regard to whose discourse should be the model to follow, they have to act according to their respective roles of learners and teachers, and they must have a unified vision of the goals of learning and of the course this learning is going to take.

The results of this stocktaking seem to justify the claim that the commognitive perspective shows signs of fulfilling its promise. It helped us in responding to old challenges and ushered us into hitherto unexplored strata of the "uniquely human." I view the commognitive accounts of what we saw as more helpful than the ones we would have been able to construct a few years ago, while working within a more traditional framework. This said, I am aware that much additional conceptual and methodological work waits to be done. In this chapter, new quandaries presented themselves just as my exposition of the commognitive framework was coming to its close. One of the most obvious outstanding questions, that of how the development of a discourse is shaped by its interaction with other discourses, led me to propose commognitive operationalization of the notion of *identity* and the systematic study of processes of *subjectification*. This, however, is but an example of forthcoming research projects. In this book, I could not possibly exhaust all the quandaries that we may have to address in the future. Because "crevices of unreason" hide in even the most careful of human constructions, new, as yet unnamed puzzles can be trusted to pop up one day, and with them the need for revisions of the commognitive discourse and for far-reaching conceptual innovations. Hence, one of the most important points to keep in mind while closing this book is that the story it told did not end before a new one began.

Glossary of Commognition

abstract discourse   discourse about **abstract objects.**

abstract object   discursive object that originates, among others, in **reification** of discursive processes.

acquisitionism   discourses (theories) on learning, grounded in the metaphor of learning as acquiring a certain entity (knowledge, concept, schema). *See also* **participationism.**

agency   ability to make one's own choices and to influence situations.

alienation   using discursive forms that present phenomena in an impersonal way, as if they were occurring of themselves, without the participation of human beings. *See also* **objectification; reification.**

applicability conditions   subset of **routine**-defining **metarules**, composed of rules that delineate, usually in a nondeterministic way, the circumstances in which the given **routine course of action** is likely to be undertaken by the person. *See also* **closing conditions.**

atomic *d*-object.   *See* **simple discursive object; atomic discursive object.**

atomic discursive object   a product of assigning a noun or nounlike symbolic artifact to a specific **primary object** (atomic discursive object is also called **simple discursive object** or **atomic *d*-object**).

authoritative discourse   term introduced by Bakhtin to denote a **discourse** that "binds us, quite independently of any power it might have to persuade us internally"; an opposite of **internally persuasive discourse**, one that is "tightly woven with one's own world" (Bakhtin, 1981, pp. 110–111). *See also* **discourse-for-others.**

automation of realizing procedures   situation that arises when one is able to perform all the components of the procedure one after another without having recourse to verbal prescriptions – without asking oneself what occurs next. *See also* **embodiment of realizing procedures.**

closing conditions (closure)   **metarules** defining circumstances that the performer is likely to interpret as signaling a successful completion of performance.

colloquial discourse   discourse used in everyday life and developing spontaneously; it is **mediated visually** mainly by **primary objects** preexisting the discourse. *See also* the complementary term **literate discourse.**

commognition   term that encompasses **thinking** (individual cognition) and (interpersonal) communicating; as a combination of the words **communication** and cognition, it stresses the fact that these two processes are different (intrapersonal and interpersonal) manifestations of the same phenomenon.

commognitive conflict   situation that arises when **communication** occurs across **incommensurable discourses** (interlocutors participating in incommensurable discourses try to communicate with one another); commognitive conflict may be interpersonal or intrapersonal.

communalization   process complementary to **individualization**, in which individual variations in historically established activities feed back into the collective forms of doing, acquire permanence, and are carried in space and time from one collective to another.

communication   a collectively performed patterned activity in which action A of an individual is followed by action B of another individual so that (1) A belongs to a certain well-defined repertoire of actions known as communicational, and (2) action B belongs to a repertoire of re-actions that fit A, that is, actions recurrently observed in conjunction with A. This latter repertoire is not exclusively a function of A, and it depends, among others, on factors such as the history of A (what happened prior to A), the situation in which A and B are performed, the identities of the actor and re-actor, and so forth.

communicational (discursive) action   action that is performed as a part of the activity of communication (this term is complementary to **practical action**; some actions may be communicational and practical at the same time).

community of discourse   all the individuals capable of participating in a given **discourse**.

compound *d*-object.   *See* **compound discursive object.**

compound discursive object   object that arises by assigning a noun or pronoun to extant objects (either discursive or primary) by **saming, encapsulating,** or **reifying.**

concept   word or other **signifier** together with its discursive use.

concrete discourse   discourse about **concrete objects.** *See also* **abstract discourse.**

concrete object   **primary object** or a **discursive object** that arises through **saming** or **encapsulating** familiar primary objects.

consolidation of discourse   one of the characteristic features of a well-developed **mathematical discourse** (along with explorization – see **explorative discourse**; and **objectification**), which expresses itself in the fact that its **routines** constitute a well-integrated network, kept together by the relation of partial equivalence (two routines are partially equivalent if they are exchangeable in certain contexts).

construction of narratives   discursive process whose result is a **narrative** about objects of this **discourse**. **Routines** of narrative construction (routines that count as completed when a narrative is produced) are called **explorations** (as opposed to routines called **deeds** that produce a change in environment and those called **rituals** whose closure is a completion of a well-defined discursive process). *See also* the complementary term **substantiation of narratives.**

d-object.   *See* **discursive object.**

deed   one of the three types of **routines**, the goal (**closing condition**) of which is a change in objects. *See also* the complementary terms **ritual** and **exploration.**

discourse   special type of communication made distinct by its repertoire of admissible actions and the way these actions are paired with re-actions; every discourse defines its own **community of discourse**; discourses in language are distinguishable by their vocabularies, visual mediators, **routines**, and **endorsed narratives.**

discourse-for-oneself   discourse in which one engages of one's own accord, while trying to solve her own problems. *See also* **internally persuasive discourse** and the complementary term **discourse-for-others.**

discourse-for-others   discourse in which one engages only with those for whom this discourse makes sense and for the sake of **communication** with these other people (as opposed to practicing this discourse in self-communication). *See also* **authoritative discourse** and the complementary term **discourse-for-oneself.**

discourse community   community of all those capable of participating in a given discourse.

discursant   participant of a discourse.

discursive compression   developmental process complementary to **discursive expansion** that occurs through intradiscursive **saming** (**endogenous** compression) or by conflating of several different discourses into one **subsuming discourse** (**exogenous** compression).

discursive deed   routine whose goal (**closing condition**) is a change in **discursive objects.**

discursive expansion   growth in the volume and complexity of a discourse; can be **endogenous** or **exogenous**. *See also* the complementary term **discursive compression.**

discursive object (*d*-object)   either **primary object** or a **compound discursive object** that arises by according a noun or pronoun to extant objects in the process of **saming, encapsulation** or **reification.**

embodiment of realizing procedures   situation that arises when visual scanning and other physical actions implemented as part of a given **realization** are remembered "by our bodies" as a series of physical movements, rather than "by our minds," as a series of discursive moves. *See also* **automation of realizing procedures.**

enacted rule   activity-regulating rule, as identified by an observer of the activity.

encapsulation   act of assigning a noun or pronoun (**signifier**) to a specific set of extant **primary** or **discursive objects**, so that some of the stories about the members of this set that have, so far, been told in plural may now be told in singular. Encapsulation is one of the three main mechanisms for the production of new discursive objects, whereas the other two are **saming** and **reification.**

endogenous discursive expansion   an increase in the amount and complexity of discursive **routines** and **endorsed narratives** within the given discourse. *See also* the complementary term **exogenous discursive expansion.**

endorsed narrative   narrative that is regarded as reflecting the state of affairs in the world and labeled as *true*. When the term appears without any mention of the endorser, it is to be understood that the narrative is concensually endorsed by the community of the relevant discourse. In mathematics, endorsed narratives are those that constitute mathematical theories.

endorsed rule   activity-regulating rule, which the implementer considers as obliging.

exogenous discursive expansion   discursive growth that expresses itself in proliferation of new discourses. *See also* **discursive compression.**

exploration   routine whose goal (**closing condition**) is production of an **endorsed narrative.** *See also* the complementary terms **deed** and **ritual.**

explorative discourse   discourse whose **routines** are **explorations** rather than **rituals.** *See also* **ritualized discourse.**

factual narratives   narratives that are subject to consensual, rules-regulated **substantiation** by the **discourse** community (the substantiation ends with either endorsement or rejection).

identity   set of reifying, significant, **endorsed narratives** about a person.

incommensurable discourses   discourses that differ in their use of words and **mediators** or in their **routines**; incommensurable discourses may allow for the endorsement of seemingly contradictory **narratives.**

individualization   process that results in the ability to enact individually an activity that previously could only be performed with others; individualization is reflexively related to **communalization.**

insider to a discourse   person who is capable of participating in the discourse.

internally persuasive discourse   term introduced by Bakhtin to denote discourse that is "tightly woven with one's own world." (Bakhtin, 1981, pp. 110–111). *See also* **discourse-for-oneself** and the complementary term **authoritative discourse.**

interpretation   a **narrative** A counts as interpretation of narrative B within a given discourse if A is regarded by its author as equivalent to (interchangeable with) B in this discourse.

interpretative elaboration   a text (series of **utterances**) that, utterance by utterance, elaborates on the text produced by the interlocutors.

isomorphic discourses   discourses A and B are called isomorphic if there is one-to-one mapping from the narratives of A to narratives of B so that all the endorsement relations, as well as all the relations between the narratives of A are preserved.

learning, discursive   changing a discourse in a lasting way.

learning-teaching agreement   situation that arises when the **discursants** are unanimous, if only tacitly, about at least three basic aspects of the communicational process: about which is the leading discourse, about the discursants' own respective roles as those who learn or those who teach, and about the nature of the expected change.

literate discourse   discourse mediated mainly by symbolic artifacts created specifically for the sake of **communication**. *See also* the complementary term **colloquial discourse.**

mathematical discourse   discourse with vocabulary that counts as mathematical (contains, for example, words that refer to numbers and operations on numbers and to geometric shapes).

mathematical theory   set of all **endorsed narratives** about a certain set of mathematical objects.

mathematist   participant in **mathematical discourse.**

mathematizing   participation in mathematical discourse; "doing" mathematics.

metadiscursive rule (metarule)   rule that defines patterns in the activity of the discursants; see the complementary term **object-level rule.**

metalevel discourse   discourse about another (object-level) discourse. *See also* the complementary term **object-level discourse.**

metalevel learning learning that expresses itself in the change in the **metarules** of the discourse; it is a transition to **incommensurable discourse** in which words are used in a different way. *See also* the complementary term **object-level learning.**

metalevel *noun*: level of discourse about discourse; *adjective*: concerning discourse about discourse.

metarule. *See* **metadiscursive rule.**

narrative a series of **utterances**, spoken or written, that is framed as a description of objects, of relations between objects, or processes with or by objects, and is subject to endorsement or rejection, that is, to being labeled as "true" or "false."

norm **metarule** that is widely endorsed and enacted within the **discourse** community.

object-level discourse discourse about objects; the term is used to distinguish this discourse from a discourse about this discourse (**metalevel discourse**).

object-level learning learning resulting in **endogenous discursive expansion** (growth in the number and complexity of **endorsed narratives** and **routines**). *See also* the complementary term **metalevel learning.**

object-level rule rule that defines regularities in the behavior of objects of the discourse. *See also* the complementary term **metadiscursive rule** or **metarule.**

objectification process in which a noun begins to be used as if it signified an extradiscursive, self-sustained entity (object), independent of human agency; the process consists of two tightly related, but not inseparable subprocesses: **reification** and **alienation.**

objectified discourse discourse whose keywords are used as if they signified extradiscursive entities, existing independently of this discourse, though, in fact, these words signify **discursive objects.**

observer person who watches and interprets a conversation between other people.

ontological collapse phenomenon of taking all the objects that are being talked about – discursive (**d-objects**), and extradiscursive (**p-objects**) – as belonging to the same ontological category of "things in the world" that preexist discourse, with their mutual relations similarly "objective" and mind-independent.

outsider to a discourse person incapable of participating in the discourse.

p-object. *See* **primary object.**

participant person who takes part in a discourse.

participationism   research discourse grounded in the metaphor of learning as improving participation in historically established forms of activity; participationist tradition grew out of the criticism of **acquisitionism.**

practical action   action that produces change in objects (in the environment).

practical deed   routine whose goal (**closing condition**) is a change in primary objects.

primary object   any perceptually accessible entity existing independently of human **discourses**, including the things we can see and touch (material objects, pictures) as well as those that can only be heard (sounds). *See also* *p*-**object** and the complementary term **discursive object.**

principle of the continuity of discourse   pedagogical principle according to which new discourses should be developed by transforming discourses in which the learner is already fluent.

realization   procedure that pairs a **signifier** with another **primary object** or the product of such procedure.

realization tree   hierarchically organized set of all the **realizations** of the given **signifier**, together with the realizations of these realizations, as well as the realizations of these latter realizations, and so forth.

recursion   feature of language thanks to which every legitimate linguistic construct may give rise to a new, more complex one, provided we replace some of its simple elements with more complex linguistic constructs. Recursivity allows for turning one commognitive act into an object of another and thus accords the property of **reflexivity** to our discourses.

reflexivity   property of binary relation expressing itself in the fact that an element may remain in this relation with itself; in case of linguistic communication the relation of aboutness is reflexive because discourses in language may be about themselves. *See also* **self-reference.**

reification   replacement of talk about processes with talk about objects; usually, reification requires introduction of a new noun or written symbol; for example, the utterance "He has a learning disability" uses the noun phrase *learning disability* to reify the utterance "He cannot cope with even the simplest arithmetic problems in spite of years of instruction."

research   discourse produced with the intention of creating **endorsed narratives** with which we can mediate and enhance our **deeds.**

ritual   routine whose goal (**closing condition**) is alignment with others and social approval (rather than any kind of self-sustained product, as is the case with **deed** and **exploration**).

ritualized discourse   discourse that is a collection of unrelated **rituals**. *See also* the complementary term **explorative discourse.**

routine   set of **metarules** defining a discursive pattern that repeats itself in certain types of situations; this set can be divided into three subsets:

applicability conditions, routine course of action (or **routine procedure**), and **closing conditions** (or closure).

routine applicability conditions. *See* **applicability conditions.**

routine closing conditions (closure). *See* **closing conditions.**

routine course of action (or procedure) set of **metarules** that determine (e.g., in numerical calculations) or just constrain (e.g., in proving or writing a poem) the way the routine sequence of actions can be executed.

routine procedure. *See* **routine course of action.**

routine prompt those elements of situations whose presence increases the likelihood of implementation of the routine.

saming assigning one **signifier** (giving one name) to a number of things previously not considered as being "the same."

self-reference talking about (referring to) oneself. *See also* **reflexivity.**

signifier primary object used in communication, that is, one for which there exist realization procedures.

simple *d*-object. *See* **simple discursive object.**

simple discursive object. *See* **atomic discursive object, atomic *d*-object.**

subjectification objectification of the **discursant** – a special case of the activity of **objectifying**, one that occurs when the discursive focus shifts from actions and their objects to the performers of the actions.

substantiation of narratives discursive process of making sure that a given narrative can be endorsed; every discourse has its own **metarules** (routines) of substantiation.

subsuming discourse discourse A subsumes discourse B if A either is a metadiscourse of B or contains an isomorphic reflection of B. *See also* **isomorphic discourses.**

thinking **individualization** of interpersonal **communication** (the process of communicating between a person and herself, one that does not have to be verbal).

understanding interpretive term used by **discursants** to assess their own or their interlocutors' ability to follow a given strand or type of **communication**; the commognitive researcher, rather than assessing participants' understanding, is interested in the interplay of the participants' first- and third-person talk about understanding and their object-level discursive activity.

utterance communicational act in language (this category includes written communicational acts along with the spoken ones).

visual mediation use of **visual mediators in communication.**

visual mediator visual **realization** of the object of a discourse. Visual mediators include primary objects that preexist the discourse and artifacts created specially for the sake of communication (e.g., written symbols).

References

Albers, D. J., & Alexanderson, G. L. (1985). *Mathematical people – profiles and interviews*. Chicago: Contemporary Books.

The American heritage second college dictionary. (1985). Boston: Houghton Mifflin.

Anderson, J. R., Reder, L. M., & Simon, H. A. (1996). Situated learning and education. *Educational Researcher, 25*(4), 5–11.

Austin, J. L. (1962). *How to do things with words* (2nd ed.). Cambridge, MA: Harvard University Press.

Bakhtin, M. (1981). *The dialogic imagination: Four essays* (M. Holquist & C. Emerson, Trans.). Austin: University of Texas Press.

Bakhtin, M. (1986). *Speech genres and other late essays* (V. W. McGee, Trans.). Austin: University of Texas Press.

Bakhtin, M. (1999). The problem of speech genres. In A. Jaworski & N. Coupland (Eds.), *The discourse reader* (pp. 121–132). London: Routledge.

Bateson, G. (1973). *Steps to the ecology of mind*. Frogmore, St. Albans, Herts, UK: Paladin Books.

Bauersfeld, H. (1988). Interaction, construction, and knowledge: Alternative perspectives for mathematics education. In T. J. Cooney & D. A. Grouws (Eds.), *Effective mathematics teaching* (pp. 27–46). Reston, VA: National Council of Teachers of Mathematics and Lawrence Erlbaum Associates.

Bauersfeld, H. (1995). "Language games" in mathematics classroom: Their function and their effects. In P. Cobb & H. Bauersfeld (Eds.), *The emergence of mathematical meaning: Interaction in classroom cultures* (pp. 271–292). Hillsdale, NJ: Lawrence Erlbaum Associates.

Bauman, Z. (1996). From Pilgrim to tourist – or a short history of identity. In S. Hall & P. du Gay (Eds.), *Questions of cultural identity* (pp. 18–36). London: Sage Publications.

Bauman, Z. (2001). Identity in the globalized world. *Social Anthropology, 9*(2), 121–129.

Beach, K. (1995). Activity as a mediator of sociocultural change and individual development: The case of school-work transition in Nepal. *Mind, Culture, and Activity, 2*(4), 285–302.

Ben-Yehuda, M., Lavy, I., Linchevski, L., & Sfard, A. (2005). Doing wrong with words: What bars students' access to arithmetical discourses. *Journal for Research in Mathematics Education, 36*(3), 176–247.

Bereiter, C. (1985). Towards a solution of the learning paradox. *Review of Educational Research, 55*, 201–226.

Berlinski, D. (2005). *Infinite ascent: A short history of mathematics.* New York: Modern Library.

Bills, C. (2002). Linguistic pointers in young children's description of mental calculations. In A. Cockburn & E. Nardi (Eds.), *Proceedings of 26th Annual Meeting of the International Group for the Psychology of Mathematics Education* (Vol. 2, pp. 97–104). Norwich, England: School of Educational and Professional Development, University of East Anglia.

Blumer, H. (1969). *Symbolic interactionism: Perspective and method.* Englewood Cliffs, NJ: Prentice-Hall.

Borges, J. L. (1962/1964). *Labyrinths: Selected stories and other writings* (D. A. Yates & J. E. Irby, Eds.). New York: New Directions.

Borges, J. L. (1998). Argumentum ornitologicum (A. Hurley, Trans.). In *Collected fictions.* New York: Viking. (Original work published 1960.)

Bourdieu, P. (1999). Structures, habits, practices. In A. Elliot (Ed.), *The Blackwell reader in contemporary social theory* (pp. 107–118). Oxford: Blackwell.

Boyer, C. B., & Merzbach, U. C. (1989). *A history of mathematics* (2nd ed.). New York: Wiley.

Bransford, J. D., Barron, B., Pea, R. D., Meltzoff, A., Kuhl, P., Bell, P., et al. (2006). Foundations and opportunities for an interdisciplinary science of learning. In R. K. Sawyer (Ed.), *The Cambridge handbook of learning sciences* (pp. 19–34). Cambridge: Cambridge University Press.

Brousseau, G. (1997). *Theory of didactical situations.* Dordrecht, The Netherlands: Kluwer Academic.

Brown, G., & Yule, G. (1983). *Discourse analysis.* Cambridge: Cambridge University Press.

Brown, J. S., & Burton, R. R. (1978). Diagnostic models for procedural bugs in basic mathematical skills. *Cognitive Science, 2*, 155–192.

Brown, J. S., Collins, A., & Duguid, P. (1989). Situated cognition and the culture of learning. *Educational Researcher, 18*(1), 32–42.

Brownell, W. A. (1935). Psychological considerations in the learning and teaching of arithmetic. In W. D. Reeve (Ed.), *The teaching of arithmetic: Tenth yearbook of the National Council of Teachers of Mathematics* (pp. 1–31). New York: Columbia University, Teachers College.

Bruner, J. S. (1986). *Actual minds, possible worlds.* Cambridge, MA: Harvard University Press.

Bruner, J. S. (1990). The proper study of man: Four lectures on mind and culture. In J. Bruner (Ed.), *Acts of meaning* (pp. 1–32). Cambridge, MA: Harvard University Press.

Burkhard, H.-D., & Schoenfeld, A. H. (2003). Improving educational research: Toward a more useful, more influential, and better-funded enterprise. *Educational Researcher, 32*(9), 3–14.

Caduri, G. (2005). *The development of discourse on infinity.* Unpublished master's thesis, University of Haifa, Haifa, Israel. (In Hebrew.)

Carroll, L. (1998). *Alice's adventures in Wonderland; And, Through the looking-glass and what Alice found there.* Oxford, England: Oxford University Press.

Carruthers, P., & Boucher, J. (Eds.). (1998). *Language and thought: Interdisciplinary themes.* Cambridge: Cambridge University Press.

Cavaillès, J. (1962). *Philosophie mathematique.* Paris: Hermann.

Cazden, C. B. (2001). *Classroom discourse: The language of teaching and learning* (2nd ed.). Portsmouth, NH: Heinemann.

Chalouh, L., & Herscovics, N. (1988). Teaching algebraic expressions in a meaningful way. In A. F. Coxford & A. P. Shulte (Eds.), *The ideas of algebra, K–12. (1988 Yearbook)* (pp. 33–42). Reston, VA: National Council of Teachers of Mathematics.

Changeaux, J.-P., & Connes, A. (1995). *Conversations on mind, matter, and mathematics* (M. B. DeBevoise, Ed. and Trans.). Princeton, NJ: Princeton University Press.

Chevallard, Y. (1985). *Transposition didactique du savoir savant au savoir enseigne.* Grenoble, France: La Pensee Sauvage Editions.

Chevallard, Y. (1990). On mathematics education and culture: Critical afterthoughts. *Educational Studies in Mathematics, 21*(1), 3–28.

Chinn, S. J. (1996). *What to do when you can't learn the times tables.* Aalborg, Denmark: Marko.

Chomsky, N. (1957). *Syntactic structures.* 's-Gravenhage, The Netherlands: Mouton.

Clark, A. (1997). *Being there: Putting brain, body, and world together again.* Cambridge, MA: MIT Press.

Cobb, P. (1996). Accounting for mathematics learning in the social context of the classroom. In C. Alsina, J. Alvarez, B. Hodgson, C. Laborde, & A. Perez (Eds.), *Eighth International Congress on Mathematical Education: Selected Lectures* (pp. 85–100). Seville, Spain: S. A. E. M. 'THALES.'

Cobb, P. (2002). A relational perspective on issues of cultural diversity and equity as they play out in the mathematics classroom. *Mathematical Thinking and Learning, 4*(2–3), 249–284.

Cobb, P., & Bowers, J. (1999). Cognitive and situated learning perspectives in theory and in practice. *Educational Researcher, 25*(4), 4–15.

Cobb, P., Gravemeijer, K. E. P., Yackel, E., McClain, K., & Whitenack, J. (1997). Situated cognition. In D. Kirshner & J. A. Whitson (Eds.), *Mathematizing and symbolizing* (pp. 151–233). Mahwah, NJ: Lawrence Erlbaum Associates.

Cobb, P., Wood, T. L., & Yackel, E. (1993). Discourse, mathematical thinking, and classroom practice. In E. Forman, N. Minick, & A. Stone (Eds.), *Contexts for learning: Sociocultural dynamics in children's development* (pp. 91–119). New York: Oxford University Press.

Cobb, P., Yackel, E., & Wood, T. L. (1992). A constructivist alternative to the representational view of mind in mathematics education. *Journal for Research in Mathematics Education, 23*(1), 2–33.

Cole, M. (1996). *Cultural psychology: A once and future discipline.* Cambridge, MA: The Belknap Press of Harvard University Press.

Cole, M., Gay, J., Glick, J. A., & Sharp, D. W. (1971). *The cultural context of learning and thinking: An exploration in experimental anthropology.* New York: Basic Books.

Confrey, J. (1990). A review of the research on student conceptions in mathematics, science, and programming. In C. B. Cazden (Ed.), *Review of research in education* (Vol. 16, pp. 3–56). Washington, DC: American Educational Research Association.

Damasio, A. R. (1999a). *The feeling of what happens: Body and emotion in the making of consciousness.* New York: Harcourt.

Damasio, A. R. (1999b, December). How the brain creates the mind. *Scientific American, 281,* 112–117.

Davis, P. J., & Hersh, R. (1981). *The mathematical experience.* London: Penguin Books.

Davis, R. (1988). The interplay of algebra, geometry, and logic. *Journal of Mathematical Behavior, 7,* 9–28.

de Abreu, G. (2000). Relationship between macro and micro socio-cultural context: Implications for the study of interactions in mathematics classroom. *Educational Studies in Mathematics, 41*(1), 1–29.

Dehaene, S. (1997). *The number sense: How the mind creates mathematics.* New York: Oxford University Press.

Dekel, L. (2003). *Colloquial and literate arithmetic discourse among children with learning difficulties and learning disabilitys in mathematics* (in Hebrew). Unpublished masters thesis. The University of Haifa, Haifa, Israel.

Dennett, D. C. (1996). *Kinds of minds: Towards an understanding of consciousness.* New York: Basic Books.

Descartes, R. (1968). *Discourse on method and the meditations* (F. E. Sutcliffe, Trans.). Harmondsworth, England: Penguin Books.

Donald, M. (1993). *Origins of modern mind.* Cambridge, MA: Harvard University Press.

Donmoyer, R. (1996). This issue: A focus of learning. *Educational Researcher, 25*(4), 4.

Dreyfus, T. (1991). On the status of visual reasoning in mathematics and mathematics education. In F. Furinghetti (Ed.), *15th Annual Conference of the International Group of the Psychology of Mathematics Education* (Vol. 1, pp. 32–48). Assisi, Italy.

Dubinsky, E. (1991). Reflective abstraction in advanced mathematical thinking. In D. Tall (Ed.), *Advanced mathematical thinking* (pp. 95–125). Dordrecht, The Netherlands: Kluwer Academic.

Edwards, D. (1993). But what do children really think? Discourse analysis and conceptual content in children's talk. *Cognition and Instruction, 11*(3–4), 207–225.

Edwards, D. (1997). *Discourse and cognition.* London: Sage.

Edwards, D., & Potter, J. (1992). *Discursive psychology.* Newbury Park, CA: Sage.

Encyclopedia Britannica. (1998). Britannica CD 98, Multimedia edition. (International version).

Encyclopedia Britannica. (n.d.). *Encylclopedia Britannica online.* Retrieved from http://www.britannica.com/search?ct=genl&query=language.

Engeström, Y. (1987). *Learning by expanding: An activity-theoretical approach to developmental research.* Helsinki: Orienta-Konsultit.

Erlwanger, S. H. (1973). Benny's conception of rules and answers in IPI mathematics. *Journal of Children's Mathematical Behavior, 1*(2), 7–26.

Ernest, P. (1993). *Conversation as a metaphor for mathematics and learning.* Paper presented at the British Society for Research into Learning Mathematics Day Conference, Manchester Metropolitan University.

Ernest, P. (1994). *Mathematics, education and philosophy: An international perspective.* London: Routledge Falmer.

Filloy, E., & Rojano, T. (1989). Solving equations: The transition from arithmetic to algebra. *For the Learning of Mathematics, 9*(2), 19–25.

Fischbein, E. (1987). *Intuition in science and mathematics*. Dordrecht, The Netherlands: Reidel.

Fischbein, E. (1989). Tactic models and mathematical reasoning. *For the Learning of Mathematics, 9*(2), 9–14.

Fischbein, E., Deri, M., Nello, M. S., & Marino, M. S. (1985). The role of implicit models in solving verbal problems in multiplication and division. *Journal for Research in Mathematics Education, 16*, 3–17.

Fisher, W. R. (1984). Narration as human communication paradigm: The case of public moral argument. *Communication Monographs, 51*, 1–22.

Fodor, J. A. (1975). *The language of thought*. New York: Crowell.

Fodor, J. A. (1983). *The modularity of mind: An essay on faculty psychology*. Cambridge, MA: MIT Press.

Forman, E. (1996). Forms of participation in classroom practice: Implications for learning mathematics. In P. Nesher, L. Steffe, P. Cobb, G. Goldin, & B. Greer (Eds.), *Theories of mathematical learning* (pp. 115–130). Hillsdale, NJ: Lawrence Erlbaum Associates.

Forman, E. A., & Ansell, E. (2002). Orchestrating the multiple voices and inscriptions of a mathematics classroom. *Journal of the Learning Sciences, 11*, 251–274.

Foucault, M. (1972). *The archaeology of knowledge; And, The discourse on language*. New York: Pantheon Books.

Fouts, R. (1998). *Next of kin: My conversations with chimpanzees*. New York: Harper Paperbacks.

Gadamer, H.-G. (1975). *Truth and method*. New York: Seabury Press.

Garfinkel, H. (1967). *Studies in ethnomethodology*. Englewood Cliffs, NJ: Prentice-Hall.

Garnett, K. (1992). Developing fluency with basic number facts: Intervention for students with learning disabilities. *Learning Disabilities Research and Practice, 7*, 210–216.

Gauker, C. (n.d.). Langue and thought. Retrieved from http://host.uniroma3.it/progetti/kant/field/lat.htm.

Geary, D. C., Hoard, M. K., & Hamson, C. O. (1999). Numerical and arithmetical cognition: Patterns of functions and deficits in children at risk for a mathematical disability. *Journal of Experimental Child Psychology, 74*(3), 213–240.

Gee, J. (1989). Literacy, discourse, and linguistics: Introduction. *Journal of Education, 171*(1), 6–17.

Gee, J. P. (1997). Thinking, learning, and reading: The situated sociocultural mind. In D. Kirshner & J. A. Whitson (Eds.), *Situated cognition: Social, semiotic, and psychological perspective* (pp. 235–260). Mahwah, NJ: Lawrence Erlbaum Associates.

Gee, J. P. (2001). Identity as an analytic lens for research in education. *Review of Research in Education, 25*, 99–125.

Geertz, C. (1973). *The interpretation of cultures*. New York: Basic Books.

Gelman, R., & Gallistel, C. R. (1978). *The child's understanding of number*. New York: Cambridge University Press.

Ginsburg, H. P. (1997). *Entering the child's mind: The clinical interview in psychological research and practice*. New York: Cambridge University Press.

Goffman, E. (1959). *The presentation of self in everyday life.* Garden City, NY: Doubleday.

Goffman, E. (1967). *Interaction ritual: Essays on face-to-face behavior.* New York: Anchor Books.

Goldman, S. R., Pelligrino, J. W., & Mertz, D. L. (1988). Extended practice of basic addition facts: Strategy changes in learning disabled students. *Cognition and Instruction, 5,* 223–265.

Goody, J. (1977). *The domestication of the savage mind.* Cambridge: Cambridge University Press.

Greeno, J. G. (1991). Number sense as a situated knowing in conceptual domain. *Journal for Research in Mathematics Education, 22*(3), 170–218.

Greeno, J. G. (1997). On claims that answer the wrong question. *Educational Researcher, 26*(1), 5–17.

Grice, H. (1975). Logic and conversation. In P. Cole & J. L. Morgan (Eds.), *Syntax and symantics: Speech acts* (Vol. 3, pp. 41–58). New York: Academic Press.

Grice, H. P. (1957). Meaning. *Philosophical Review, 66,* 377–388.

Groome, D. (1999). *An introduction to cognitive psychology: Processes and disorders.* London: Routledge.

Gurnik, M., & Saban, A. (2003). *Solving mathematical word problems with real-life content in mathematics and language lessons.* Haifa, Israel: University of Haifa. Unpublished manuscript.

Hadamard, J. (1954). *An essay on the psychology of invention in the mathematical field.* New York: Dover.

Hall, S., & du Gay, P. (1996). *Questions of cultural identity.* London: Sage Publications.

Halliday, M. A. K. (1978). *Language as social semiotics.* London: Edward Arnold.

Halliday, M. A. K. (2003). *On language and linguistics.* London: Continuum.

Halliday, M. A. K., & Martin, J. R. (1993). *Writing science.* Pittsburgh: University of Pittsburgh Press.

Halliday, M. A. K., & Matthiessen, C. M. I. M. (2004). *An introduction to functional grammar* (3rd ed.). London: Arnold.

Halmos, P. R. (1985). *I want to be a mathematician – an automathography in three parts.* Washington, DC: Mathematical Association of America.

Hanks, P. (Ed.). (1986). *Collins dictionary of the English language.* London: Collins.

Harel, G., Behr, M., Post, T., & Lesh, R. (1989). Fishbein's theory: A further consideration. In G. Vergnaud, J. Rogalski, & M. Artigue (Eds.), *Proceedings of the 13th Annual Conference of the Psychology of Mathematics Education* (pp. 52–59): Paris: University of Paris.

Harré, R., & Gillett, G. (1995). *The discursive mind.* Thousand Oaks, CA: Sage Publications.

Hauser, M. D., Chomsky, N., & Fitch, W. T. (2002). The language faculty: What is it, who has it, and how did it evolve? *Science, 298,* 1569–1579.

Heider, F. (1958). *The psychology of interpersonal relations.* New York: Wiley.

Herder, J. G. (1771/1967). Abhandlung über Ursprung der Sprache. In B. Suphon (Ed.), *Herder, J. G., Sämtliche Werke V.* George Olms.

Hershkowitz, R. (1989). Visualisation in geometry – two sides of the coin. *Focus on Learning Problems in Mathematics, 11*(1), 61–75.

Hesse, M. B. (1966). *Models and analogies in science.* Notre Dame, IN: University of Notre Dame Press.

Hiebert, J., & Carpenter, T. P. (1992). Learning and teaching with understanding. In D. A. Grouws (Ed.), *The handbook of research on mathematics teaching and learning* (pp. 65–100). New York: Macmillan.

Holland, D., Lachicotte, W. J., Skinner, D., & Cain, C. (1998). *Identity and agency in cultural worlds.* Cambridge, MA: Harvard University Press.

Holquist, M. (1990). *Dialogism: Bakhtin and his world.* London: Routledge.

Horn, L. R., & Ward, G. (Eds.). (2004). *Handbook of pragmatics.* Malden, MA: Blackwell.

Hoyles, C., Noss, R., & Pozzi, S. (2001). Proportional reasoning in nursing practices. *Journal for Research in Mathematics Education, 32*(1), 4–27.

Hutchins, E. (1995). *Cognition in the wild.* Cambridge, MA: MIT Press.

Jacoby, S., & Ochs, E. (1995). Co-construction: An introduction. *Research on Language and Social Interaction, 28*(3), 171–183.

Johnson, M. (1987). *The body in the mind: The bodily basis of meaning, imagination, and reason.* Chicago: University of Chicago Press.

Jourdain, P. E. B. (1956). The nature of mathematics. In J. P. Newman (Ed.), *The world of mathematics.* New York: Simon & Schuster.

Kavale, K. A., & Forness, S. R. (1997). Defining learning disabilities: Consonance and dissonance. In J. W. Lloyd, E. J. Kame'euni, & D. J. Chard (Eds.), *Issues in educating students with disabilities* (pp. 3–25). Mahwah, NJ: Lawrence Erlbaum Associates.

Kieran, C. (1981). Concepts associated with the equality symbol. *Educational Studies in Mathematocs, 12*(3), 317–326.

Kieran, C., & Sfard, A. (1999). Seeing through symbols: The case of equivalent expressions. *Focus on Learning Problems in Mathematics, 21*(1), 1–17.

Kilpatrick, J., Swafford, J., & Findell, B. (Eds.). (2001). *Adding it up: Helping children learn mathematics.* Washington, DC: National Academy Press.

Kipling, R. (1894). *The jungle book.* Retrieved July 12, 2007, from http://whitewolf. newcastle.edu.au/words/authors/K/KiplingRudyard/prose/JungleBook/index. html.

Kleiner, I. (1989). Evolution of the function concept: A brief survey. *The College Mathematics Journal, 20*(4), 282–300.

Kline, M. (1980). *Mathematics: The loss of certainty.* New York: Oxford University Press.

Kosc, L. (1974). Developmental dyscalculia. *Journal of Learning Disabilities, 7,* 46–89.

Kozulin, A. (1990). *Vygotsky's psychology: A biography of ideas.* New York: Harvester Wheatsheaf.

Kristal, L. (2005). *The development of discourse on derivative of lower placement 11th grade mathematics students.* Unpublished master's thesis, University of Haifa, Haifa, Israel.

Krummheuer, G. (1995). The ethnography of argumentation. In P. Cobb & H. Bauersfeld (Eds.), *The emergence of mathematical meaning: Interactions in classroom culture* (pp. 229–269). Hillsdale, NJ: Lawrence Erlbaum Associates.

Kuhn, T. (1962). *The structure of scientific revolutions* (2nd ed.). Chicago: University of Chicago Press.

Labov, W., & Waletzky, J. (1967). Narrative analysis: Oral versions of personal experience. In J. Helm (Ed.), *Essays on the verbal and visual arts: Proceedings of the 1966 Annual Spring meeting of the American Ethnological Society* (pp. 12–44). Seattle: University of Washington Press.

Lacan, J. (1966). *Ecrits 1*. Paris: Editions du Seuil.

Lakatos, I. (1976). *Proofs and refutations*. Cambridge: Cambridge University Press.

Lakoff, G. (1987). *Women, fire and dangerous things: What categories reveal about the mind*. Chicago: University of Chicago Press.

Lakoff, G. (1993). The contemporary theory of metaphor. In A. Ortony (Ed.), *Metaphor and thought* (pp. 202–250). Cambridge: Cambridge University Press.

Lakoff, G., & Johnson, M. (1980). *The metaphors we live by*. Chicago: University of Chicago Press.

Latour, B. (1987). *Science in action*. Cambridge, MA: Harvard University Press.

Lave, J. (1988). *Cognition in practice*. Cambridge: Cambridge University Press.

Lave, J., & Wenger, E. (1991). *Situated learning: Legitimate peripheral participation*. Cambridge: Cambridge University Press.

Lemke, J. L. (1993). *Talking science: Language, learning, and values*. Norwood, NJ: Ablex.

Lemke, J. L. (2000). Across the scales of time: Artifacts, activities, and meanings in ecosocial systems. *Mind, Culture, and Activity, 7*(4), 273–290.

Leont'ev, A. N. (1930). Studies in the cultural development of the child: 2. The development of voluntary attention in the child. *Journal of Genetic Psychology, 37*, 52–81.

Leont'ev, A. N. (1981). *Psychology and the language learning process*. Oxford, England: Pergamon Press.

Lerman, S. (1998). A moment in the zoom of a lens: Towards a discursive psychology of mathematics teaching and learning. In A. Olivier & K. Newstead (Eds.), *Proceedings of the 22nd Annual Meeting of the International Group for the Psychology of Mathematics Education*. Stellenbosch, South Africa.

Lerman, S. (1999). Culturally situated knowledge and the problem of transfer in the learning of mathematics. In L. Burton (Ed.), *Learning mathematics: From hierarchies to networks*. London: Falmer Press.

Levinson, S. (1983). *Pragmatics*. Cambridge: Cambridge University Press.

Lucy, J. A. (1997). Linguistic relativity. *Annual Review of Anthropology, 26*, 291–313.

Lucy, J. A., & Shweder, R. (1979). Whorf and his critics: Linguistic and nonlinguistic influences on color memory. *American Anthropologist, 81*, 581–615.

Malik, M. A. (1980). Historical and pedagogical aspects of definition of function. *International Journal of Math Science and Technology, 1*(4), 489–492.

Markova, I. (2003). *Dialogicality and social representations: The dynamics of mind*. Cambridge: Cambridge University Press.

Markovits, Z., Eylon, B., & Bruckheimer, M. (1986). Functions today and yesterday. *For the Learning of Mathematics, 6*(2), 18–24.

Maturana, H. R. and Varela, F. J. (1987). *The Three of Knowledge*. Boston: Shambhala.

Mayer, R. E. (1983). *Thinking, problem solving, cognition*. New York: W. H. Freeman.

McDermott, R. P. (1993). The acquisition of a child by a learning disability. In S. Chaiklin & J. Lave (Eds.), *Understanding practice*. Cambridge: Cambridge University Press.

McGarrigle, J., & Donaldson, M. (1974). Conservation accidents. *Cognition, 3*, 341–350.

Mead, G. H. (1934). *Mind, self, and society from the standpoint of a social behaviorist* (C. W. Morris, Ed.). Chicago: University of Chicago Press.

Mehan, H. (1979). *Learning lessons: Social organization in the classroom*. Cambridge, MA: Harvard University Press.

Mehan, H. (1996). The construction of an LD student: A case study in the politics of representation. In M. Silverstein & G. Urban (Eds.), *Natural histories of discourse* (pp. 253–276). Chicago: University of Chicago Press.

Mehler, J., & Bever, T. G. (1967). Cognitive capacity of very young children. *Science, 158*, 141–142.

Minick, N. (1987). Development of Vygotsky's thought: An introduction. In R. W. Rieber & A. S. Carton (Eds.), *The collected works of L. S. Vgotsiy* (Vol. 1, pp. 17–38). New York: Plenum Press.

Minsky, M. (1985). *The society of mind*. New York: Simon and Schuster.

Nardi, B. (Ed.). (1996). *Context and consciousness: Activity theory and human-computer interaction*. Cambridge, MA: MIT Press.

National Council of Teachers of Mathematics. (2000). *Principles and standards for school mathematics*. Reston, VA: Author.

Neisser, U. (Ed.). (1987). *Concepts and conceptual development: Ecological and intellectual factors in categorization*. Cambridge: Cambridge University Press.

Nunes, T., & Bryant, P. (1996). *Children doing mathematics*. Oxford: Blackwell.

Nunes, T., Schliemann, A., & Carraher, D. (1993). *Street mathematics and school mathematics*. Cambridge: Cambridge University Press.

O'Connor, M. C. (1998). Language socialization in the mathematics classroom: Discourse practices in group discussions. In M. Lampert & M. Blunk (Eds.), *Talking mathematics: Studies of teaching and learning in school* (pp. 17–55). Cambridge: Cambridge University Press.

O'Connor, M. C., & Michaels, S. (1996). Shifting participant frameworks: Orchestrating thinking practices in group discussions. In D. Hicks (Ed.), *Discourse, learning, and schooling* (pp. 63–103). Cambridge: Cambridge University Press.

Olby, R. C. (1974). *The path to the double helix*. Seattle: University of Washington Press.

Ortony, A. (1993). *Metaphor and thought*. Cambridge: Cambridge University Press.

Overbye, D. (2006, August 15). An elusive proof and its elusive prover. *New York Times*, Section F, p. 1.

Peirce, C. (1931–1935). *Collected papers of Charles Sanders Peirce* (Vol. 1–6). Cambridge, MA: Harvard University Press.

Peirce, C. (1955). *Philosophical writings of Peirce*. New York: Dover.

Perkins, D. (2001). *Eureka effect: The art and logic of breakthrough thinking*. New York: W. W. Norton.

Piaget, J. (1952). *The origins of intelligence of the child*. London: Routledge and Kegan Paul.

Piaget, J. & Garcia, R. (1989). *Psychogenesis and the history of science*. New York: Columbia University Press.

Pinker, S. (1994). *The language instinct*. New York: HarperCollins.

Pinker, S. (2003). *Blank slate: The modern denial of human nature*. London: Penguin.

Plato. (1949). *Meno*. New York: Liberal Arts Press.

Poincaré, H. (1952). *Science and method*. New York: Dover.

Pullum, G. K. (1991). *The great Eskimo hoax, and other irreverent essays on the study of language*. Chicago: University of Chicago Press.

Reddy, M. J. (1979). The conduit metaphor: A case of frame conflict in our language about language. In A. Ortony (Ed.), *Metaphor and thought*. Cambridge: Cambridge University Press.

Reed, H. J., & Lave, J. (1979). Arithmetic as a tool for investigating the relations between culture and cognition. *American Ethnologist, 6,* 568–582.

Richter, D. J. (n.d.). Ludwig Wittgenstein (1889–1951). In *The Internet encyclopedia of philosophy*. Retrieved from http://www.iep.utm.edu/w/wittgens.htm.

Ricoeur, P. (1977). *The rule of metaphor: Multidisciplinary studies of the creation of meaning in language*. Toronto: University of Toronto Press.

Rogoff, B. (1990). *Apprenticeship in thinking: Cognitive development in social context*. Oxford: Oxford University Press.

Rogoff, B. (1995). Observing sociocultural activity on three planes: Participatory appropriation, guided participation, and apprenticeship. In J. V. Wertsch, P. Del Rio, & A. Alvarez (Eds.), *Sociocultural studies of mind*. Cambridge: Cambridge University Press.

Rorty, R. (1979). *Philosophy and the mirror of nature*. Princeton, NJ: Princeton University Press.

Rorty, R. (1989). *Contingency, irony, solidarity*. Cambridge: Cambridge University Press.

Rosch, E. (1978). Principles of categorization. In E. Rosch & B. B. Lloyd (Eds.), *Cognition and categorization*. Hillsdale, NJ: Lawrence Erlbaum Associates.

Russell, B. (1904). Recent works on the principles of mathematics. *International Monthly, 4,* 84.

Russell, B. (1956). *Portraits from memory, and other essays*. New York: Simon and Schuster.

Rutherford, E. (n.d.). Retrieved in June 1999 from http://epmalab.uoregon.edu/weird/Rutherford%20Story.pdf.

Ruthing, D. (1984). Some definitions of the concept of function from John Bernoulli to N. Bourbaki. *Mathematical Intelligence, 6*(4), 72–77.

Ryle, G. (1949/2000). *The concept of mind*. Chicago: University of Chicago Press.

Sacks, S. (Ed.). (1978). *On metaphor*. Chicago: University of Chicago Press. Sacks, H. (1992). *Lectures on conversation*. Oxford: Blackwell.

Säljö, R., & Wyndhamn, J. (1993). Solving everyday problems in the formal setting: An empirical study of the school as context for thought. In S. Chaiklin & J. Lave (Eds.), *Understanding practice: Perspectives on activity and context* (pp. 327–342). Cambridge: Cambridge University Press.

Sapir, E. (1949). *Selected writings in language, culture, and personality*. Berkeley: University of California Press.

Saxe, G. B., & Esmonde, I. (2005). Studying cognition in flux: A historical treatment of "Fu" in the shifting structure of Oksapmin mathematics. *Mind, Culture, and Activity, 13*(2), 171–225.

Scheffler, I. (1991). Educational metaphors. In I. Scheffler (Ed.), *In praise of the cognitive emotions and other essays in the philosophy of education* (pp. 45–55). New York: Routledge.

Schnotz, W., Vosniadou, S., & Carretero, M. (Eds.). (1999). *New perspectives on conceptual change.* Oxford: Pergamon.

Schoenfeld, A. H. (1998). Making mathematics and making pasta: From cookbook procedures to really cooking. In J. G. Greeno & S. V. Goldman (Eds.), *Thinking practices in mathematics and science learning* (pp. 299–319). Mahwah, NJ: Lawrence Erlbaum Associates.

Schutz, A. (1967). *Collected papers: The problem of social reality.* The Hague, The Netherlands: Martinus Nijhoff.

Schutz, A., & Luckmann, T. (1973). *The structures of the life world.* Evanston, IL: Northwestern University Press.

Scribner, S. (1997). Mind in action: A functional approach to thinking. In M. Cole, Y. Engstrom, & O. Vasquez (Eds.), *Mind, culture, and activity: Seminal papers from the Laboratory of Comparative Human Cognition* (pp. 354–368). Cambridge: Cambridge University Press. (Original work published in 1983.)

Scribner, S., & Cole, M. (1981). *The psychology of literacy.* Cambridge, MA: Harvard University Press.

Searle, J. R. (2002). *Consciousness and language.* Cambridge: Cambridge University Press.

Searle, J. R. (2004). *Mind: A brief introduction.* New York: Oxford University Press.

Sebeok, T. A. (2001). Nonverbal communication. In P. Cobley (Ed.), *The Routledge companion to semiotics and linguistics.* London: Routledge.

Sfard, A. (1987). *Teaching the theory of algorithms in high school.* Unpublished doctoral dissertation, Hebrew University of Jerusalem, Jerusalem, Israel. (In Hebrew.)

Sfard, A. (1991). On the dual nature of mathematical conceptions: Reflections on processes and objects as different sides of the same coin. *Educational Studies in Mathematics, 22,* 1–36.

Sfard, A. (1992). Operational origin of mathematical objects and the quandary of reification – the case of function. In E. Dubinsky & G. Harel (Eds.), *The Concept of function: Aspects of epistemology and pedagogy (MAA Notes No. 25)* (pp. 59–84). Washington, DC: Mathematical Association of America.

Sfard, A. (1994). Reification as a birth of a metaphor. *For the Learning of Mathematics, 14*(1), 44–55.

Sfard, A. (1995). The development of algebra: Confronting historical and psychological perspectives. *Journal of Mathematic Behavior, 14,* 15–39.

Sfard, A. (1997). Commentary: On metaphorical roots of conceptual growth. In L. D. English (Ed.), *Mathematical reasoning: Analogies, metaphors, and images* (pp. 339–371). Mahwah, NJ: Lawrence Erlbaum Associates.

Sfard, A. (1998). Two metaphors for learning and the dangers of choosing just one. *Educational Researcher, 27*(2), 4–13.

Sfard, A. (2003). Balancing the unbalanceable: The NCTM Standards in the light of theories of learning mathematics. In J. Kilpatrick, W. G. Martin,

& D. Schifter (Eds.), *A research companion to principles and standards for school mathematics* (pp. 353–392). Reston, VA: National Council of Teachers of Mathematics.

Sfard, A. (2005). What could be more practical than good research? On mutual relations between research and practice of mathematics education. *Educational Studies in Mathematics, 58*(3), 393–413.

Sfard, A. (2007). When the rules of discourse change, but nobody tells you: Making sense of mathematics learning from a cognitive standpoint. *Journal for Learning Sciences.*

Sfard, A., & Kieran, C. (2001a). Cognition as communication: Rethinking learning-by-talking through multi-faceted analysis of students' mathematical interactions. *Mind, Culture, and Activity, 8*(1), 42–76.

Sfard, A., & Kieran, C. (2001b). Preparing teachers for handling students' mathematical communication: Gathering knowledge and building tools. In F. L. Lin & T. J. Cooney (Eds.), *Making sense of mathematics teacher education.* Dordrecht, The Netherlands: Kluwer Academic.

Sfard, A., & Lavie, I. (2005). Why cannot children see as the same what grown-ups cannot see as different? Early numerical thinking revisited. *Cognition and Instruction 23*(2), 237–309.

Sfard, A., & Linchevski, L. (1994). The gains and the pitfalls of reification: The case of algebra. *Educational Studies in Mathematics, 26,* 191–228.

Sfard, A., & Prusak, A. (2005). Telling identities: In search of an analytic tool for investigating learning as a culturally shaped activity. *Educational Researcher, 34*(4), 14–22.

Shannon, C. E., & Weaver, W. (1949). *The mathematical theory of communication.* Urbana: University of Illinois Press.

Shaywitz, S., Escobar, M., Shaywitz, B., Fletchers, J., & Makuch, R. (1992). Evidence that dyslexia may represent the lower tail of a normal distribution of reading ability. *New England Journal of Medicine, 326*(3), 145–150.

Simon, T., Hespos, S. J., & Rochat, P. (1994). Do infants understand simple arithmetic? A replication of Wynn (1992). *Cognitive Development, 10*(2), 253–269.

Sinclair, J. M., & Coulthard, M. (1975). *Toward an analysis of discourse: The English used by teachers and pupils.* London: Oxford University Press.

Smith, H. (n.d.). Quotation retrieved from http://brainyquote.com/quotes/quotes/h/hustonsmit220777.html.

Smith, J. P., diSessa, A. A., & Rochelle, J. (1993). Misconceptions reconceived: A constructivist analysis of knowledge in transition. *The Journal of the Learning Sciences, 3*(2), 115–163.

Sperber, D., & Wilson, D. (1986). *Relevance: Communication and cognition.* Malden, MA: Blackwell.

Sperber, D., & Wilson, D. (1995). *Relevance: Communication and cognition.* Cambridge, MA: Blackwell.

Starkey, P., & Cooper, R. (1980). Perception of numbers by human infants. *Science, 210*(28), 1033–1034.

Steeves, K. J., & Tomey, H. A. (1998). *Mathematics and dyslexia: The individual who learns differently may still be successful in math.* Unpublished manuscript.

Stern, D. G. (1995). *Wittgenstein on mind and language*. New York: Oxford University Press.

Suchman, L. (2007). *Human-machine reconfigurations: Plans and situated actions*. Cambridge: Cambridge University Press.

Tall, D., & Schwartzenberger, R. (1978). Conflicts in the learning of real numbers and limits. *Mathematics Teaching, 82,* 44–49.

Tall, D., & Vinner, S. (1981). Concept image and concept definition in mathematics with particular reference to limits and continuity. *Educational Studies in Mathematics, 12,* 151–169.

Tannen, D., & Wallat, C. (1999). Interactive frames and knowledge schemas in interactions. In A. Jaworski & N. Coupland (Eds.), *The discourse reader* (pp. 346–366). New York: Routledge.

Thom, R. (1971). Modern mathematics: An educational and philosophical error? *American Scientist, 59,* 695–699.

Thurston, W. P. (1990). Mathematical education. *Notices of the American Mathematical Society, 37*(7), 844–850.

Thurston, W. P. (1994). On proof and progress in mathematics. *Bulletin of the American Mathematical Society, 30,* 161–177.

Tomasello, M. (1999). *The cultural origins of human cognition*. Cambridge, MA: Harvard University Press.

Toulmin, S. (1972). *Human understanding. Vol. 1.General Introduction and Part 1*. Oxford: Calderon Press.

Turing, A. M. (1950). Computing machinery and intelligence. *Mind, 59,* 443–460.

Van Dooren, W., DeBock, D., Janssens, D., & Verschaffel, L. (2005). *Students' overreliance on linearity: An effect of school-like word problems?* Paper presented at the 29th Conference of the International Group for the Psychology of Mathematics Education, Melbourne, Australia.

van Hiele, P. M. (1985). A child's thought and geometry. In D. Fuys, D. Geddes, & R. Tischler (Eds.), *English translation of selected writing of Dina van Hiele-Geldorf and Pierre M. van Hiele* (pp. 243–252). Brooklyn, NY: Brooklyn College, School of Education.

van Hiele, P. M. (2004/1959). A child's thought and geometry. In T. P. Carpenter, J. A. Dossey, & J. L. Koelher (Eds.), *Classics in mathematics education research* (pp. 60–67). Reston, VA: National Council of Teachers of Mathematics.

Varela, F. J., Thompson, E., & Rosch, E. (1991). *The embodied mind: Cognitive science and human experience*. Cambridge, MA: MIT Press.

Varenne, H., & McDermott, R. P. (1998). *Successful failure: The school America builds*. Boulder, CO: Westview Press.

Vinner, S. (1983). Concept definition, concept image and the notion of function. *International Journal of Mathematical Education in Science and Technology, 14*(3), 293–305.

Vinner, S. (1991). The role of definitions in the teaching and learning of mathematics. In D. Tall (Ed.), *Advanced mathematical thinking*. Dordrecht, The Netherlands: Kluwer Academic.

Vinner, S., & Dreyfus, T. (1989). Images and definitions for the concept of function. *Journal for Research in Mathematics Education, 20*(4), 356–366.

Voigt, J. (1985). Patterns and routines in classroom interaction. *Recherches en Didactique des Mathématiques, 6*(1), 69–118.

Voigt, J. (1994). Negotiation of mathematical meaning and learning mathematics. *Educational Studies in Mathematics, 26,* 275–298.

Voigt, J. (1995). Thematic patterns of interaction and sociomathematical norms. In P. Cobb & H. Bauersfeld (Eds.), *The emergence of mathematical meaning: Interaction in classroom cultures* (pp. 163–201). Hillsdale, NJ: Lawrence Erlbaum Associates.

Voigt, J. (1996). Negotiation of mathematical meaning in classroom processes: Social interaction and learning mathematics. In L. Steffe, P. Nesher, P. Cobb, G. Goldin, & B. Greer (Eds.), *Theories of mathematical learning* (pp. 21–50). Mahwah, NJ: Kluwer Academic.

Vosniadou, S. (1994). Capturing and modeling the process of conceptual change. *Learning and Instruction, 4,* 45–69.

Vosniadou, S., Baltas, A., & Vamvakoussi, X. (Eds.). (2007). *Reframing the conceptual change approach in learnign and instruction.* Amsterdam: Elsevier.

Vygotsky, L. S. (1978). *Mind in society: The development of higher psychological processes.* Cambridge, MA: Harvard University Press.

Vygotsky, L. S. (1982). Consciousness as a problem in the psychology of behavior. In L. S. Vygotsky (Ed.), *Collected works: Problems of the theory and history of psychology.* Moscow: Pedagogica. (In Russian.)

Vygotsky, L. S. (1986). *Thought and language* (A. Kozulin, Trans.). Cambridge, MA: MIT Press.

Vygotsky, L. S. (1987). Thinking and speech. In R. W. Rieber, & A. C. Carton (Eds.), *The collected works of L. S. Vygotsky.* New York: Plenum Press.

Walkerdine, V. (1988). *The mastery of reason.* London: Routledge.

Watson, J. D. (2001). *The double helix: A personal account of the discovery of the structure of DNA.* New York: Touchstone.

Wenger, E. (1998). *Communities of practice: Learning, meaning, and identity.* New York: Cambridge University Press.

Whorf, B. L. (1940). Science and linguistics. *Technology Review, 42*(6), 229–231, 247–228.

Wikipedia. (n.d.). Language. Retrieved from http://en.wikipedia.org/wiki/Language.

Wikipedia. (n.d.). Occam's razor. Retrieved from http://en.wikipedia.org/wiki/Occam's_Razor.

William of Ockham. (1974). *Ockham's theory of terms: Part I of the Summa logicae* (M. J. Loux, Trans.). Notre Dame, IN: University of Notre Dame Press.

William of Ockham. (1984). *Venerabilis inceptoris Guillelmi de Ockham brevis summa libri physicorum; Summula philosophiae naturalis; et Quaestiones in libros physicorum Aristotelis* (S. Brown, Trans.). St. Bonaventure, NY: St. Bonaventure University.

William of Ockham. (1990). *Philosophical writings: A selection* (P. Boehner, Trans.). Indianapolis, IN: Hackett.

Wittgenstein, L. (1953/2003). *Philosophical investigations: The German text, with a revised English translation* (3rd ed., G. E. M. Anscombe, Trans.). Malden, MA: Blackwell.

Wittgenstein, L. (1961). *Tractatus logico-philosophicus* (D. F. Pears & B. F. McGuiness, Trans.). London: Routledge & Paul.

Wittgenstein, L. (1969). *On certainty* (G. E. M. Anscombe & G. H. von Wright, Eds.) (D. Paul & G. E. M. Anscombe, Trans.). Oxford: Blackwell.

Wittgenstein, L. (1978). *Remarks on the foundations of mathematics*. Oxford: Blackwell.

Wittgenstein, L. (1980). *Remarks on the philosophy of psychology* (Vol. 2, G. H. von Wright & H. Nyman, Eds.) (C. G. Luckhardt & M. A. E. Aue, Trans.). Oxford: Blackwell.

Wittgenstein, L. (1981). *Zettel* (2nd ed., G. E. M. Anscombe & G. H. V. Wright, Eds.). Oxford: Blackwell.

Woodfield, A. (1993). Do your concepts develop? In C. Hookway & D. Peterson (Eds.), *Philosophy and cognitive science* (pp. 41–67). Cambridge: Cambridge University Press.

Wu, H. (1997). The mathematics education reform: Why you should be concerned and what you can do. *American Mathematical Monthly, 104,* 954–962.

Wynn, K. (1992). Addition and subtraction by human infants. *Nature, 358,* 749–750.

Wynn, K. (1995). Origins of numerical knowledge. *Psychological Science, 7,* 164–169.

Xu, F., & Carey, S. (1996). Infants' metaphysics: The case of numerical identity. *Cognitive Psychology, 30,* 111–153.

Yackel, E., & Cobb, P. (1996). Sociomathematical norms, argumentation, and autonomy in mathematics. *Journal for Research in Mathematics Education, 27*(4), 58–477.

Name Index

Name Index

Subject Index

The Learning in Doing series was founded in 1987 by Roy Pea and John Seely Brown.